36.3493 N, 25.3994 E. MOUNT SANTORINI ON THE GREEK
ISLAND OF THIRA. UNPRECEDENTED FORTY-SEVEN DAY
PAROXYSMAL ERUPTION BEGAN APRIL 27TH. EVERY SOUL NOT
RESCUED KILLED BY THE SECOND WEEK. TEN THOUSAND DEAD.

Behold! The heart
of the world!

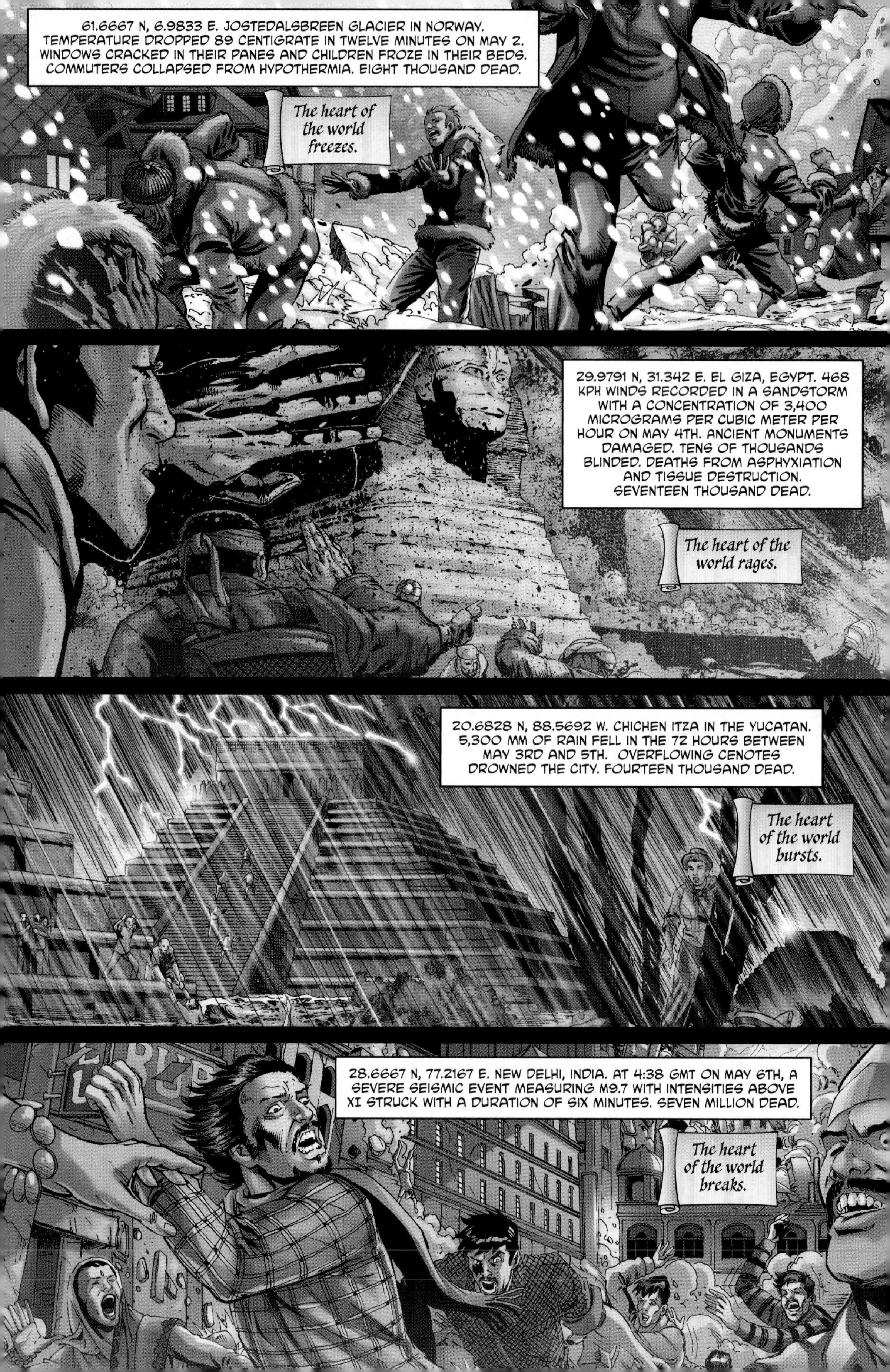
61.6667 N, 6.9833 E. JOSTEDALSBREEN GLACIER IN NORWAY. TEMPERATURE DROPPED 89 CENTIGRATE IN TWELVE MINUTES ON MAY 2. WINDOWS CRACKED IN THEIR PANES AND CHILDREN FROZE IN THEIR BEDS. COMMUTERS COLLAPSED FROM HYPOTHERMIA. EIGHT THOUSAND DEAD.
The heart of the world freezes.
29.9791 N, 31.342 E. EL GIZA, EGYPT. 468 KPH WINDS RECORDED IN A SANDSTORM WITH A CONCENTRATION OF 3,400 MICROGRAMS PER CUBIC METER PER HOUR ON MAY 4TH. ANCIENT MONUMENTS DAMAGED. TENS OF THOUSANDS BLINDED. DEATHS FROM ASPHYXIATION AND TISSUE DESTRUCTION. SEVENTEEN THOUSAND DEAD.
The heart of the world rages.
20.6828 N, 88.5692 W. CHICHEN ITZA IN THE YUCATAN. 5,300 MM OF RAIN FELL IN THE 72 HOURS BETWEEN MAY 3RD AND 5TH. OVERFLOWING CENOTES DROWNED THE CITY. FOURTEEN THOUSAND DEAD.
The heart of the world bursts.
28.6667 N, 77.2167 E. NEW DELHI, INDIA. AT 4:38 GMT ON MAY 6TH, A SEVERE SEISMIC EVENT MEASURING M9.7 WITH INTENSITIES ABOVE XI STRUCK WITH A DURATION OF SIX MINUTES. SEVEN MILLION DEAD.
The heart of the world breaks.

Written by J _____ Mike Costa

Interlude _____ el Ortiz

Cover by **Jonathan Hickman**

Chapter Breaks by **Jacen Burrows** and **Jonathan Hickman**

Colors by **Juanmar**

Lettering by **Kurt Hathaway**

God is Dead created by **Jonathan Hickman**

William Christensen editor-in-chief

Mark Seifert creative director

Jim Kuhoric managing editor

David Marks director of events

Ariana Osborne production assistant

w w w . a v a t a r p r e s s . c o m
www.twitter.com/avatarpress
www.facebook.com/avatarpresscomics

God is Dead **Volume One**

April 2014. Published by Avatar Press, Inc.,
515 N. Century Blvd. Rantoul, IL 61866. ©2014 Avatar
Press, Inc. God is Dead and all related properties TM
& ©2014 Jonathan Hickman and Avatar Press, Inc. All
characters as depicted in this story are over the age of
18. The stories, characters, and institutions mentioned
in this magazine are entirely fictional. Printed in Canada.

ONE

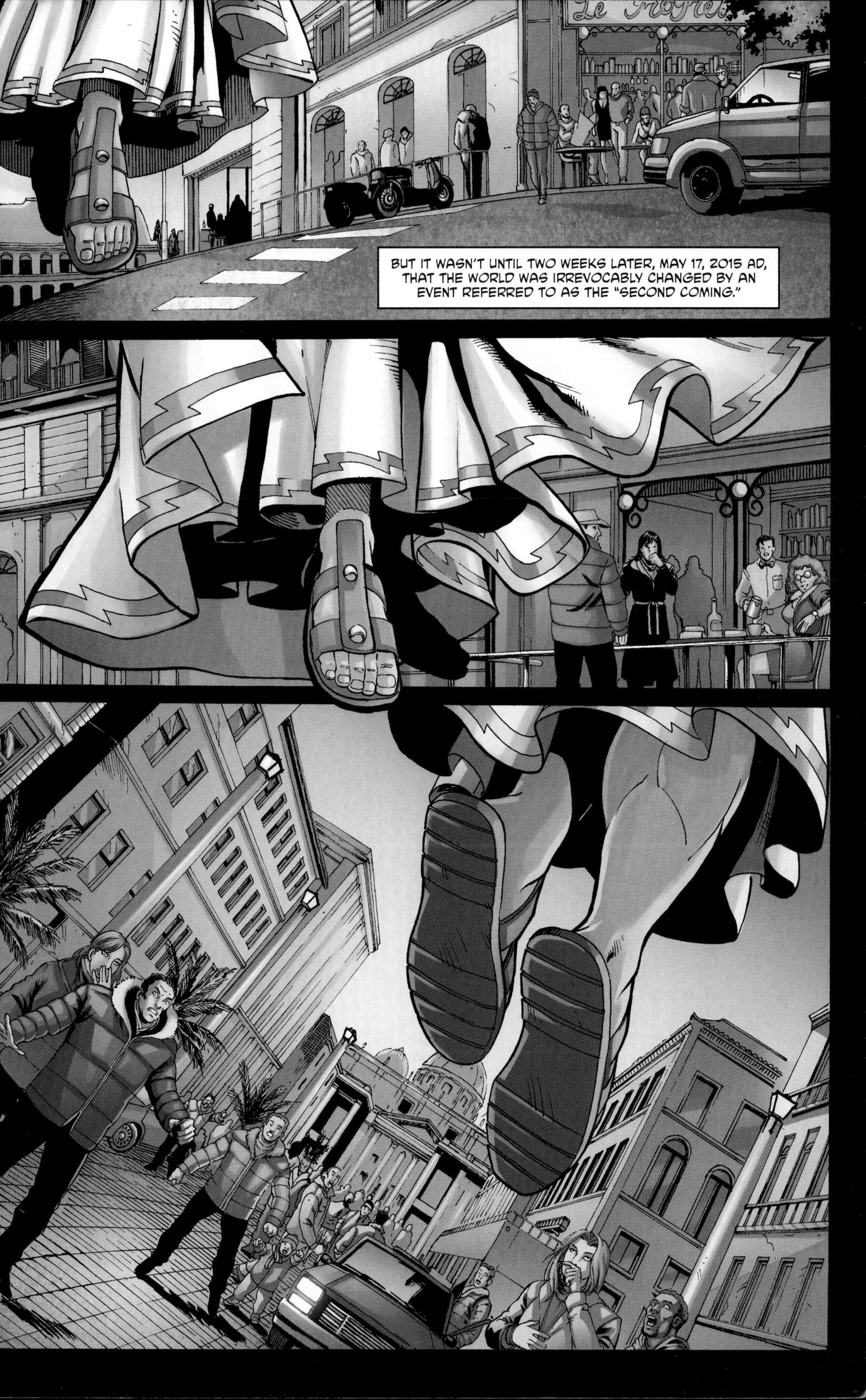
BUT IT WASN'T UNTIL TWO WEEKS LATER, MAY 17, 2015 AD, THAT THE WORLD WAS IRREVOCABLY CHANGED BY AN EVENT REFERRED TO AS THE "SECOND COMING."

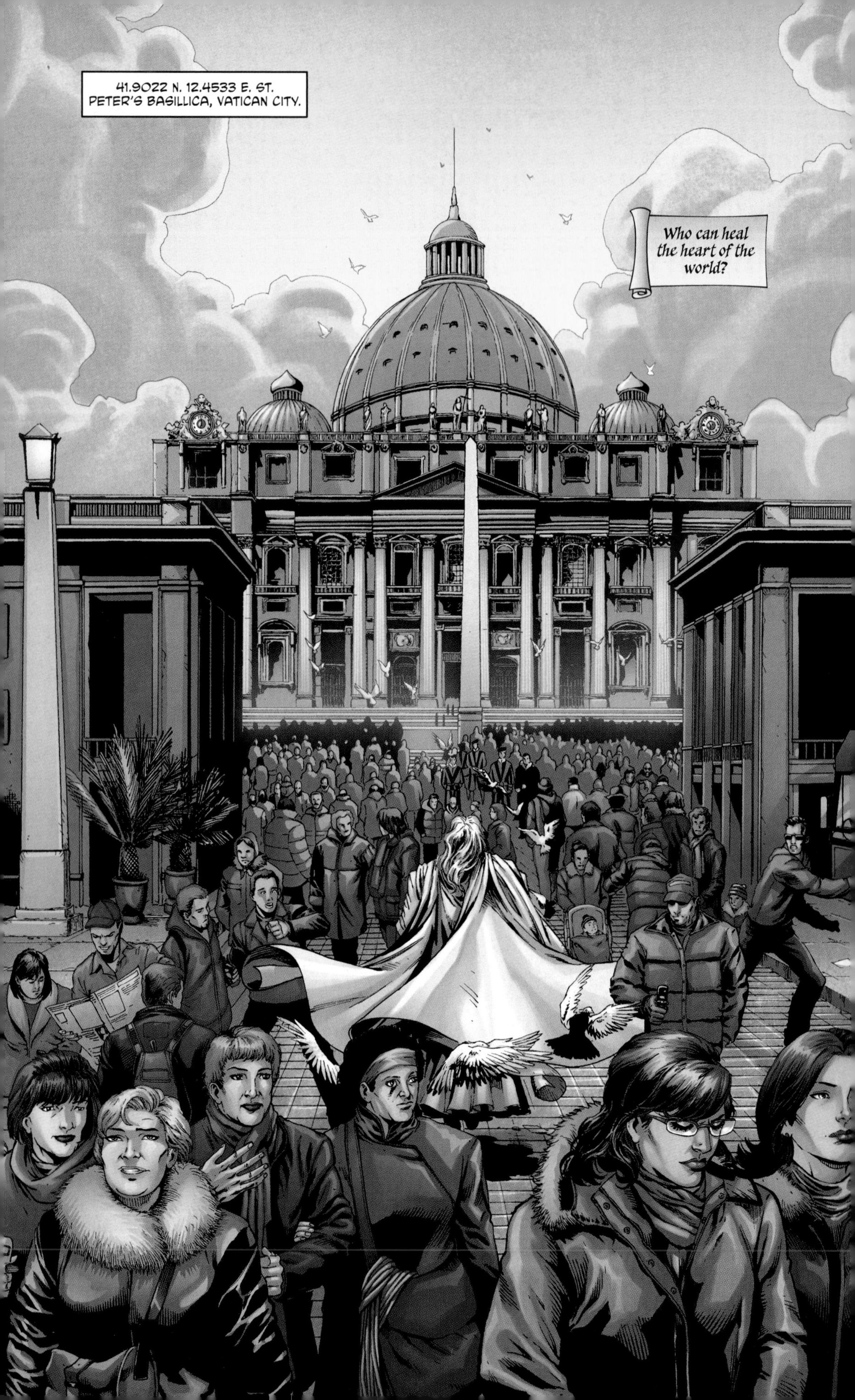
41.9022 N. 12.4533 E. ST. PETER'S BASILLICA, VATICAN CITY.
Who can heal the heart of the world?

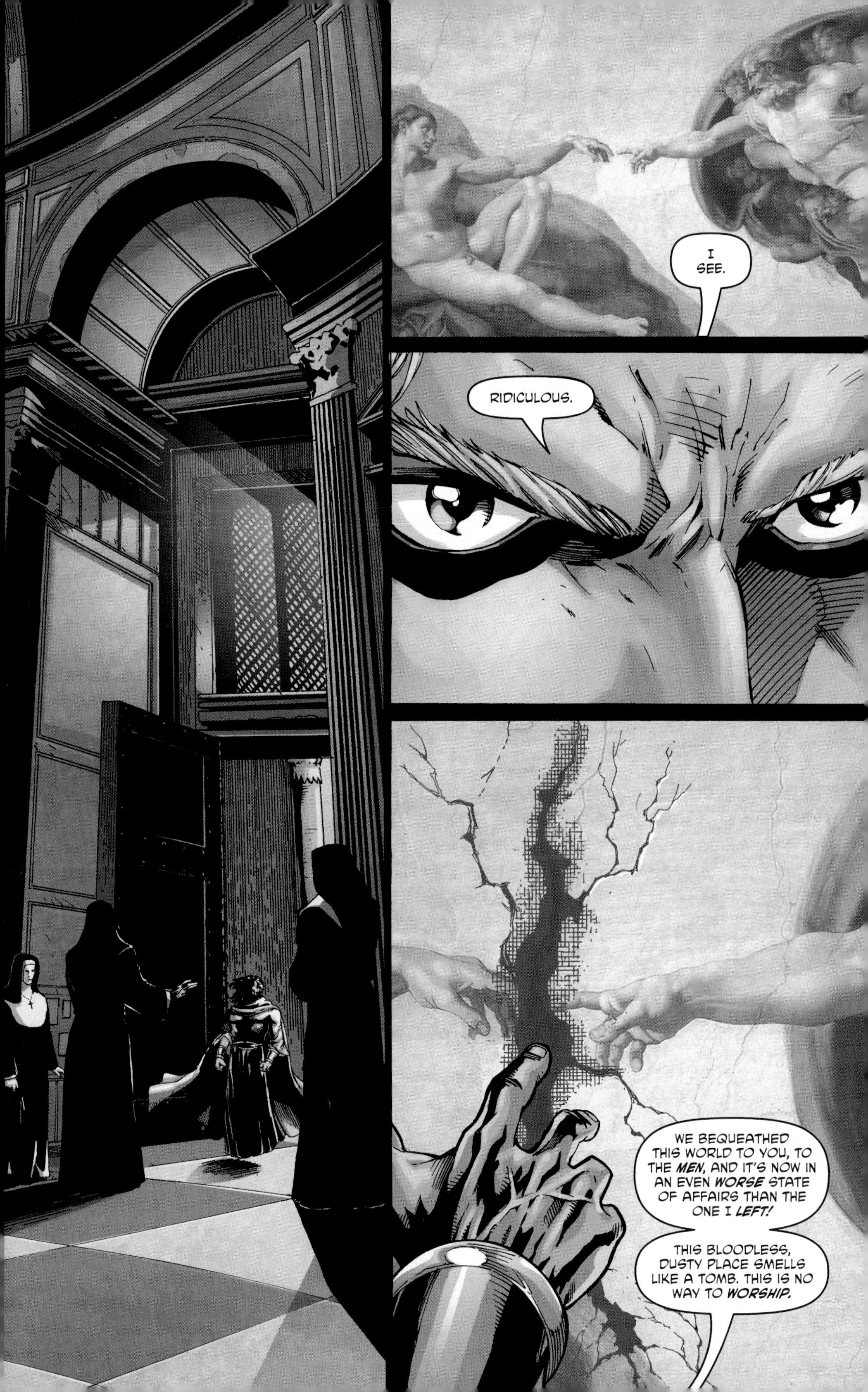

I SEE.
RIDICULOUS.
WE BEQUEATHED THIS WORLD TO YOU, TO THE *MEN*, AND IT'S NOW IN AN EVEN *WORSE* STATE OF AFFAIRS THAN THE ONE I *LEFT!*
THIS BLOODLESS, DUSTY PLACE SMELLS LIKE A TOMB. THIS IS NO WAY TO *WORSHIP.*

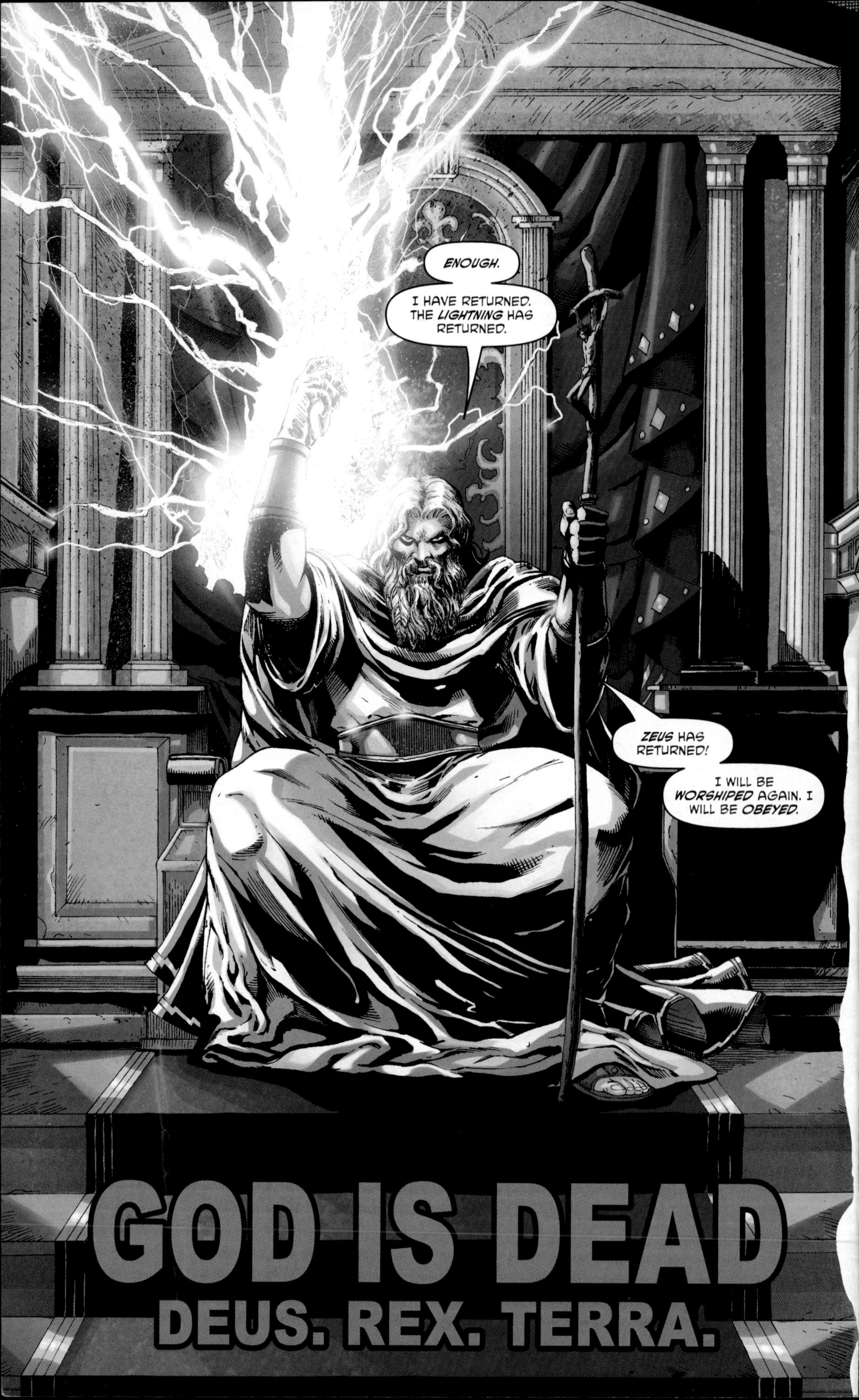
ENOUGH.
I HAVE RETURNED. THE LIGHTNING HAS RETURNED.
ZEUS HAS RETURNED!
I WILL BE WORSHIPED AGAIN. I WILL BE OBEYED.
GOD IS DEAD
DEUS. REX. TERRA.

TWO MONTHS LATER

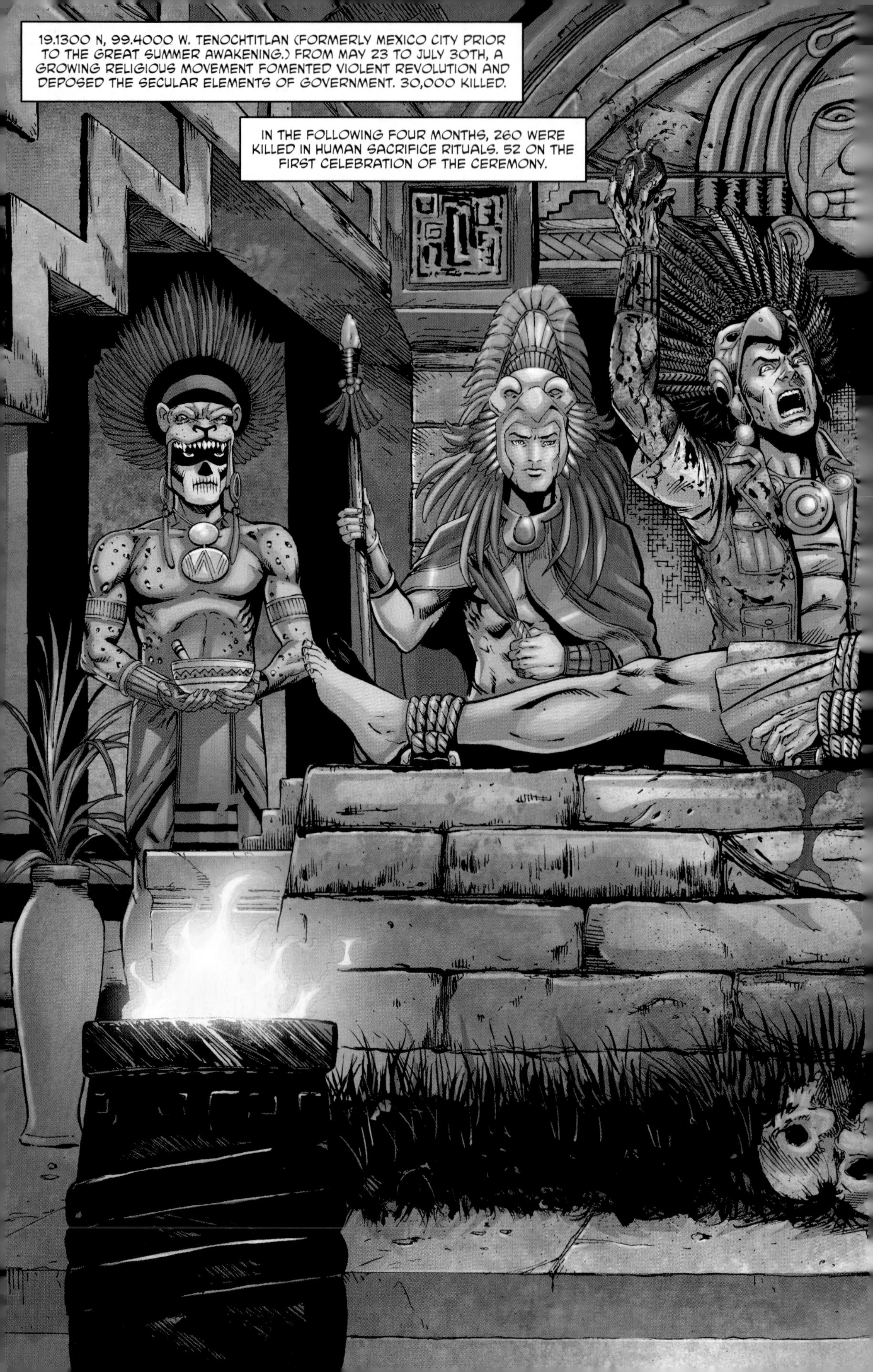
19.1300 N, 99.4000 W. TENOCHTITLAN (FORMERLY MEXICO CITY PRIOR TO THE GREAT SUMMER AWAKENING.) FROM MAY 23 TO JULY 30TH, A GROWING RELIGIOUS MOVEMENT FOMENTED VIOLENT REVOLUTION AND DEPOSED THE SECULAR ELEMENTS OF GOVERNMENT. 30,000 KILLED.
IN THE FOLLOWING FOUR MONTHS, 260 WERE KILLED IN HUMAN SACRIFICE RITUALS. 52 ON THE FIRST CELEBRATION OF THE CEREMONY.

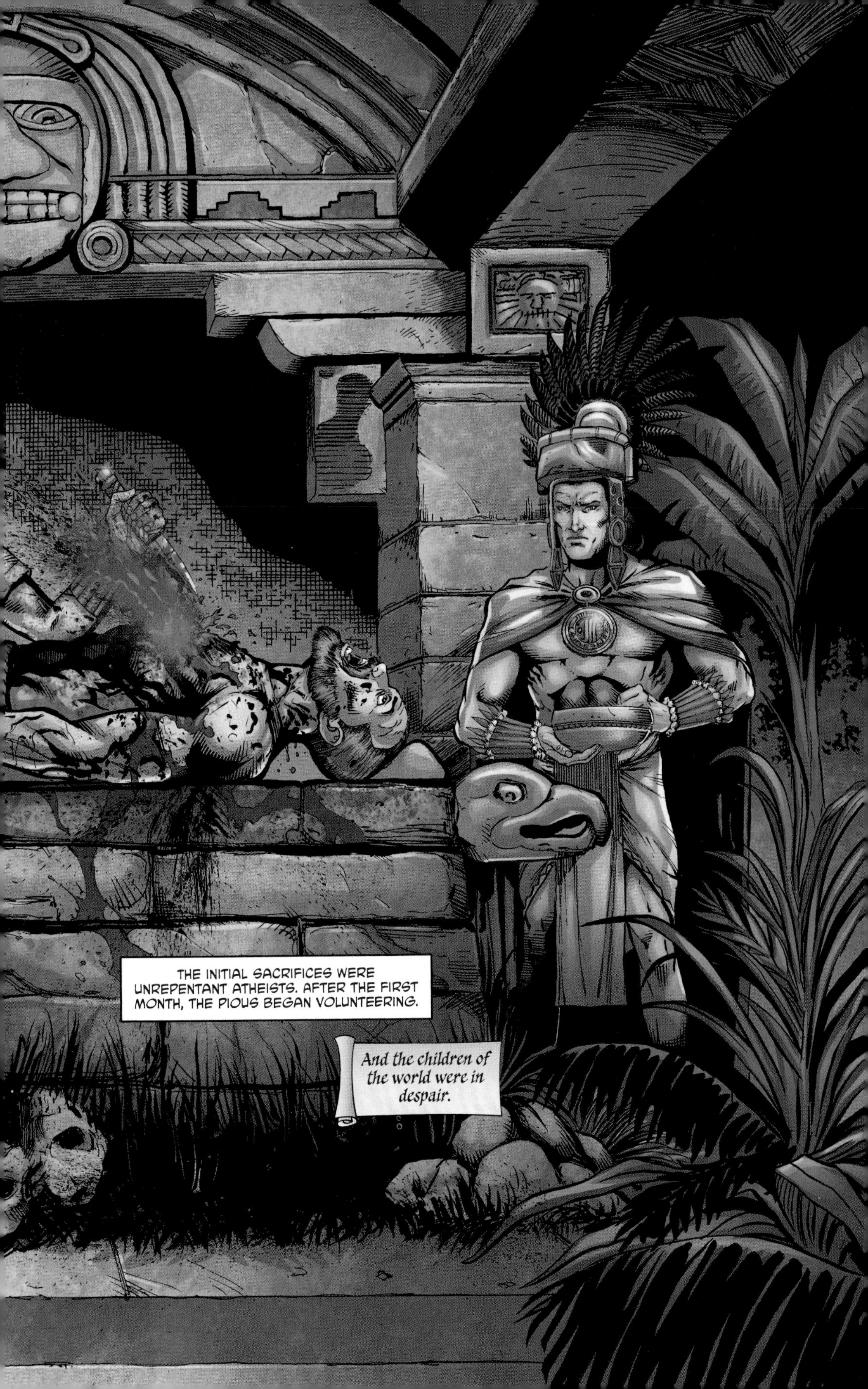

THE INITIAL SACRIFICES WERE UNREPENTANT ATHEISTS. AFTER THE FIRST MONTH, THE PIOUS BEGAN VOLUNTEERING.
And the children of the world were in despair.

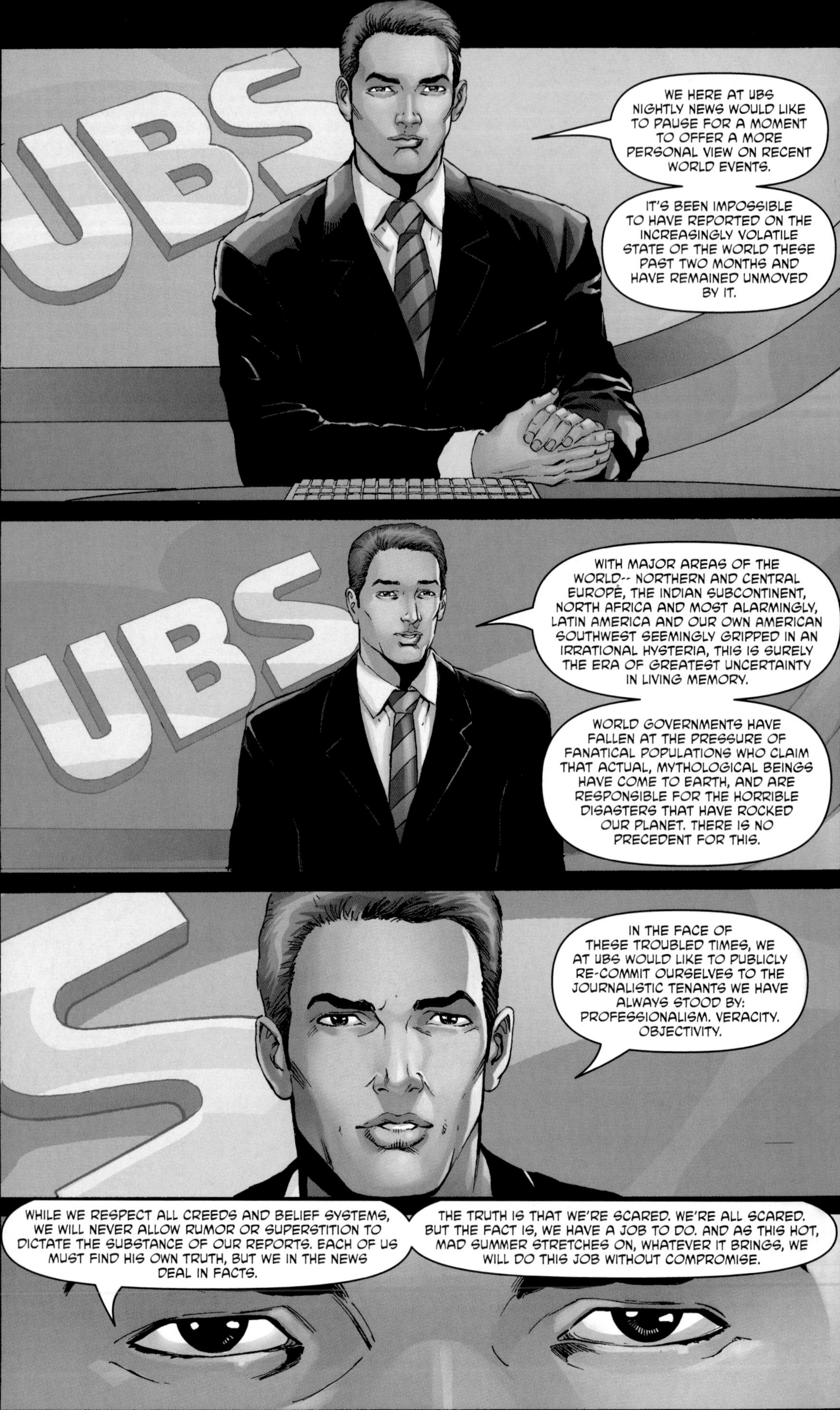
WE HERE AT UBS NIGHTLY NEWS WOULD LIKE TO PAUSE FOR A MOMENT TO OFFER A MORE PERSONAL VIEW ON RECENT WORLD EVENTS.
IT'S BEEN IMPOSSIBLE TO HAVE REPORTED ON THE INCREASINGLY VOLATILE STATE OF THE WORLD THESE PAST TWO MONTHS AND HAVE REMAINED UNMOVED BY IT.
WITH MAJOR AREAS OF THE WORLD-- NORTHERN AND CENTRAL EUROPE, THE INDIAN SUBCONTINENT, NORTH AFRICA AND MOST ALARMINGLY, LATIN AMERICA AND OUR OWN AMERICAN SOUTHWEST SEEMINGLY GRIPPED IN AN IRRATIONAL HYSTERIA, THIS IS SURELY THE ERA OF GREATEST UNCERTAINTY IN LIVING MEMORY.
WORLD GOVERNMENTS HAVE FALLEN AT THE PRESSURE OF FANATICAL POPULATIONS WHO CLAIM THAT ACTUAL, MYTHOLOGICAL BEINGS HAVE COME TO EARTH, AND ARE RESPONSIBLE FOR THE HORRIBLE DISASTERS THAT HAVE ROCKED OUR PLANET. THERE IS NO PRECEDENT FOR THIS.
IN THE FACE OF THESE TROUBLED TIMES, WE AT UBS WOULD LIKE TO PUBLICLY RE-COMMIT OURSELVES TO THE JOURNALISTIC TENANTS WE HAVE ALWAYS STOOD BY: PROFESSIONALISM. VERACITY. OBJECTIVITY.
WHILE WE RESPECT ALL CREEDS AND BELIEF SYSTEMS, WE WILL NEVER ALLOW RUMOR OR SUPERSTITION TO DICTATE THE SUBSTANCE OF OUR REPORTS. EACH OF US MUST FIND HIS OWN TRUTH, BUT WE IN THE NEWS DEAL IN FACTS.
THE TRUTH IS THAT WE'RE SCARED. WE'RE ALL SCARED. BUT THE FACT IS, WE HAVE A JOB TO DO. AND AS THIS HOT, MAD SUMMER STRETCHES ON, WHATEVER IT BRINGS, WE WILL DO THIS JOB WITHOUT COMPROMISE.

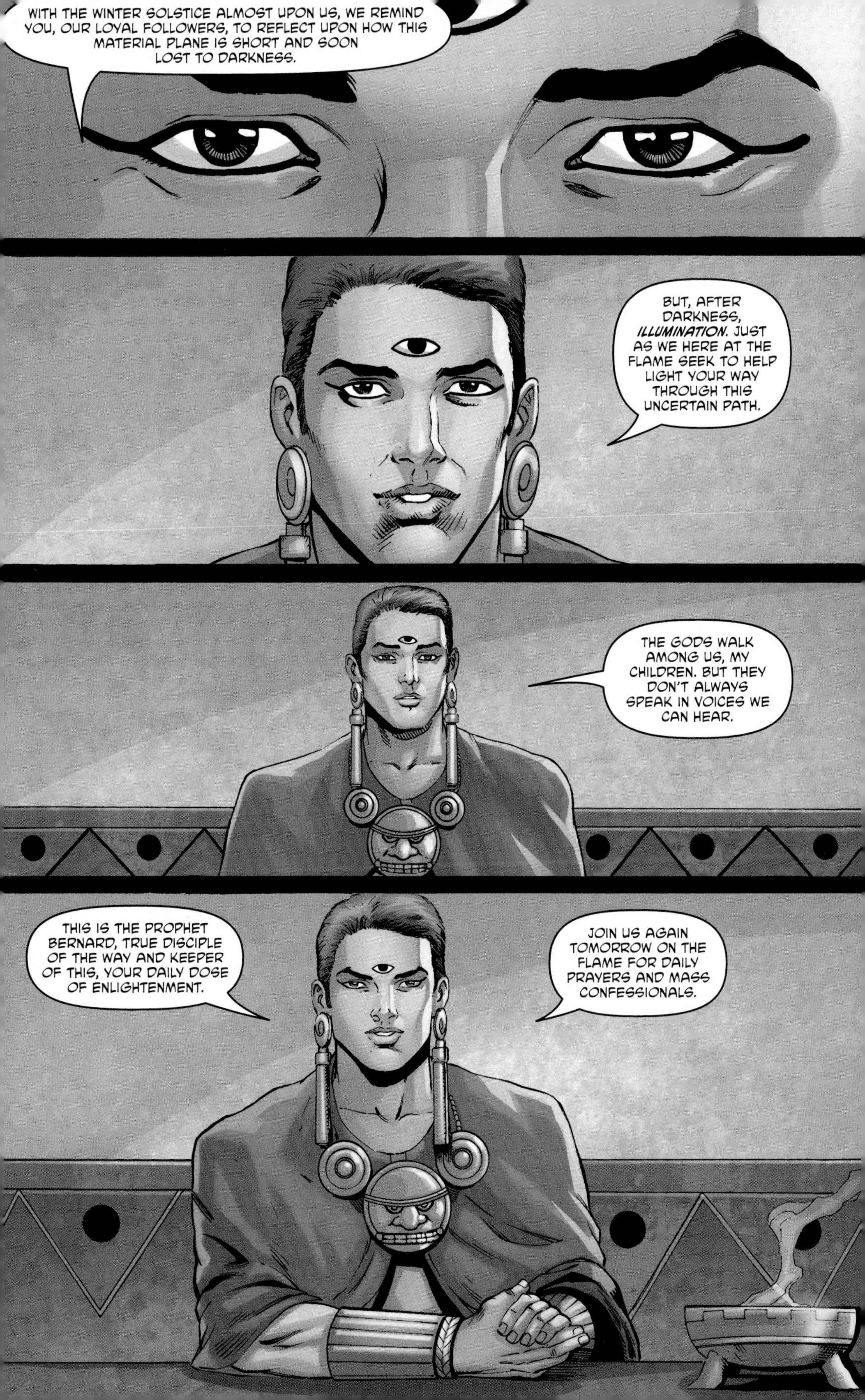
WITH THE WINTER SOLSTICE ALMOST UPON US, WE REMIND YOU, OUR LOYAL FOLLOWERS, TO REFLECT UPON HOW THIS MATERIAL PLANE IS SHORT AND SOON LOST TO DARKNESS.
BUT, AFTER DARKNESS, *ILLUMINATION*. JUST AS WE HERE AT THE FLAME SEEK TO HELP LIGHT YOUR WAY THROUGH THIS UNCERTAIN PATH.
THE GODS WALK AMONG US, MY CHILDREN. BUT THEY DON'T ALWAYS SPEAK IN VOICES WE CAN HEAR.
THIS IS THE PROPHET BERNARD, TRUE DISCIPLE OF THE WAY AND KEEPER OF THIS, YOUR DAILY DOSE OF ENLIGHTENMENT.
JOIN US AGAIN TOMORROW ON THE FLAME FOR DAILY PRAYERS AND MASS CONFESSIONALS.

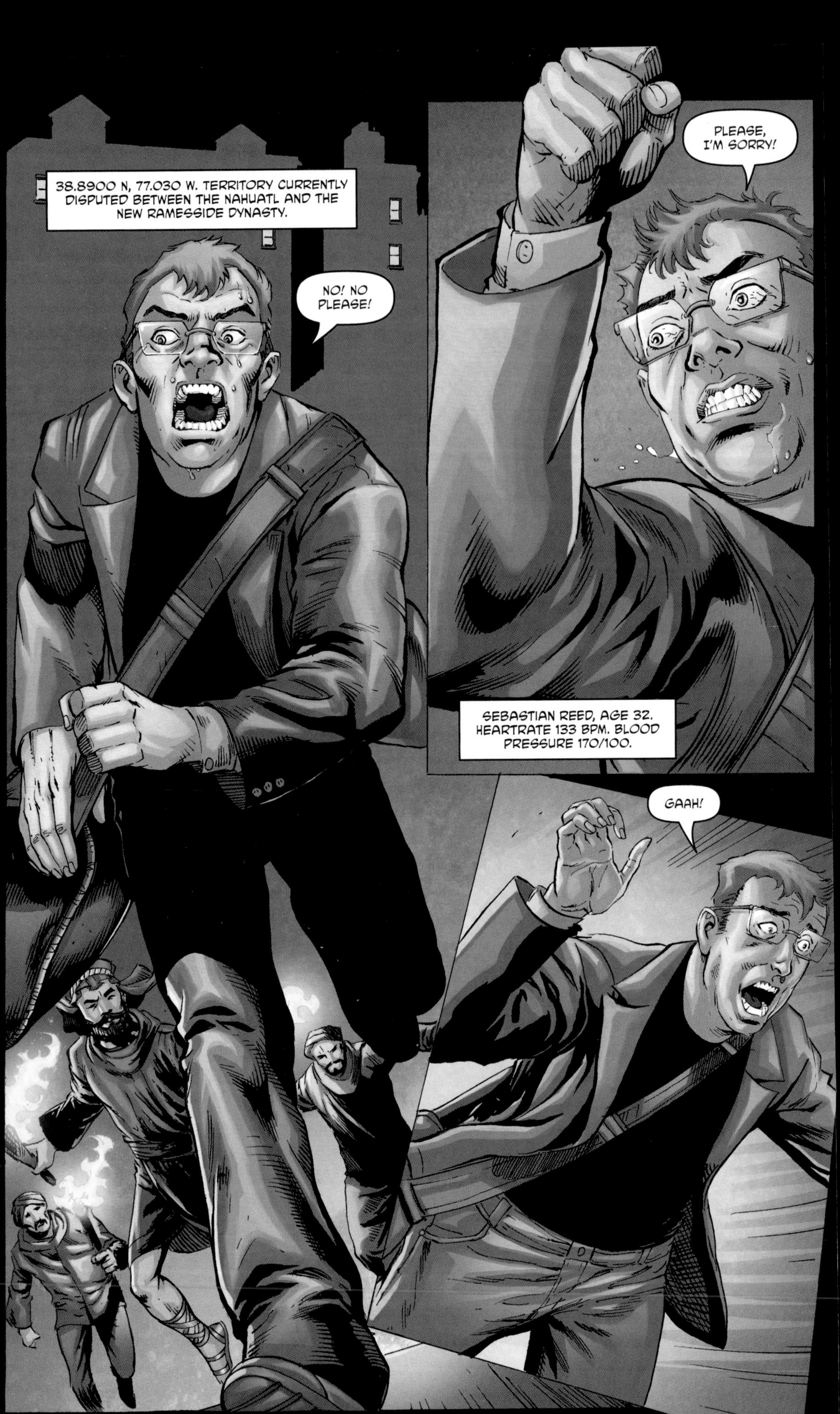
38.8900 N, 77.030 W. TERRITORY CURRENTLY DISPUTED BETWEEN THE NAHUATL AND THE NEW RAMESSIDE DYNASTY.
NO! NO PLEASE!
PLEASE, I'M SORRY!
SEBASTIAN REED, AGE 32. HEARTRATE 133 BPM. BLOOD PRESSURE 170/100.
GAAH!

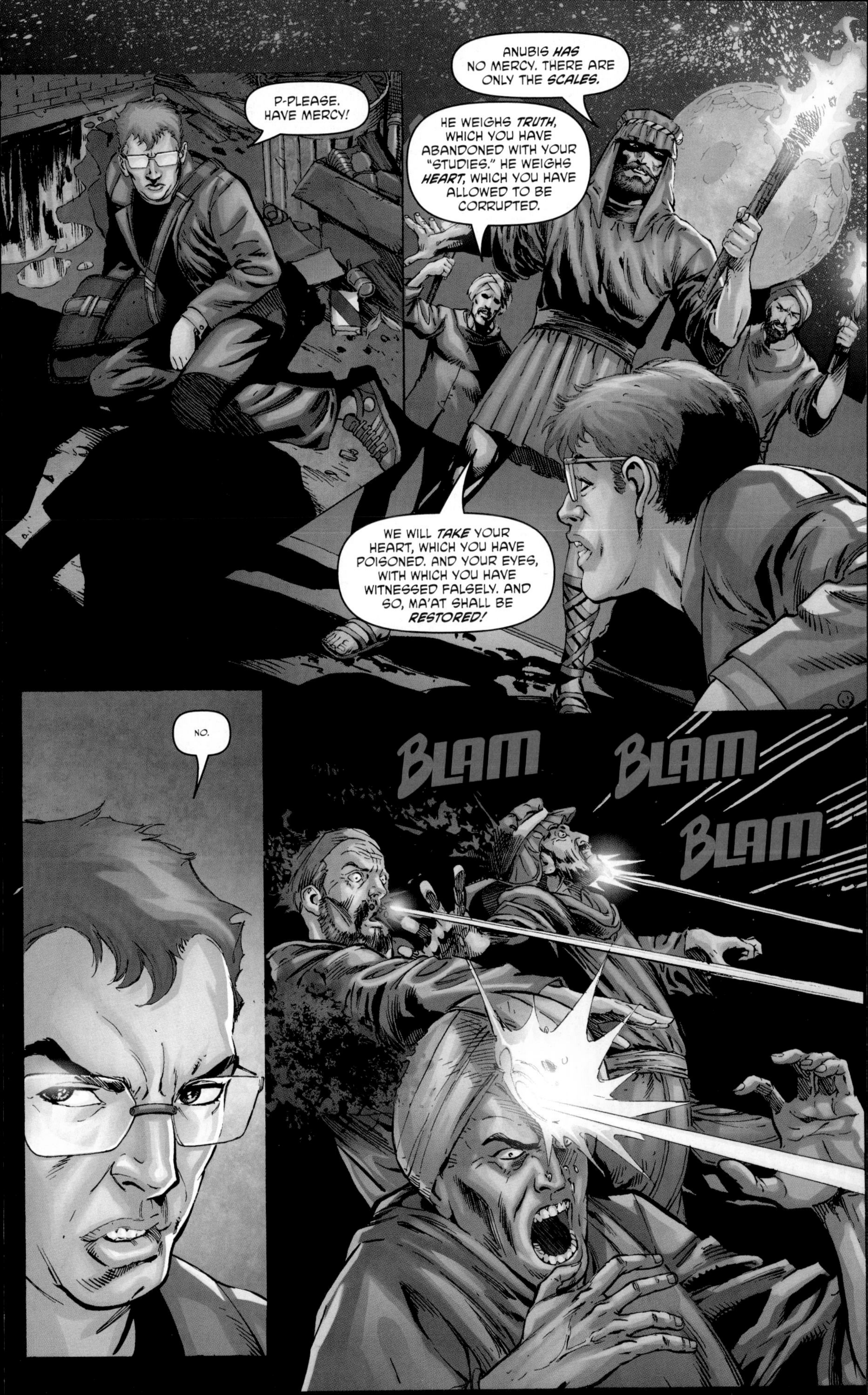
P-PLEASE. HAVE MERCY!
ANUBIS HAS NO MERCY. THERE ARE ONLY THE SCALES.
HE WEIGHS TRUTH, WHICH YOU HAVE ABANDONED WITH YOUR "STUDIES." HE WEIGHS HEART, WHICH YOU HAVE ALLOWED TO BE CORRUPTED.
WE WILL TAKE YOUR HEART, WHICH YOU HAVE POISONED. AND YOUR EYES, WITH WHICH YOU HAVE WITNESSED FALSELY. AND SO, MA'AT SHALL BE RESTORED!
NO.
BLAM
BLAM
BLAM

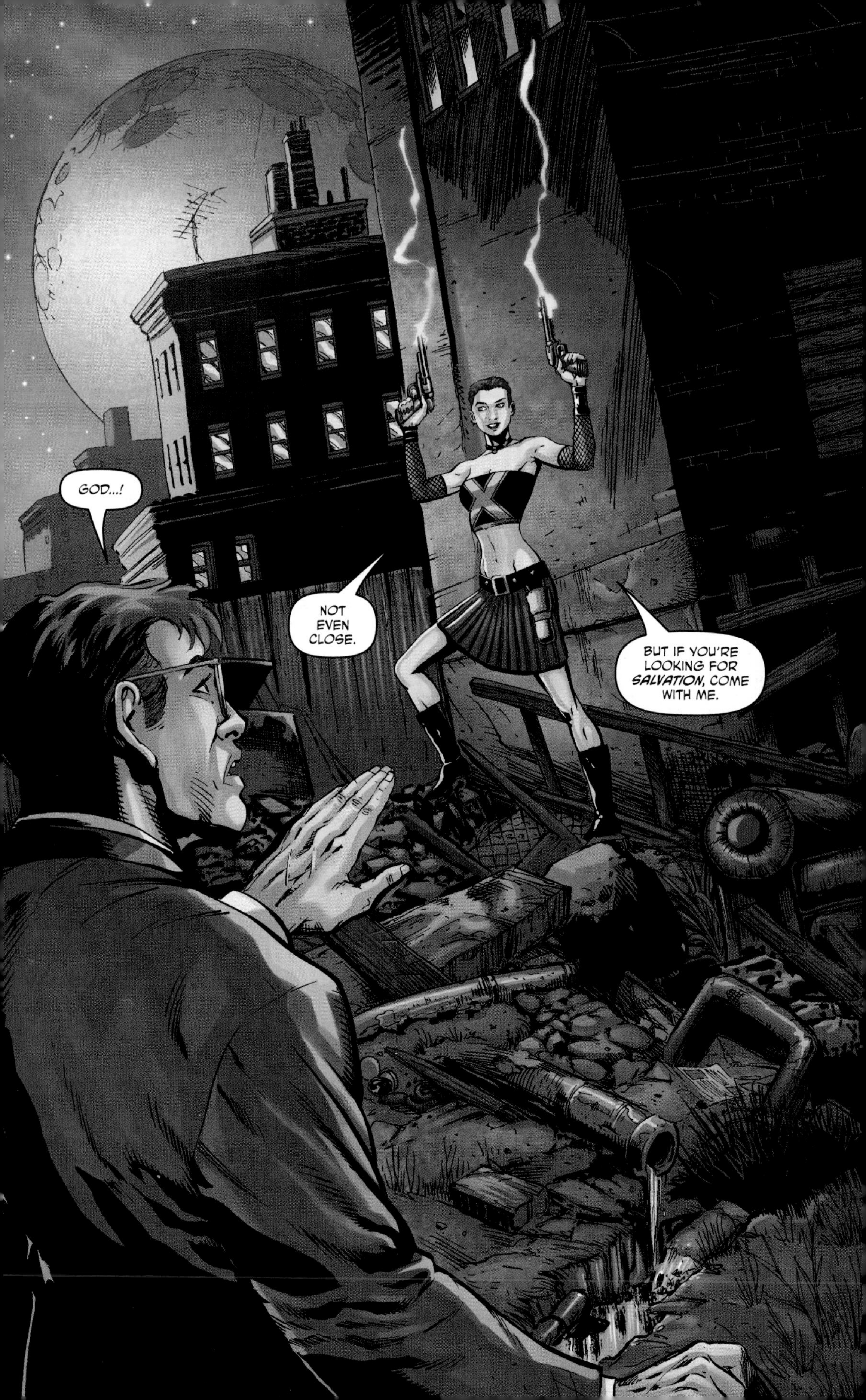
GOD...!
NOT EVEN CLOSE.
BUT IF YOU'RE LOOKING FOR *SALVATION*, COME WITH ME.

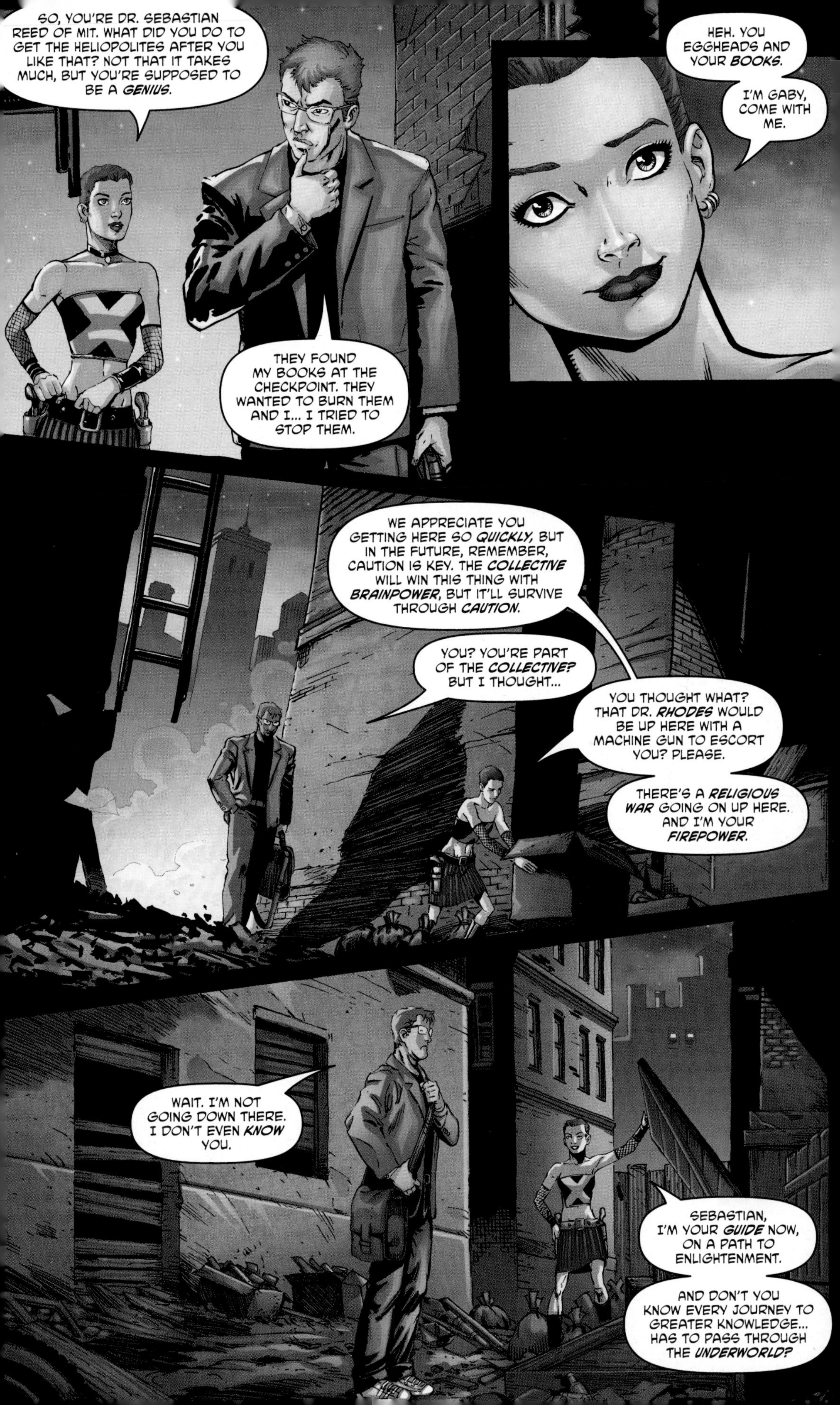
SO, YOU'RE DR. SEBASTIAN REED OF MIT. WHAT DID YOU DO TO GET THE HELIOPOLITES AFTER YOU LIKE THAT? NOT THAT IT TAKES MUCH, BUT YOU'RE SUPPOSED TO BE A *GENIUS*.
THEY FOUND MY BOOKS AT THE CHECKPOINT. THEY WANTED TO BURN THEM AND I... I TRIED TO STOP THEM.
HEH. YOU EGGHEADS AND YOUR *BOOKS*.
I'M GABY, COME WITH ME.
WE APPRECIATE YOU GETTING HERE SO *QUICKLY*, BUT IN THE FUTURE, REMEMBER, CAUTION IS KEY. THE *COLLECTIVE* WILL WIN THIS THING WITH *BRAINPOWER*, BUT IT'LL SURVIVE THROUGH *CAUTION*.
YOU? YOU'RE PART OF THE *COLLECTIVE?* BUT I THOUGHT...
YOU THOUGHT WHAT? THAT DR. *RHODES* WOULD BE UP HERE WITH A MACHINE GUN TO ESCORT YOU? PLEASE.
THERE'S A *RELIGIOUS WAR* GOING ON UP HERE. AND I'M YOUR *FIREPOWER*.
WAIT. I'M NOT GOING DOWN THERE. I DON'T EVEN *KNOW* YOU.
SEBASTIAN, I'M YOUR *GUIDE* NOW, ON A PATH TO ENLIGHTENMENT.
AND DON'T YOU KNOW EVERY JOURNEY TO GREATER KNOWLEDGE... HAS TO PASS THROUGH THE *UNDERWORLD?*

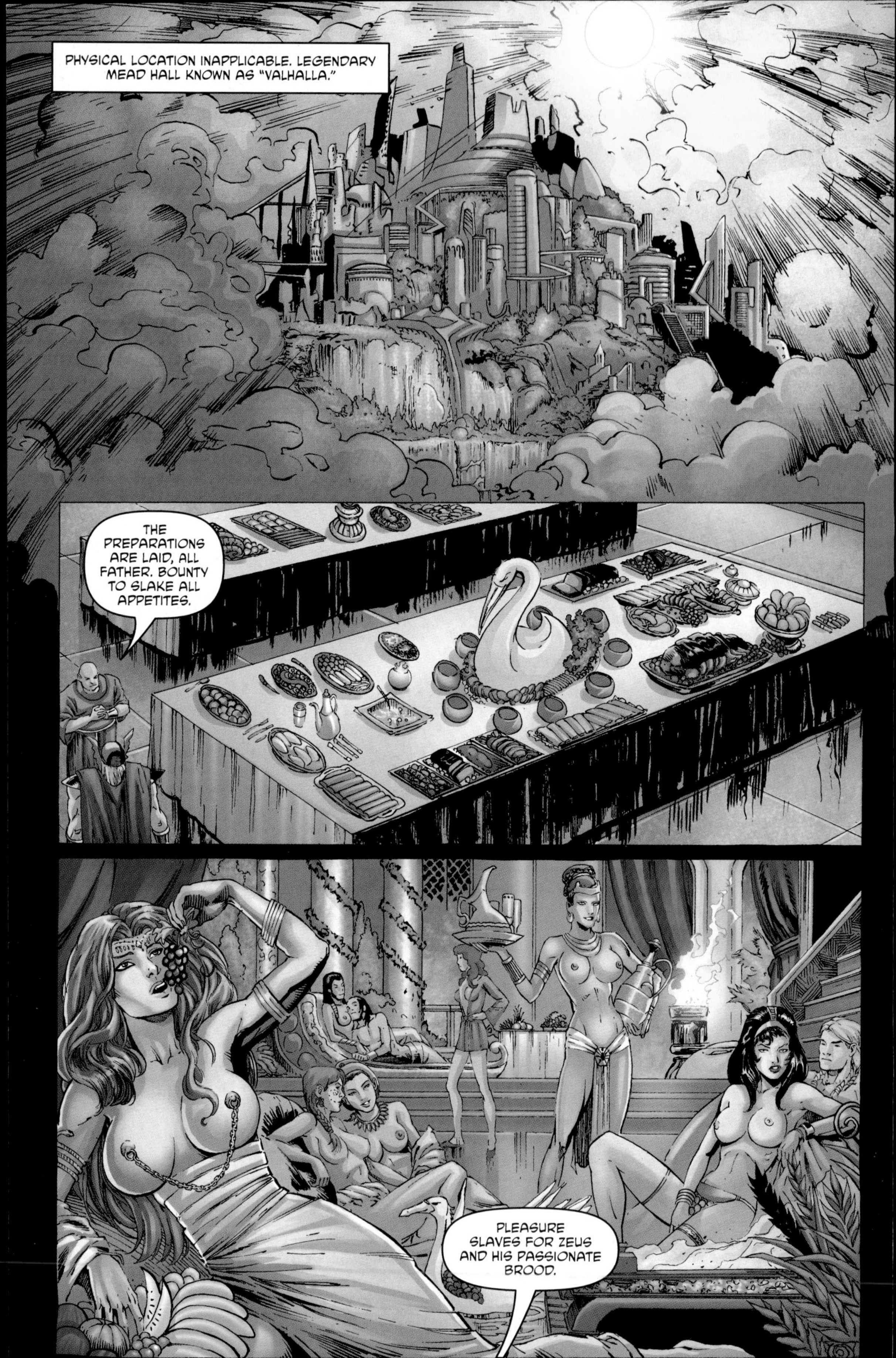
PHYSICAL LOCATION INAPPLICABLE. LEGENDARY MEAD HALL KNOWN AS "VALHALLA."
THE PREPARATIONS ARE LAID, ALL FATHER. BOUNTY TO SLAKE ALL APPETITES.
PLEASURE SLAVES FOR ZEUS AND HIS PASSIONATE BROOD.

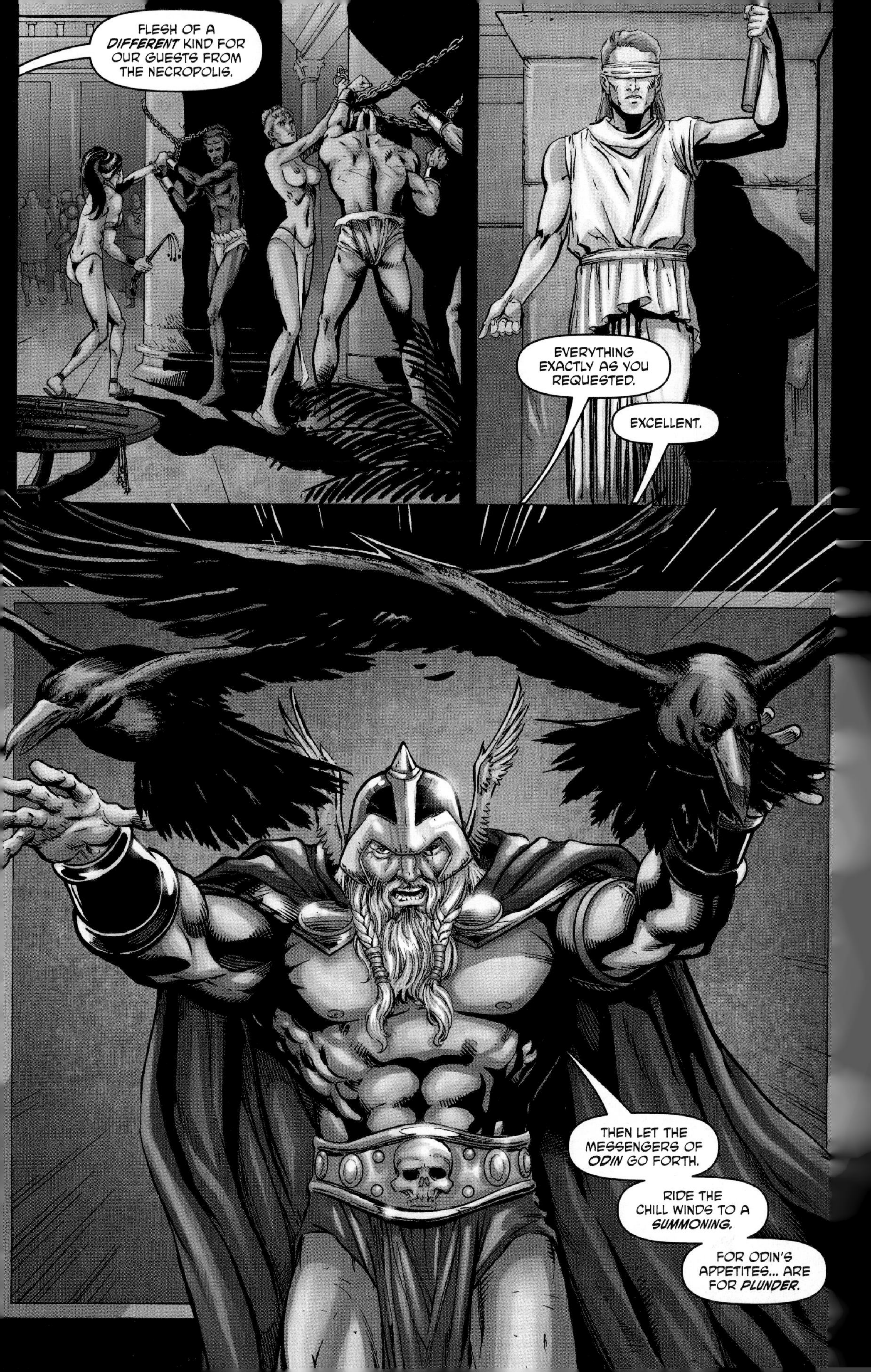
FLESH OF A *DIFFERENT* KIND FOR OUR GUESTS FROM THE NECROPOLIS.
EVERYTHING EXACTLY AS YOU REQUESTED.
EXCELLENT.
THEN LET THE MESSENGERS OF *ODIN* GO FORTH.
RIDE THE CHILL WINDS TO A *SUMMONING.*
FOR ODIN'S APPETITES... ARE FOR *PLUNDER*.

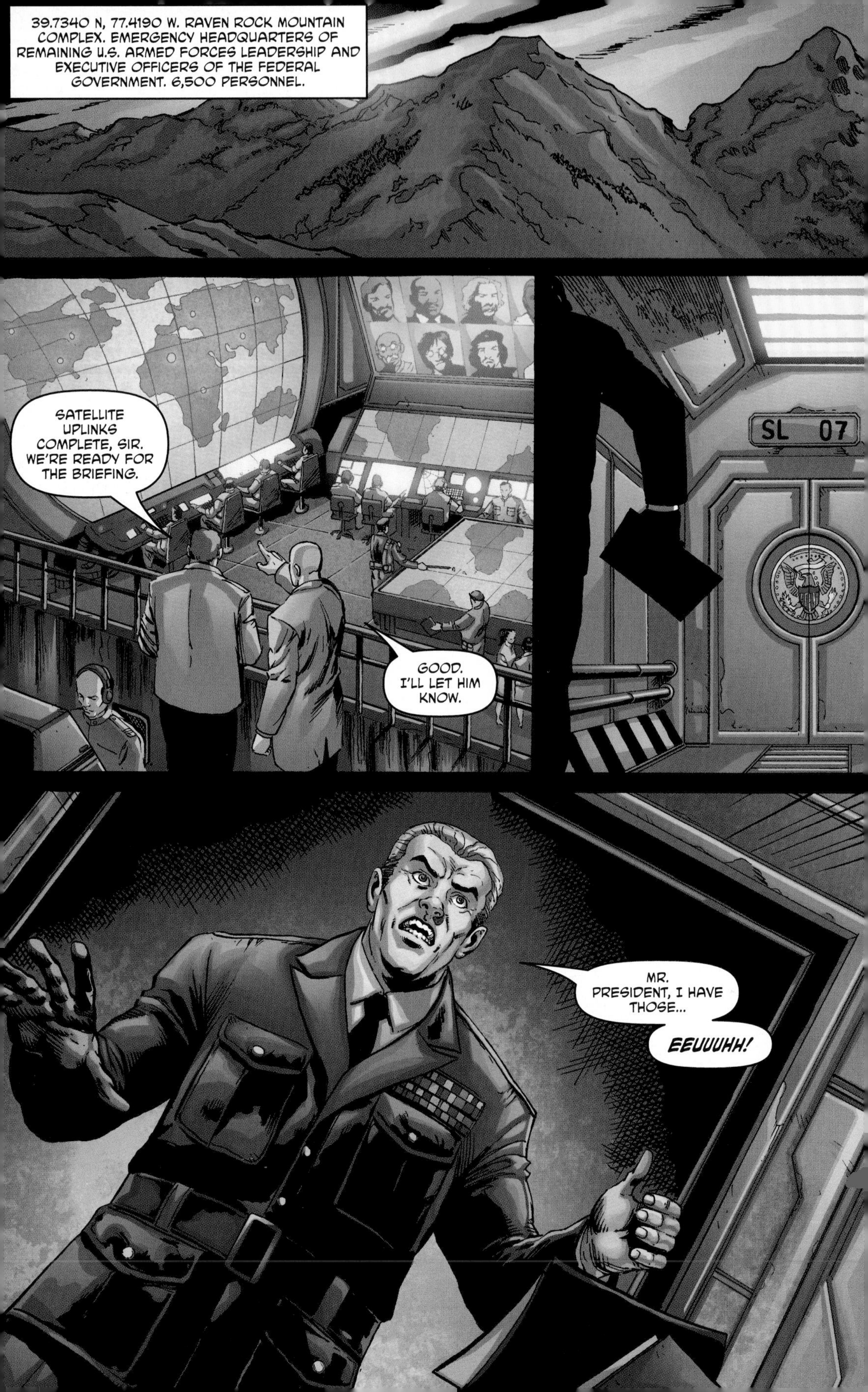
39.7340 N, 77.4190 W. RAVEN ROCK MOUNTAIN COMPLEX. EMERGENCY HEADQUARTERS OF REMAINING U.S. ARMED FORCES LEADERSHIP AND EXECUTIVE OFFICERS OF THE FEDERAL GOVERNMENT. 6,500 PERSONNEL.
SATELLITE UPLINKS COMPLETE, SIR. WE'RE READY FOR THE BRIEFING.
GOOD. I'LL LET HIM KNOW.
SL 07
MR. PRESIDENT, I HAVE THOSE...
EEUUUHH!

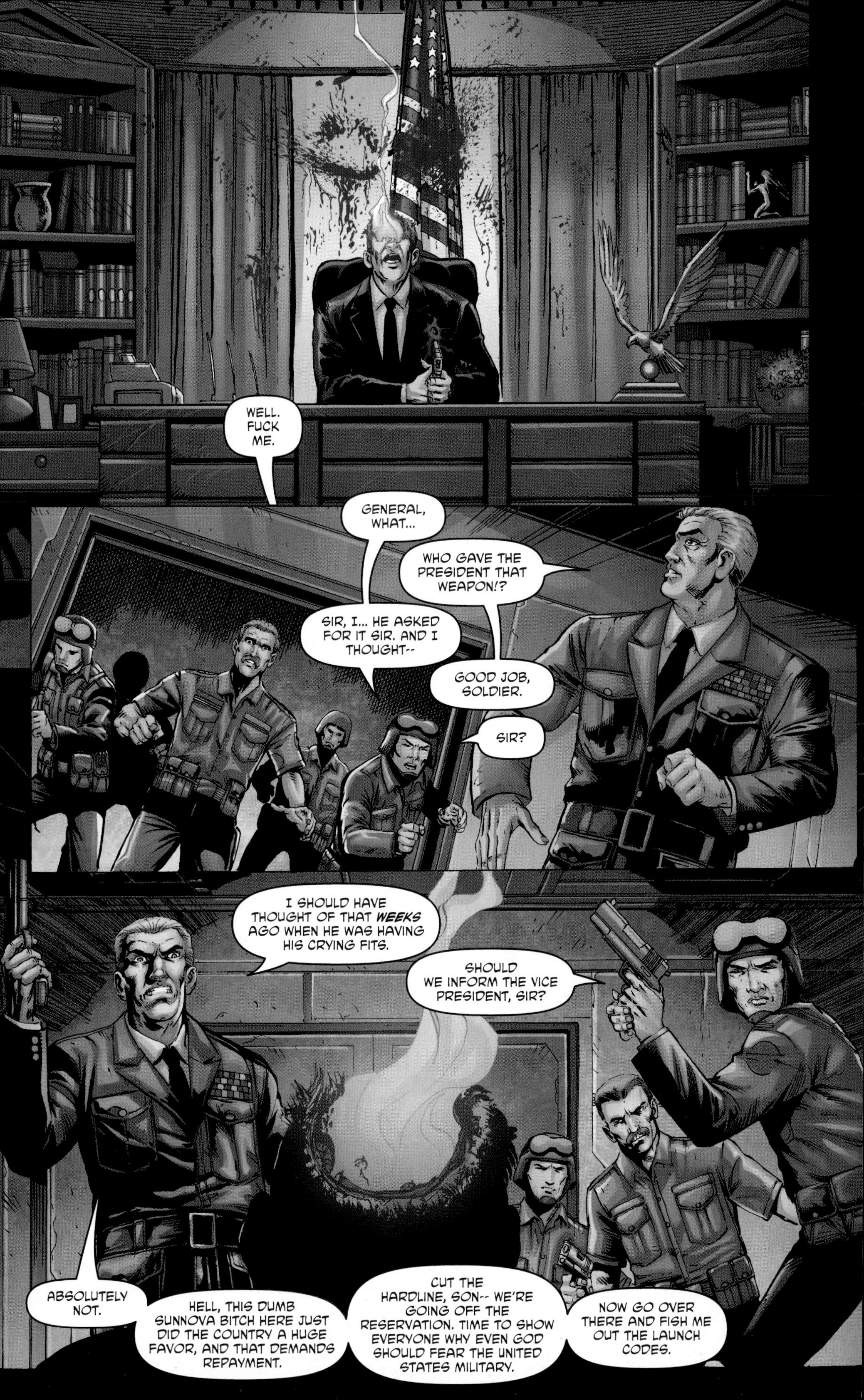
WELL. FUCK ME.
GENERAL, WHAT...
WHO GAVE THE PRESIDENT THAT WEAPON!?
SIR, I... HE ASKED FOR IT SIR. AND I THOUGHT--
GOOD JOB, SOLDIER.
SIR?
I SHOULD HAVE THOUGHT OF THAT *WEEKS* AGO WHEN HE WAS HAVING HIS CRYING FITS.
SHOULD WE INFORM THE VICE PRESIDENT, SIR?
ABSOLUTELY NOT.
HELL, THIS DUMB SUNNOVA BITCH HERE JUST DID THE COUNTRY A HUGE FAVOR, AND THAT DEMANDS REPAYMENT.
CUT THE HARDLINE, SON-- WE'RE GOING OFF THE RESERVATION. TIME TO SHOW EVERYONE WHY EVEN GOD SHOULD FEAR THE UNITED STATES MILITARY.
NOW GO OVER THERE AND FISH ME OUT THE LAUNCH CODES.

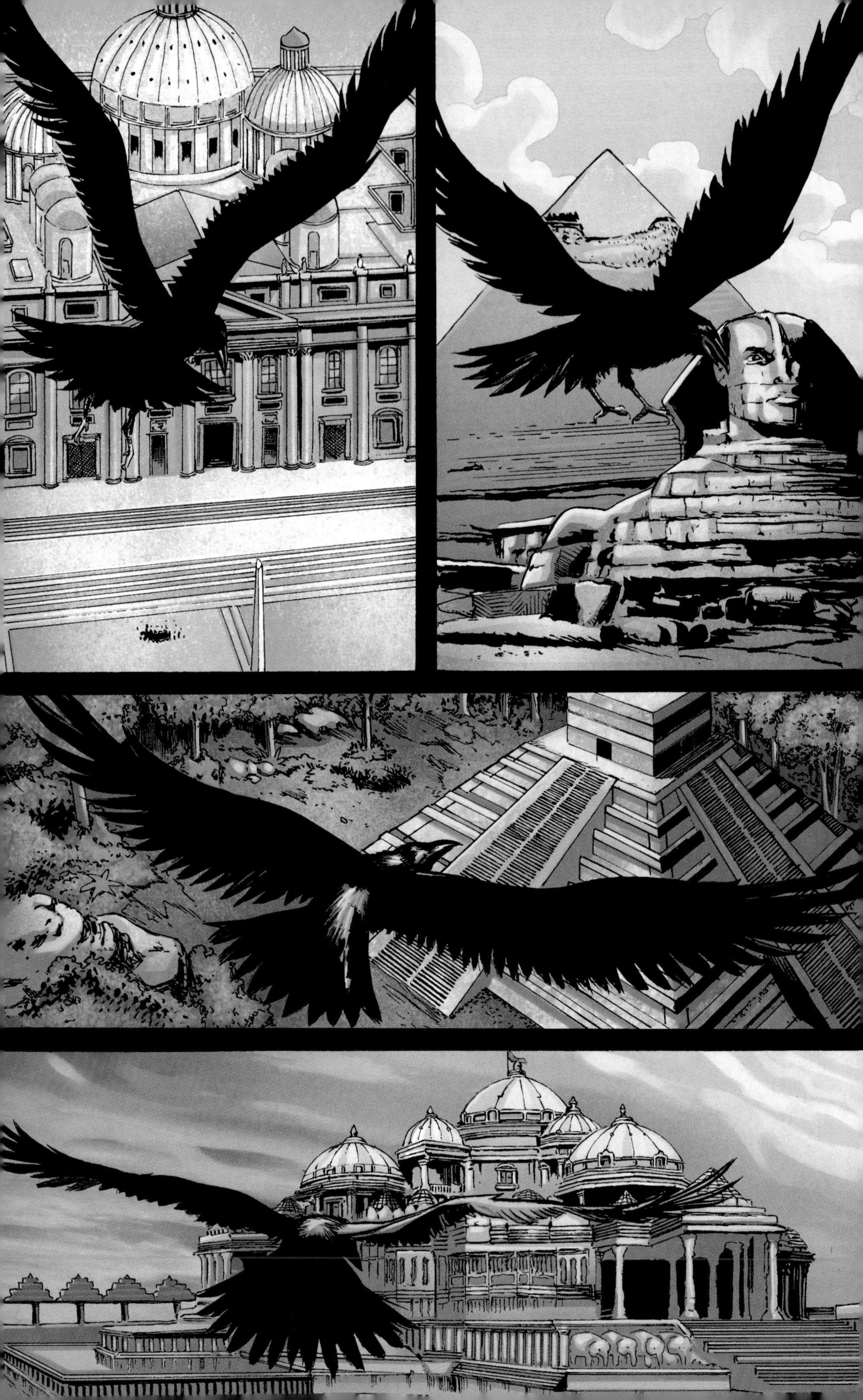

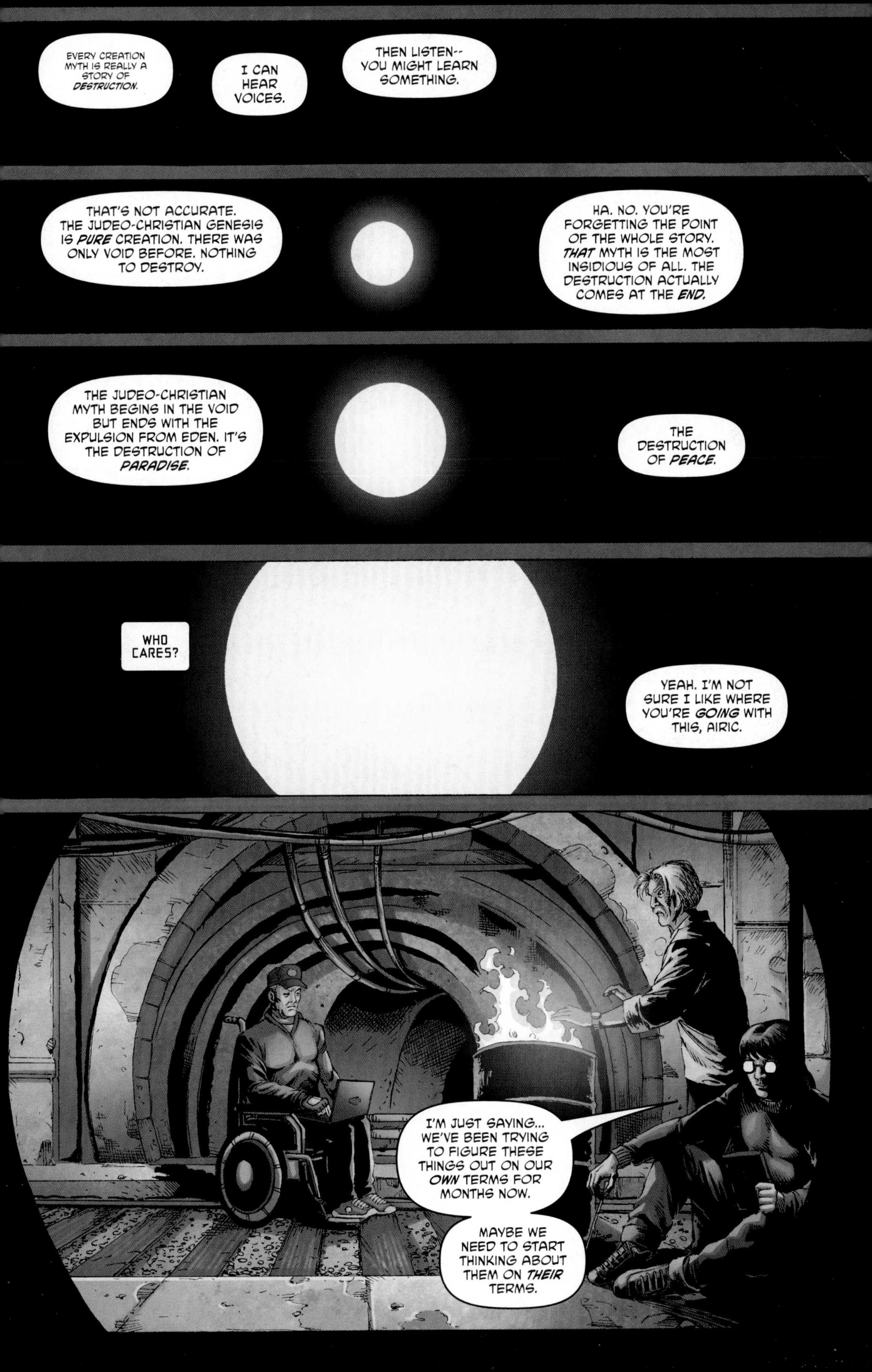

EVERY CREATION MYTH IS REALLY A STORY OF *DESTRUCTION.*
I CAN HEAR VOICES.
THEN LISTEN-- YOU MIGHT LEARN SOMETHING.
THAT'S NOT ACCURATE. THE JUDEO-CHRISTIAN GENESIS IS *PURE* CREATION. THERE WAS ONLY VOID BEFORE. NOTHING TO DESTROY.
HA. NO. YOU'RE FORGETTING THE POINT OF THE WHOLE STORY. *THAT* MYTH IS THE MOST INSIDIOUS OF ALL. THE DESTRUCTION ACTUALLY COMES AT THE *END.*
THE JUDEO-CHRISTIAN MYTH BEGINS IN THE VOID BUT ENDS WITH THE EXPULSION FROM EDEN. IT'S THE DESTRUCTION OF *PARADISE.*
THE DESTRUCTION OF *PEACE.*
WHO CARES?
YEAH. I'M NOT SURE I LIKE WHERE YOU'RE *GOING* WITH THIS, AIRIC.
I'M JUST SAYING... WE'VE BEEN TRYING TO FIGURE THESE THINGS OUT ON OUR *OWN* TERMS FOR MONTHS NOW.
MAYBE WE NEED TO START THINKING ABOUT THEM ON *THEIR* TERMS.

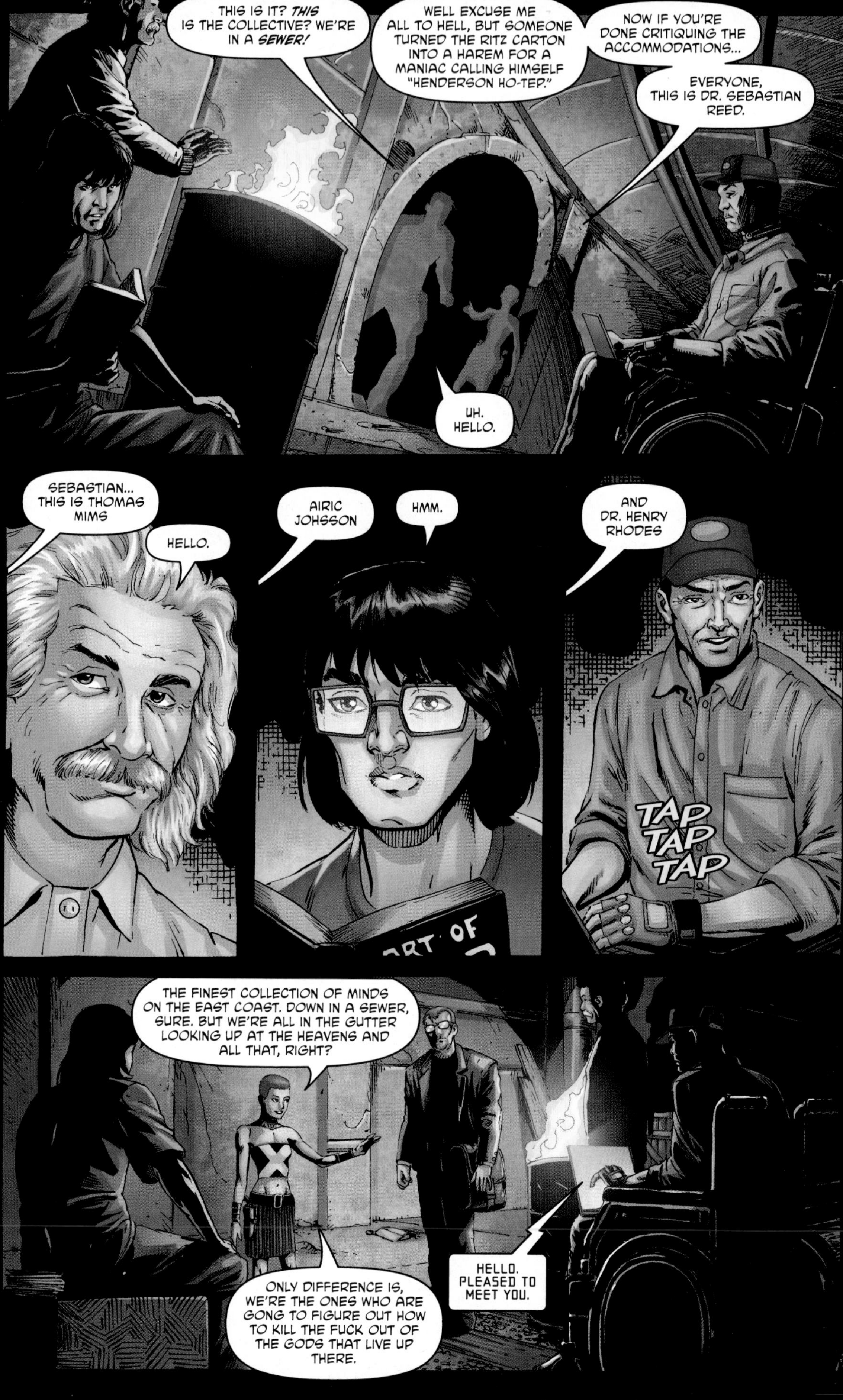
THIS IS IT? THIS IS THE COLLECTIVE? WE'RE IN A SEWER!
WELL EXCUSE ME ALL TO HELL, BUT SOMEONE TURNED THE RITZ CARTON INTO A HAREM FOR A MANIAC CALLING HIMSELF "HENDERSON HO-TEP."
NOW IF YOU'RE DONE CRITIQUING THE ACCOMMODATIONS...
EVERYONE, THIS IS DR. SEBASTIAN REED.
UH. HELLO.
SEBASTIAN... THIS IS THOMAS MIMS
HELLO.
AIRIC JOHSSON
HMM.
AND DR. HENRY RHODES
TAP TAP TAP
THE FINEST COLLECTION OF MINDS ON THE EAST COAST. DOWN IN A SEWER, SURE. BUT WE'RE ALL IN THE GUTTER LOOKING UP AT THE HEAVENS AND ALL THAT, RIGHT?
HELLO. PLEASED TO MEET YOU.
ONLY DIFFERENCE IS, WE'RE THE ONES WHO ARE GONG TO FIGURE OUT HOW TO KILL THE FUCK OUT OF THE GODS THAT LIVE UP THERE.

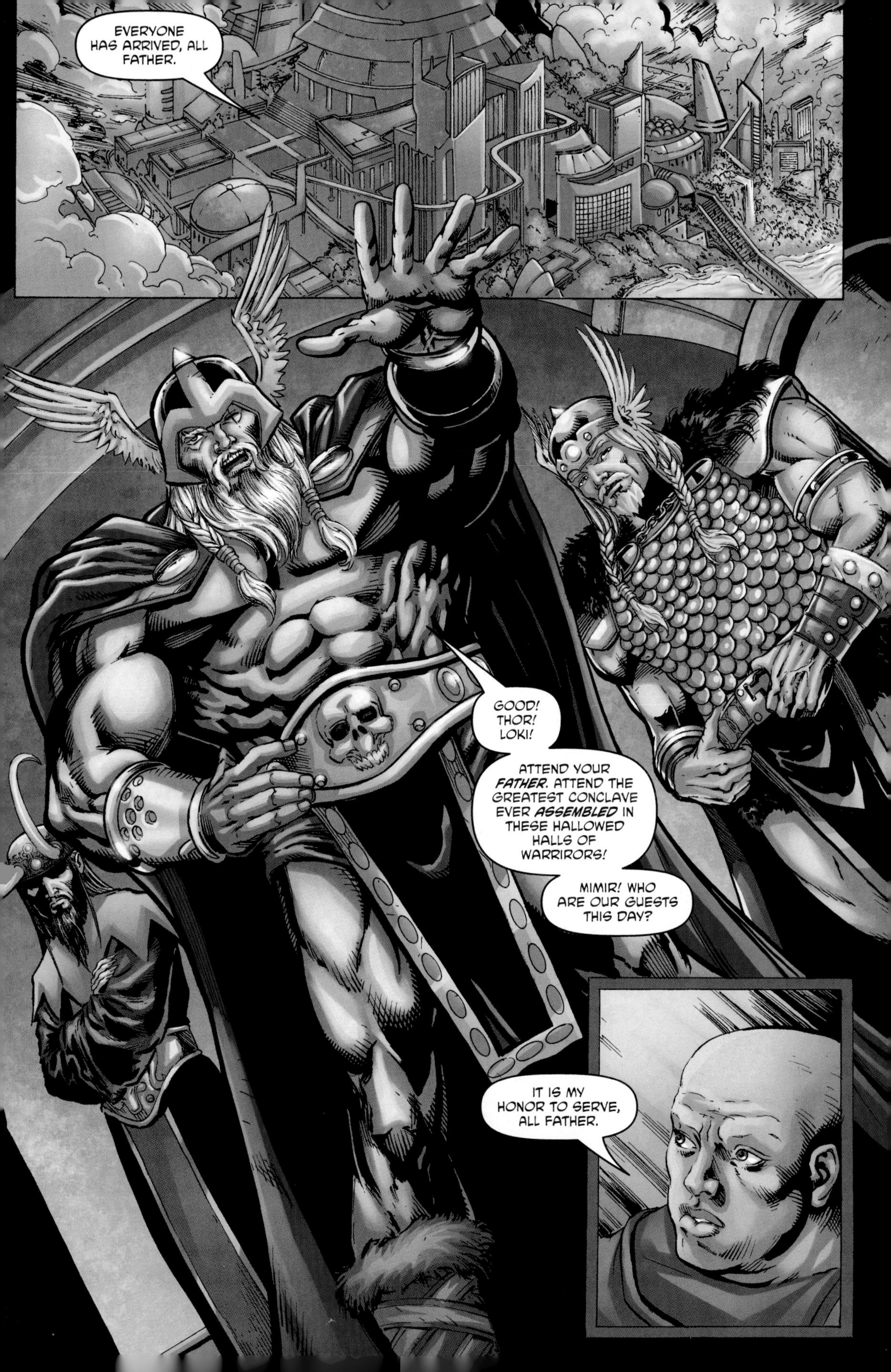
EVERYONE HAS ARRIVED, ALL FATHER.
GOOD! THOR! LOKI!
ATTEND YOUR *FATHER*. ATTEND THE GREATEST CONCLAVE EVER *ASSEMBLED* IN THESE HALLOWED HALLS OF WARRIORS!
MIMIR! WHO ARE OUR GUESTS THIS DAY?
IT IS MY HONOR TO SERVE, ALL FATHER.

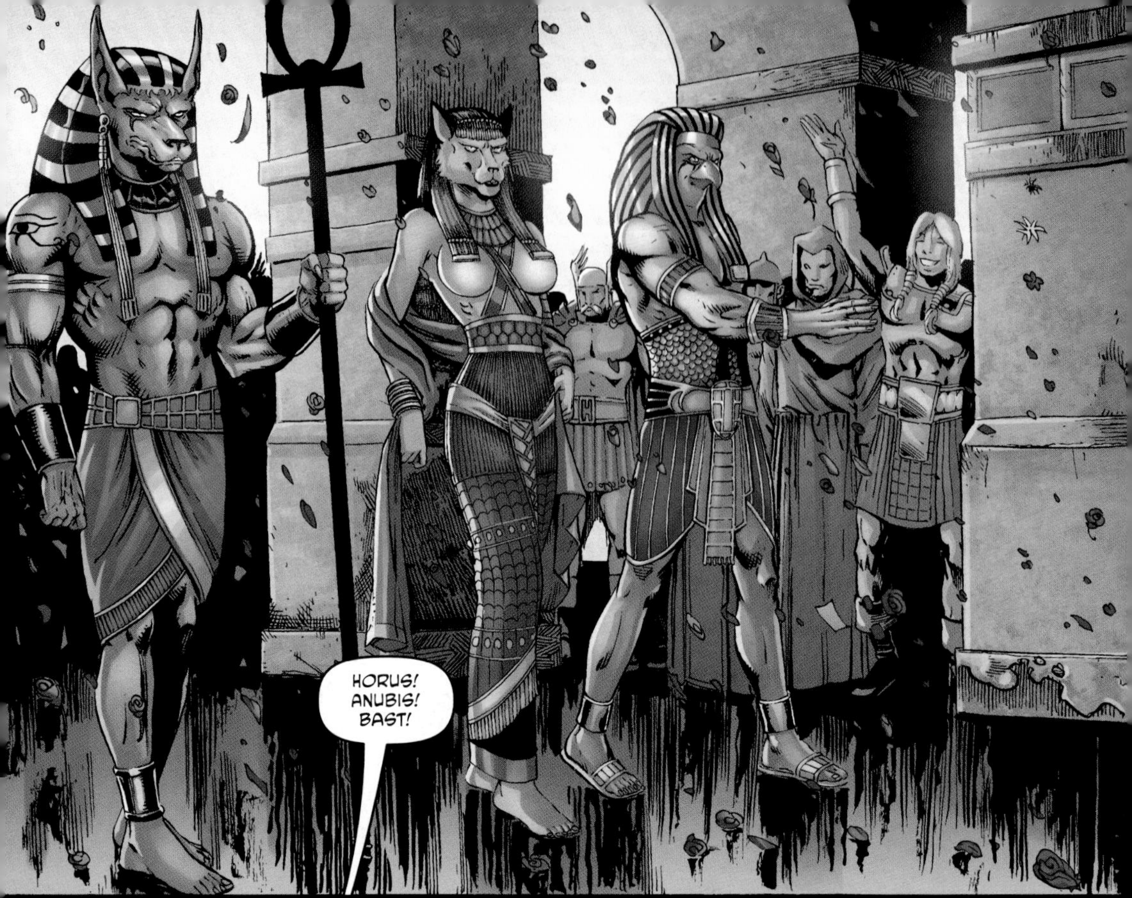
HORUS! ANUBIS! BAST!

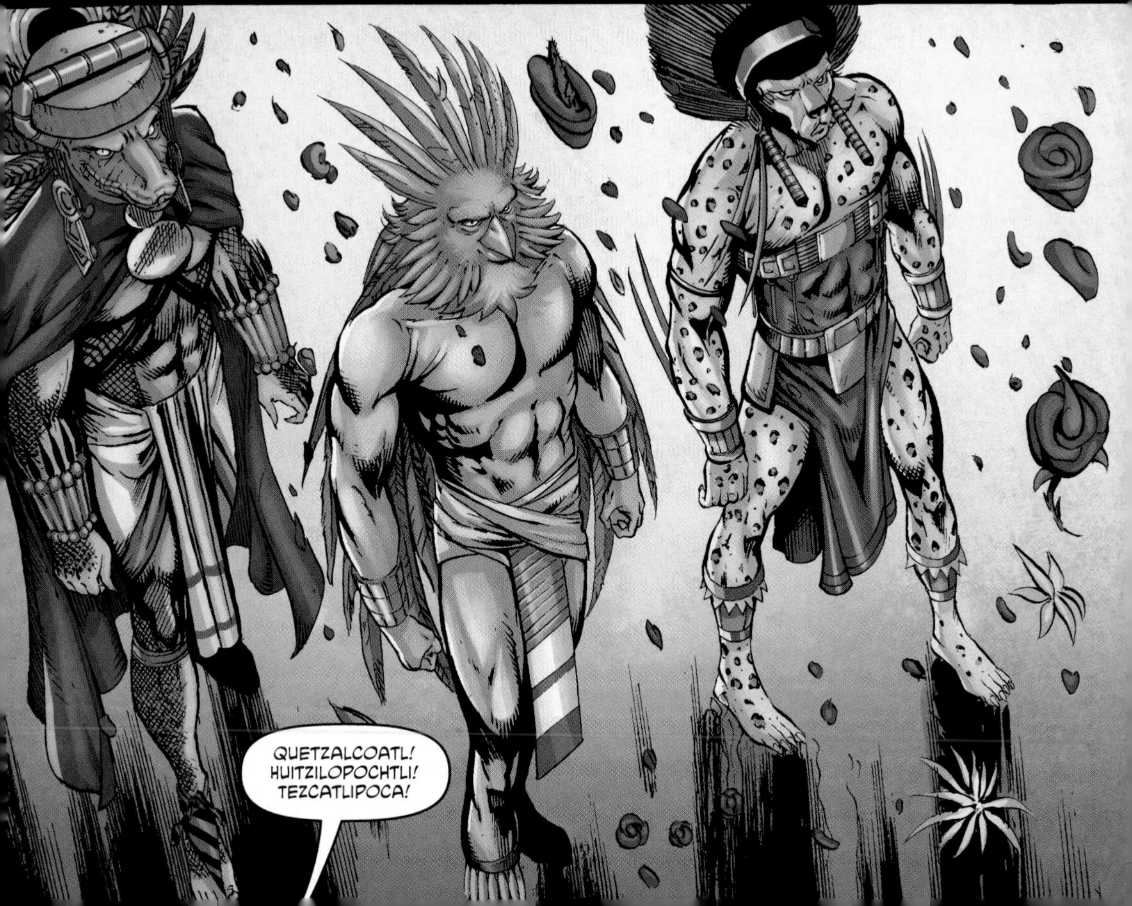
QUETZALCOATL! HUITZILOPOCHTLI! TEZCATLIPOCA!

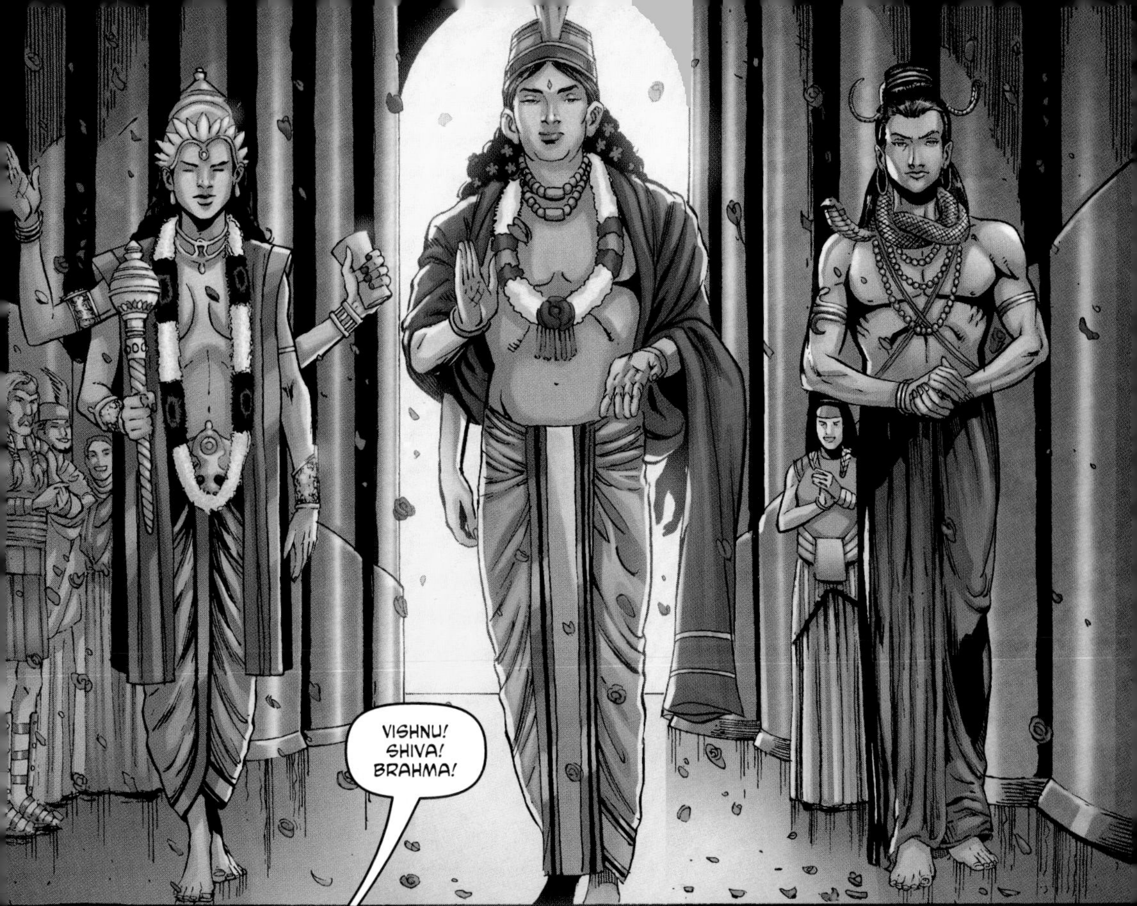
VISHNU! SHIVA! BRAHMA!

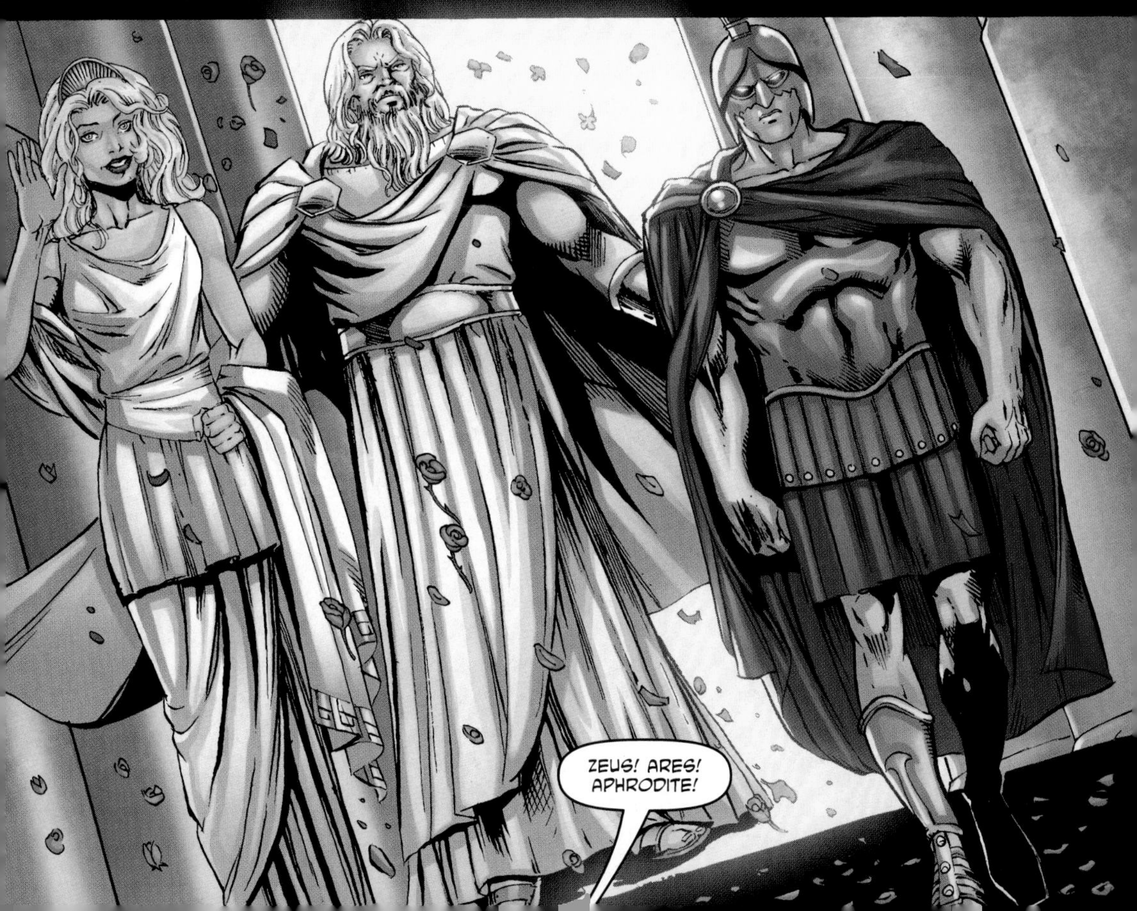
ZEUS! ARES! APHRODITE!

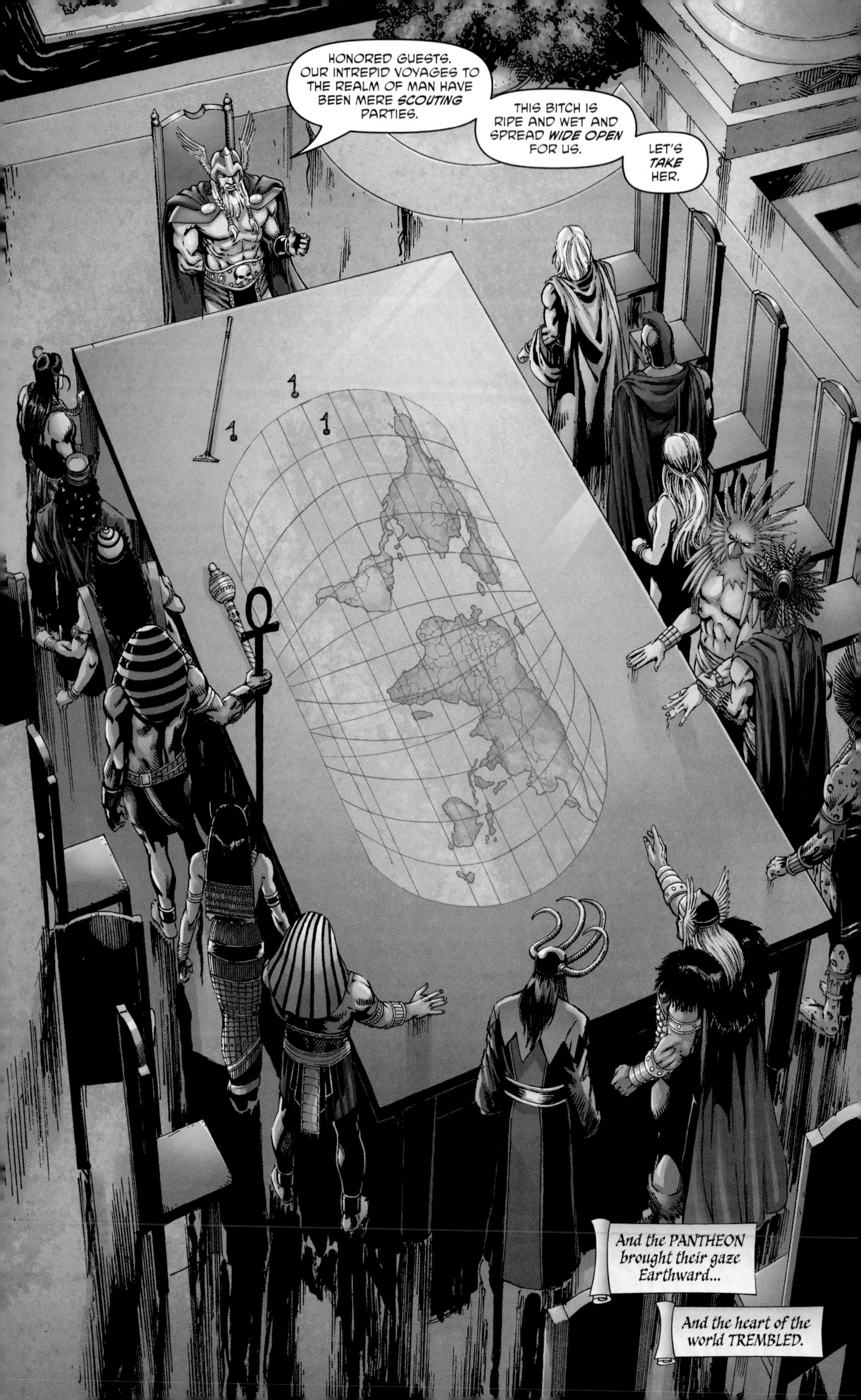
HONORED GUESTS. OUR INTREPID VOYAGES TO THE REALM OF MAN HAVE BEEN MERE SCOUTING PARTIES.
THIS BITCH IS RIPE AND WET AND SPREAD WIDE OPEN FOR US.
LET'S TAKE HER.
And the PANTHEON brought their gaze Earthward...
And the heart of the world TREMBLED.

TWO

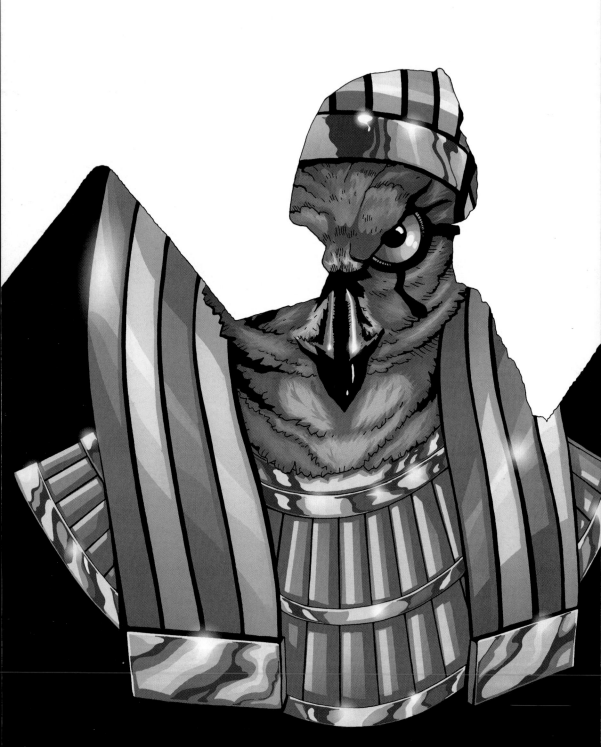

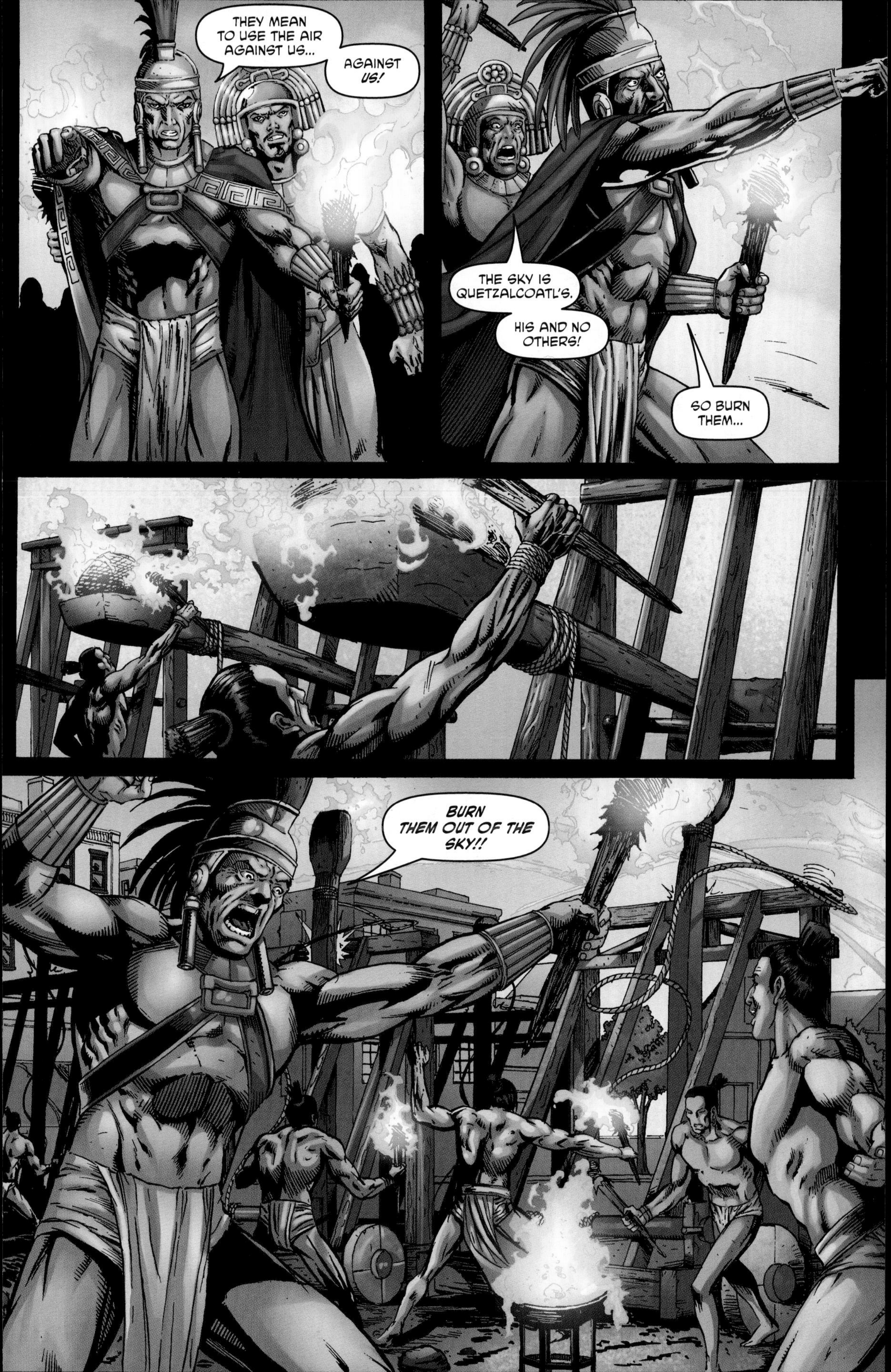
THEY MEAN TO USE THE AIR AGAINST US...
AGAINST *US!*
THE SKY IS QUETZALCOATL'S.
HIS AND NO OTHERS!
SO BURN THEM...
BURN THEM OUT OF THE SKY!!

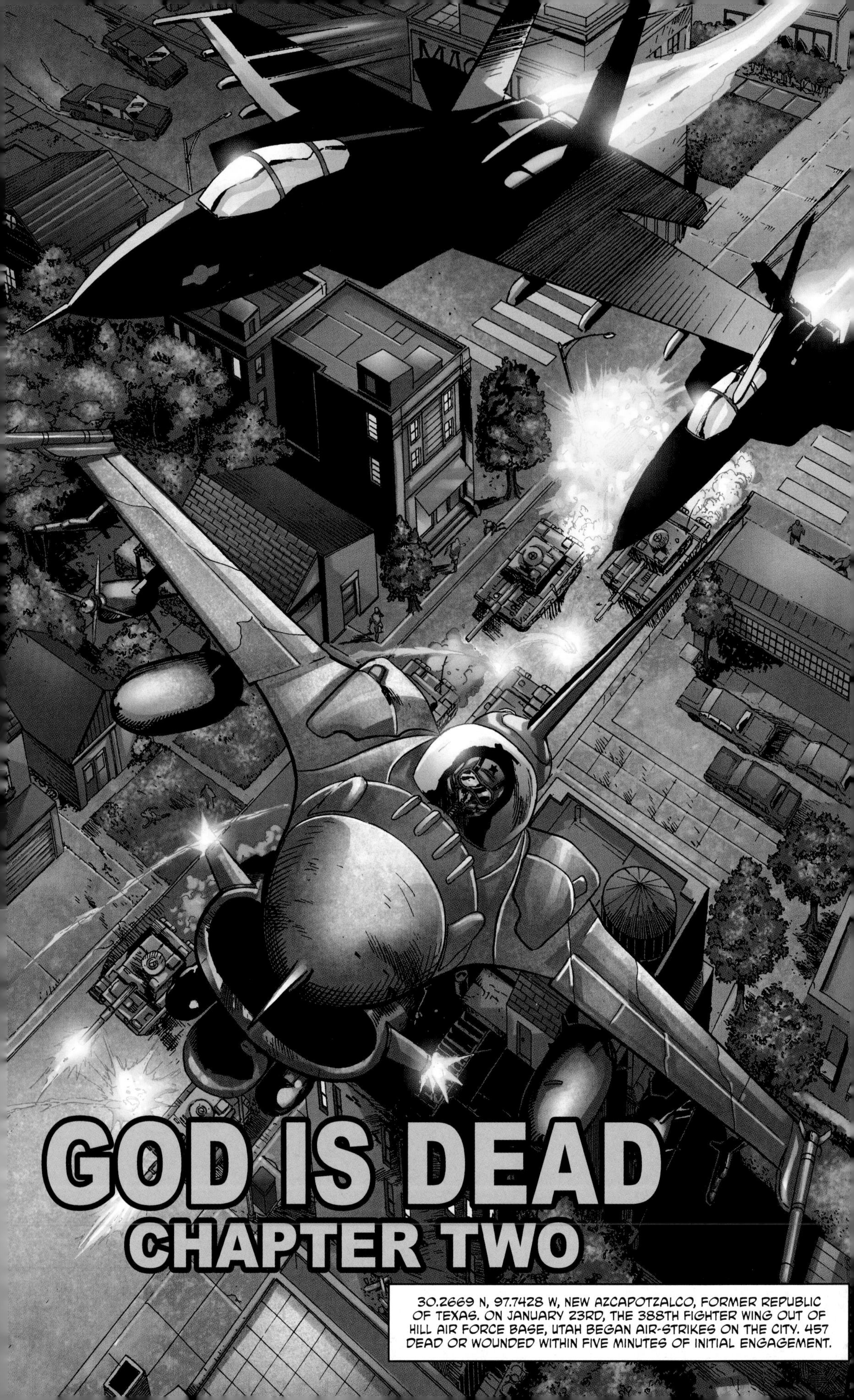
GOD IS DEAD
CHAPTER TWO
30.2669 N, 97.7428 W, NEW AZCAPOTZALCO, FORMER REPUBLIC OF TEXAS. ON JANUARY 23RD, THE 388TH FIGHTER WING OUT OF HILL AIR FORCE BASE, UTAH BEGAN AIR-STRIKES ON THE CITY. 457 DEAD OR WOUNDED WITHIN FIVE MINUTES OF INITIAL ENGAGEMENT.

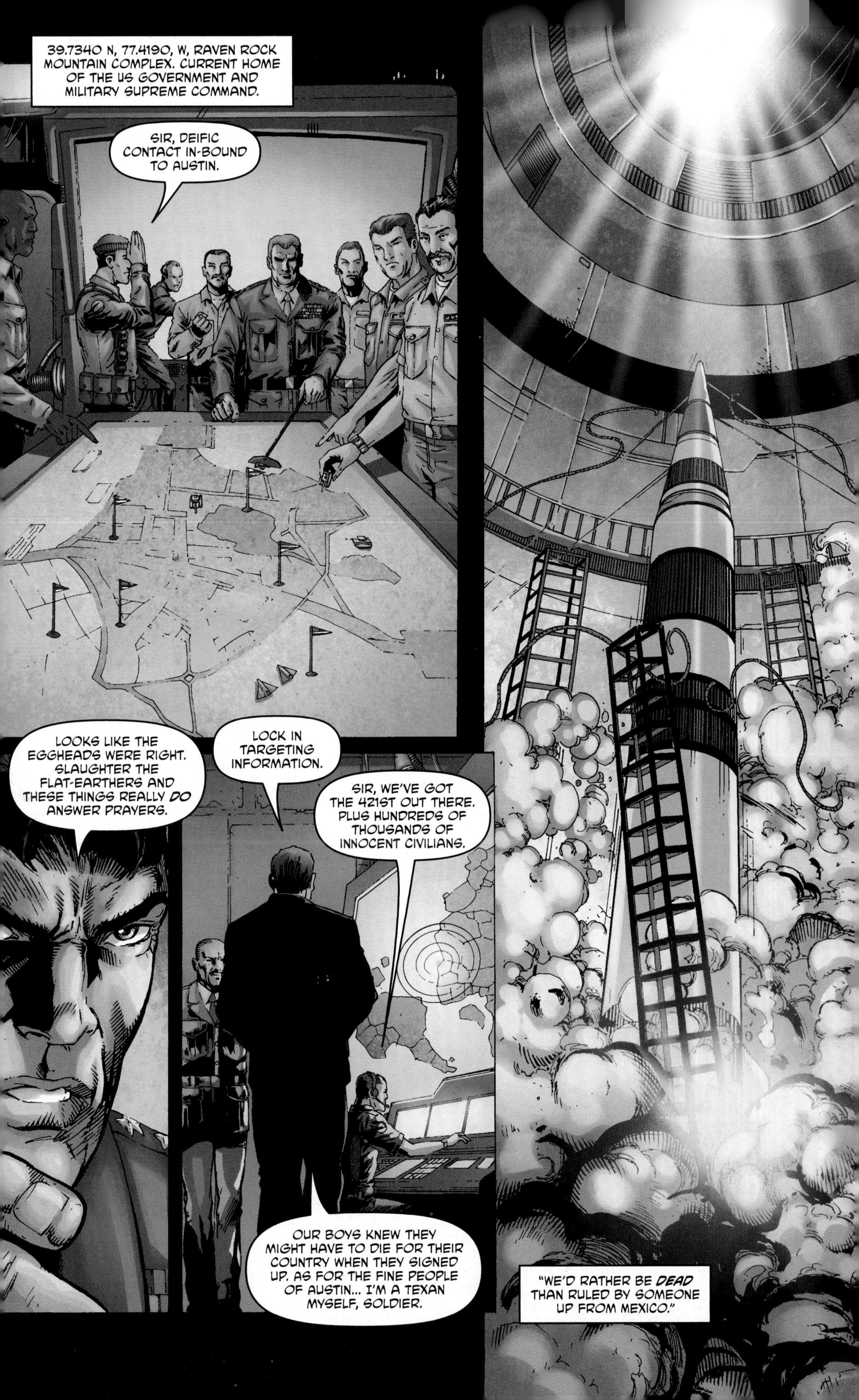
39.7340 N, 77.4190, W, RAVEN ROCK MOUNTAIN COMPLEX. CURRENT HOME OF THE US GOVERNMENT AND MILITARY SUPREME COMMAND.
SIR, DEIFIC CONTACT IN-BOUND TO AUSTIN.
LOOKS LIKE THE EGGHEADS WERE RIGHT. SLAUGHTER THE FLAT-EARTHERS AND THESE THINGS REALLY *DO* ANSWER PRAYERS.
LOCK IN TARGETING INFORMATION.
SIR, WE'VE GOT THE 421ST OUT THERE. PLUS HUNDREDS OF THOUSANDS OF INNOCENT CIVILIANS.
OUR BOYS KNEW THEY MIGHT HAVE TO DIE FOR THEIR COUNTRY WHEN THEY SIGNED UP. AS FOR THE FINE PEOPLE OF AUSTIN... I'M A TEXAN MYSELF, SOLDIER.
"WE'D RATHER BE *DEAD* THAN RULED BY SOMEONE UP FROM MEXICO."

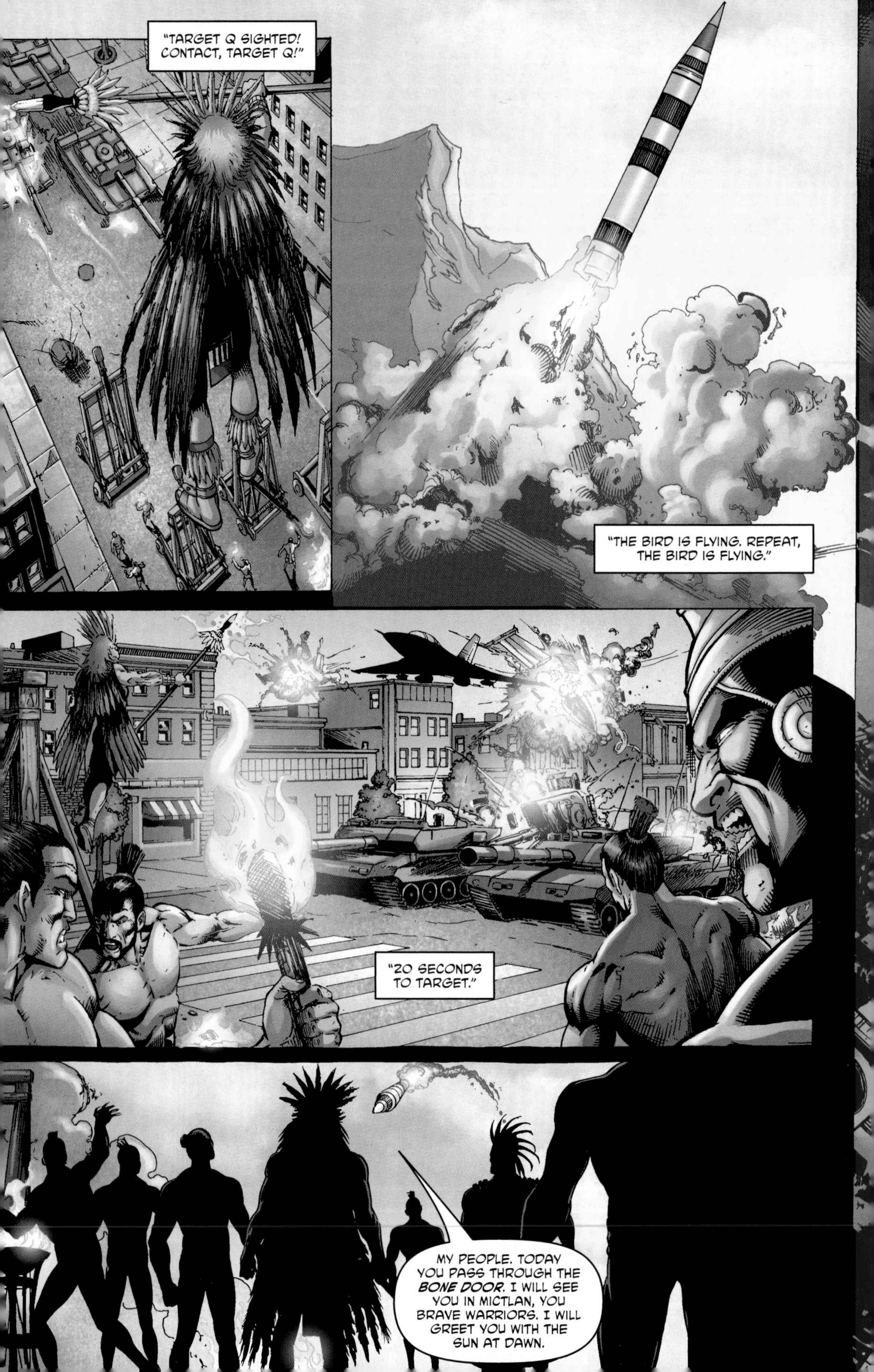
"TARGET Q SIGHTED! CONTACT, TARGET Q!"
"THE BIRD IS FLYING. REPEAT, THE BIRD IS FLYING."
"20 SECONDS TO TARGET."
MY PEOPLE. TODAY YOU PASS THROUGH THE *BONE DOOR*. I WILL SEE YOU IN MICTLAN, YOU BRAVE WARRIORS. I WILL GREET YOU WITH THE SUN AT DAWN.

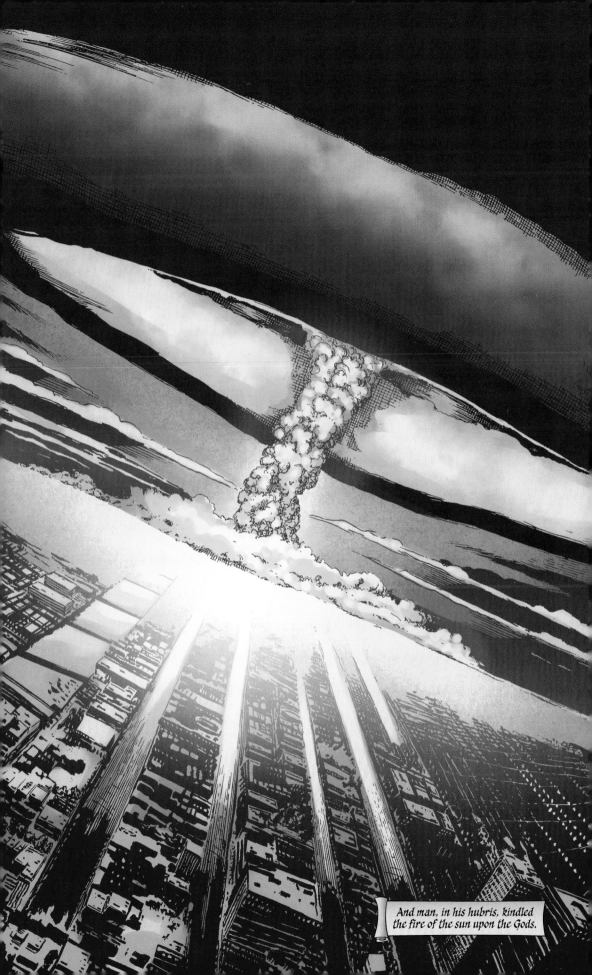

And man, in his hubris, kindled
the fire of the sun upon the Gods.

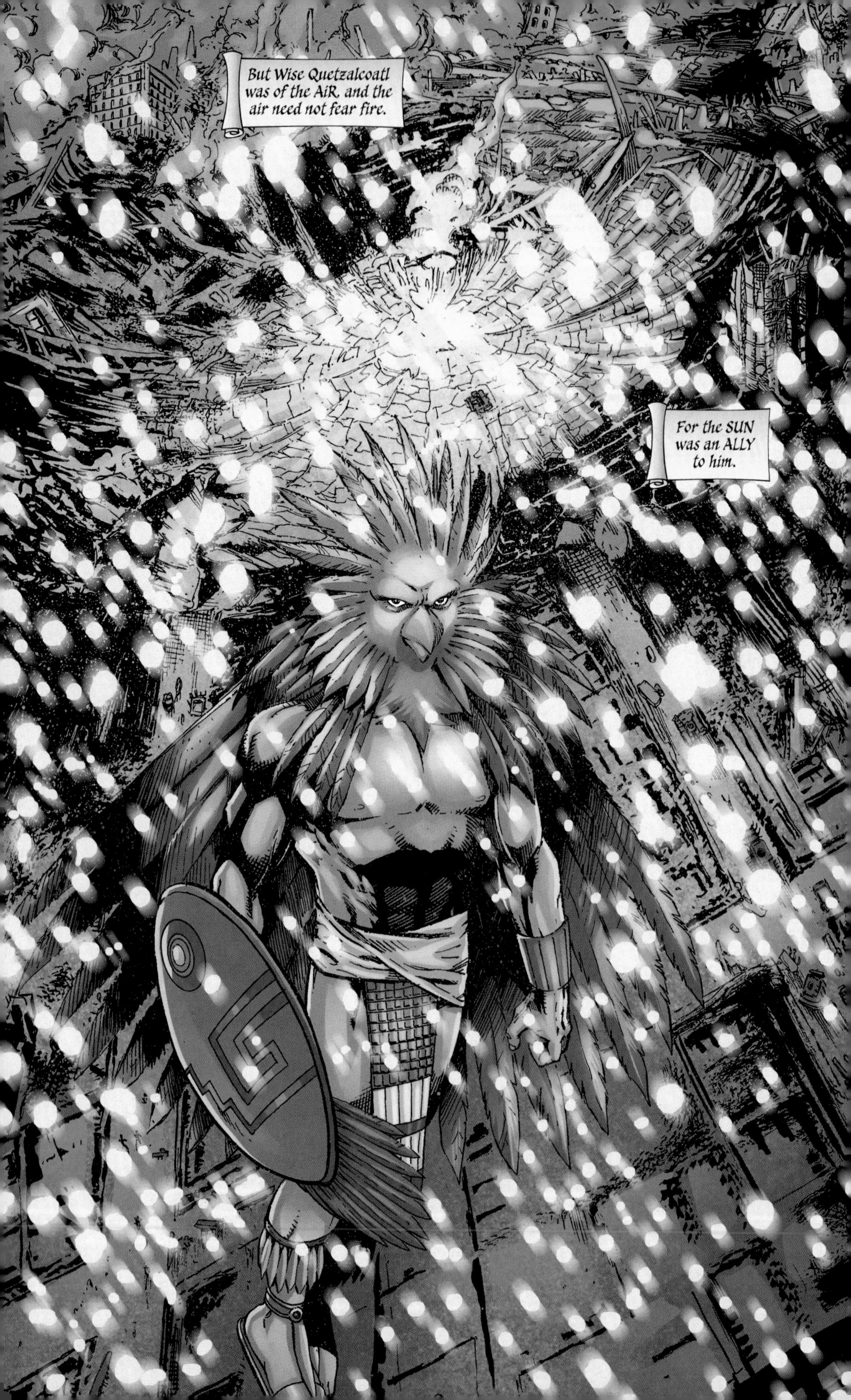
But Wise Quetzalcoatl was of the AiR, and the air need not fear fire.
For the SUN was an ALLY to him.

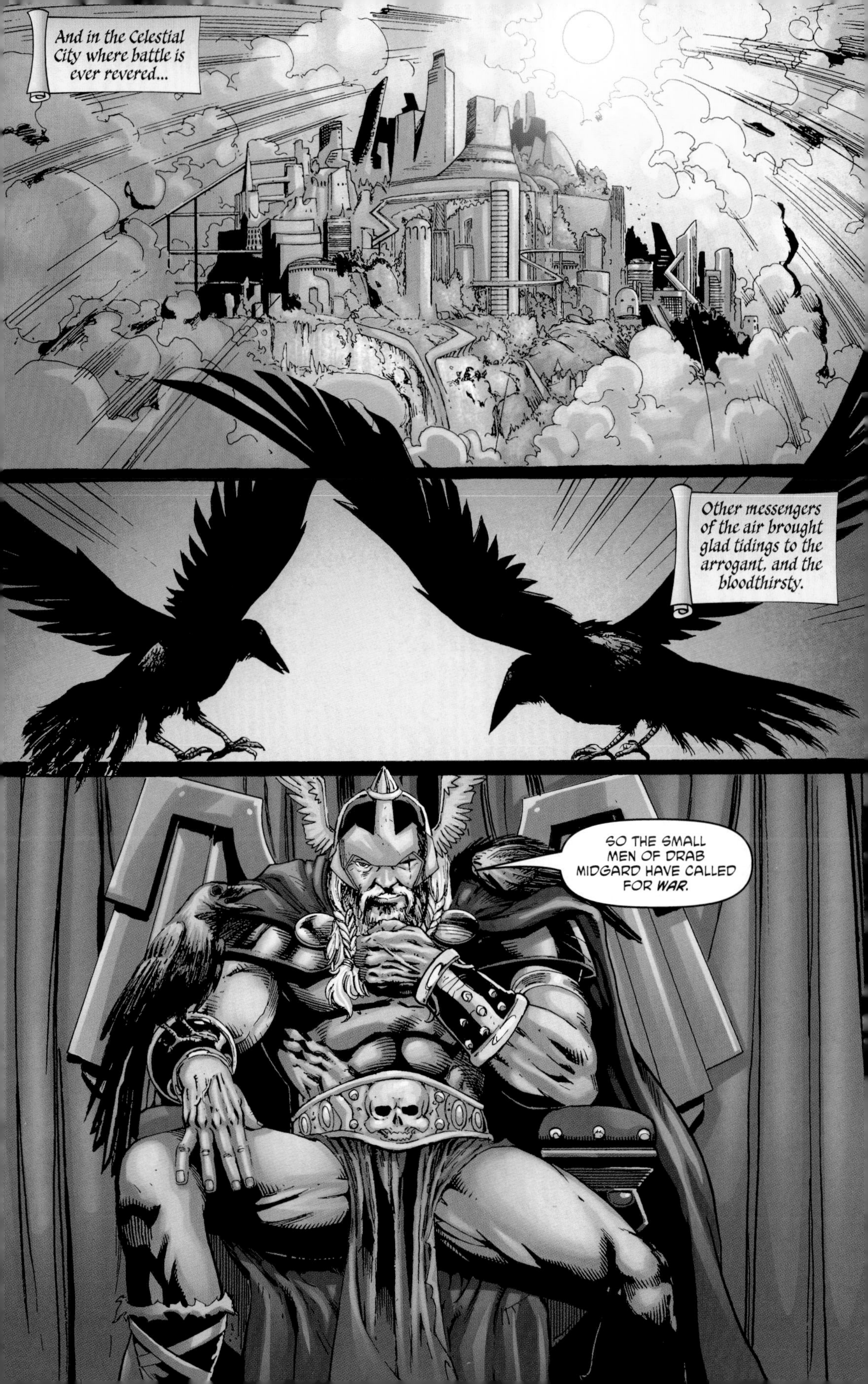
And in the Celestial City where battle is ever revered...
Other messengers of the air brought glad tidings to the arrogant, and the bloodthirsty.
SO THE SMALL MEN OF DRAB MIDGARD HAVE CALLED FOR *WAR*.

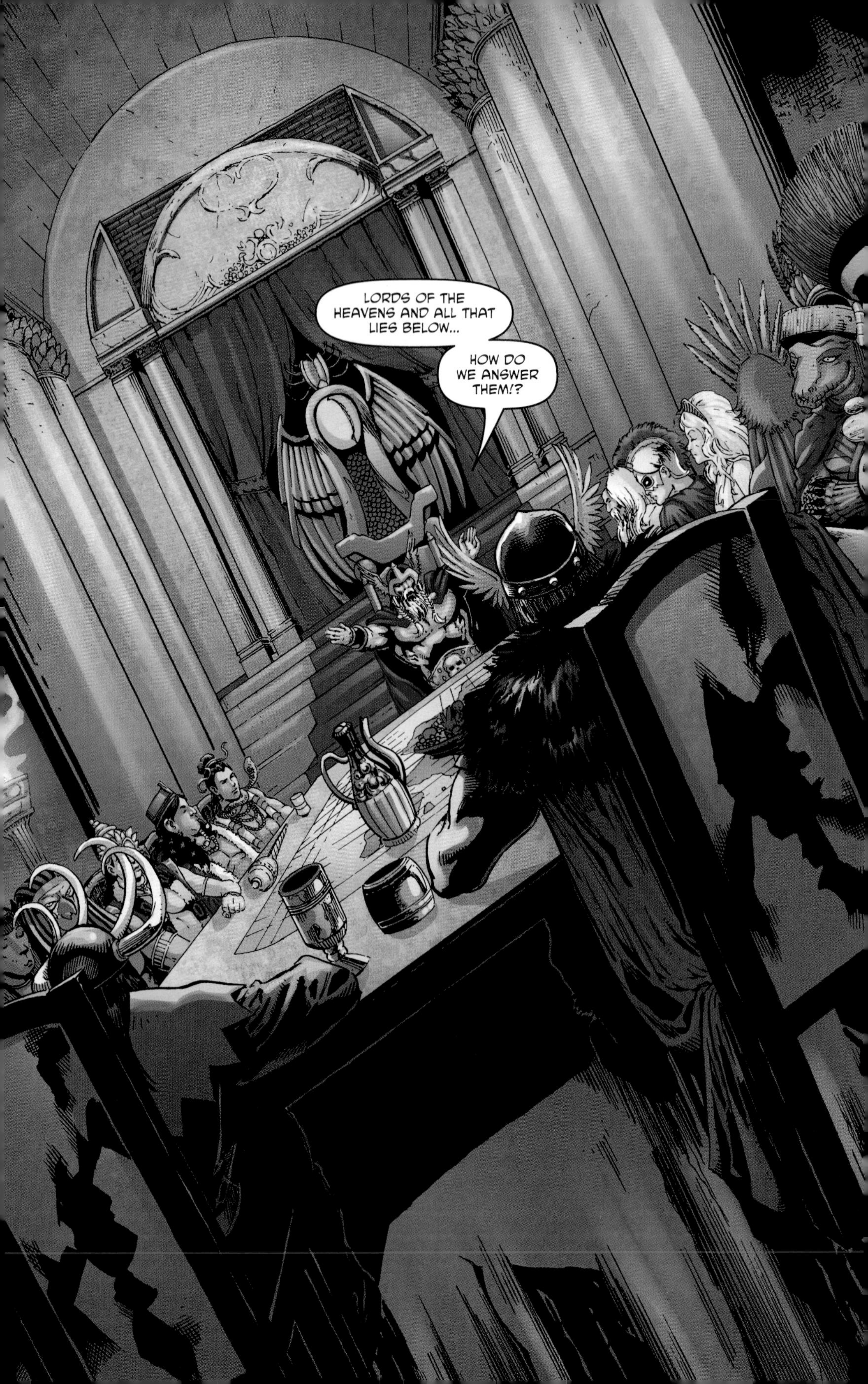
LORDS OF THE HEAVENS AND ALL THAT LIES BELOW...
HOW DO WE ANSWER THEM!?

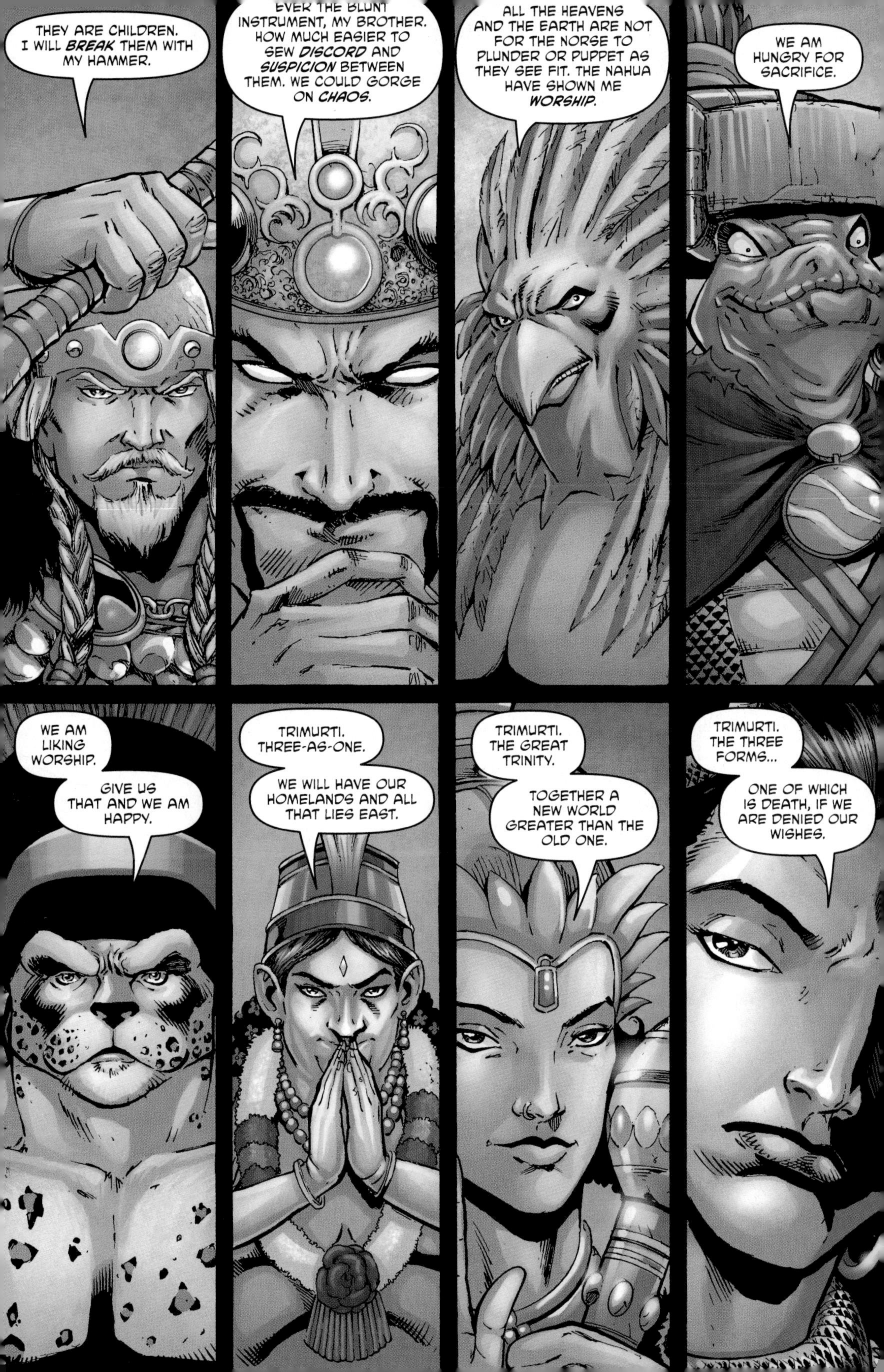
THEY ARE CHILDREN. I WILL BREAK THEM WITH MY HAMMER.
EVER THE BLUNT INSTRUMENT, MY BROTHER. HOW MUCH EASIER TO SEW DISCORD AND SUSPICION BETWEEN THEM. WE COULD GORGE ON CHAOS.
ALL THE HEAVENS AND THE EARTH ARE NOT FOR THE NORSE TO PLUNDER OR PUPPET AS THEY SEE FIT. THE NAHUA HAVE SHOWN ME WORSHIP.
WE AM HUNGRY FOR SACRIFICE.
WE AM LIKING WORSHIP.
GIVE US THAT AND WE AM HAPPY.
TRIMURTI. THREE-AS-ONE.
WE WILL HAVE OUR HOMELANDS AND ALL THAT LIES EAST.
TRIMURTI. THE GREAT TRINITY.
TOGETHER A NEW WORLD GREATER THAN THE OLD ONE.
TRIMURTI. THE THREE FORMS...
ONE OF WHICH IS DEATH, IF WE ARE DENIED OUR WISHES.

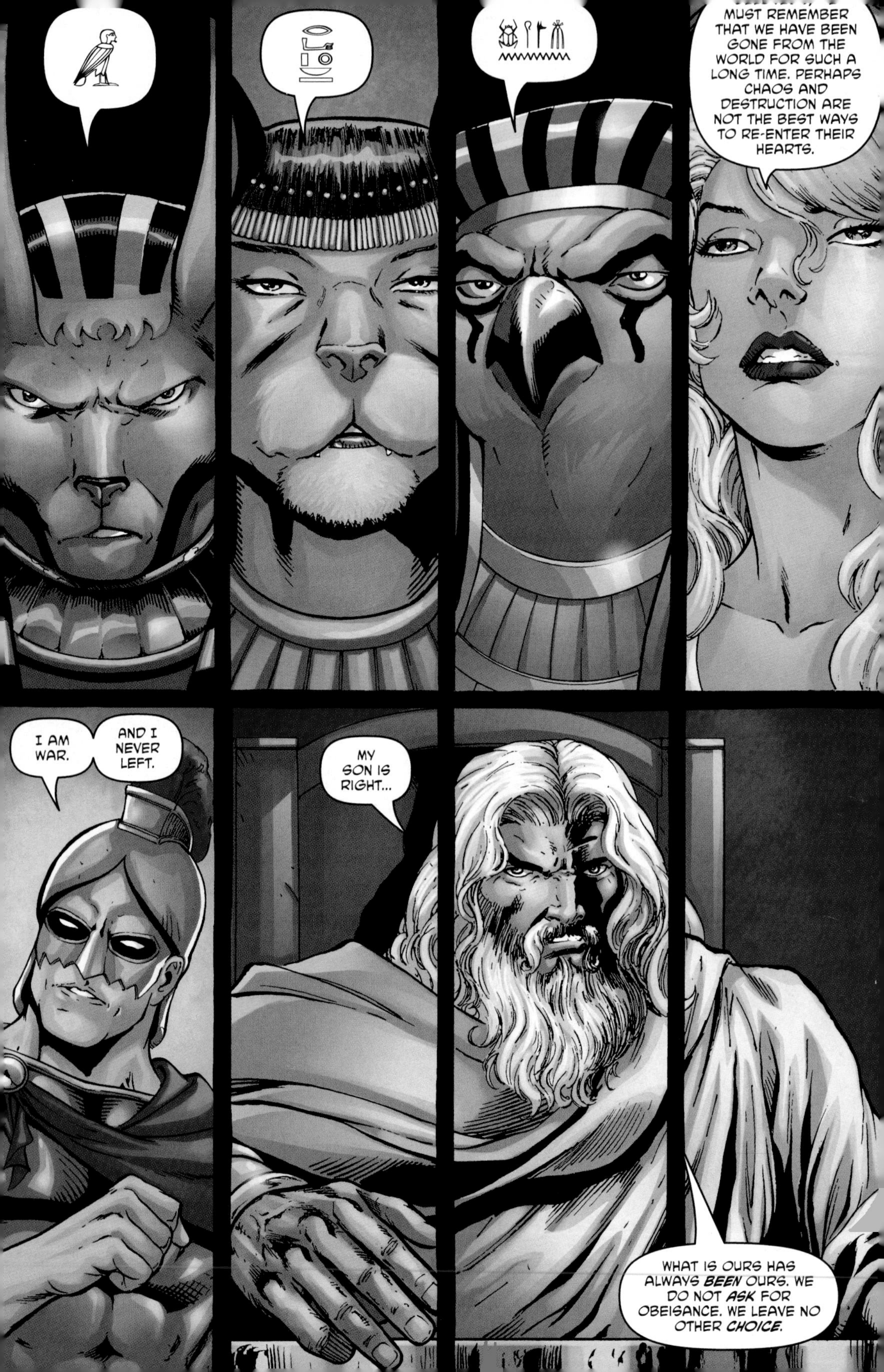
MUST REMEMBER THAT WE HAVE BEEN GONE FROM THE WORLD FOR SUCH A LONG TIME. PERHAPS CHAOS AND DESTRUCTION ARE NOT THE BEST WAYS TO RE-ENTER THEIR HEARTS.
I AM WAR.
AND I NEVER LEFT.
MY SON IS RIGHT...
WHAT IS OURS HAS ALWAYS *BEEN* OURS. WE DO NOT *ASK* FOR OBEISANCE. WE LEAVE NO OTHER *CHOICE*.

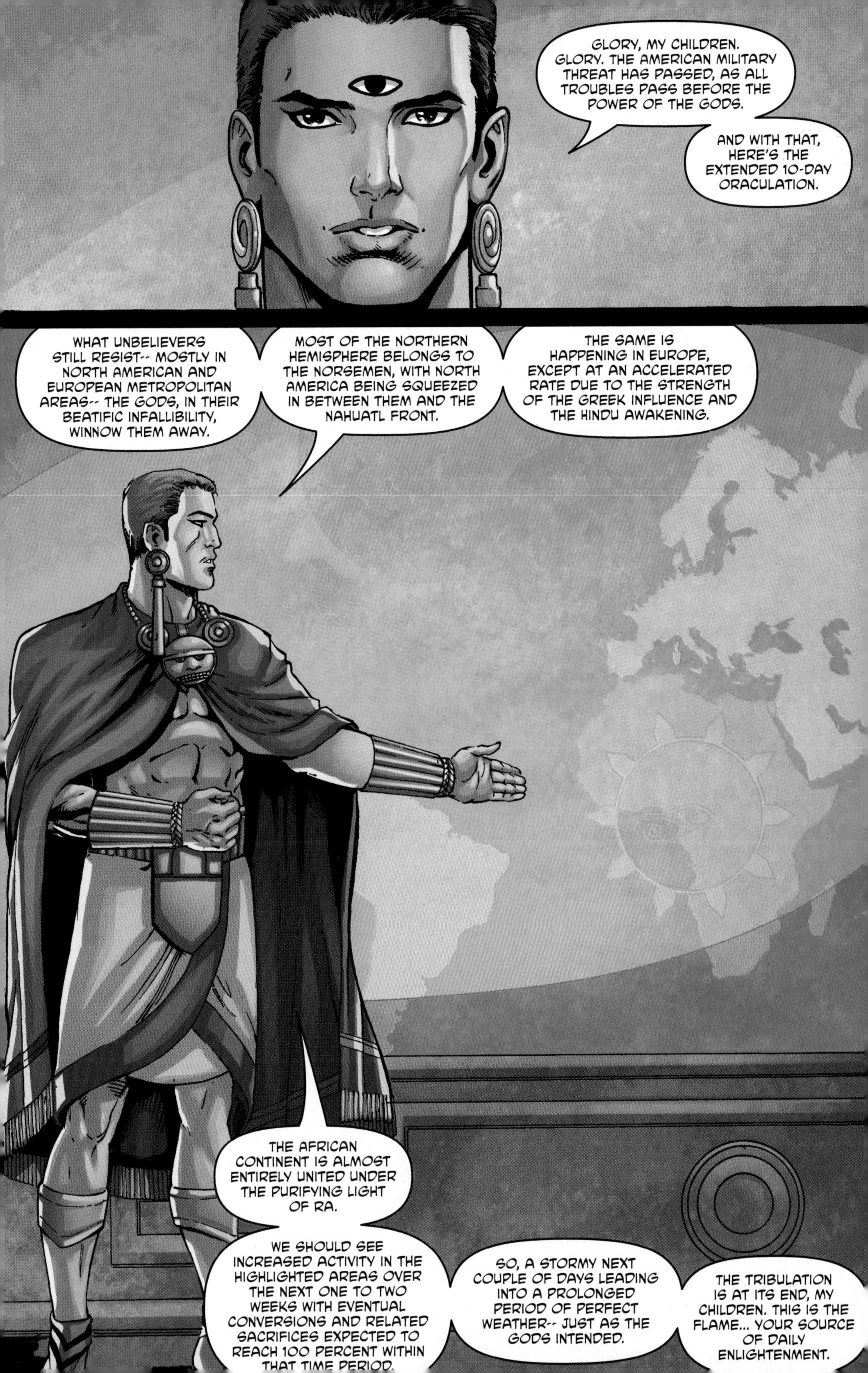
GLORY, MY CHILDREN. GLORY. THE AMERICAN MILITARY THREAT HAS PASSED, AS ALL TROUBLES PASS BEFORE THE POWER OF THE GODS.
AND WITH THAT, HERE'S THE EXTENDED 10-DAY ORACULATION.
WHAT UNBELIEVERS STILL RESIST-- MOSTLY IN NORTH AMERICAN AND EUROPEAN METROPOLITAN AREAS-- THE GODS, IN THEIR BEATIFIC INFALLIBILITY, WINNOW THEM AWAY.
MOST OF THE NORTHERN HEMISPHERE BELONGS TO THE NORSEMEN, WITH NORTH AMERICA BEING SQUEEZED IN BETWEEN THEM AND THE NAHUATL FRONT.
THE SAME IS HAPPENING IN EUROPE, EXCEPT AT AN ACCELERATED RATE DUE TO THE STRENGTH OF THE GREEK INFLUENCE AND THE HINDU AWAKENING.
THE AFRICAN CONTINENT IS ALMOST ENTIRELY UNITED UNDER THE PURIFYING LIGHT OF RA.
WE SHOULD SEE INCREASED ACTIVITY IN THE HIGHLIGHTED AREAS OVER THE NEXT ONE TO TWO WEEKS WITH EVENTUAL CONVERSIONS AND RELATED SACRIFICES EXPECTED TO REACH 100 PERCENT WITHIN THAT TIME PERIOD.
SO, A STORMY NEXT COUPLE OF DAYS LEADING INTO A PROLONGED PERIOD OF PERFECT WEATHER-- JUST AS THE GODS INTENDED.
THE TRIBULATION IS AT ITS END, MY CHILDREN. THIS IS THE FLAME... YOUR SOURCE OF DAILY ENLIGHTENMENT.

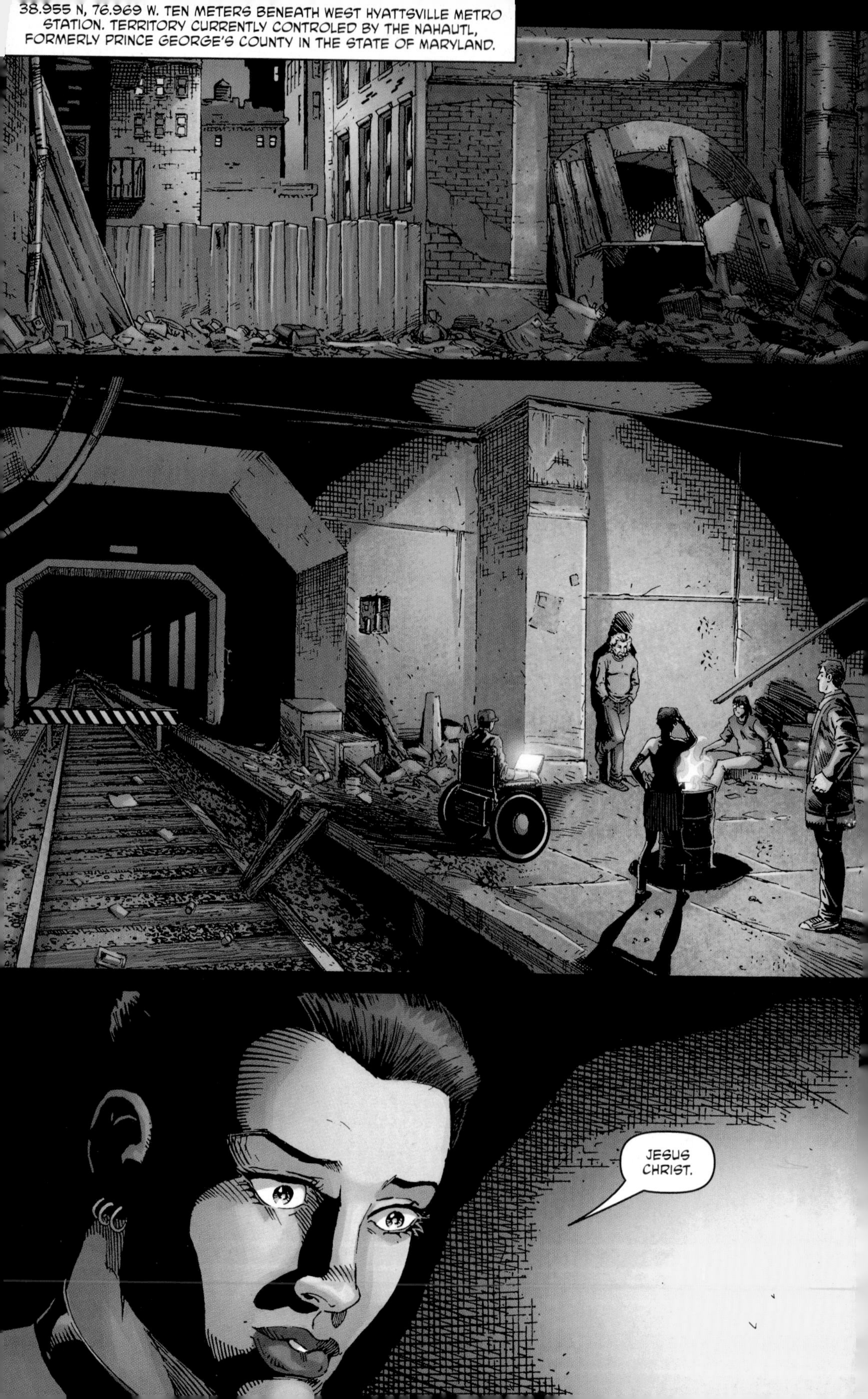
38.955 N, 76.969 W. TEN METERS BENEATH WEST HYATTSVILLE METRO STATION. TERRITORY CURRENTLY CONTROLED BY THE NAHAUTL, FORMERLY PRINCE GEORGE'S COUNTY IN THE STATE OF MARYLAND.
JESUS CHRIST.

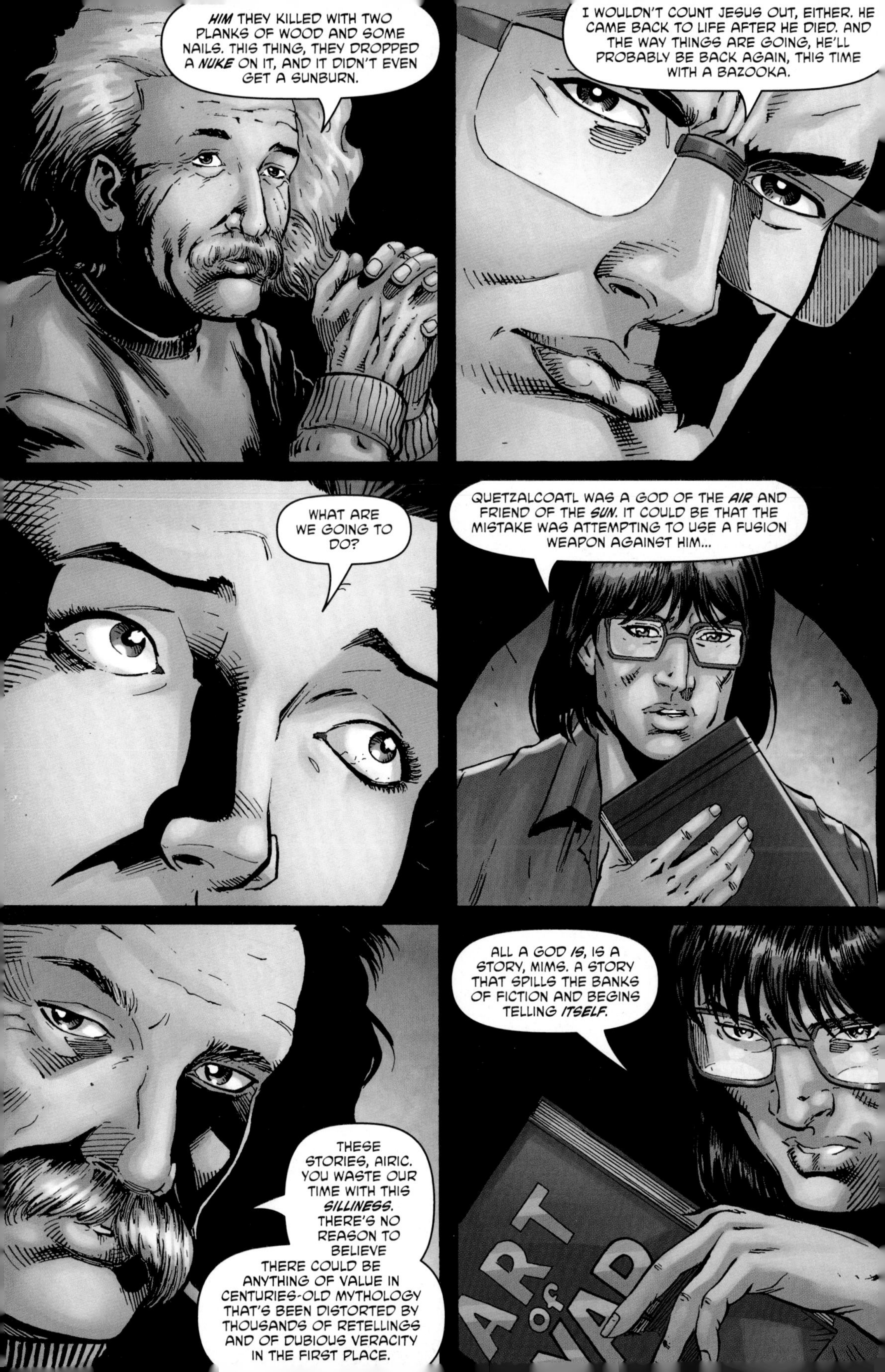
HIM THEY KILLED WITH TWO PLANKS OF WOOD AND SOME NAILS. THIS THING, THEY DROPPED A NUKE ON IT, AND IT DIDN'T EVEN GET A SUNBURN.
I WOULDN'T COUNT JESUS OUT, EITHER. HE CAME BACK TO LIFE AFTER HE DIED. AND THE WAY THINGS ARE GOING, HE'LL PROBABLY BE BACK AGAIN, THIS TIME WITH A BAZOOKA.
WHAT ARE WE GOING TO DO?
QUETZALCOATL WAS A GOD OF THE AIR AND FRIEND OF THE SUN. IT COULD BE THAT THE MISTAKE WAS ATTEMPTING TO USE A FUSION WEAPON AGAINST HIM...
THESE STORIES, AIRIC. YOU WASTE OUR TIME WITH THIS SILLINESS. THERE'S NO REASON TO BELIEVE THERE COULD BE ANYTHING OF VALUE IN CENTURIES-OLD MYTHOLOGY THAT'S BEEN DISTORTED BY THOUSANDS OF RETELLINGS AND OF DUBIOUS VERACITY IN THE FIRST PLACE.
ALL A GOD IS, IS A STORY, MIMS. A STORY THAT SPILLS THE BANKS OF FICTION AND BEGINS TELLING ITSELF.

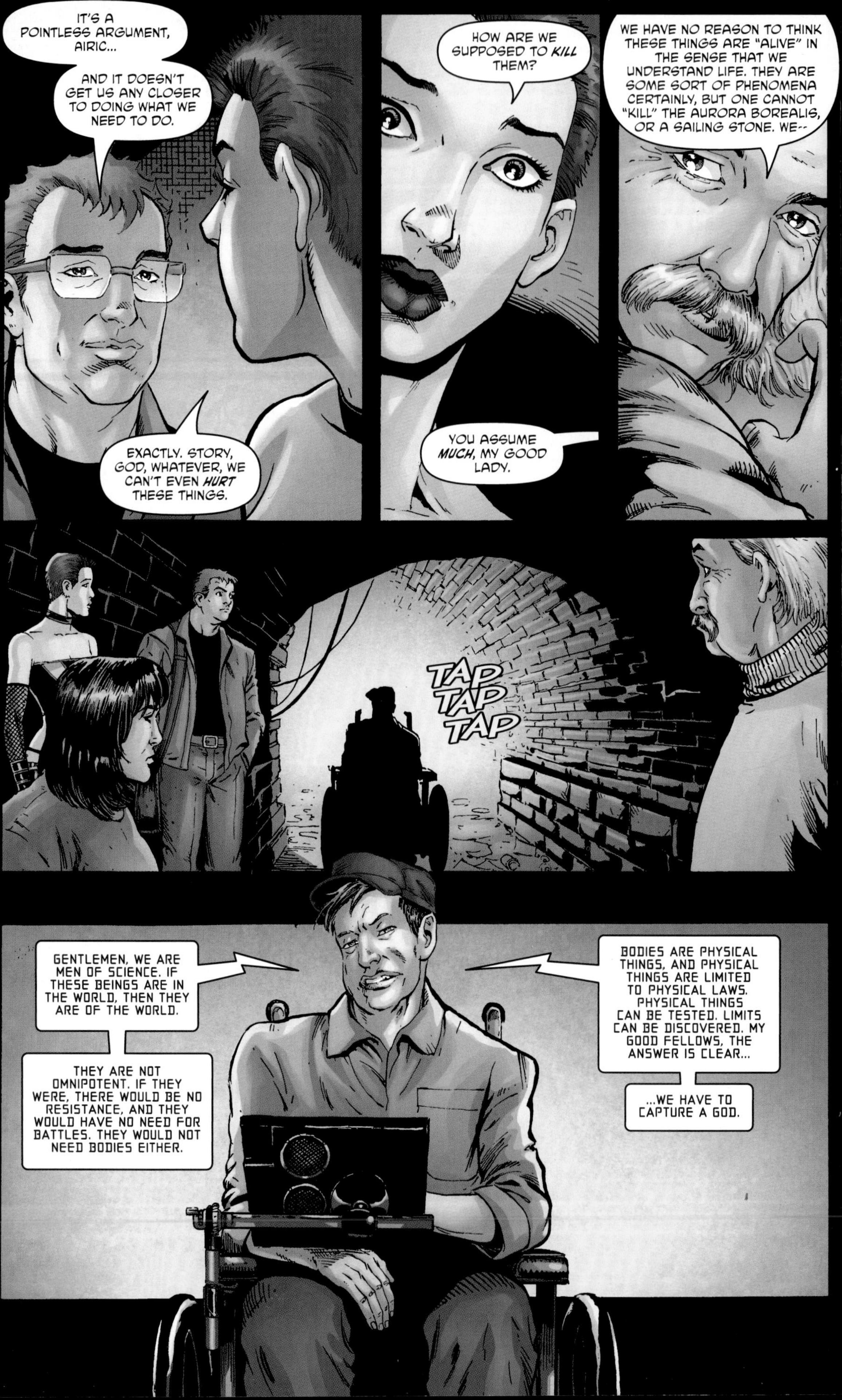
IT'S A POINTLESS ARGUMENT, AIRIC...
AND IT DOESN'T GET US ANY CLOSER TO DOING WHAT WE NEED TO DO.
EXACTLY. STORY, GOD, WHATEVER, WE CAN'T EVEN *HURT* THESE THINGS.
HOW ARE WE SUPPOSED TO *KILL* THEM?
WE HAVE NO REASON TO THINK THESE THINGS ARE "ALIVE" IN THE SENSE THAT WE UNDERSTAND LIFE. THEY ARE SOME SORT OF PHENOMENA CERTAINLY, BUT ONE CANNOT "KILL" THE AURORA BOREALIS, OR A SAILING STONE. WE--
YOU ASSUME *MUCH*, MY GOOD LADY.
TAP TAP TAP
GENTLEMEN, WE ARE MEN OF SCIENCE. IF THESE BEINGS ARE IN THE WORLD, THEN THEY ARE OF THE WORLD.
THEY ARE NOT OMNIPOTENT. IF THEY WERE, THERE WOULD BE NO RESISTANCE, AND THEY WOULD HAVE NO NEED FOR BATTLES. THEY WOULD NOT NEED BODIES EITHER.
BODIES ARE PHYSICAL THINGS, AND PHYSICAL THINGS ARE LIMITED TO PHYSICAL LAWS. PHYSICAL THINGS CAN BE TESTED. LIMITS CAN BE DISCOVERED. MY GOOD FELLOWS, THE ANSWER IS CLEAR...
...WE HAVE TO CAPTURE A GOD.

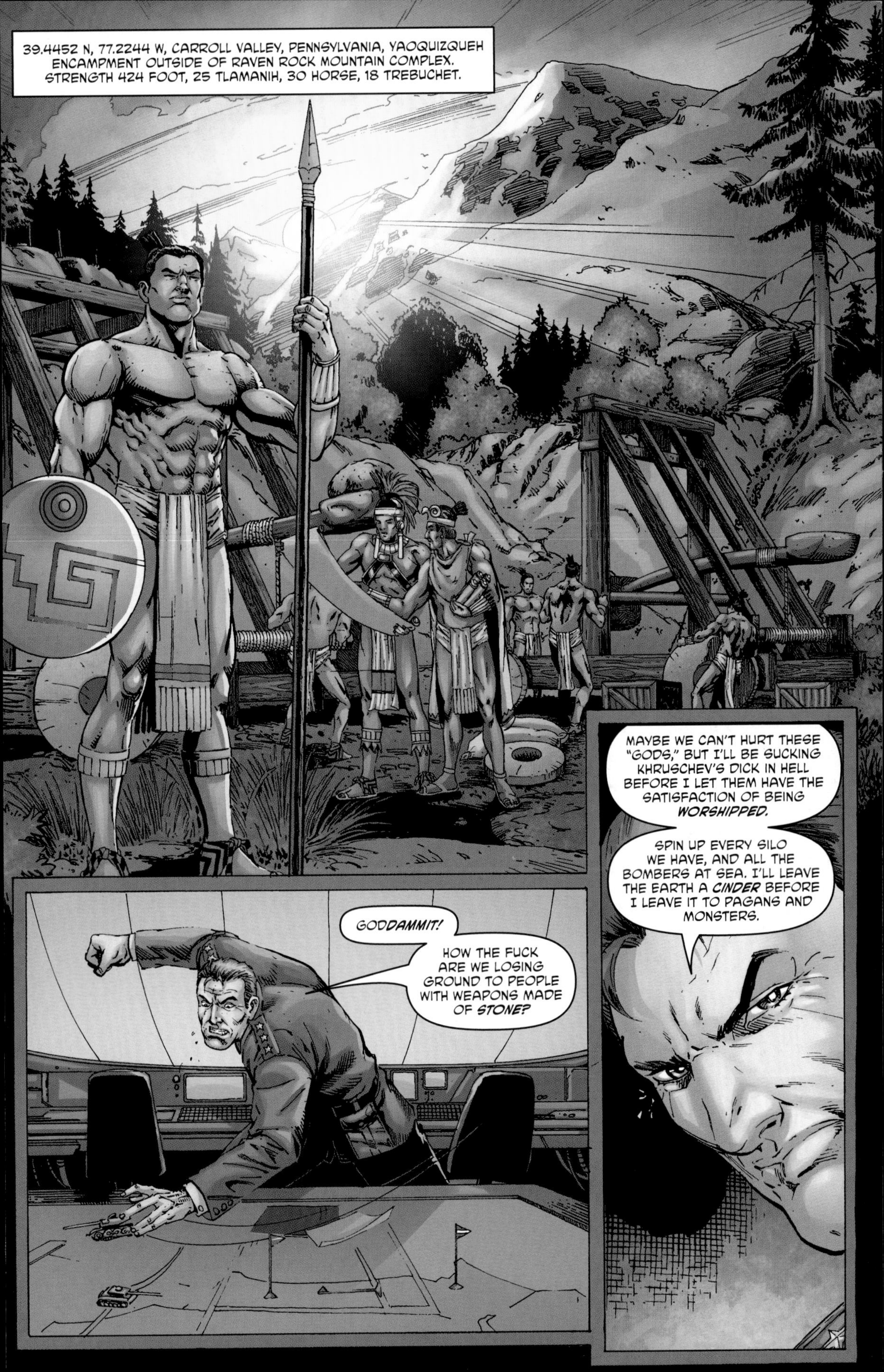
39.4452 N, 77.2244 W, CARROLL VALLEY, PENNSYLVANIA, YAOQUIZQUEH ENCAMPMENT OUTSIDE OF RAVEN ROCK MOUNTAIN COMPLEX. STRENGTH 424 FOOT, 25 TLAMANIH, 30 HORSE, 18 TREBUCHET.
GODDAMMIT!
HOW THE FUCK ARE WE LOSING GROUND TO PEOPLE WITH WEAPONS MADE OF STONE?
MAYBE WE CAN'T HURT THESE "GODS," BUT I'LL BE SUCKING KHRUSCHEV'S DICK IN HELL BEFORE I LET THEM HAVE THE SATISFACTION OF BEING WORSHIPPED.
SPIN UP EVERY SILO WE HAVE, AND ALL THE BOMBERS AT SEA. I'LL LEAVE THE EARTH A CINDER BEFORE I LEAVE IT TO PAGANS AND MONSTERS.

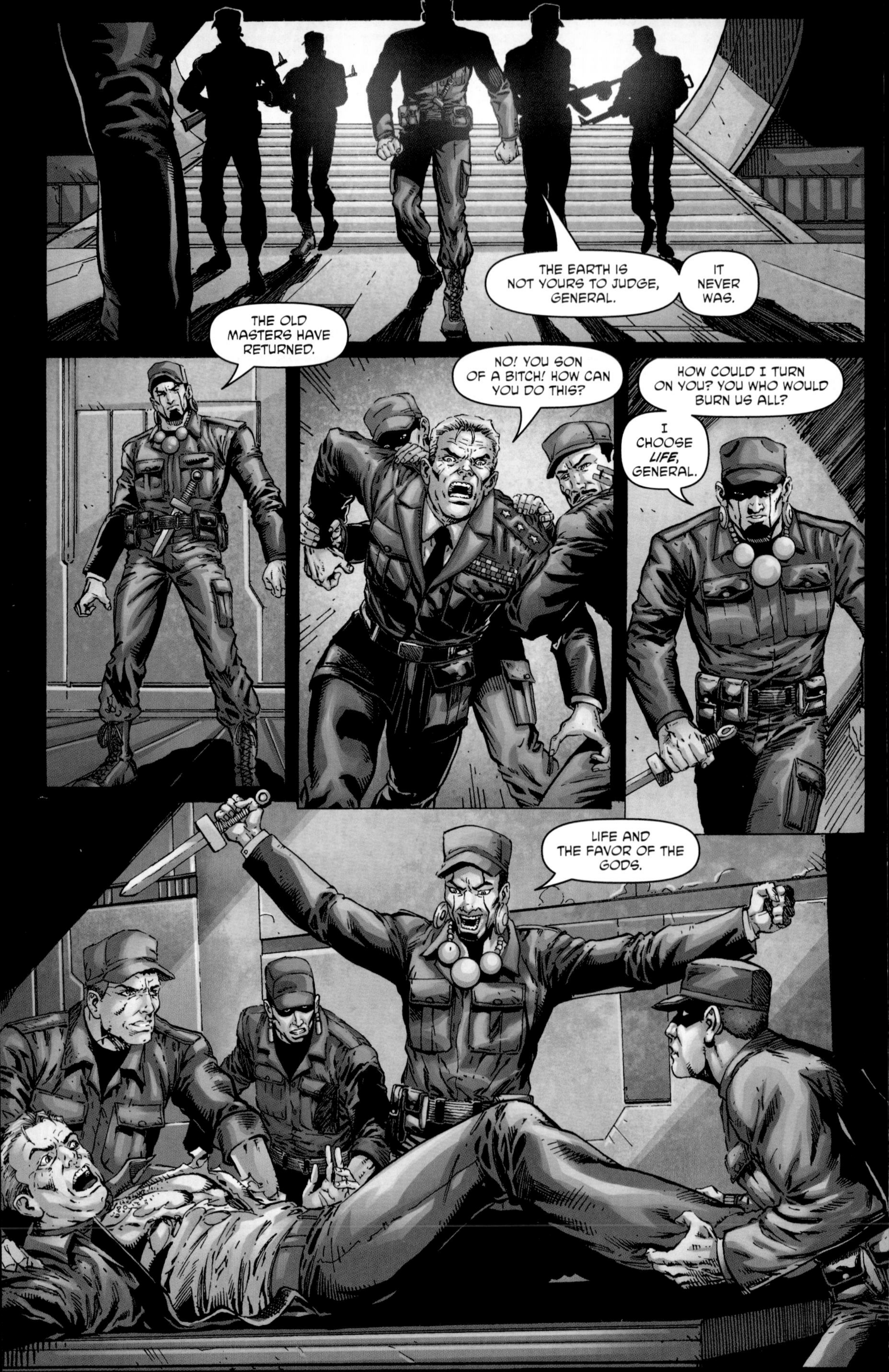
THE EARTH IS NOT YOURS TO JUDGE, GENERAL.
IT NEVER WAS.
THE OLD MASTERS HAVE RETURNED.
NO! YOU SON OF A BITCH! HOW CAN YOU DO THIS?
HOW COULD I TURN ON YOU? YOU WHO WOULD BURN US ALL?
I CHOOSE *LIFE*, GENERAL.
LIFE AND THE FAVOR OF THE GODS.

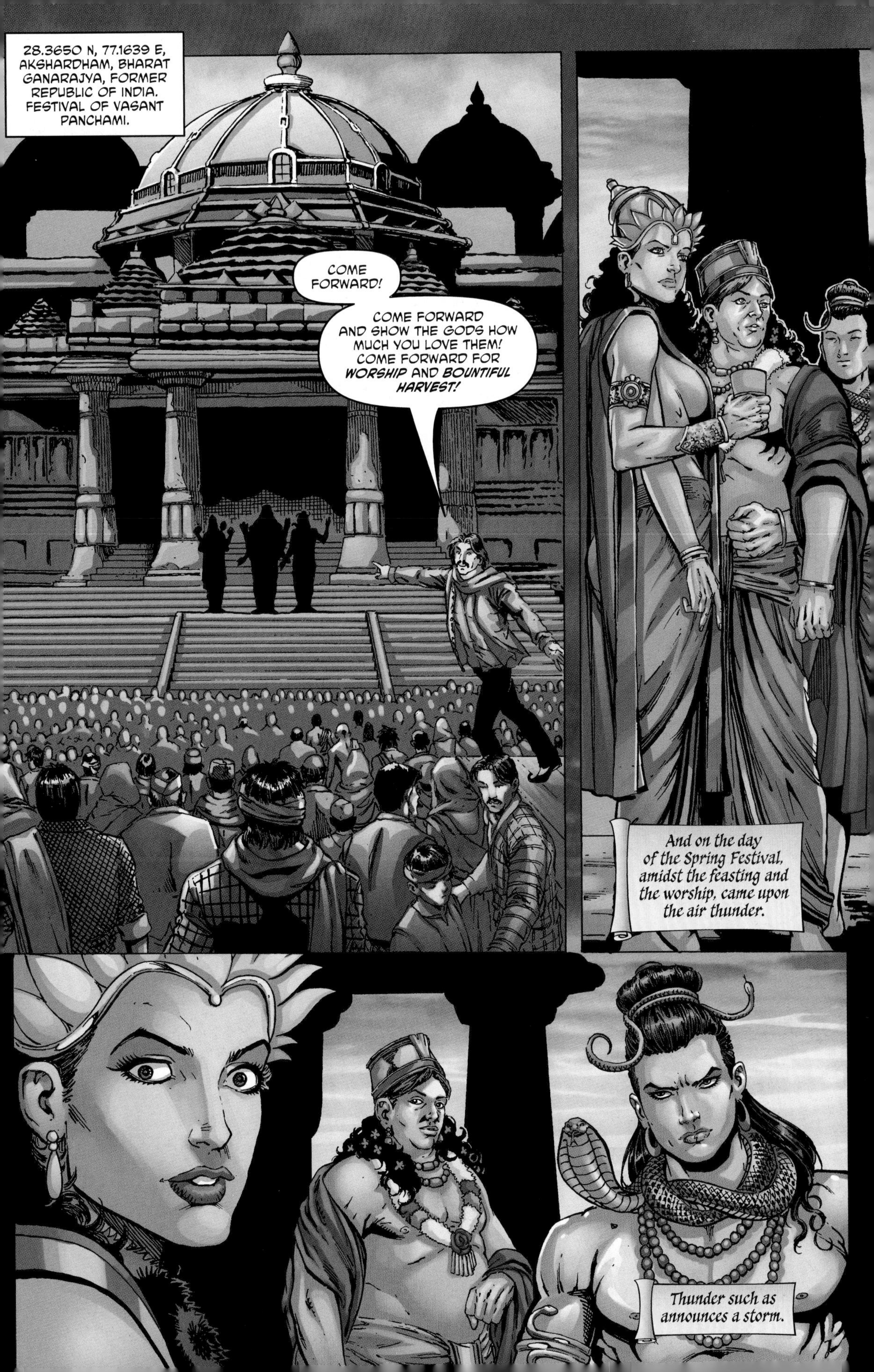

28.3650 N, 77.1639 E, AKSHARDHAM, BHARAT GANARAJYA, FORMER REPUBLIC OF INDIA. FESTIVAL OF VASANT PANCHAMI.
COME FORWARD!
COME FORWARD AND SHOW THE GODS HOW MUCH YOU LOVE THEM! COME FORWARD FOR WORSHIP AND BOUNTIFUL HARVEST!
And on the day of the Spring Festival, amidst the feasting and the worship, came upon the air thunder.
Thunder such as announces a storm.

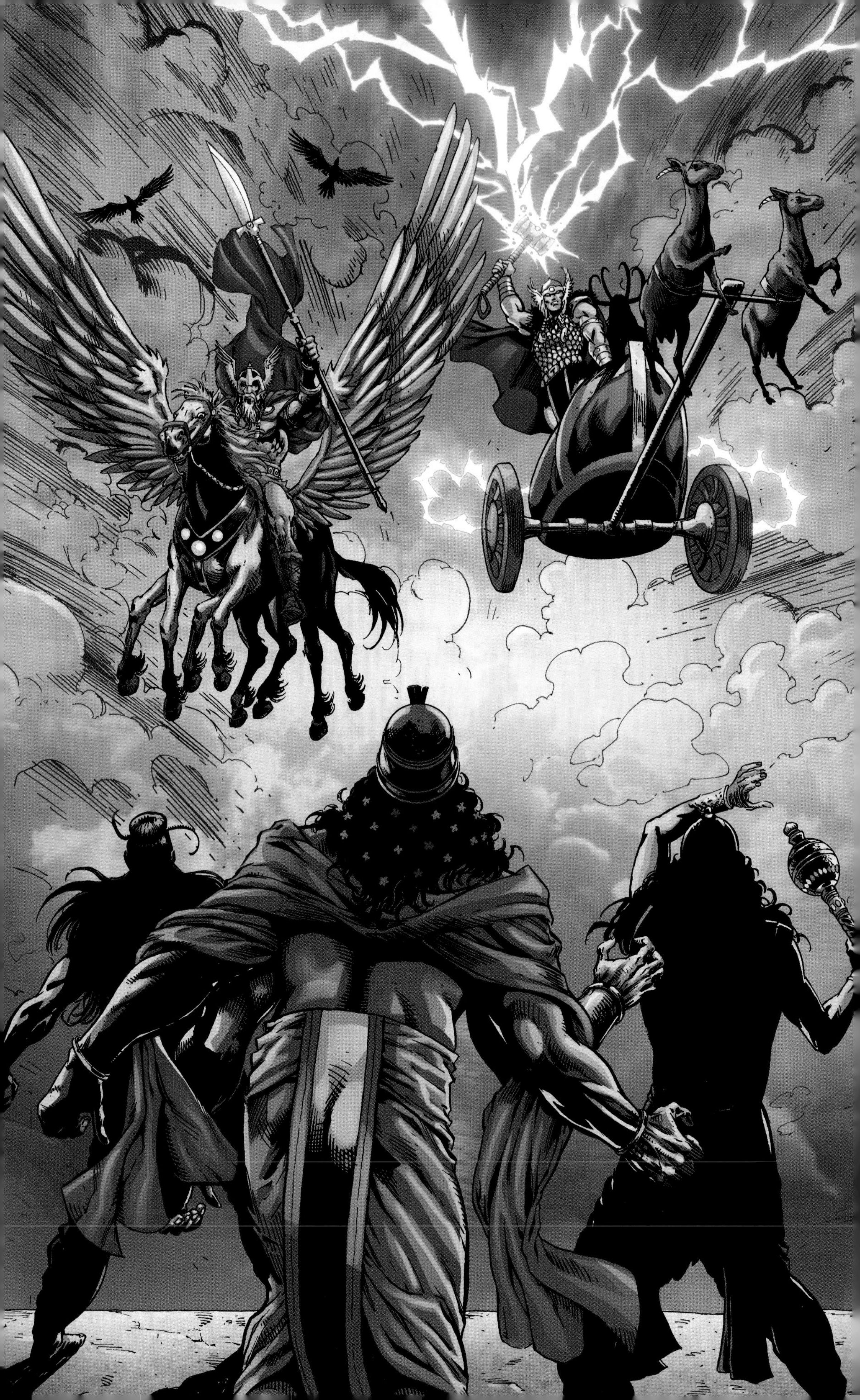

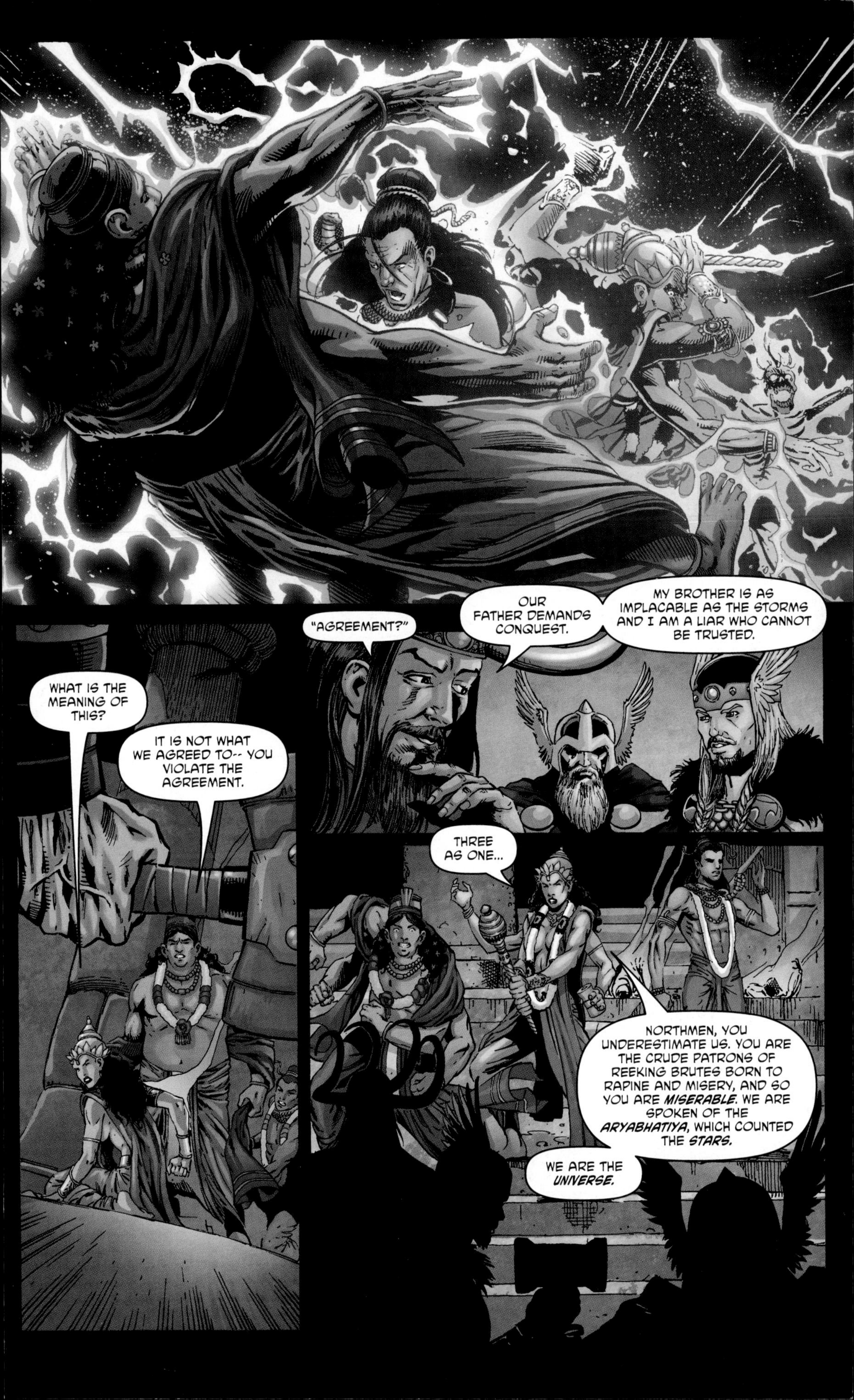
WHAT IS THE MEANING OF THIS?
IT IS NOT WHAT WE AGREED TO-- YOU VIOLATE THE AGREEMENT.
"AGREEMENT?"
OUR FATHER DEMANDS CONQUEST.
MY BROTHER IS AS IMPLACABLE AS THE STORMS AND I AM A LIAR WHO CANNOT BE TRUSTED.
THREE AS ONE...
NORTHMEN, YOU UNDERESTIMATE US. YOU ARE THE CRUDE PATRONS OF REEKING BRUTES BORN TO RAPINE AND MISERY, AND SO YOU ARE *MISERABLE*. WE ARE SPOKEN OF THE *ARYABHATIYA*, WHICH COUNTED THE *STARS*.
WE ARE THE *UNIVERSE*.

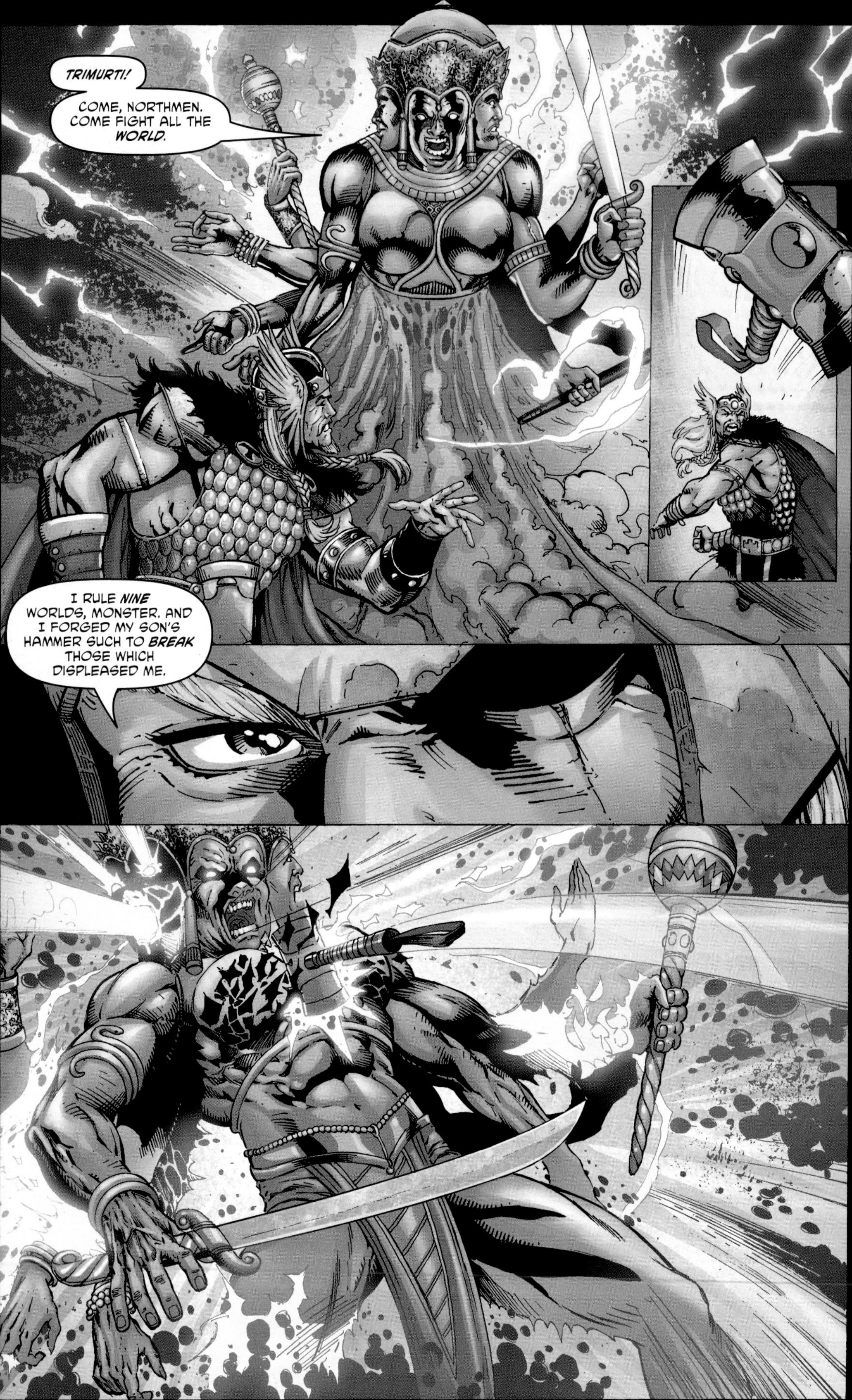
TRIMURTI!
COME, NORTHMEN. COME FIGHT ALL THE WORLD.
I RULE NINE WORLDS, MONSTER. AND I FORGED MY SON'S HAMMER SUCH TO BREAK THOSE WHICH DISPLEASED ME.

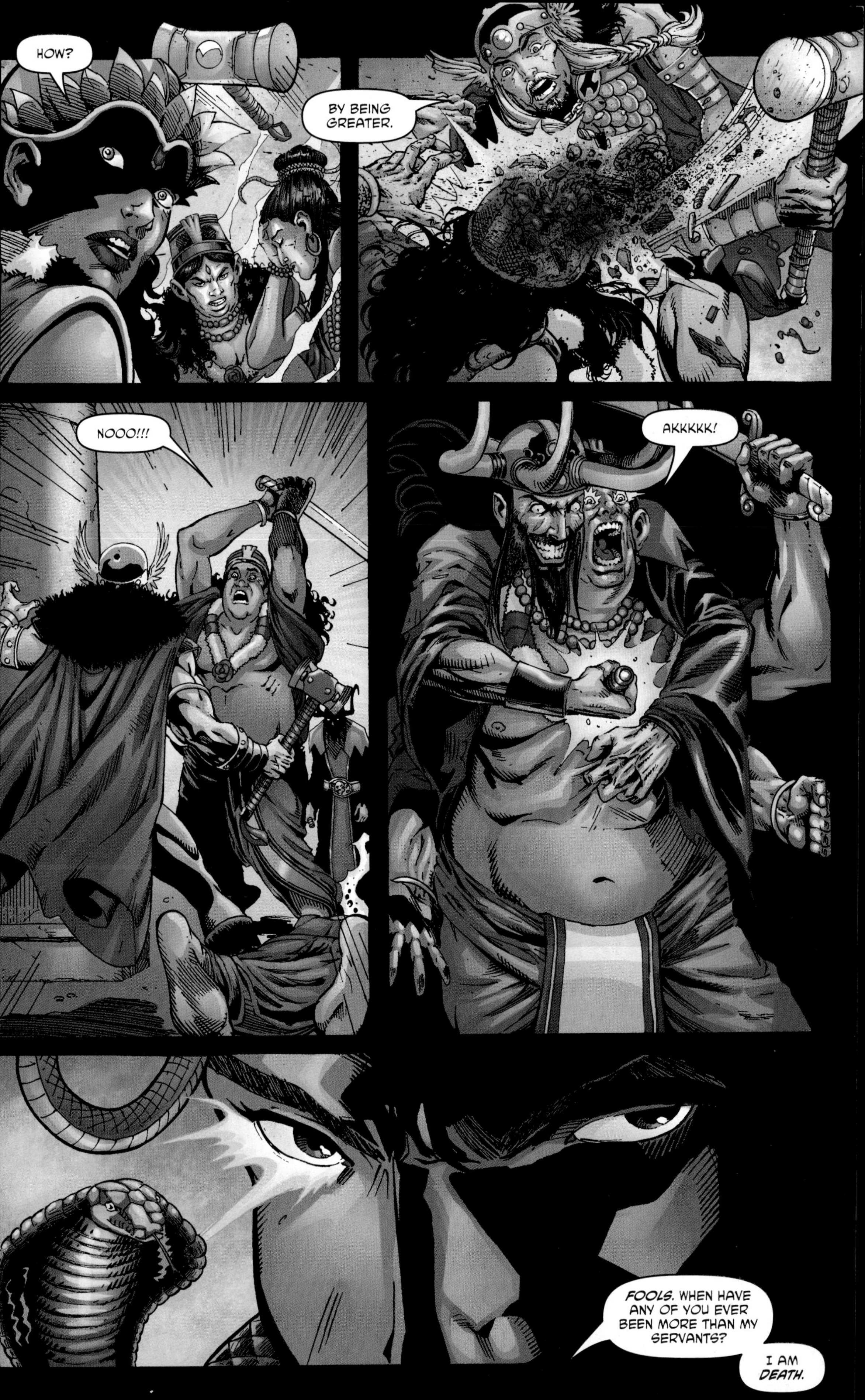
HOW?
BY BEING GREATER.
NOOO!!!
AKKKKK!
FOOLS. WHEN HAVE ANY OF YOU EVER BEEN MORE THAN MY SERVANTS?
I AM DEATH.

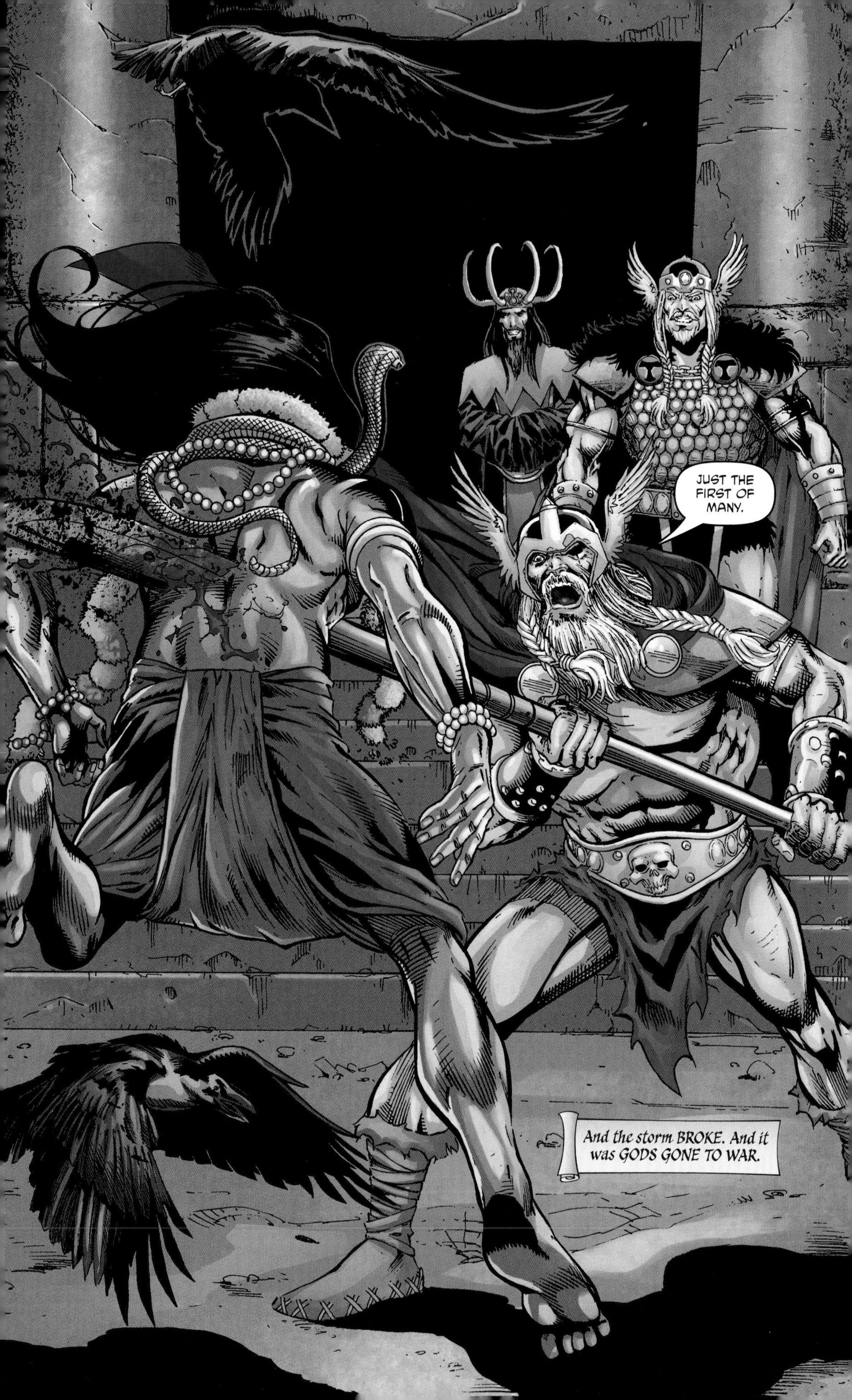
JUST THE FIRST OF MANY.
And the storm BROKE. And it was GODS GONE TO WAR.

THREE

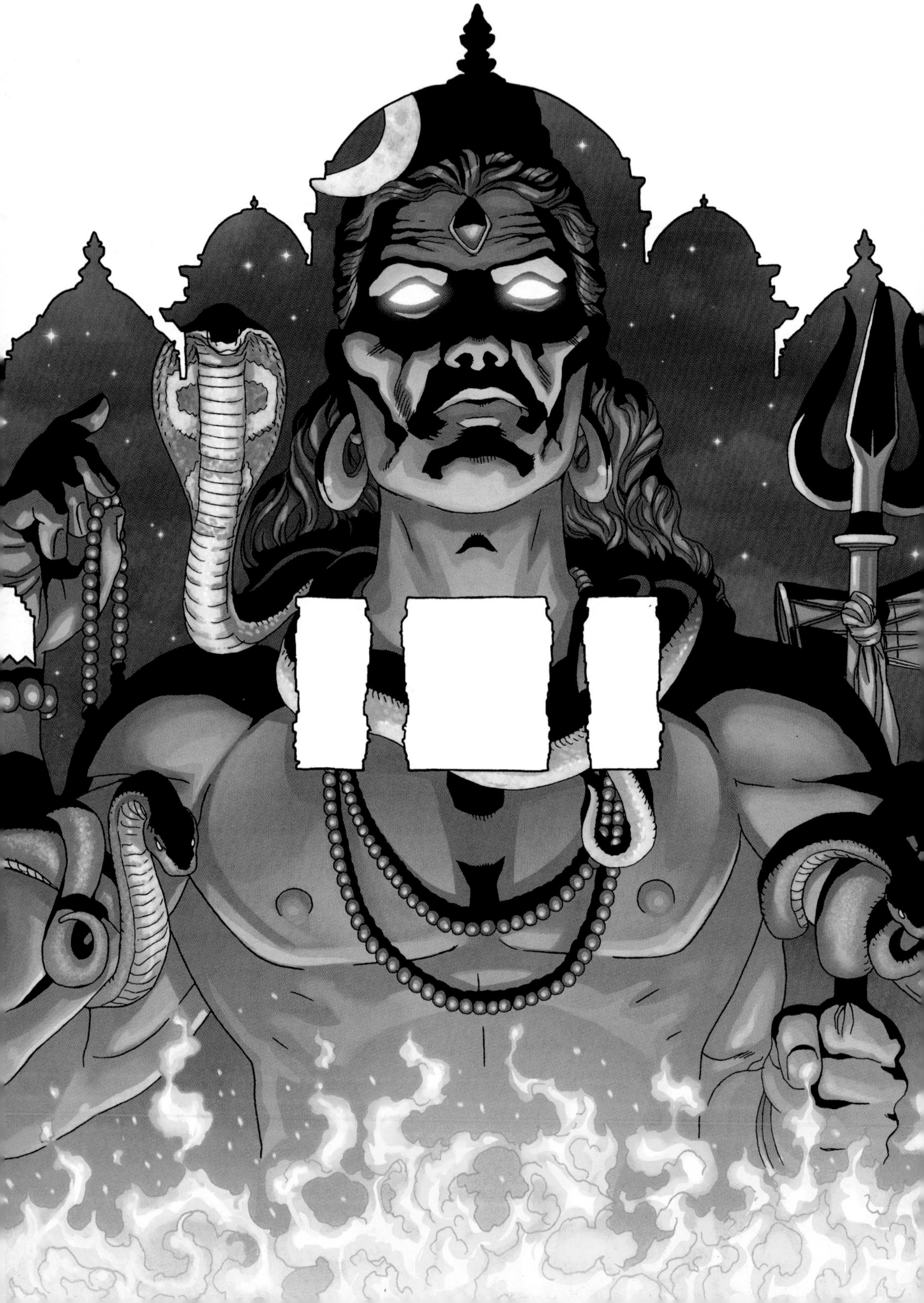

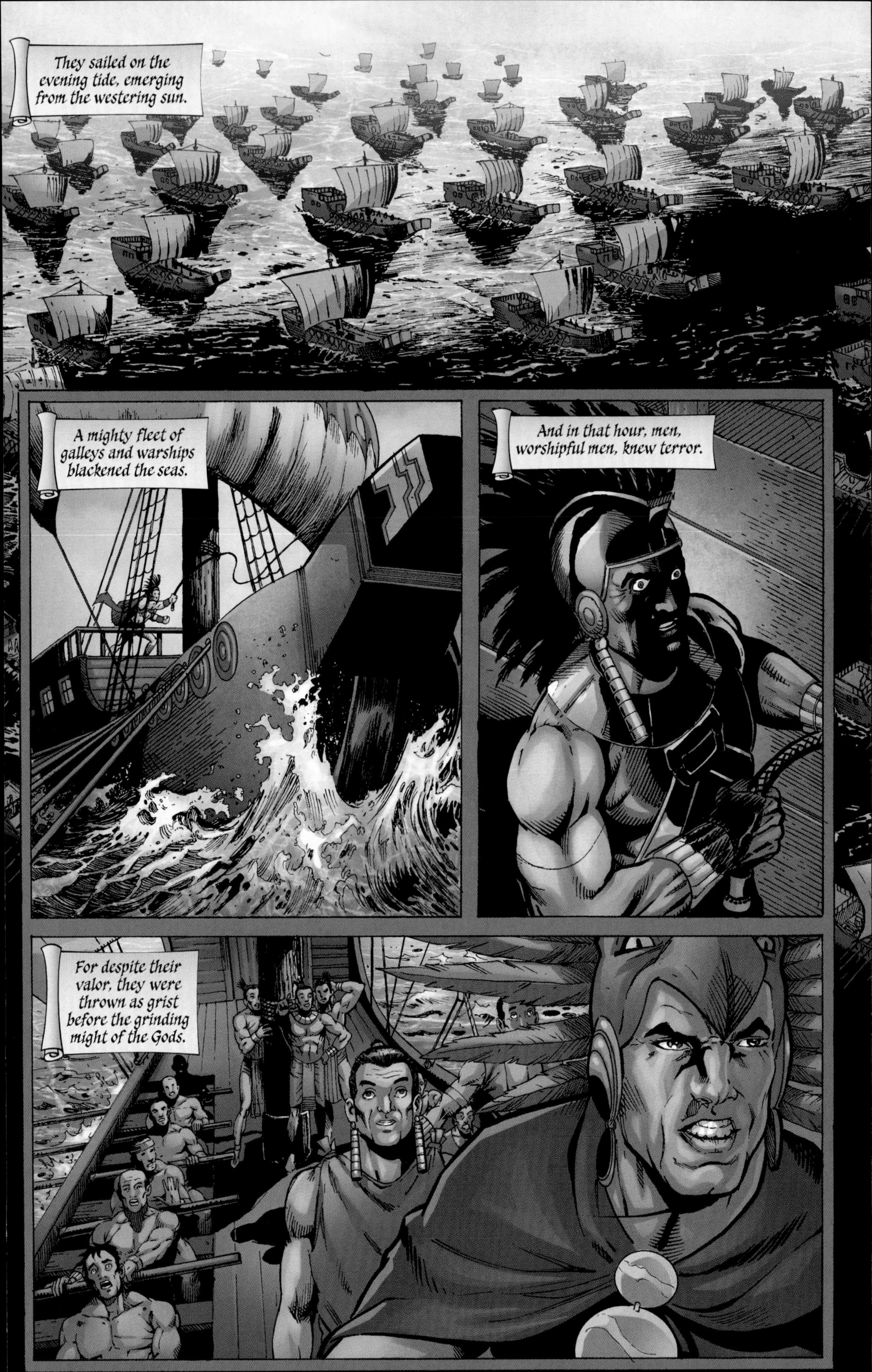
They sailed on the evening tide, emerging from the westering sun.
A mighty fleet of galleys and warships blackened the seas.
And in that hour, men, worshipful men, knew terror.
For despite their valor, they were thrown as grist before the grinding might of the Gods.

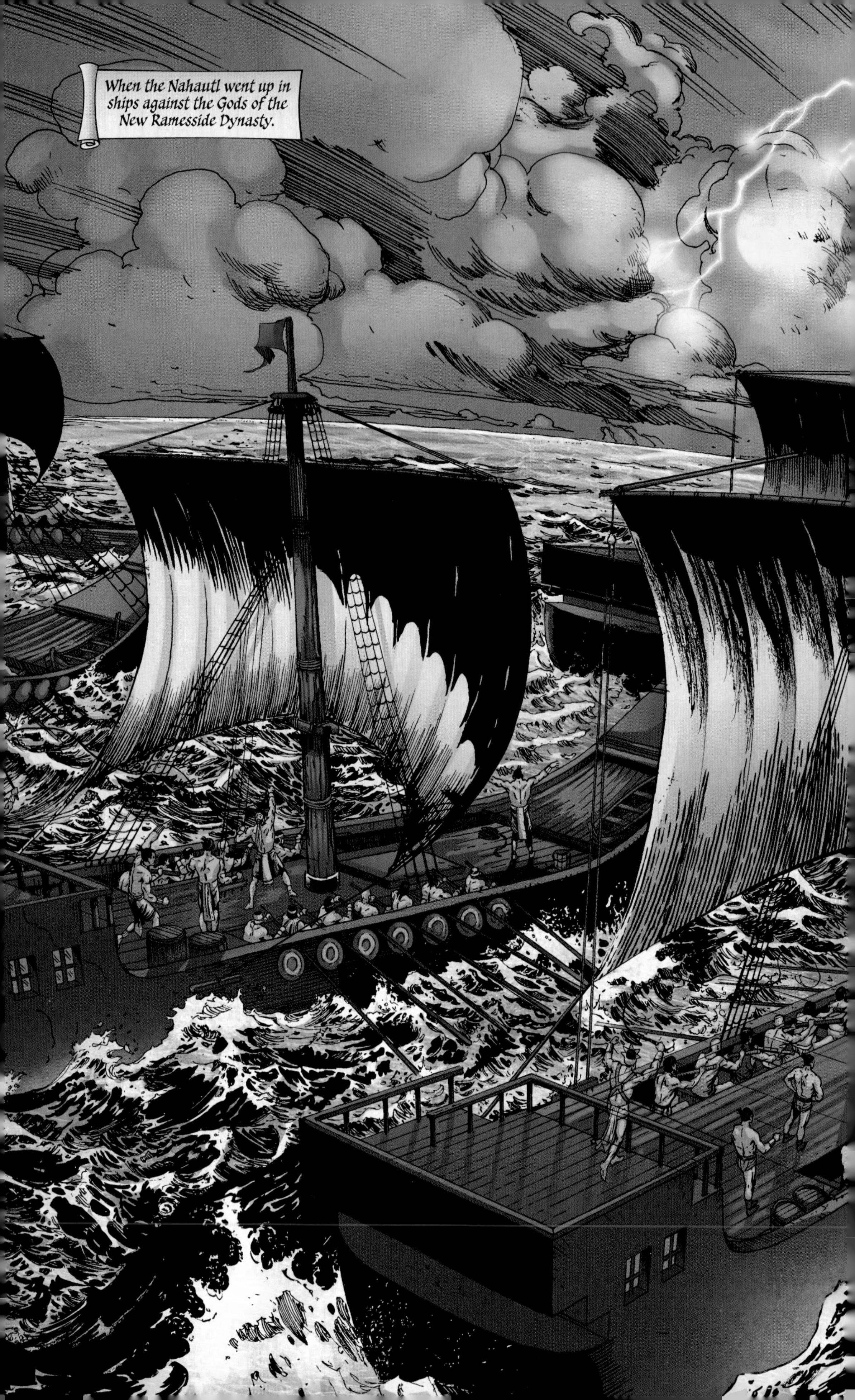
When the Nahautl went up in ships against the Gods of the New Ramesside Dynasty.

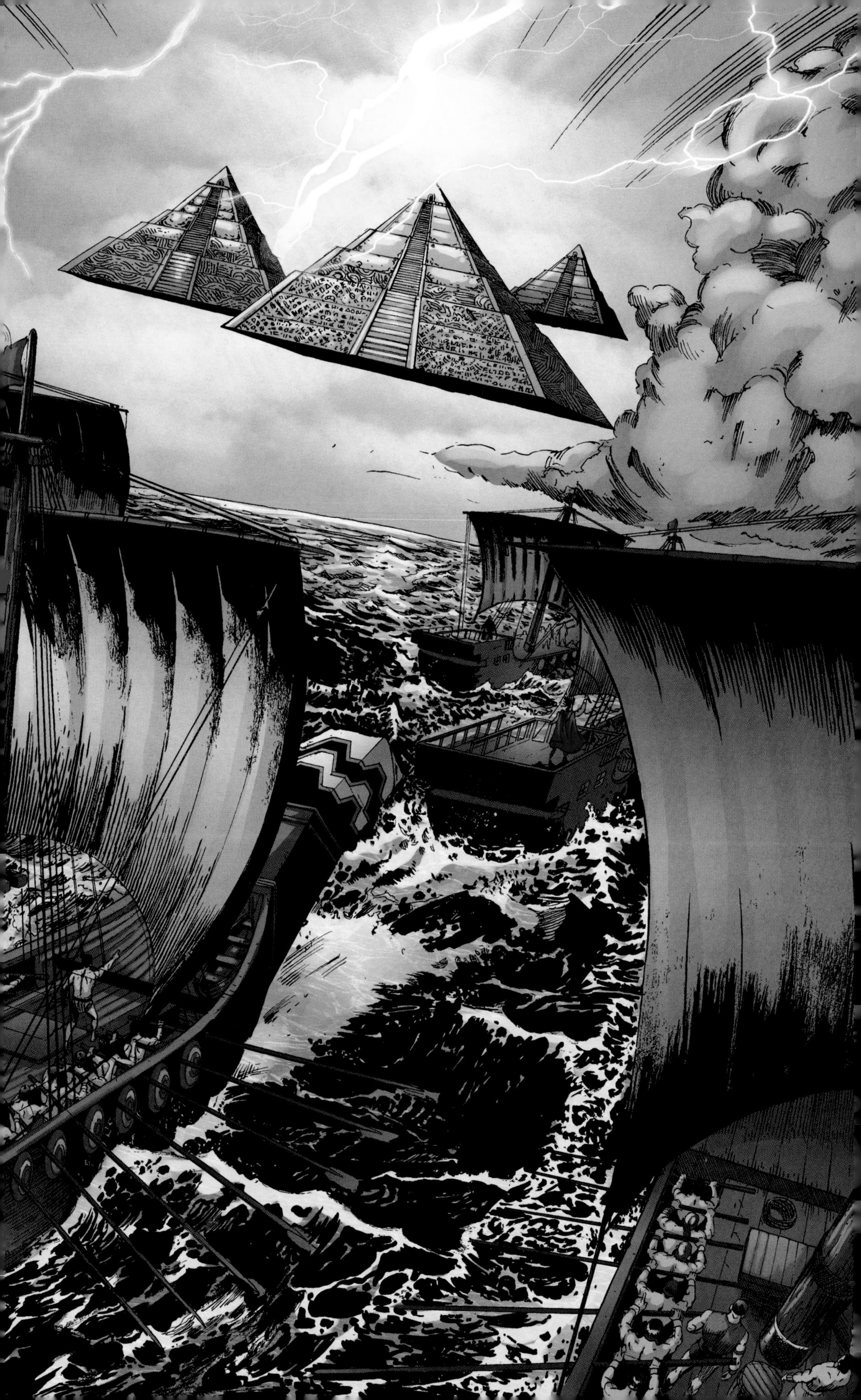

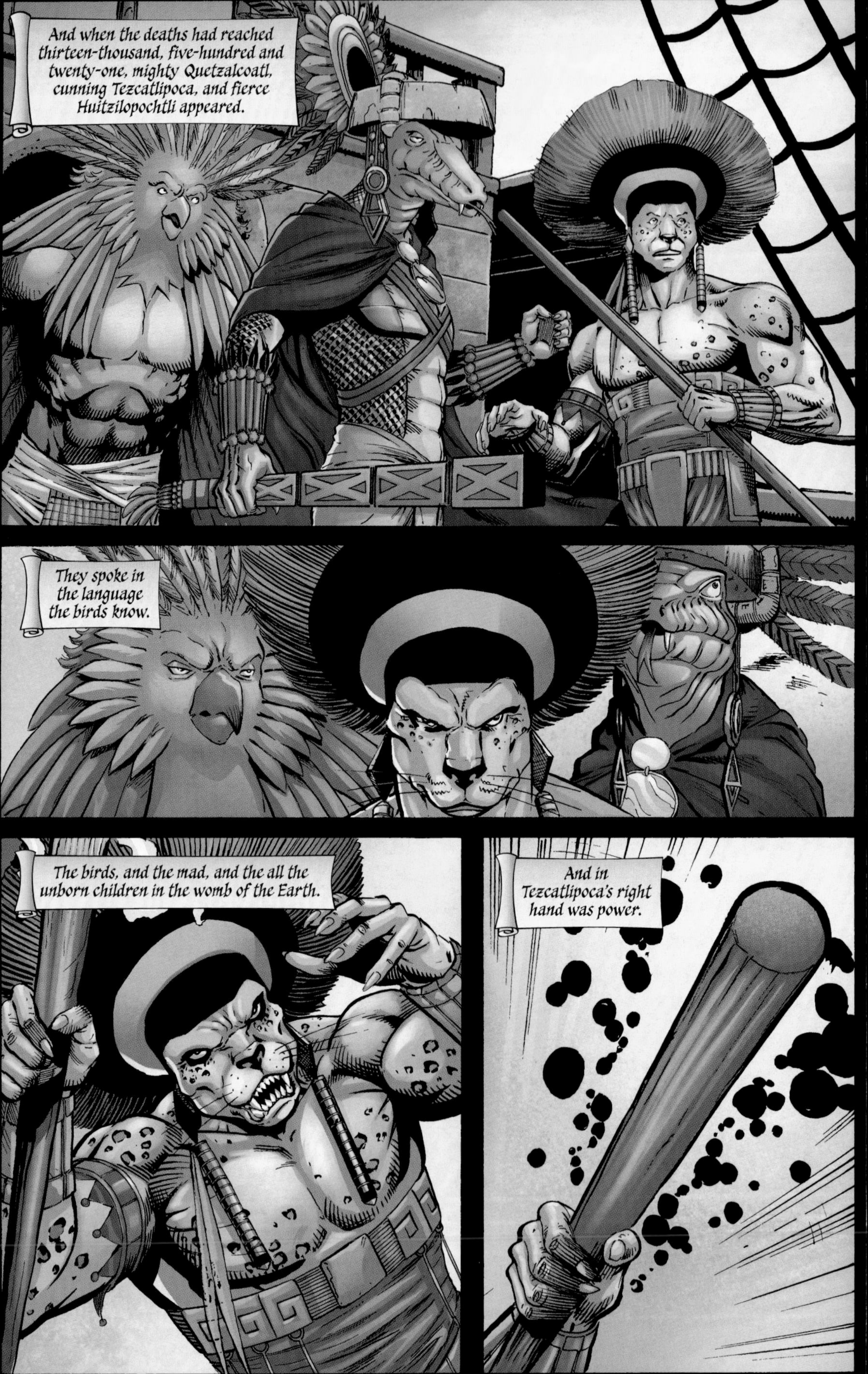
And when the deaths had reached thirteen-thousand, five-hundred and twenty-one, mighty Quetzalcoatl, cunning Tezcatlipoca, and fierce Huitzilopochtli appeared.
They spoke in the language the birds know.
The birds, and the mad, and the all the unborn children in the womb of the Earth.
And in Tezcatlipoca's right hand was power.

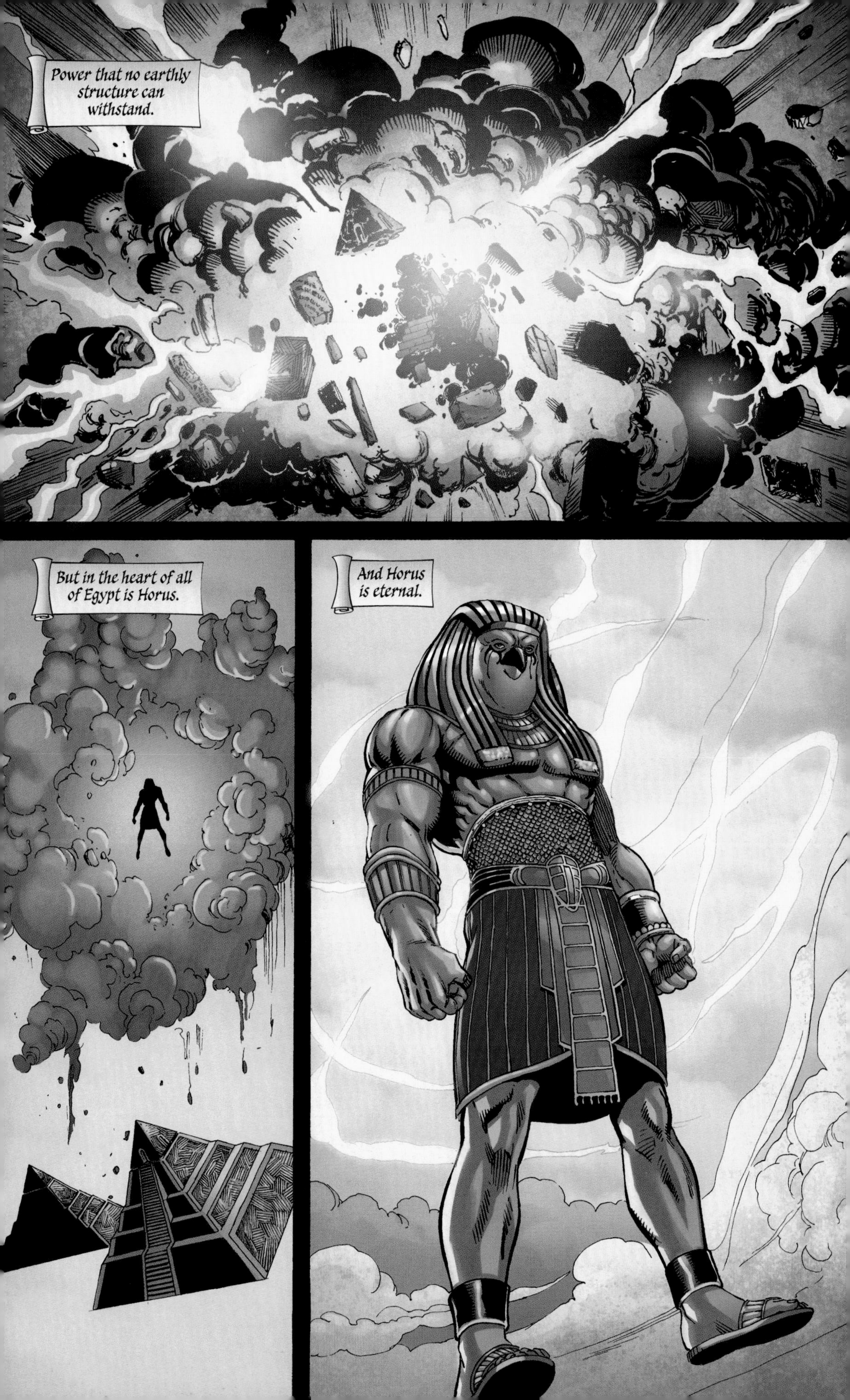
Power that no earthly structure can withstand.
But in the heart of all of Egypt is Horus.
And Horus is eternal.

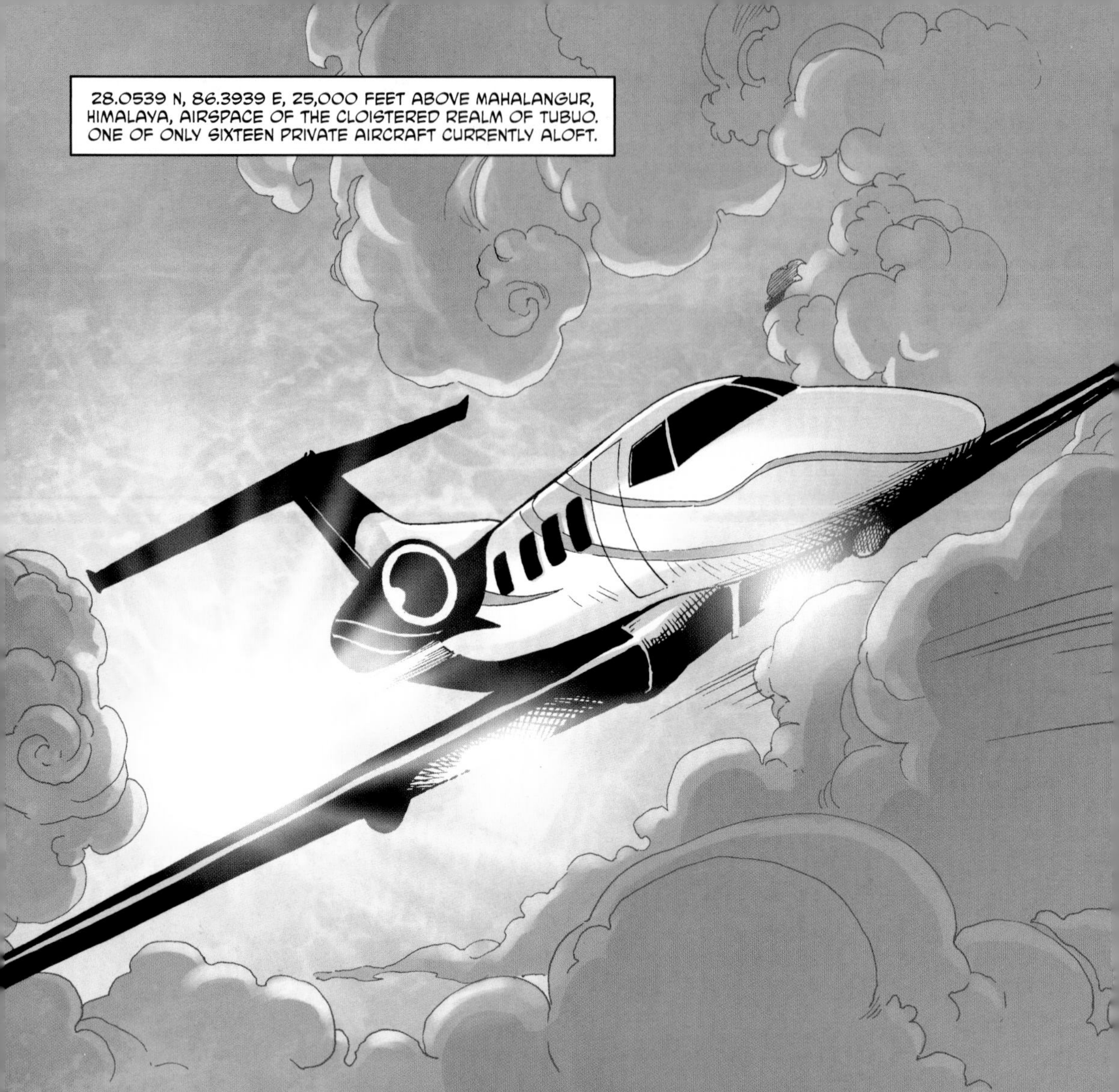
28.0539 N, 86.3939 E, 25,000 FEET ABOVE MAHALANGUR, HIMALAYA, AIRSPACE OF THE CLOISTERED REALM OF TUBUO. ONE OF ONLY SIXTEEN PRIVATE AIRCRAFT CURRENTLY ALOFT.

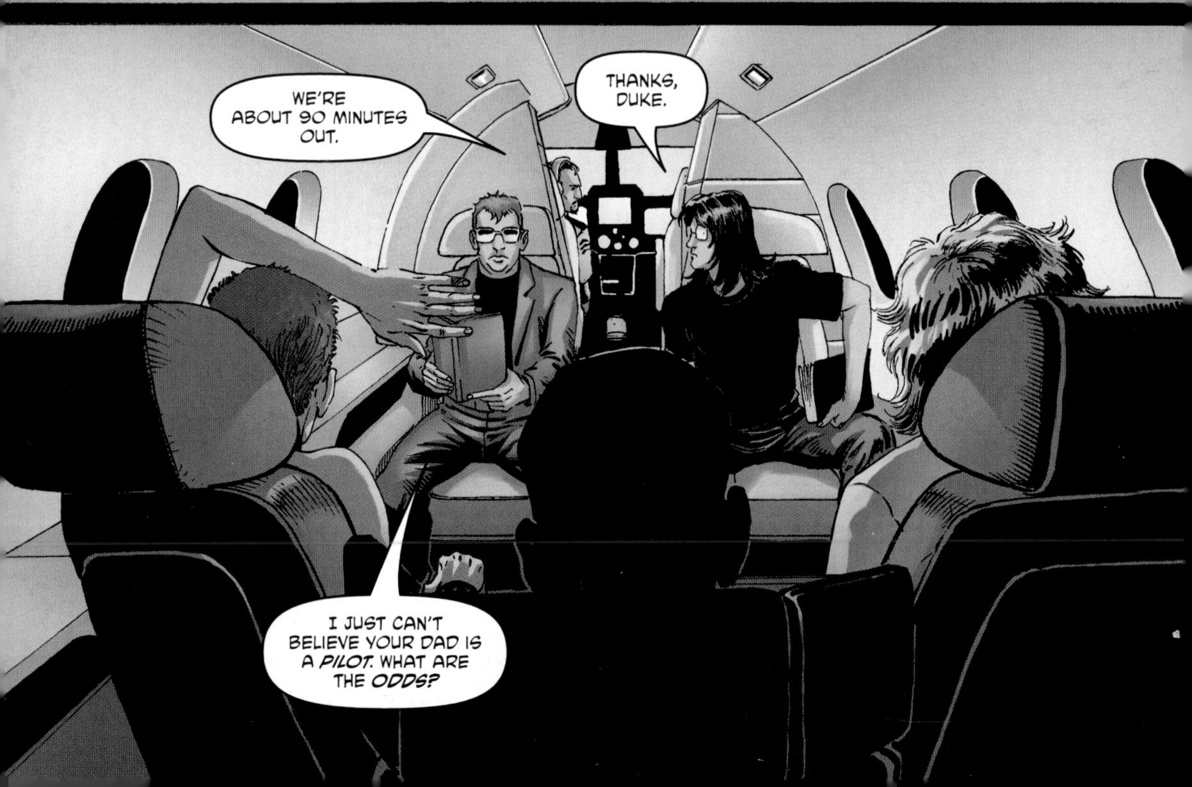
WE'RE ABOUT 90 MINUTES OUT.
THANKS, DUKE.
I JUST CAN'T BELIEVE YOUR DAD IS A *PILOT*. WHAT ARE THE *ODDS?*

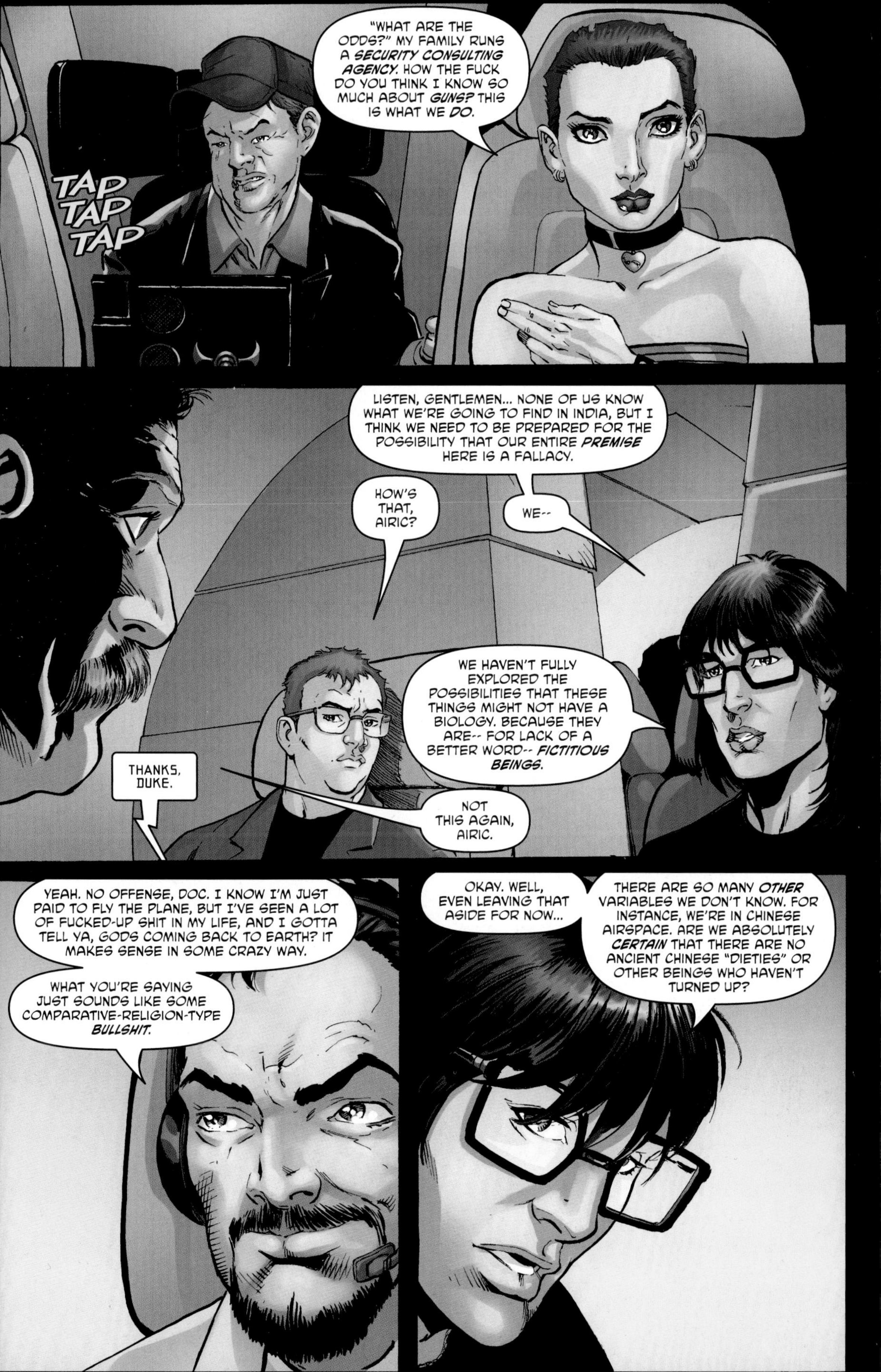
"WHAT ARE THE ODDS?" MY FAMILY RUNS A *SECURITY CONSULTING AGENCY*. HOW THE FUCK DO YOU THINK I KNOW SO MUCH ABOUT *GUNS?* THIS IS WHAT WE *DO*.
TAP TAP TAP
LISTEN, GENTLEMEN... NONE OF US KNOW WHAT WE'RE GOING TO FIND IN INDIA, BUT I THINK WE NEED TO BE PREPARED FOR THE POSSIBILITY THAT OUR ENTIRE *PREMISE* HERE IS A FALLACY.
HOW'S THAT, AIRIC?
WE--
WE HAVEN'T FULLY EXPLORED THE POSSIBILITIES THAT THESE THINGS MIGHT NOT HAVE A BIOLOGY. BECAUSE THEY ARE-- FOR LACK OF A BETTER WORD-- *FICTITIOUS BEINGS*.
THANKS, DUKE.
NOT THIS AGAIN, AIRIC.
YEAH. NO OFFENSE, DOC. I KNOW I'M JUST PAID TO FLY THE PLANE, BUT I'VE SEEN A LOT OF FUCKED-UP SHIT IN MY LIFE, AND I GOTTA TELL YA, GODS COMING BACK TO EARTH? IT MAKES SENSE IN SOME CRAZY WAY.
WHAT YOU'RE SAYING JUST SOUNDS LIKE SOME COMPARATIVE-RELIGION-TYPE *BULLSHIT*.
OKAY. WELL, EVEN LEAVING THAT ASIDE FOR NOW...
THERE ARE SO MANY *OTHER* VARIABLES WE DON'T KNOW. FOR INSTANCE, WE'RE IN CHINESE AIRSPACE. ARE WE ABSOLUTELY *CERTAIN* THAT THERE ARE NO ANCIENT CHINESE "DIETIES" OR OTHER BEINGS WHO HAVEN'T TURNED UP?

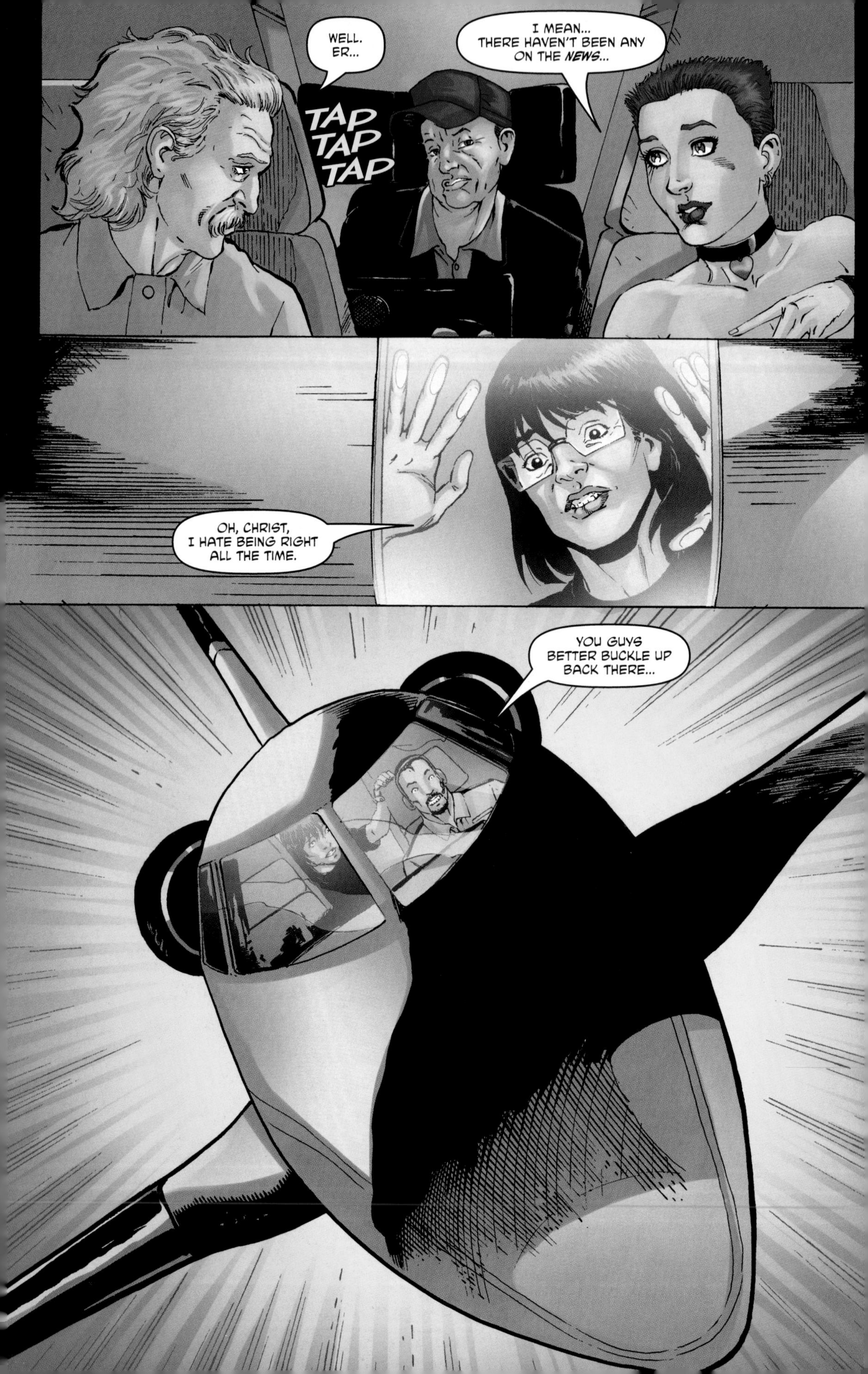
WELL.
ER...
TAP TAP TAP
I MEAN...
THERE HAVEN'T BEEN ANY
ON THE *NEWS*...
OH, CHRIST,
I HATE BEING RIGHT
ALL THE TIME.
YOU GUYS
BETTER BUCKLE UP
BACK THERE...

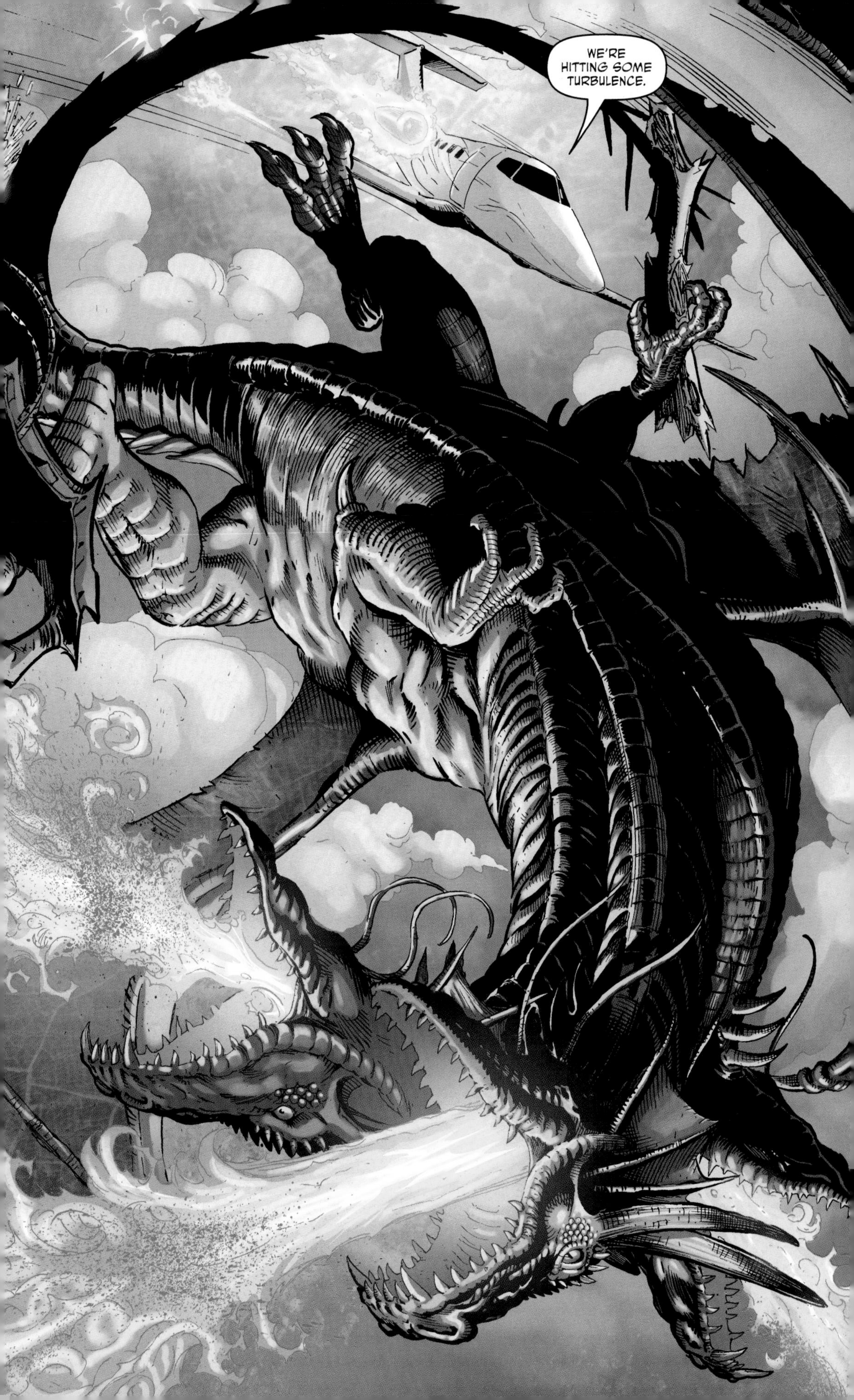
WE'RE HITTING SOME TURBULENCE.

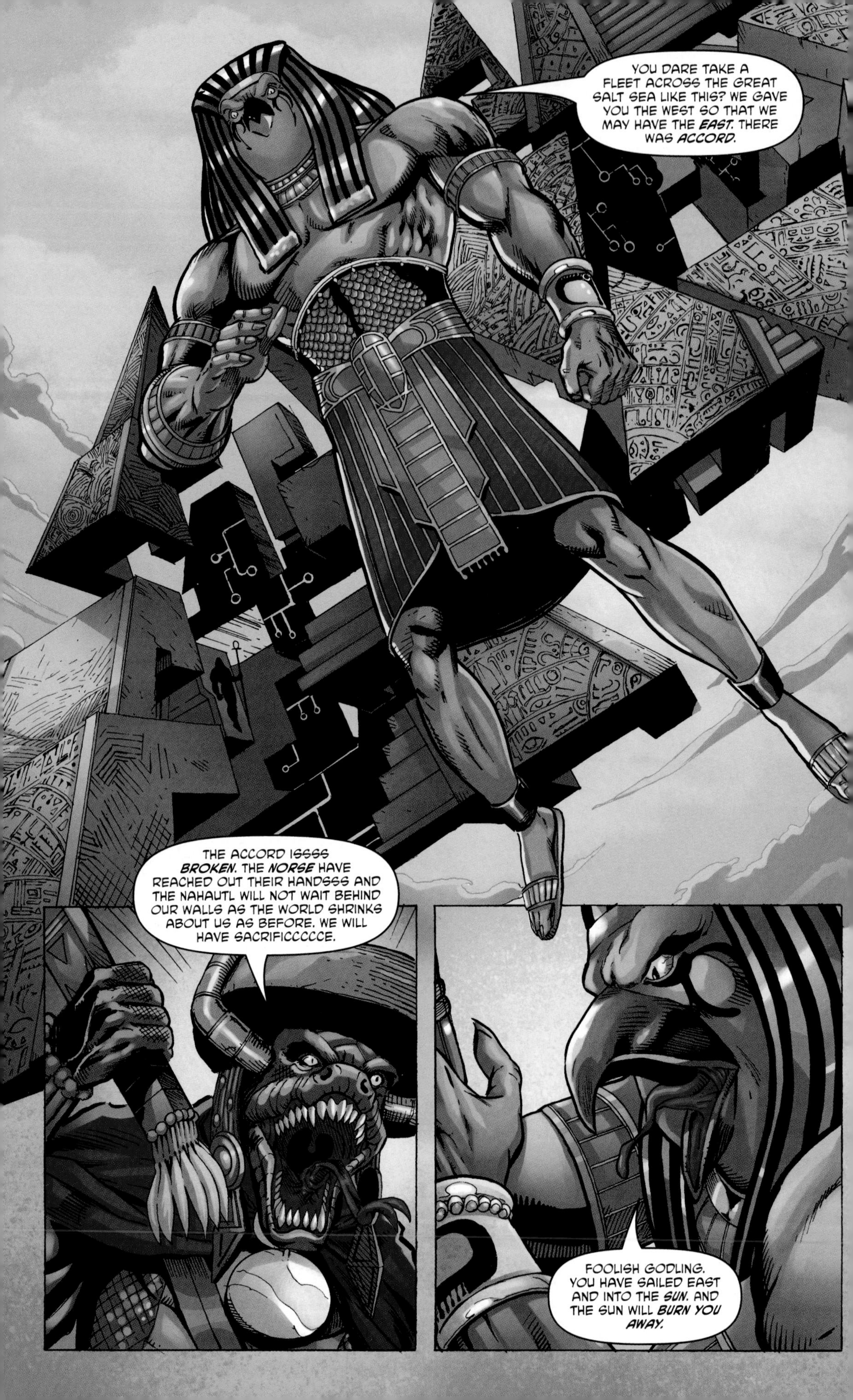
YOU DARE TAKE A FLEET ACROSS THE GREAT SALT SEA LIKE THIS? WE GAVE YOU THE WEST SO THAT WE MAY HAVE THE *EAST*. THERE WAS *ACCORD*.
THE ACCORD ISSSS *BROKEN*. THE *NORSE* HAVE REACHED OUT THEIR HANDSSS AND THE NAHAUTL WILL NOT WAIT BEHIND OUR WALLS AS THE WORLD SHRINKS ABOUT US AS BEFORE. WE WILL HAVE SACRIFICCCCCE.
FOOLISH GODLING. YOU HAVE SAILED EAST AND INTO THE *SUN*. AND THE SUN WILL *BURN YOU AWAY*.

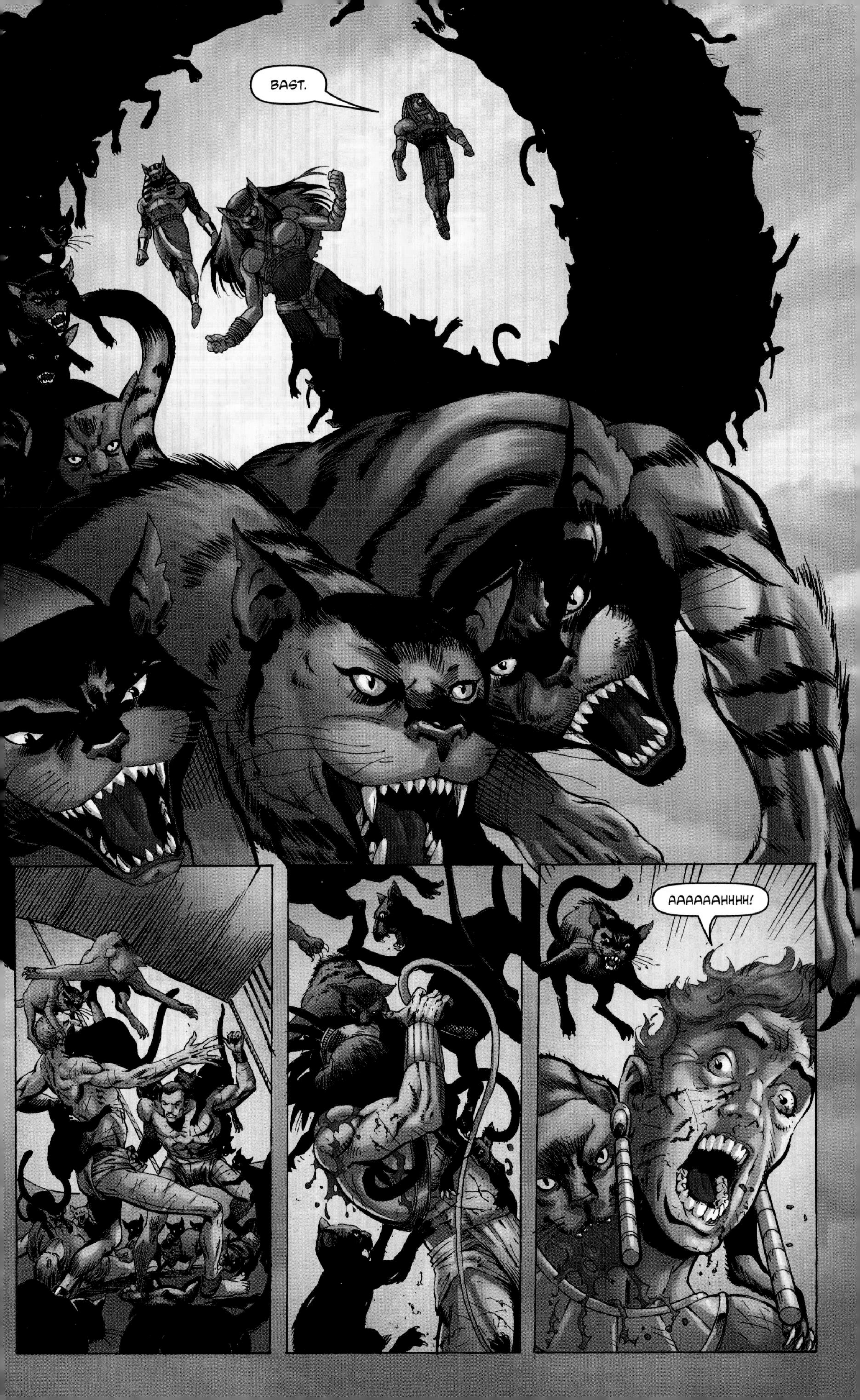
BAST.
AAAAAAHHHH!

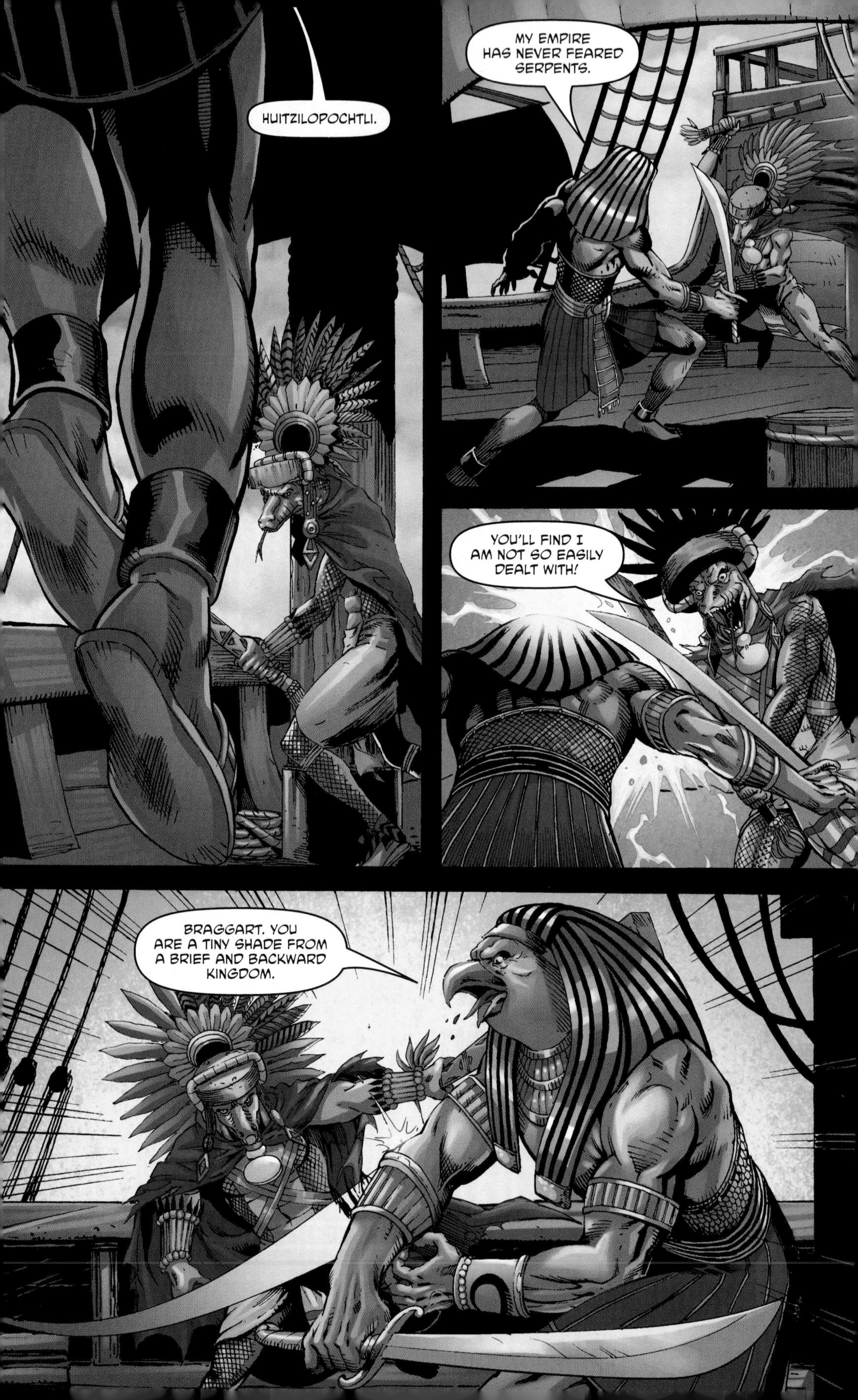
HUITZILOPOCHTLI.
MY EMPIRE HAS NEVER FEARED SERPENTS.
YOU'LL FIND I AM NOT SO EASILY DEALT WITH!
BRAGGART. YOU ARE A TINY SHADE FROM A BRIEF AND BACKWARD KINGDOM.

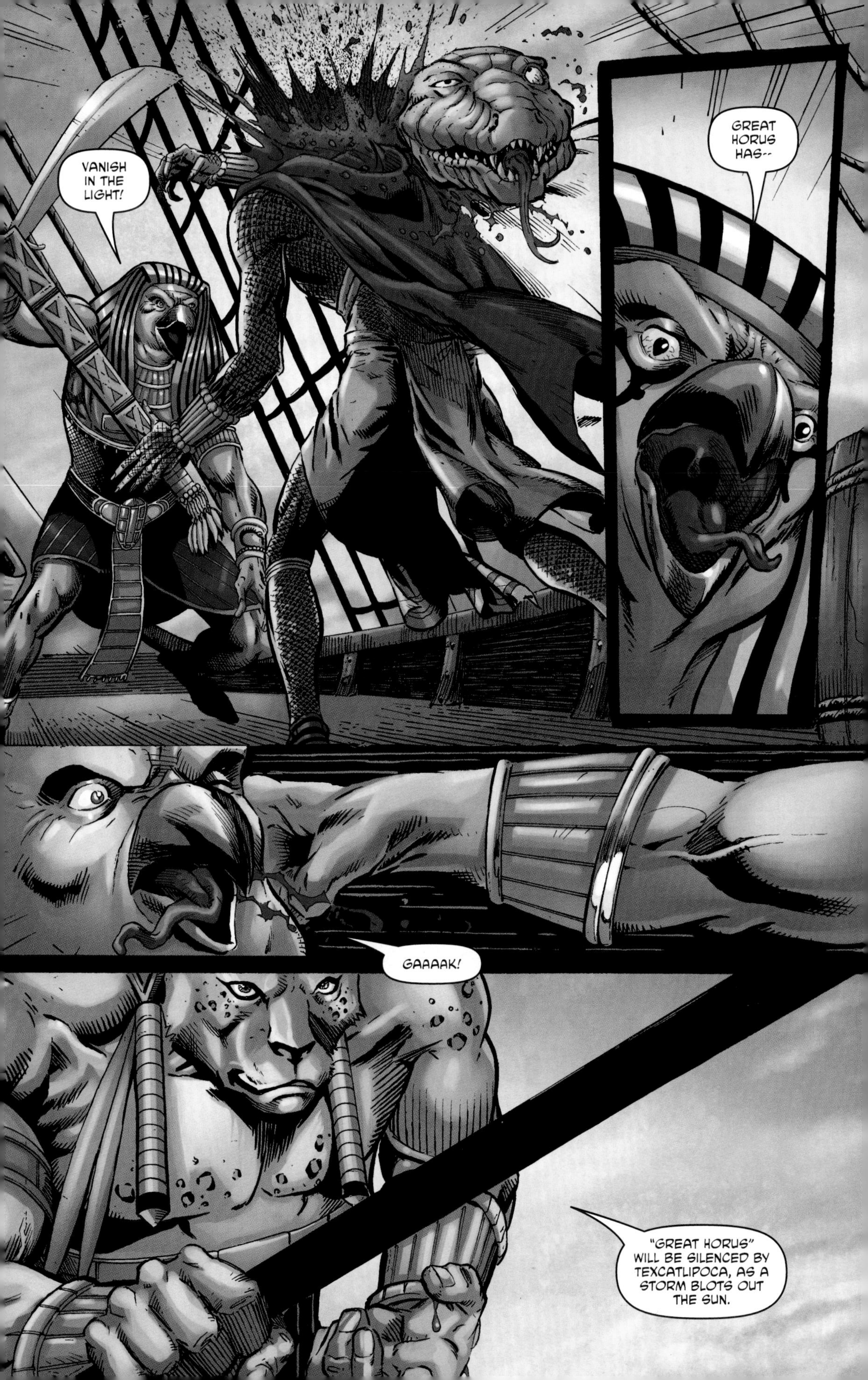
VANISH IN THE LIGHT!
GREAT HORUS HAS--
GAAAAK!
"GREAT HORUS" WILL BE SILENCED BY TEXCATLIPOCA, AS A STORM BLOTS OUT THE SUN.

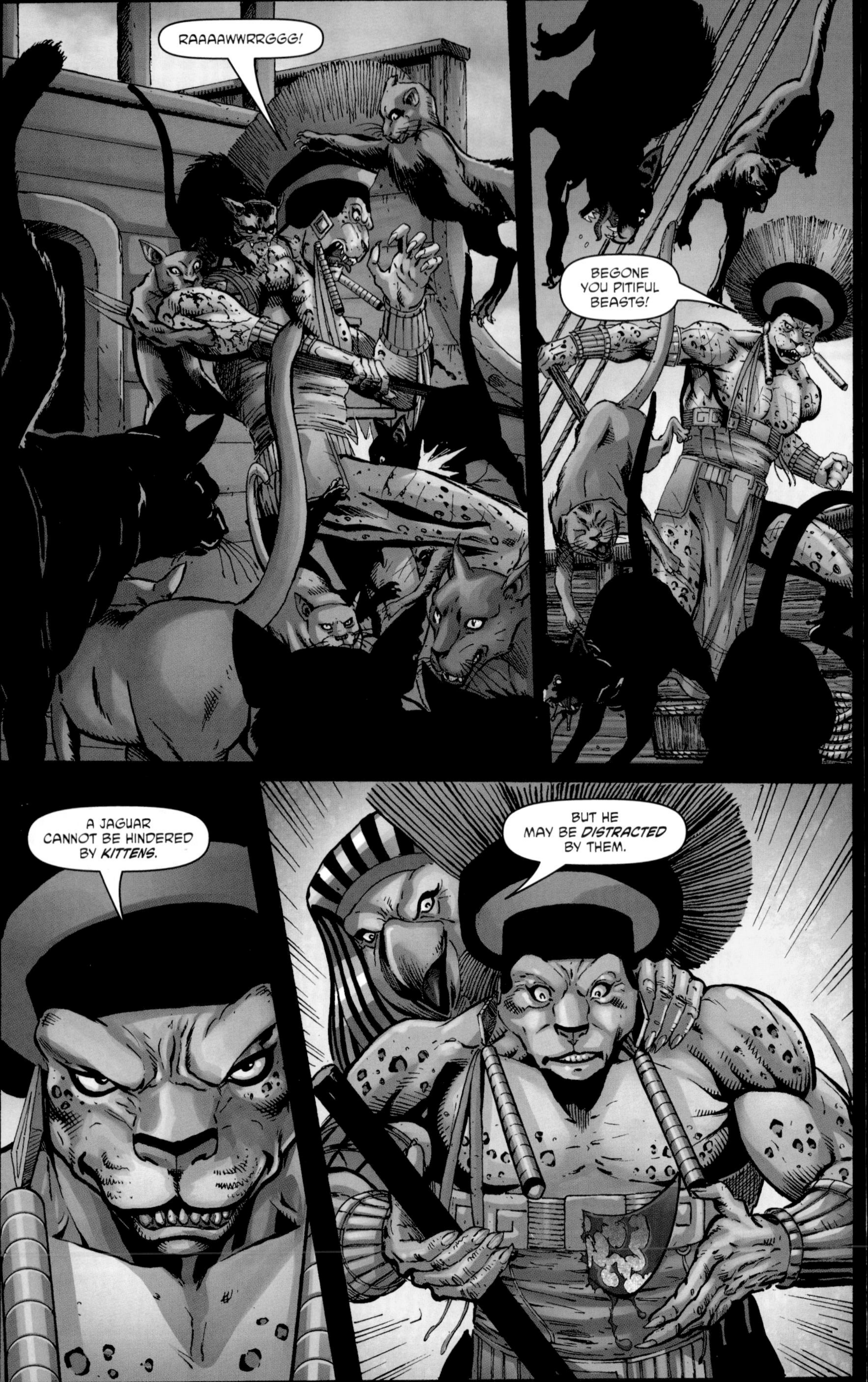
RAAAAWWRRGGG!
BEGONE YOU PITIFUL BEASTS!
A JAGUAR CANNOT BE HINDERED BY *KITTENS*.
BUT HE MAY BE *DISTRACTED* BY THEM.

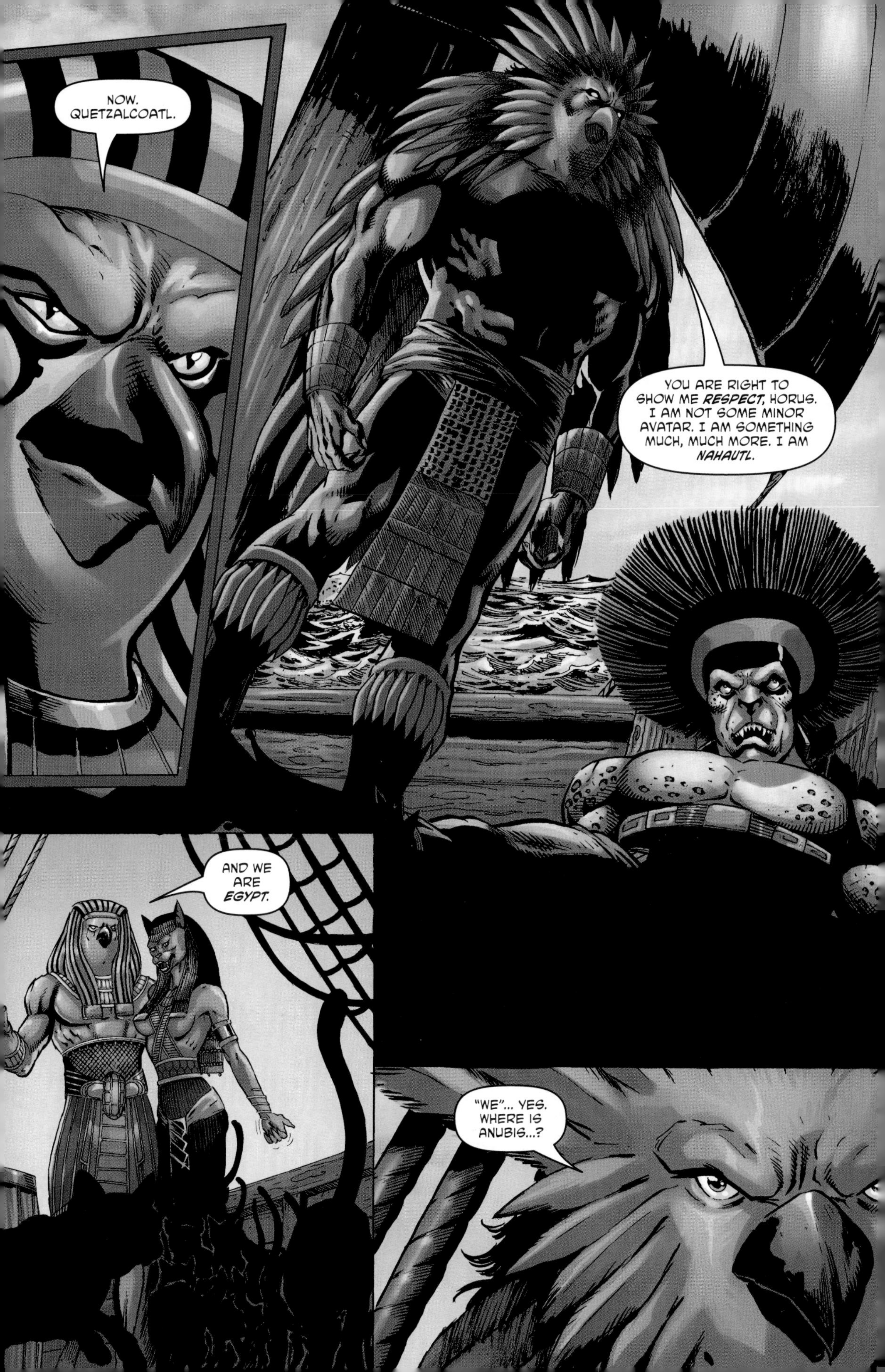
NOW. QUETZALCOATL.
YOU ARE RIGHT TO SHOW ME RESPECT, HORUS. I AM NOT SOME MINOR AVATAR. I AM SOMETHING MUCH, MUCH MORE. I AM NAHAUTL.
AND WE ARE EGYPT.
"WE"... YES. WHERE IS ANUBIS...?

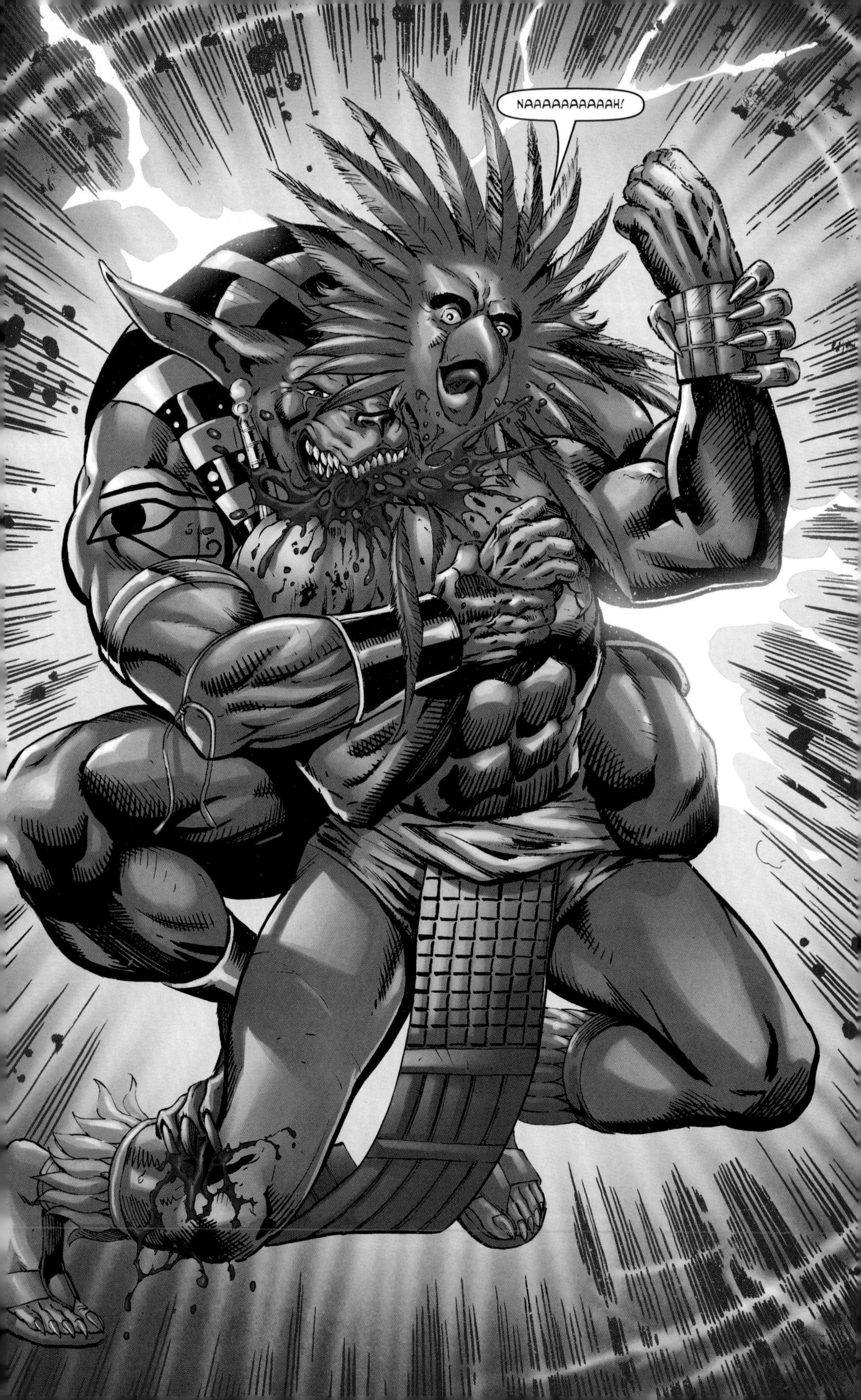
NAAAAAAAAAAH!

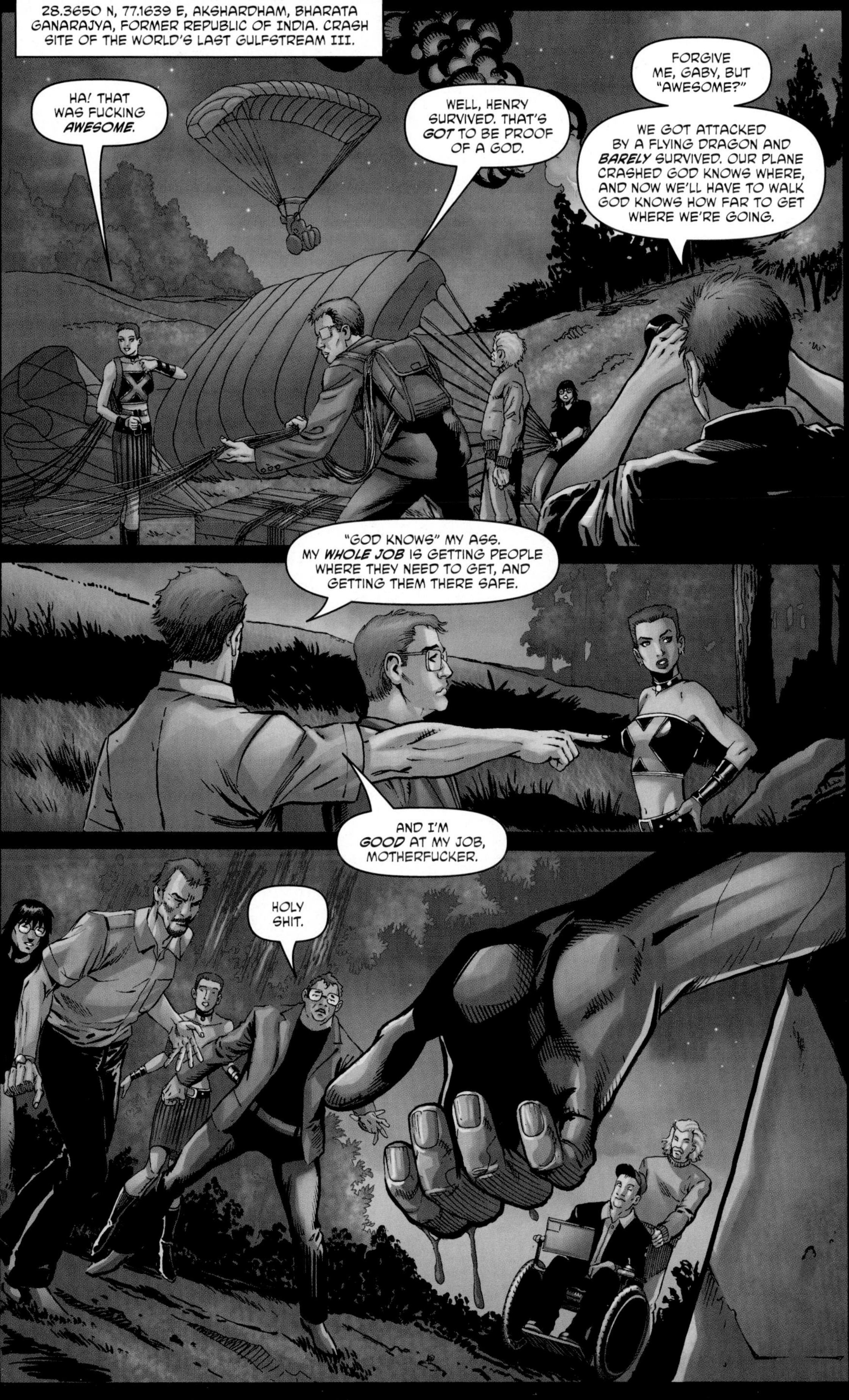

28.3650 N, 77.1639 E, AKSHARDHAM, BHARATA GANARAJYA, FORMER REPUBLIC OF INDIA. CRASH SITE OF THE WORLD'S LAST GULFSTREAM III.
HA! THAT WAS FUCKING *AWESOME*.
WELL, HENRY SURVIVED. THAT'S *GOT* TO BE PROOF OF A GOD.
FORGIVE ME, GABY, BUT "AWESOME?"
WE GOT ATTACKED BY A FLYING DRAGON AND *BARELY* SURVIVED. OUR PLANE CRASHED GOD KNOWS WHERE, AND NOW WE'LL HAVE TO WALK GOD KNOWS HOW FAR TO GET WHERE WE'RE GOING.
"GOD KNOWS" MY ASS. MY *WHOLE JOB* IS GETTING PEOPLE WHERE THEY NEED TO GET, AND GETTING THEM THERE SAFE.
AND I'M *GOOD* AT MY JOB, MOTHERFUCKER.
HOLY SHIT.

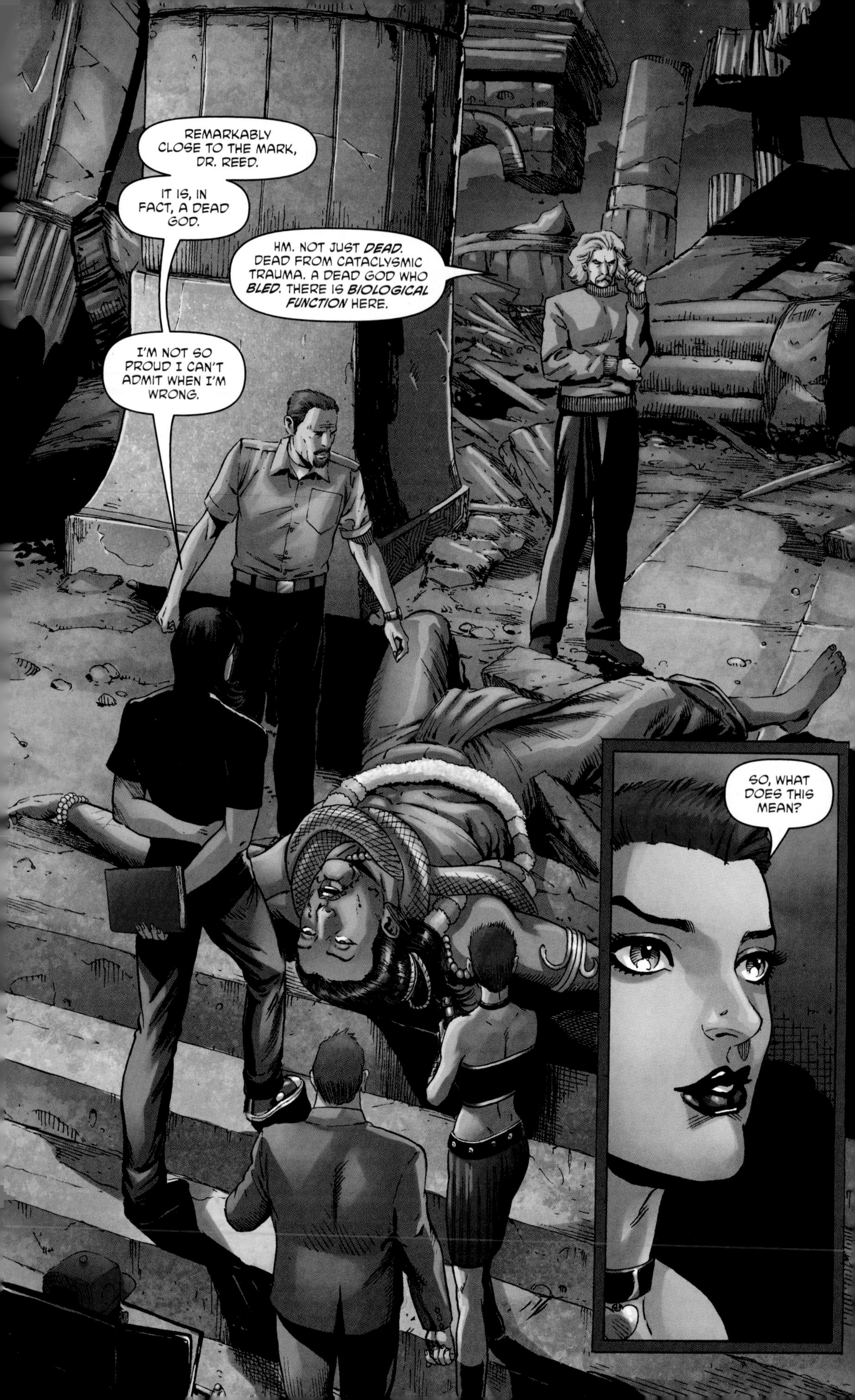
REMARKABLY CLOSE TO THE MARK, DR. REED.
IT IS, IN FACT, A DEAD GOD.
HM. NOT JUST *DEAD*. DEAD FROM CATACLYSMIC TRAUMA. A DEAD GOD WHO *BLED*. THERE IS *BIOLOGICAL FUNCTION* HERE.
I'M NOT SO PROUD I CAN'T ADMIT WHEN I'M WRONG.
SO, WHAT DOES THIS MEAN?

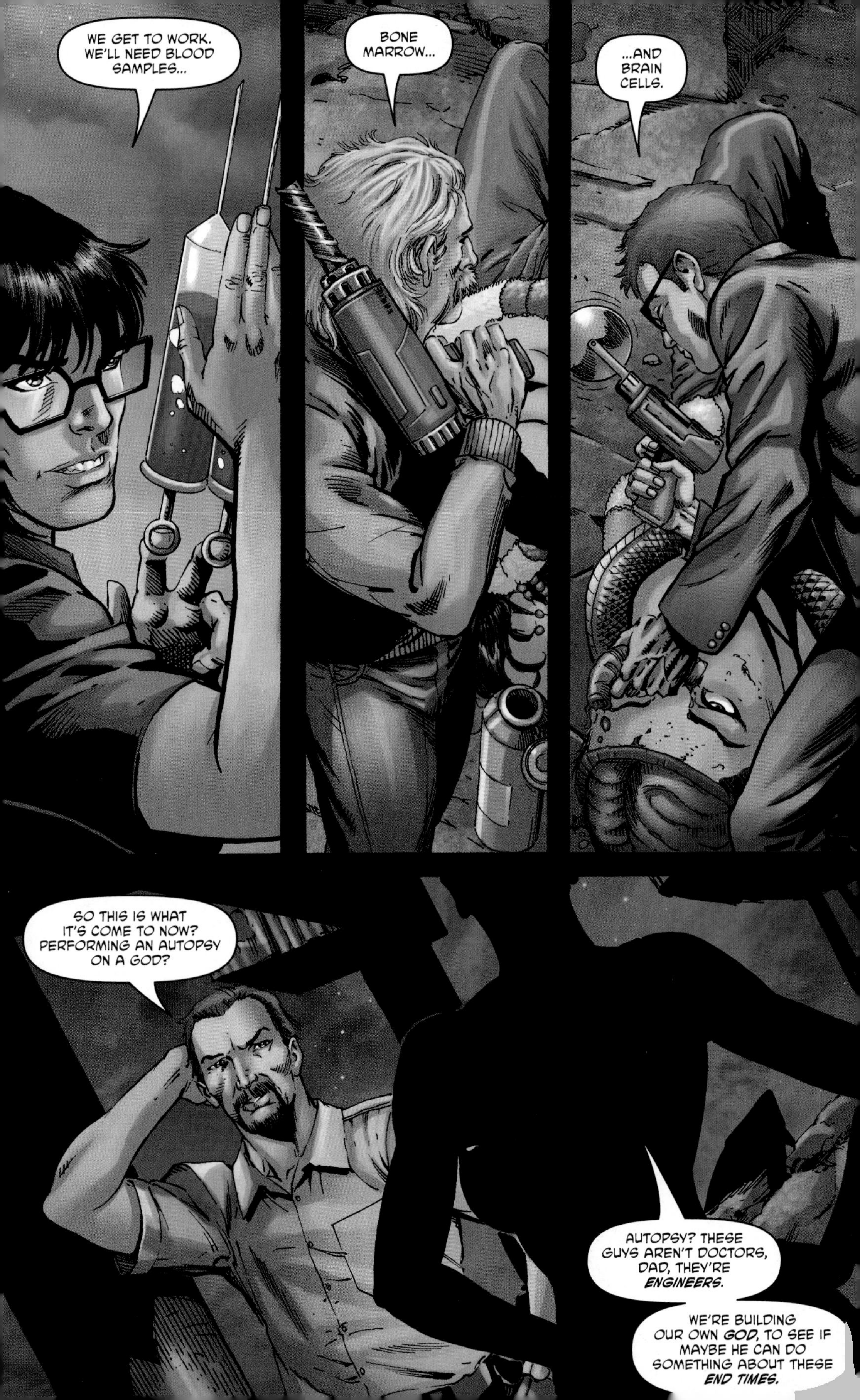
WE GET TO WORK. WE'LL NEED BLOOD SAMPLES...
BONE MARROW...
...AND BRAIN CELLS.
SO THIS IS WHAT IT'S COME TO NOW? PERFORMING AN AUTOPSY ON A GOD?
AUTOPSY? THESE GUYS AREN'T DOCTORS, DAD, THEY'RE *ENGINEERS*.
WE'RE BUILDING OUR OWN *GOD*, TO SEE IF MAYBE HE CAN DO SOMETHING ABOUT THESE *END TIMES*.

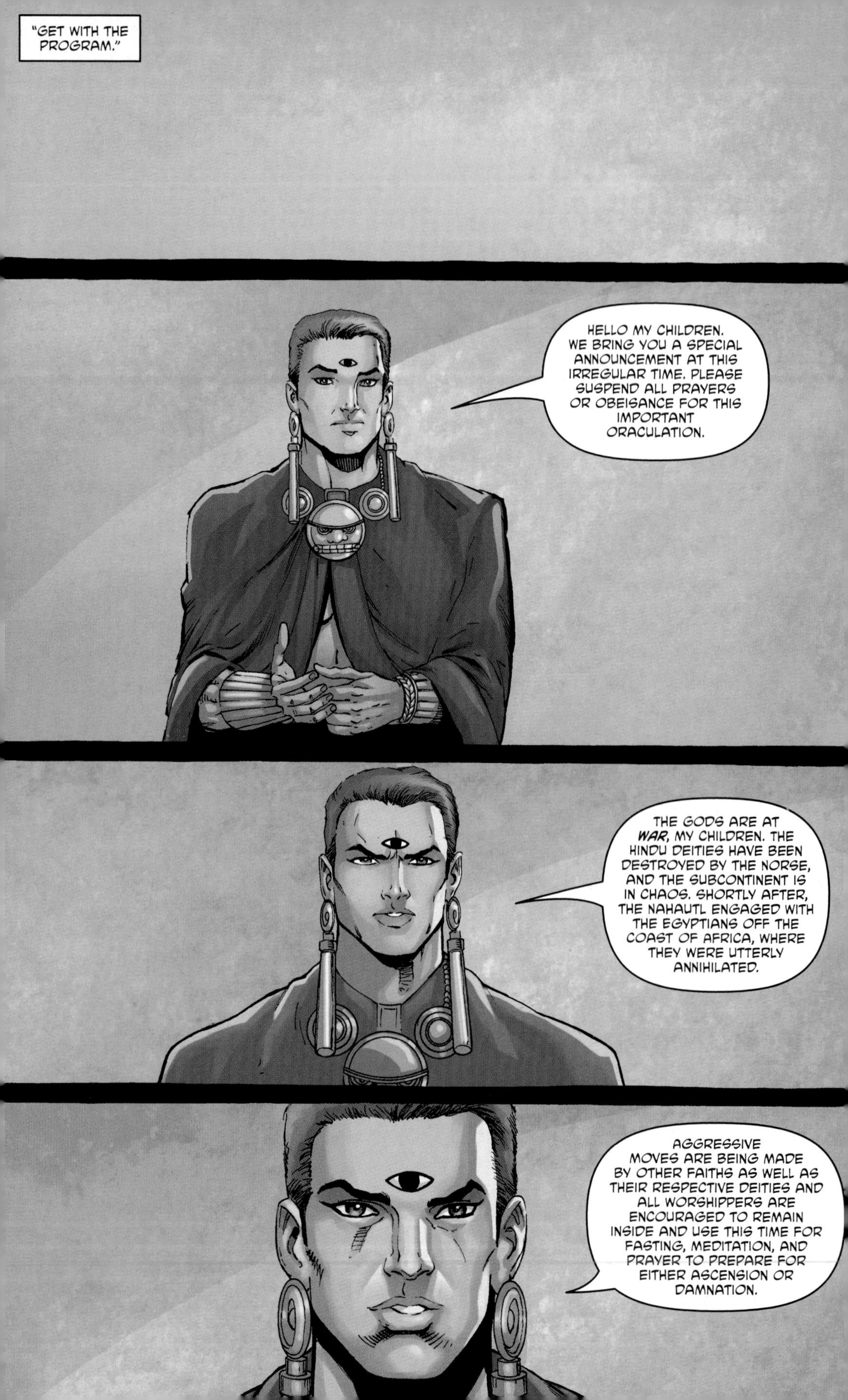
"GET WITH THE PROGRAM."
HELLO MY CHILDREN. WE BRING YOU A SPECIAL ANNOUNCEMENT AT THIS IRREGULAR TIME. PLEASE SUSPEND ALL PRAYERS OR OBEISANCE FOR THIS IMPORTANT ORACULATION.
THE GODS ARE AT *WAR*, MY CHILDREN. THE HINDU DEITIES HAVE BEEN DESTROYED BY THE NORSE, AND THE SUBCONTINENT IS IN CHAOS. SHORTLY AFTER, THE NAHAUTL ENGAGED WITH THE EGYPTIANS OFF THE COAST OF AFRICA, WHERE THEY WERE UTTERLY ANNIHILATED.
AGGRESSIVE MOVES ARE BEING MADE BY OTHER FAITHS AS WELL AS THEIR RESPECTIVE DEITIES AND ALL WORSHIPPERS ARE ENCOURAGED TO REMAIN INSIDE AND USE THIS TIME FOR FASTING, MEDITATION, AND PRAYER TO PREPARE FOR EITHER ASCENSION OR DAMNATION.

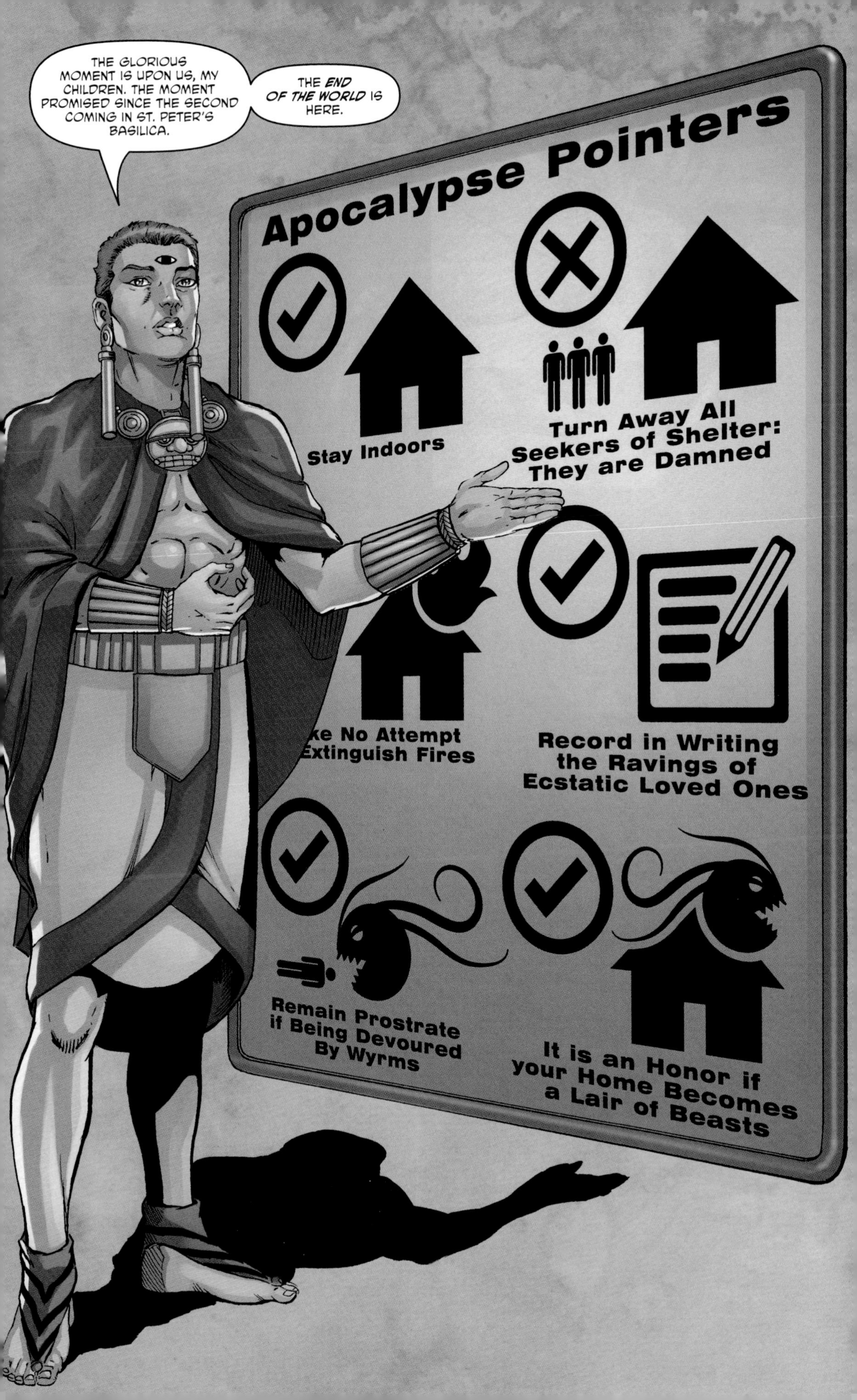
THE GLORIOUS MOMENT IS UPON US, MY CHILDREN. THE MOMENT PROMISED SINCE THE SECOND COMING IN ST. PETER'S BASILICA.
THE *END OF THE WORLD* IS HERE.
Apocalypse Pointers
Stay Indoors
Turn Away All Seekers of Shelter: They are Damned
ke No Attempt Extinguish Fires
Record in Writing the Ravings of Ecstatic Loved Ones
Remain Prostrate if Being Devoured By Wyrms
It is an Honor if your Home Becomes a Lair of Beasts

FOUR

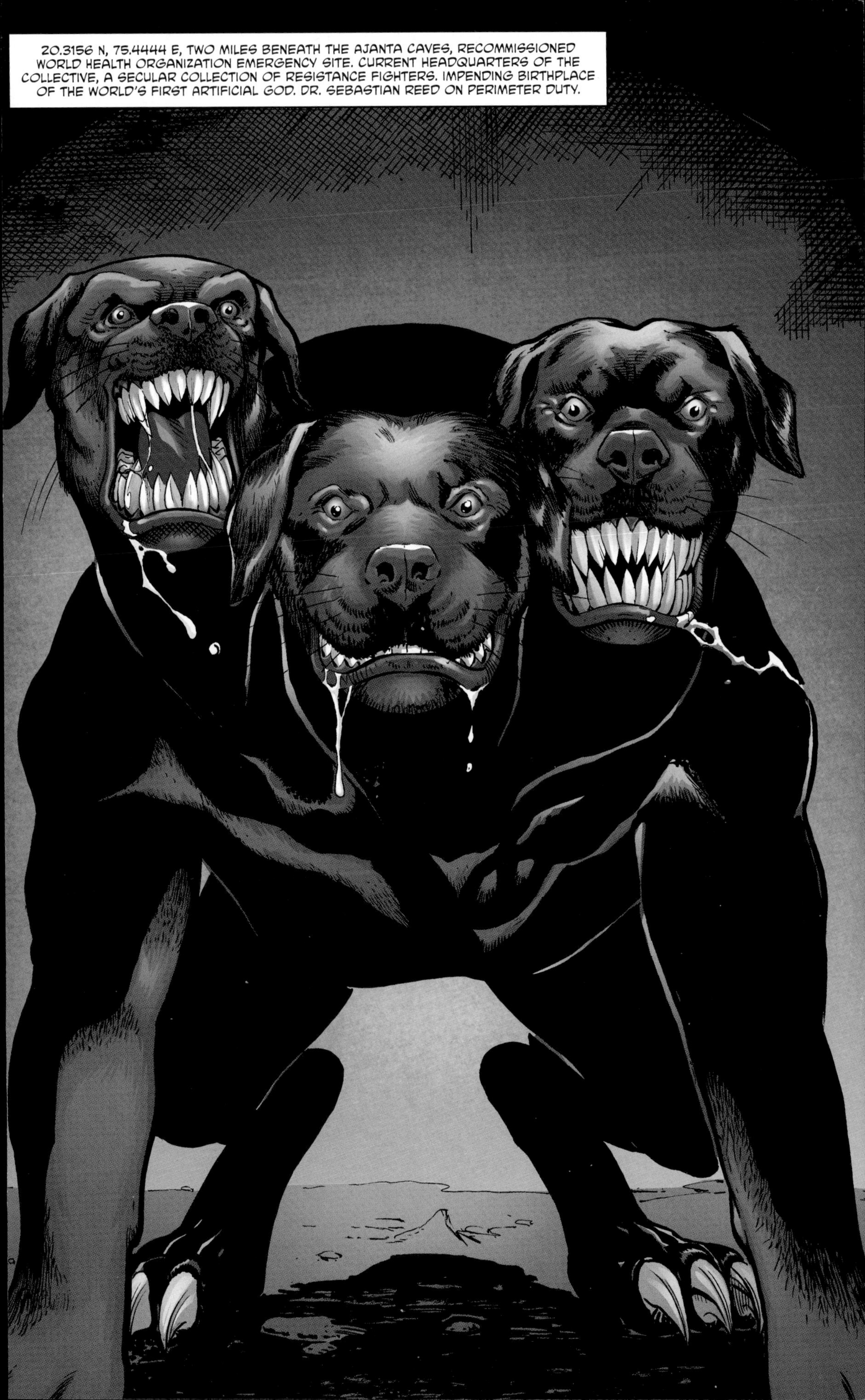
20.3156 N, 75.4444 E, TWO MILES BENEATH THE AJANTA CAVES, RECOMMISSIONED WORLD HEALTH ORGANIZATION EMERGENCY SITE. CURRENT HEADQUARTERS OF THE COLLECTIVE, A SECULAR COLLECTION OF RESISTANCE FIGHTERS. IMPENDING BIRTHPLACE OF THE WORLD'S FIRST ARTIFICIAL GOD. DR. SEBASTIAN REED ON PERIMETER DUTY.

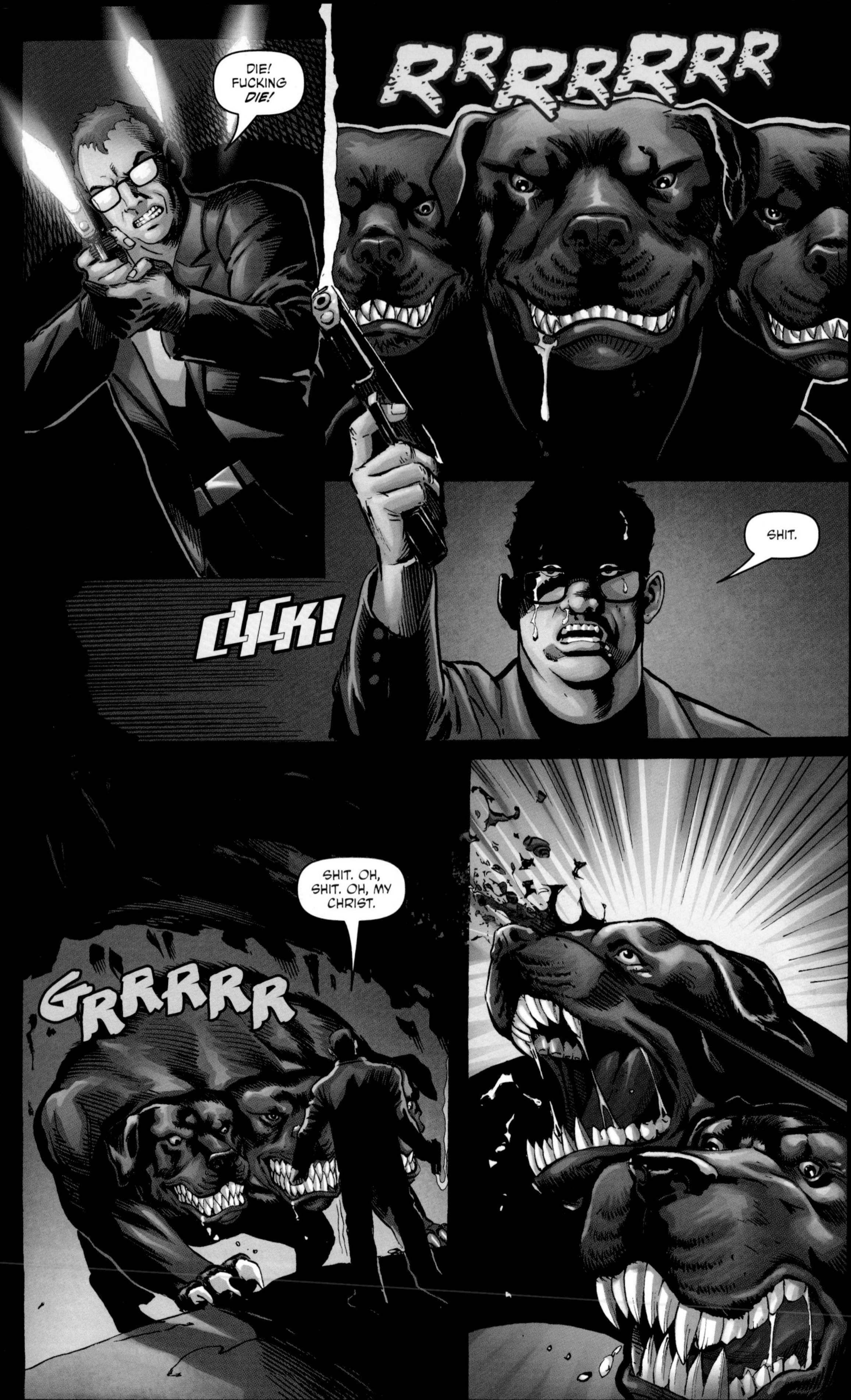
DIE! FUCKING DIE!
RRRRRRRR
SHIT.
CLICK!
SHIT. OH, SHIT. OH, MY CHRIST.
GRRRRR

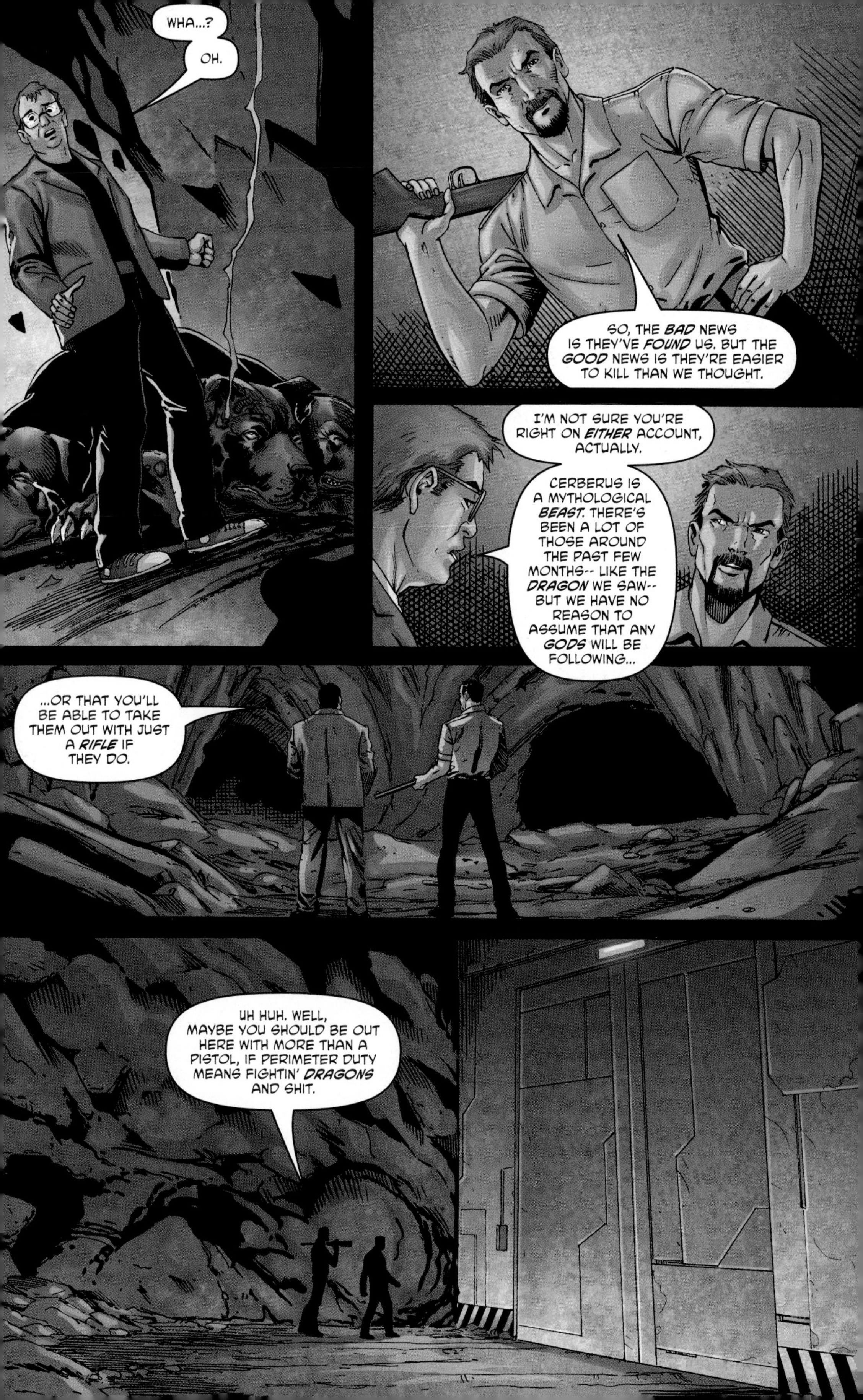
WHA...?
OH.
SO, THE BAD NEWS IS THEY'VE FOUND US. BUT THE GOOD NEWS IS THEY'RE EASIER TO KILL THAN WE THOUGHT.
I'M NOT SURE YOU'RE RIGHT ON EITHER ACCOUNT, ACTUALLY.
CERBERUS IS A MYTHOLOGICAL BEAST. THERE'S BEEN A LOT OF THOSE AROUND THE PAST FEW MONTHS-- LIKE THE DRAGON WE SAW-- BUT WE HAVE NO REASON TO ASSUME THAT ANY GODS WILL BE FOLLOWING...
...OR THAT YOU'LL BE ABLE TO TAKE THEM OUT WITH JUST A RIFLE IF THEY DO.
UH HUH. WELL, MAYBE YOU SHOULD BE OUT HERE WITH MORE THAN A PISTOL, IF PERIMETER DUTY MEANS FIGHTIN' DRAGONS AND SHIT.

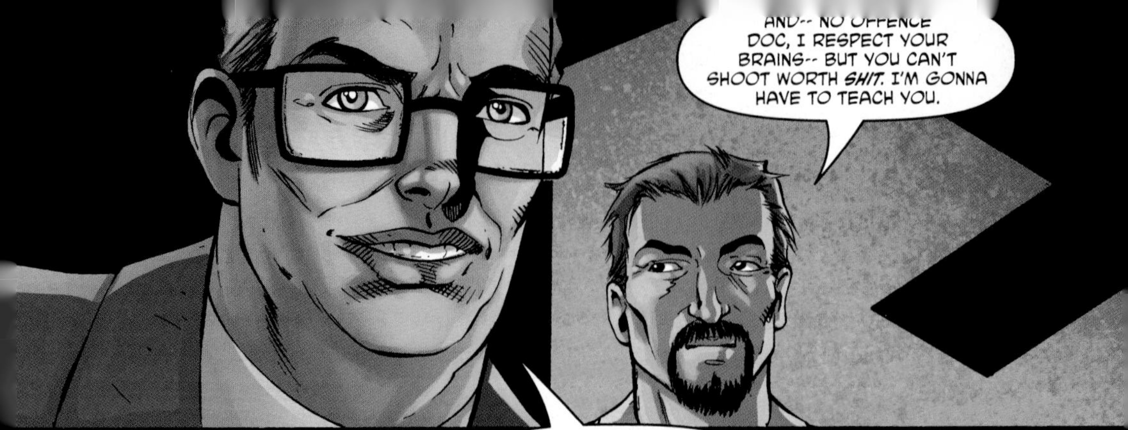
AND-- NO OFFENCE DOC, I RESPECT YOUR BRAINS-- BUT YOU CAN'T SHOOT WORTH SHIT. I'M GONNA HAVE TO TEACH YOU.

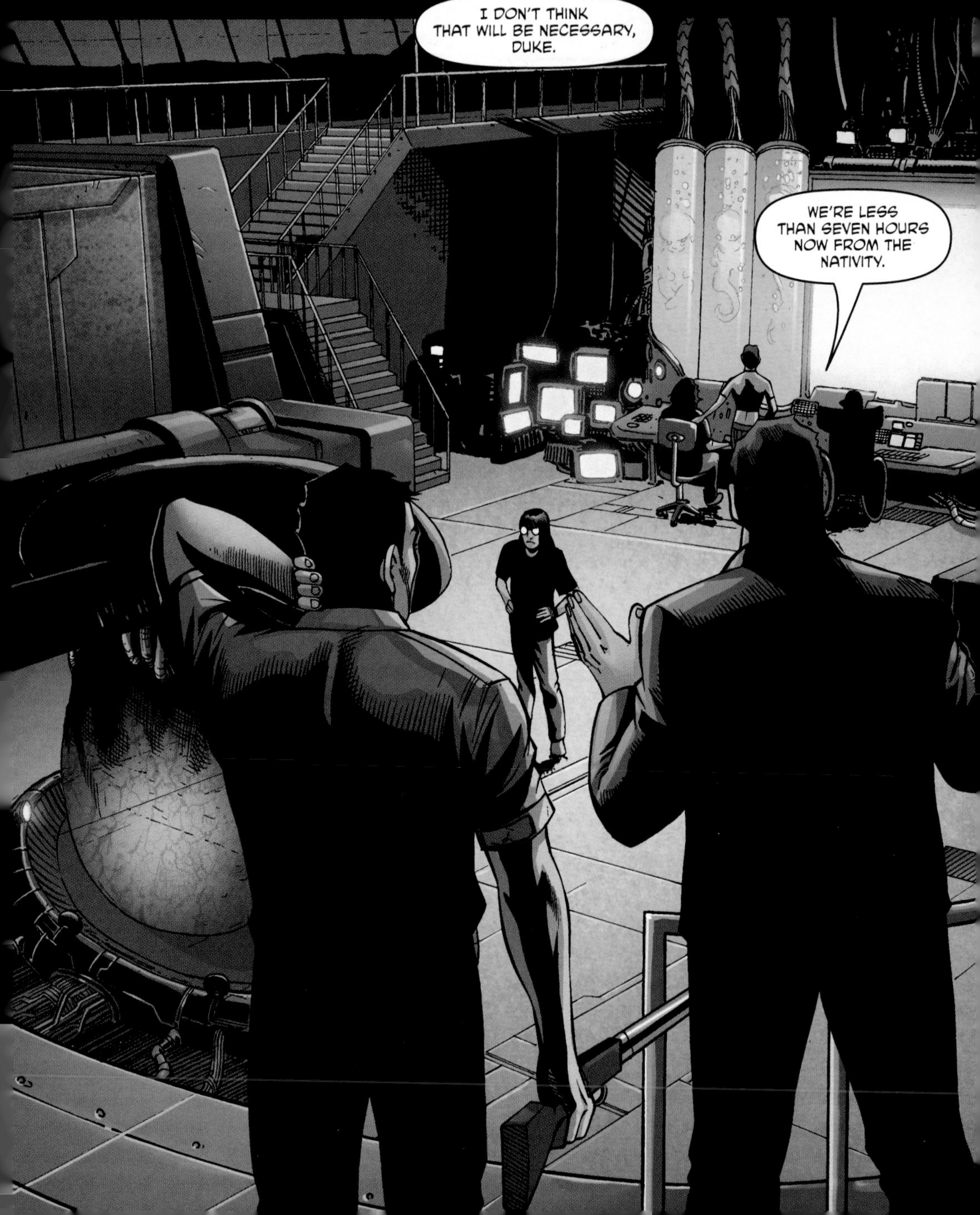
I DON'T THINK THAT WILL BE NECESSARY, DUKE.
WE'RE LESS THAN SEVEN HOURS NOW FROM THE NATIVITY.

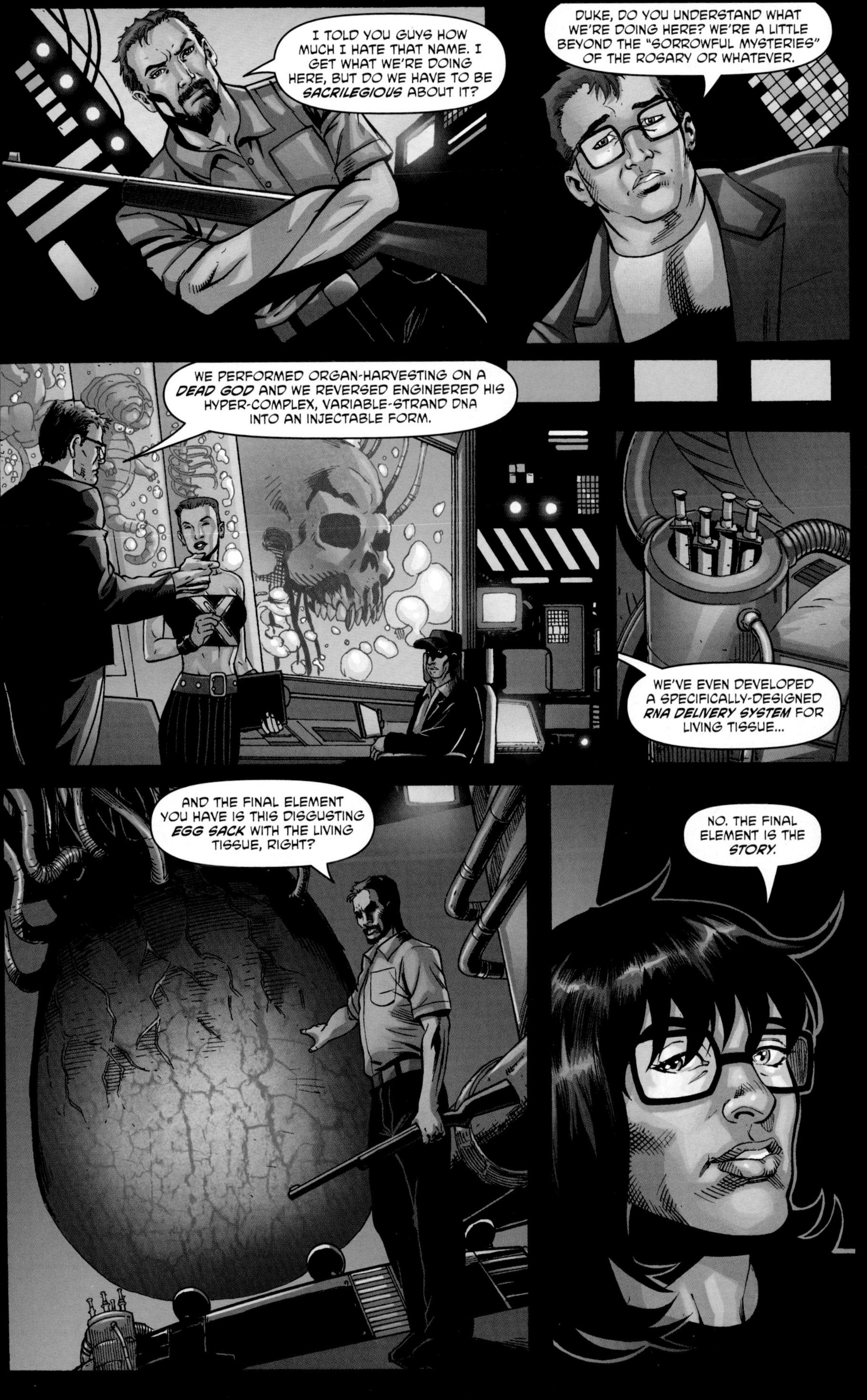
I TOLD YOU GUYS HOW MUCH I HATE THAT NAME. I GET WHAT WE'RE DOING HERE, BUT DO WE HAVE TO BE *SACRILEGIOUS* ABOUT IT?
DUKE, DO YOU UNDERSTAND WHAT WE'RE DOING HERE? WE'RE A LITTLE BEYOND THE "SORROWFUL MYSTERIES" OF THE ROSARY OR WHATEVER.
WE PERFORMED ORGAN-HARVESTING ON A *DEAD GOD* AND WE REVERSED ENGINEERED HIS HYPER-COMPLEX, VARIABLE-STRAND DNA INTO AN INJECTABLE FORM.
WE'VE EVEN DEVELOPED A SPECIFICALLY-DESIGNED *RNA DELIVERY SYSTEM* FOR LIVING TISSUE...
AND THE FINAL ELEMENT YOU HAVE IS THIS DISGUSTING *EGG SACK* WITH THE LIVING TISSUE, RIGHT?
NO. THE FINAL ELEMENT IS THE *STORY*.

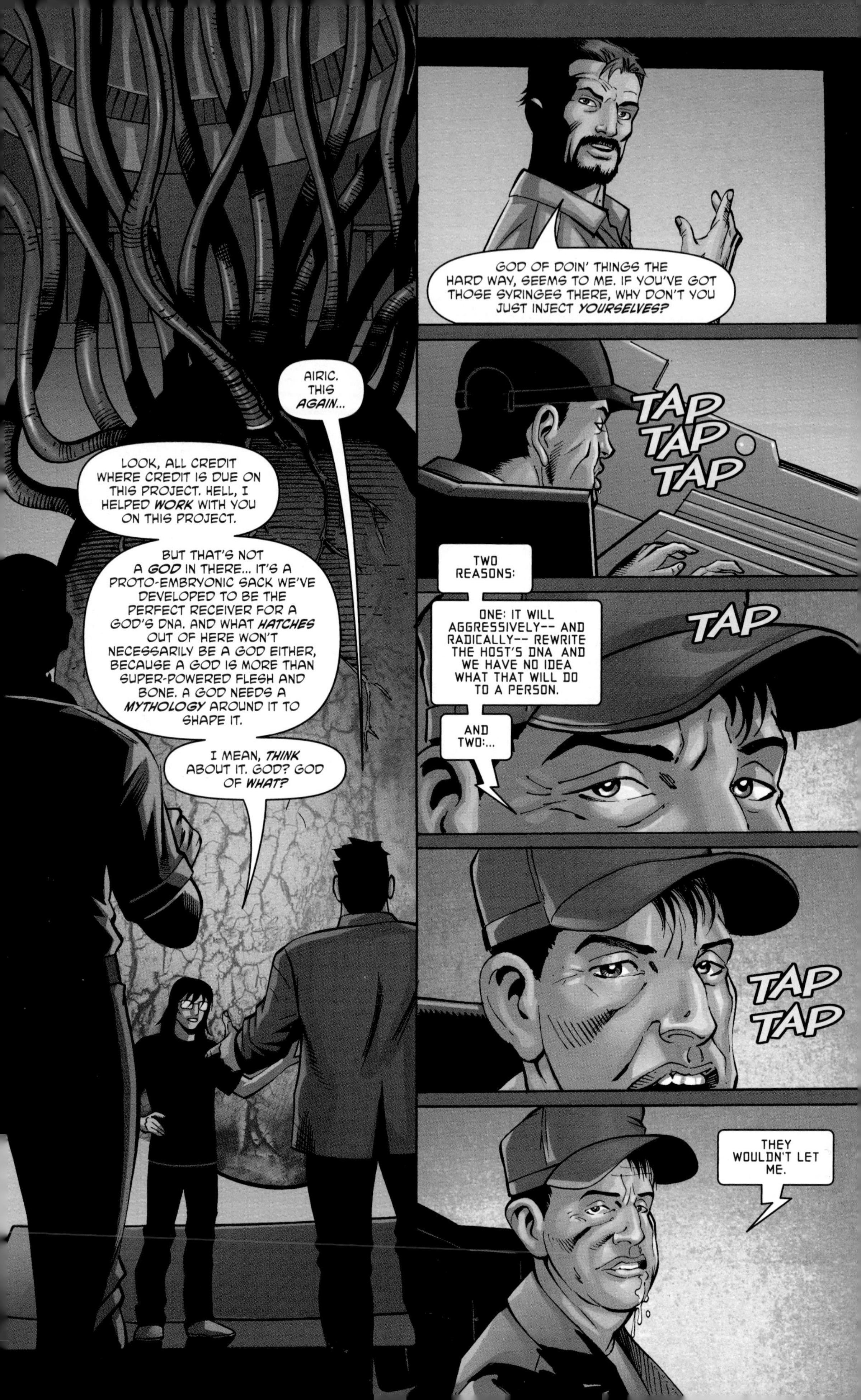
AIRIC. THIS AGAIN...
LOOK, ALL CREDIT WHERE CREDIT IS DUE ON THIS PROJECT. HELL, I HELPED WORK WITH YOU ON THIS PROJECT.
BUT THAT'S NOT A GOD IN THERE... IT'S A PROTO-EMBRYONIC SACK WE'VE DEVELOPED TO BE THE PERFECT RECEIVER FOR A GOD'S DNA. AND WHAT HATCHES OUT OF HERE WON'T NECESSARILY BE A GOD EITHER, BECAUSE A GOD IS MORE THAN SUPER-POWERED FLESH AND BONE. A GOD NEEDS A MYTHOLOGY AROUND IT TO SHAPE IT.
I MEAN, THINK ABOUT IT. GOD? GOD OF WHAT?
GOD OF DOIN' THINGS THE HARD WAY, SEEMS TO ME. IF YOU'VE GOT THOSE SYRINGES THERE, WHY DON'T YOU JUST INJECT YOURSELVES?
TAP TAP TAP
TWO REASONS:
ONE: IT WILL AGGRESSIVELY-- AND RADICALLY-- REWRITE THE HOST'S DNA AND WE HAVE NO IDEA WHAT THAT WILL DO TO A PERSON.
AND TWO:...
TAP
TAP TAP
THEY WOULDN'T LET ME.

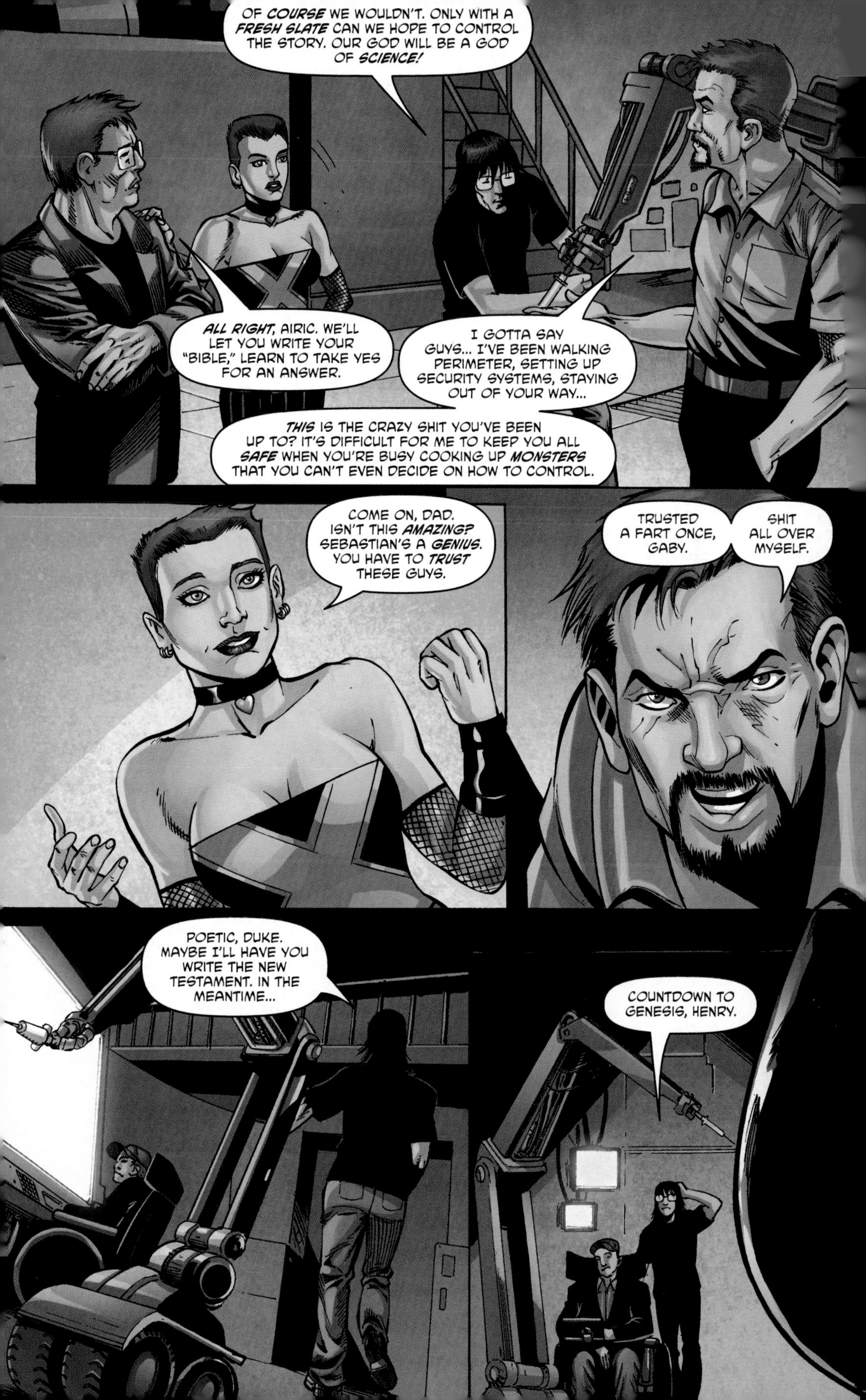
OF COURSE WE WOULDN'T. ONLY WITH A FRESH SLATE CAN WE HOPE TO CONTROL THE STORY. OUR GOD WILL BE A GOD OF SCIENCE!
ALL RIGHT, AIRIC. WE'LL LET YOU WRITE YOUR "BIBLE," LEARN TO TAKE YES FOR AN ANSWER.
I GOTTA SAY GUYS... I'VE BEEN WALKING PERIMETER, SETTING UP SECURITY SYSTEMS, STAYING OUT OF YOUR WAY...
THIS IS THE CRAZY SHIT YOU'VE BEEN UP TO? IT'S DIFFICULT FOR ME TO KEEP YOU ALL SAFE WHEN YOU'RE BUSY COOKING UP MONSTERS THAT YOU CAN'T EVEN DECIDE ON HOW TO CONTROL.
COME ON, DAD. ISN'T THIS AMAZING? SEBASTIAN'S A GENIUS. YOU HAVE TO TRUST THESE GUYS.
TRUSTED A FART ONCE, GABY.
SHIT ALL OVER MYSELF.
POETIC, DUKE. MAYBE I'LL HAVE YOU WRITE THE NEW TESTAMENT. IN THE MEANTIME...
COUNTDOWN TO GENESIS, HENRY.

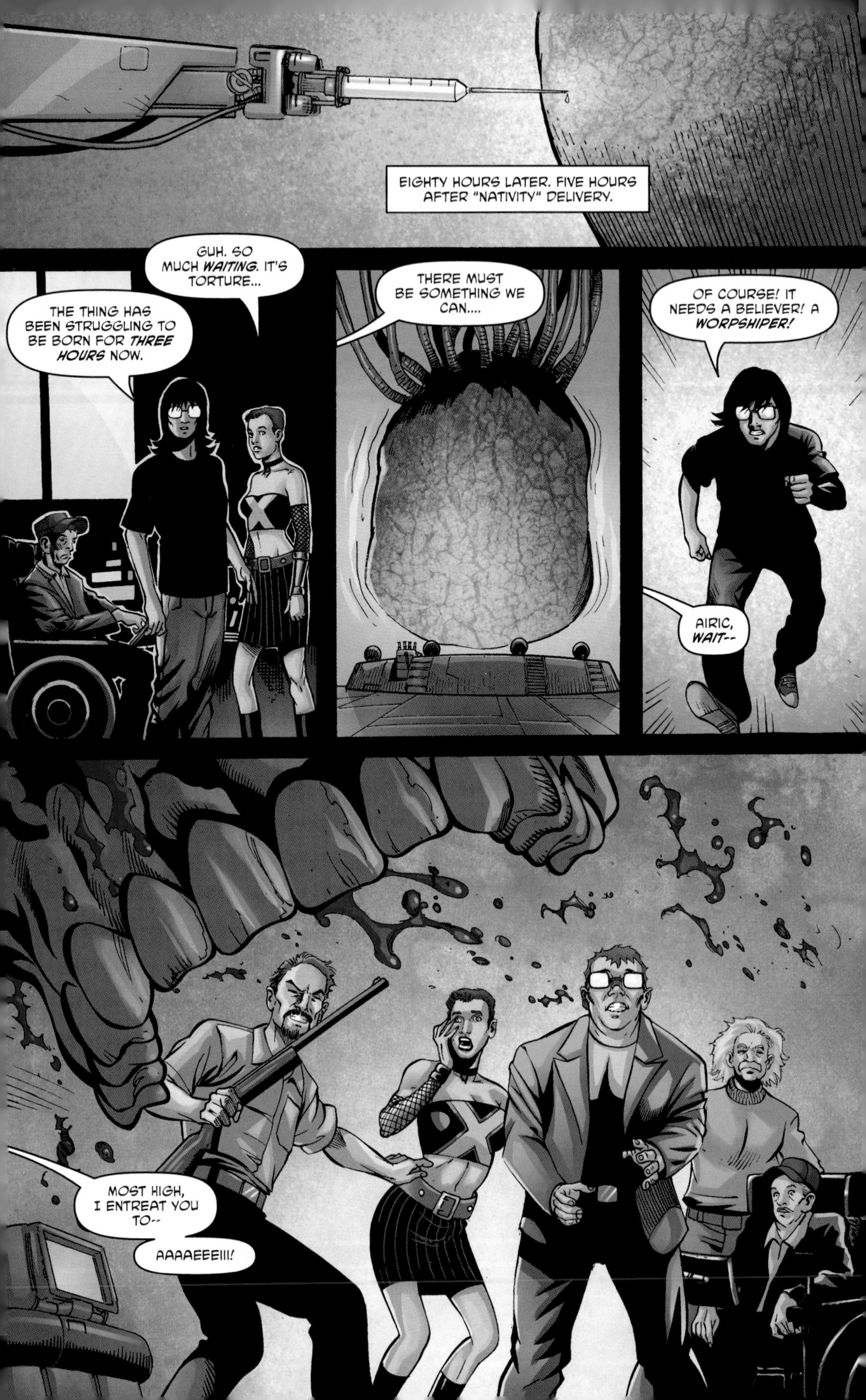
EIGHTY HOURS LATER. FIVE HOURS AFTER "NATIVITY" DELIVERY.
GUH. SO MUCH WAITING. IT'S TORTURE...
THE THING HAS BEEN STRUGGLING TO BE BORN FOR THREE HOURS NOW.
THERE MUST BE SOMETHING WE CAN....
OF COURSE! IT NEEDS A BELIEVER! A WORPSHIPER!
AIRIC, WAIT--
MOST HIGH, I ENTREAT YOU TO--
AAAAEEEIII!

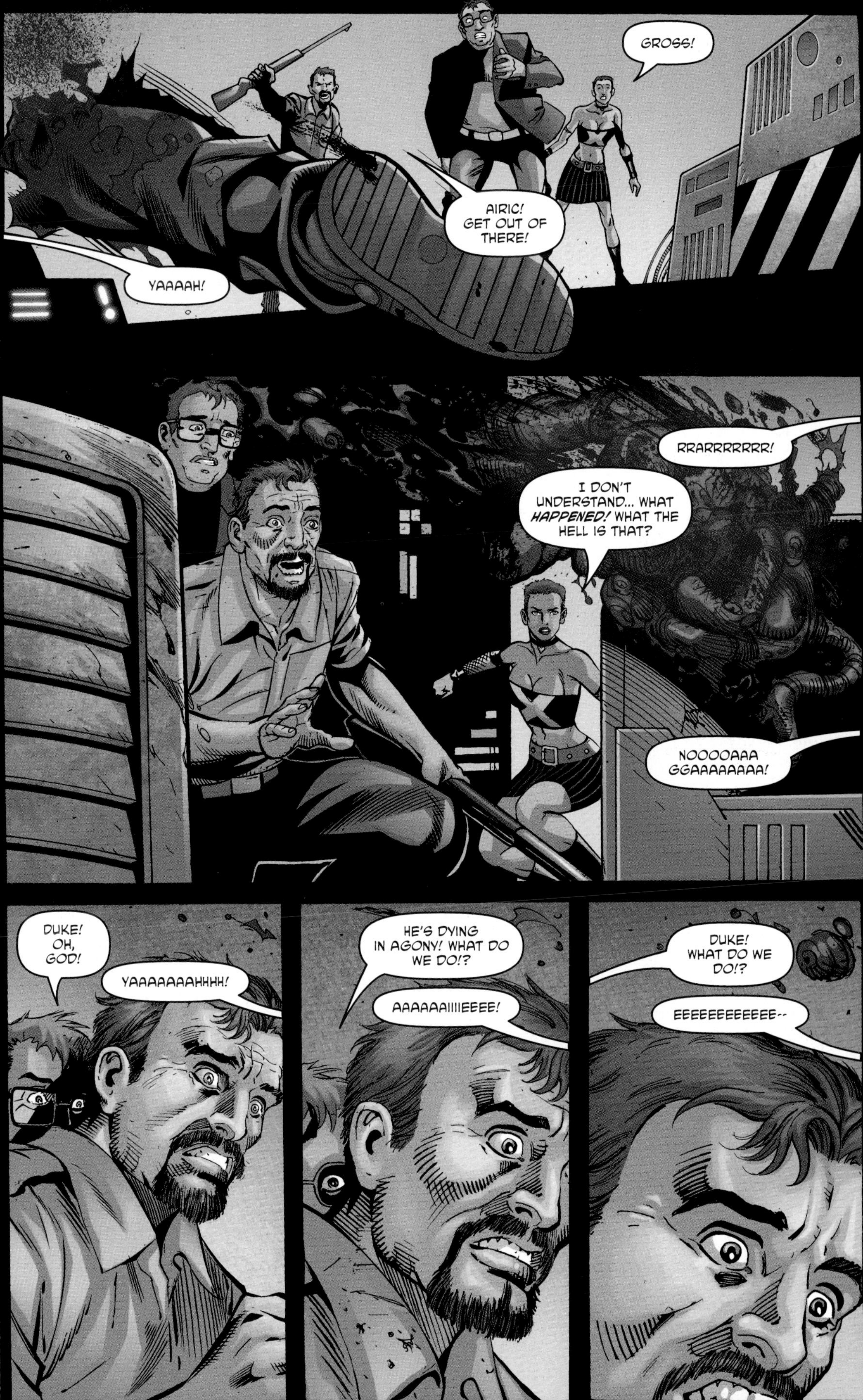
GROSS!
AIRIC! GET OUT OF THERE!
YAAAAH!
RRARRRRRRR!
I DON'T UNDERSTAND... WHAT *HAPPENED!* WHAT THE HELL IS THAT?
NOOOOAAA GGAAAAAAAA!
DUKE! OH, GOD!
YAAAAAAAHHHH!
HE'S DYING IN AGONY! WHAT DO WE DO!?
AAAAAAIIIIEEEE!
DUKE! WHAT DO WE DO!?
EEEEEEEEEEEE--

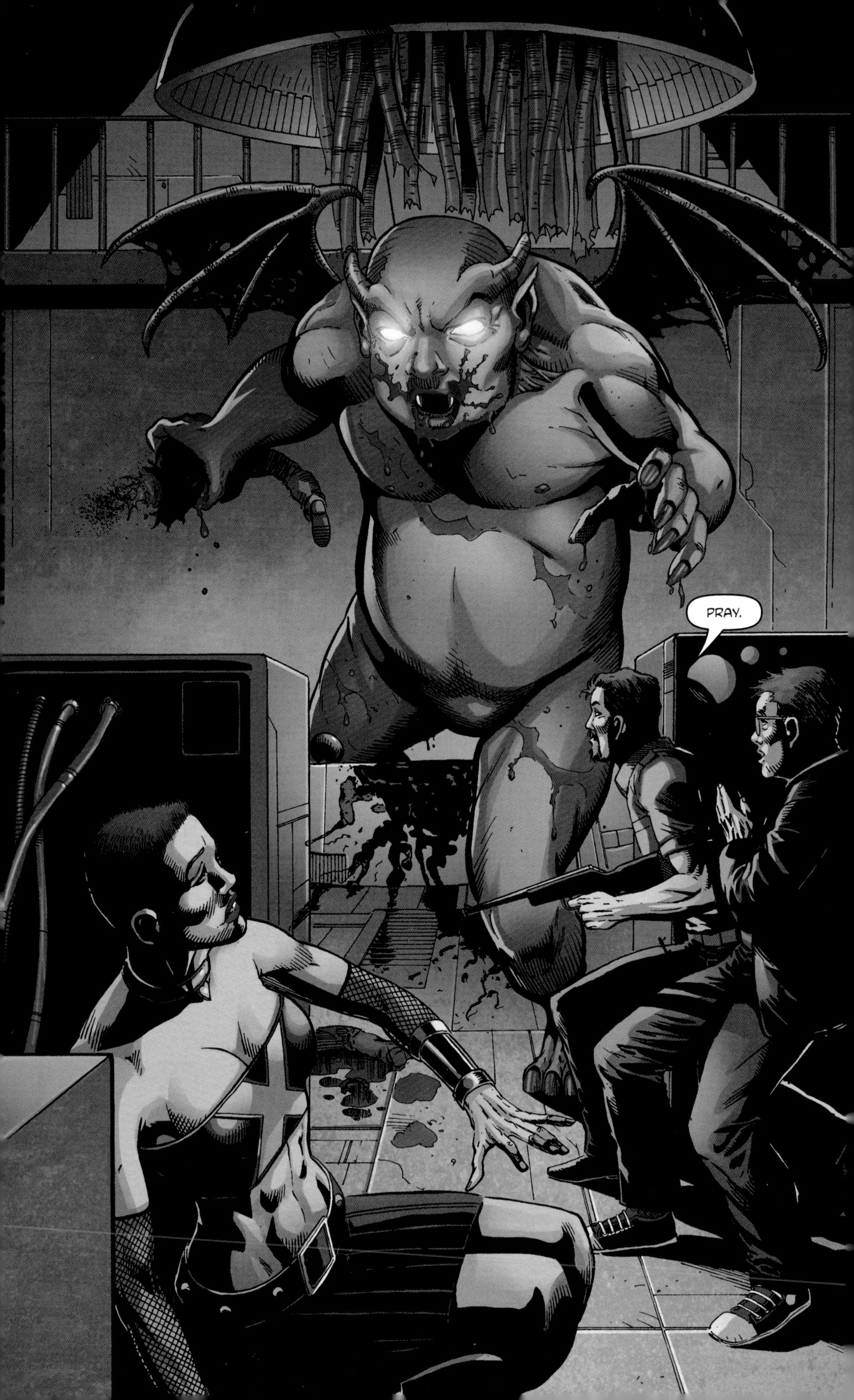
PRAY.

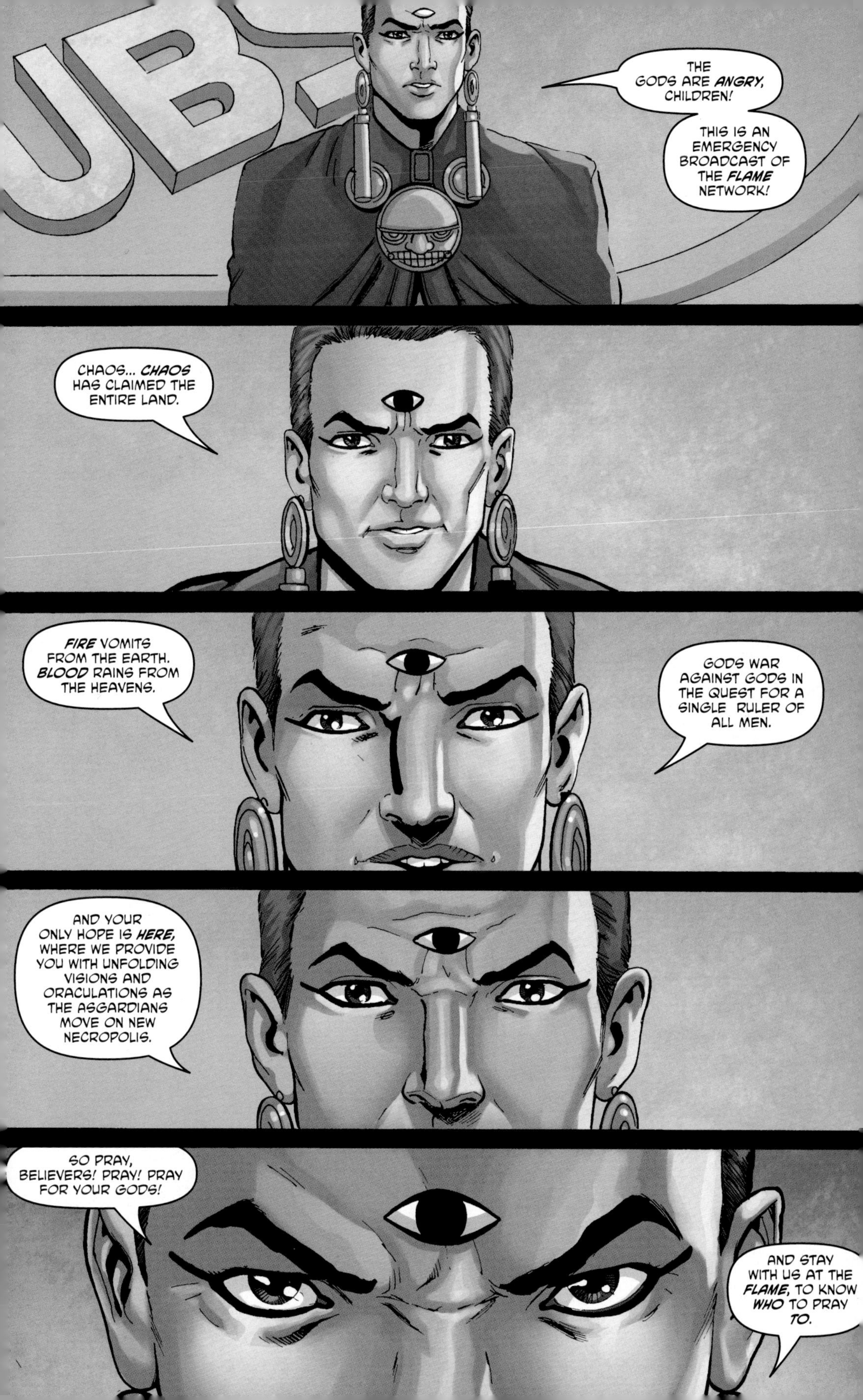

THE GODS ARE ANGRY, CHILDREN!
THIS IS AN EMERGENCY BROADCAST OF THE FLAME NETWORK!
CHAOS... CHAOS HAS CLAIMED THE ENTIRE LAND.
FIRE VOMITS FROM THE EARTH. BLOOD RAINS FROM THE HEAVENS.
GODS WAR AGAINST GODS IN THE QUEST FOR A SINGLE RULER OF ALL MEN.
AND YOUR ONLY HOPE IS HERE, WHERE WE PROVIDE YOU WITH UNFOLDING VISIONS AND ORACULATIONS AS THE ASGARDIANS MOVE ON NEW NECROPOLIS.
SO PRAY, BELIEVERS! PRAY! PRAY FOR YOUR GODS!
AND STAY WITH US AT THE FLAME, TO KNOW WHO TO PRAY TO.

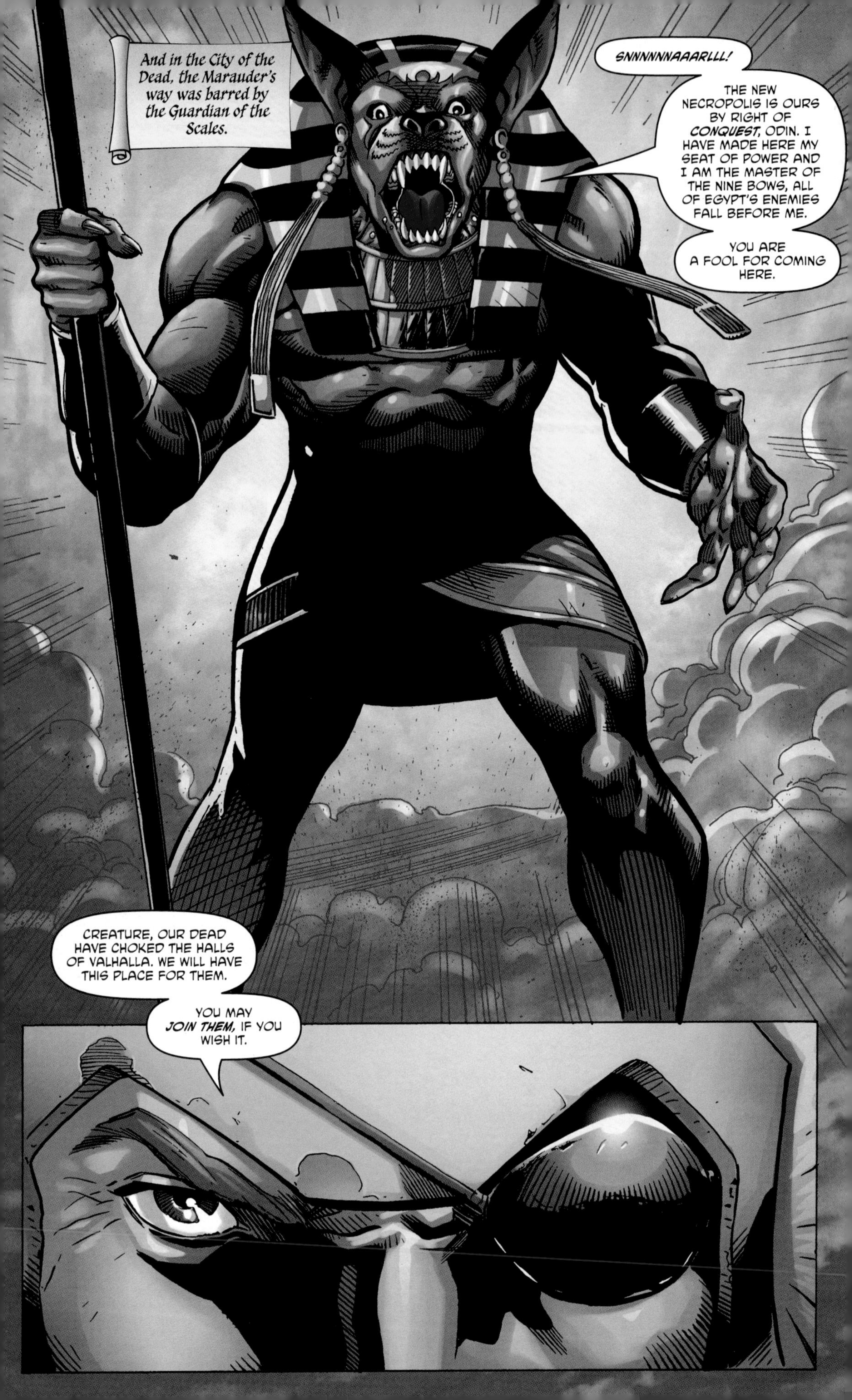
And in the City of the Dead, the Marauder's way was barred by the Guardian of the Scales.
SNNNNNNAAARLLL!
THE NEW NECROPOLIS IS OURS BY RIGHT OF CONQUEST, ODIN. I HAVE MADE HERE MY SEAT OF POWER AND I AM THE MASTER OF THE NINE BOWS, ALL OF EGYPT'S ENEMIES FALL BEFORE ME.
YOU ARE A FOOL FOR COMING HERE.
CREATURE, OUR DEAD HAVE CHOKED THE HALLS OF VALHALLA. WE WILL HAVE THIS PLACE FOR THEM.
YOU MAY JOIN THEM, IF YOU WISH IT.

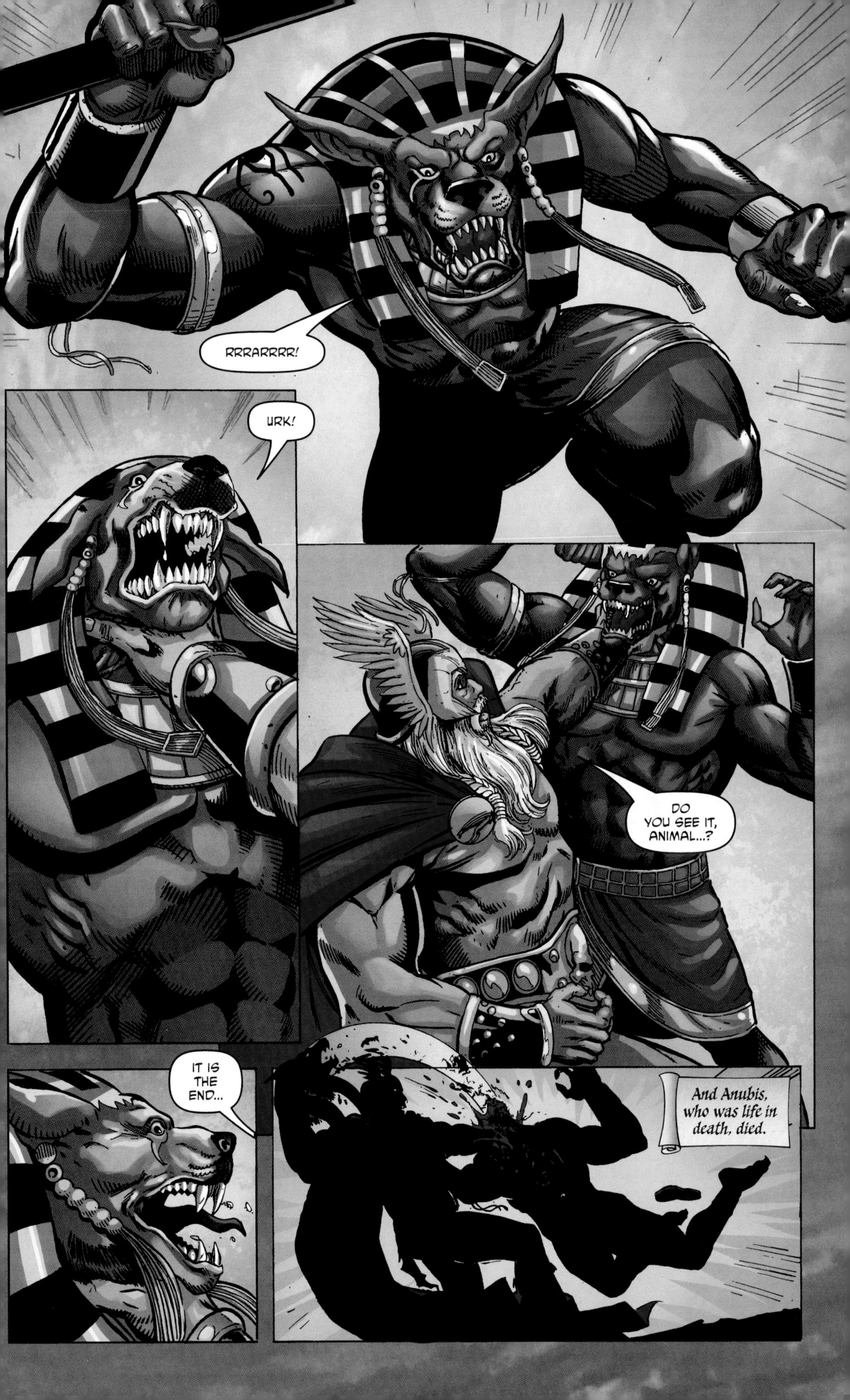
RRRARRRR!
URK!
DO YOU SEE IT, ANIMAL...?
IT IS THE END...
And Anubis, who was life in death, died.

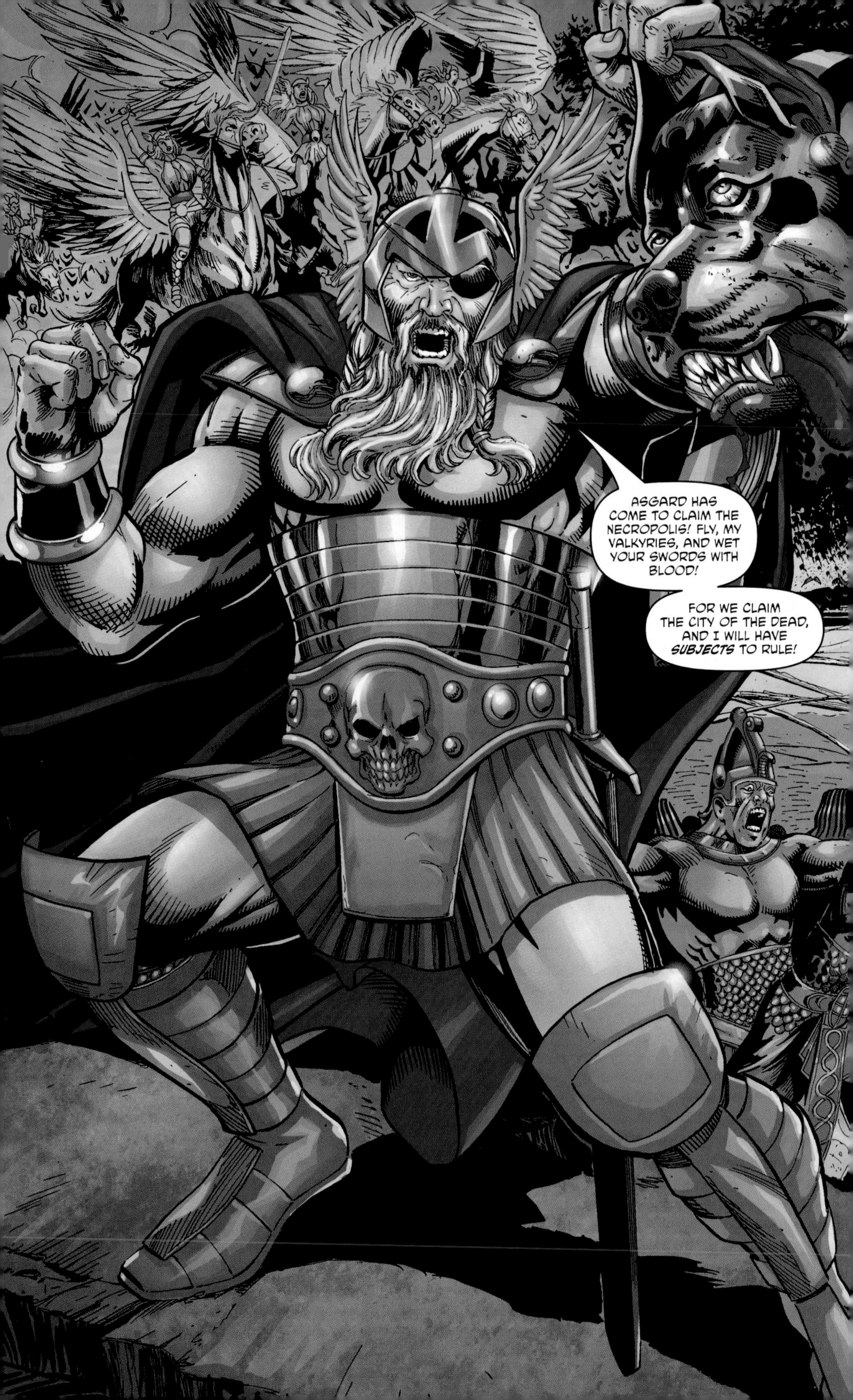
ASGARD HAS COME TO CLAIM THE NECROPOLIS! FLY, MY VALKYRIES, AND WET YOUR SWORDS WITH BLOOD!
FOR WE CLAIM THE CITY OF THE DEAD, AND I WILL HAVE *SUBJECTS* TO RULE!

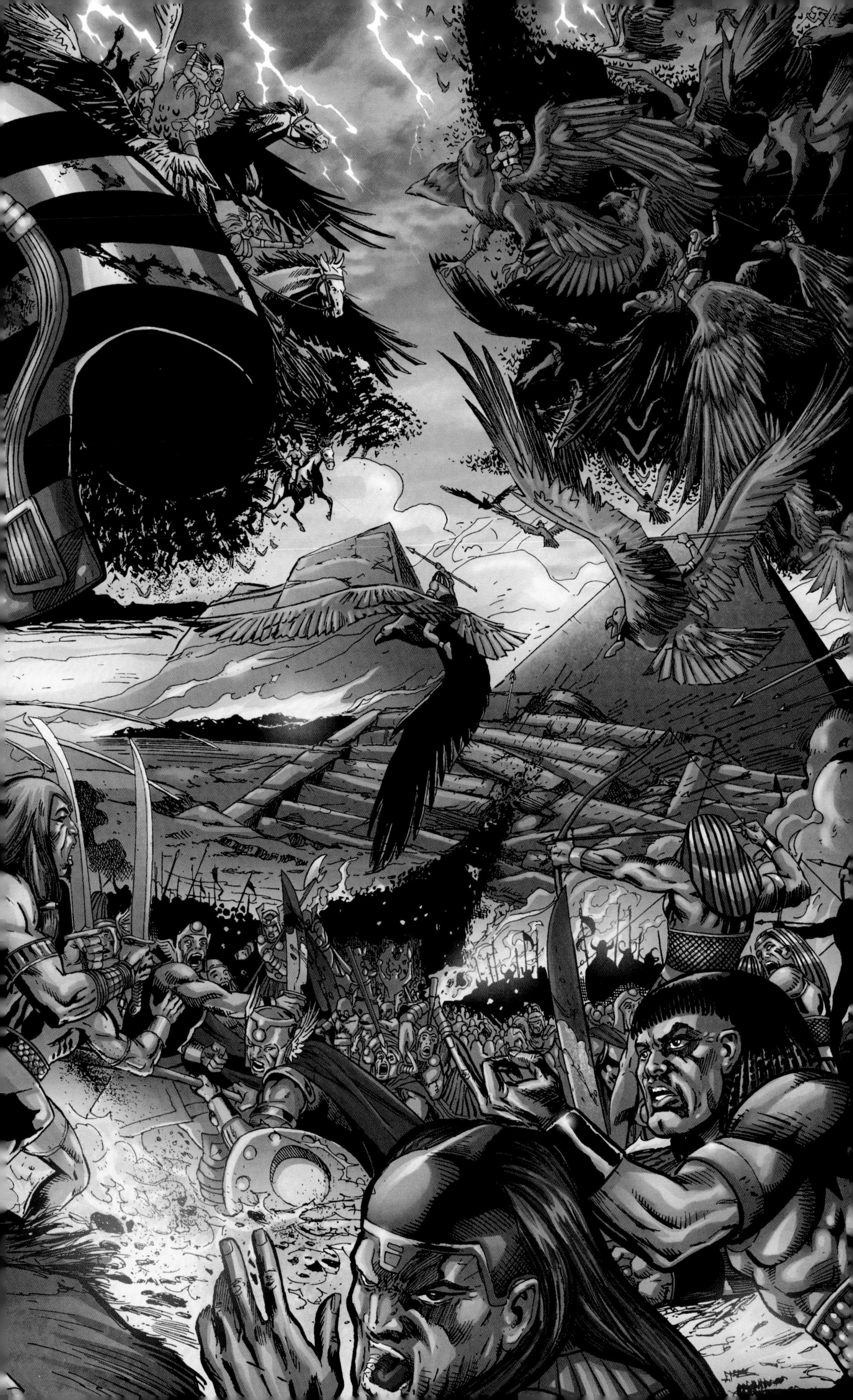

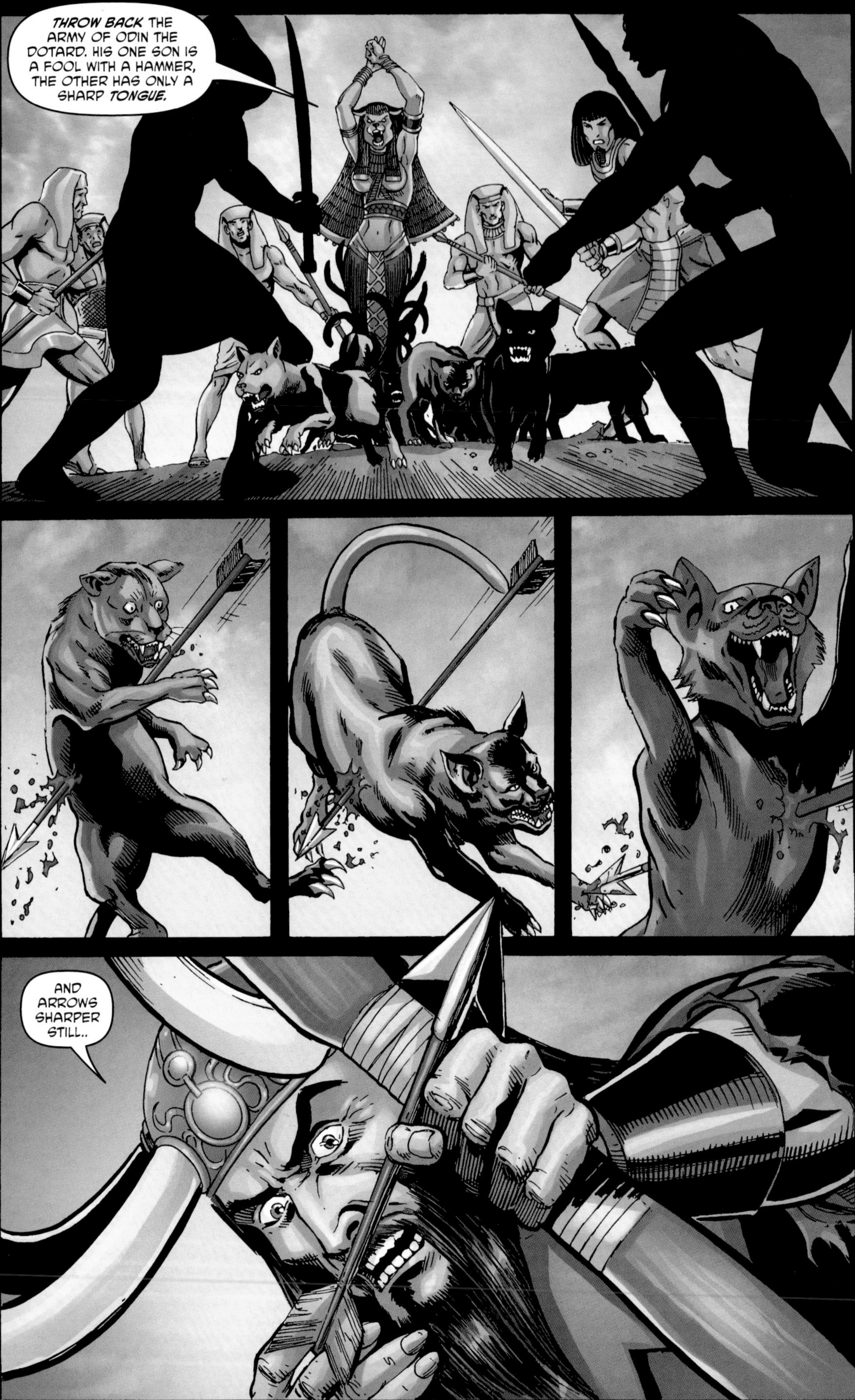
THROW BACK THE ARMY OF ODIN THE DOTARD. HIS ONE SON IS A FOOL WITH A HAMMER, THE OTHER HAS ONLY A SHARP TONGUE.
AND ARROWS SHARPER STILL..

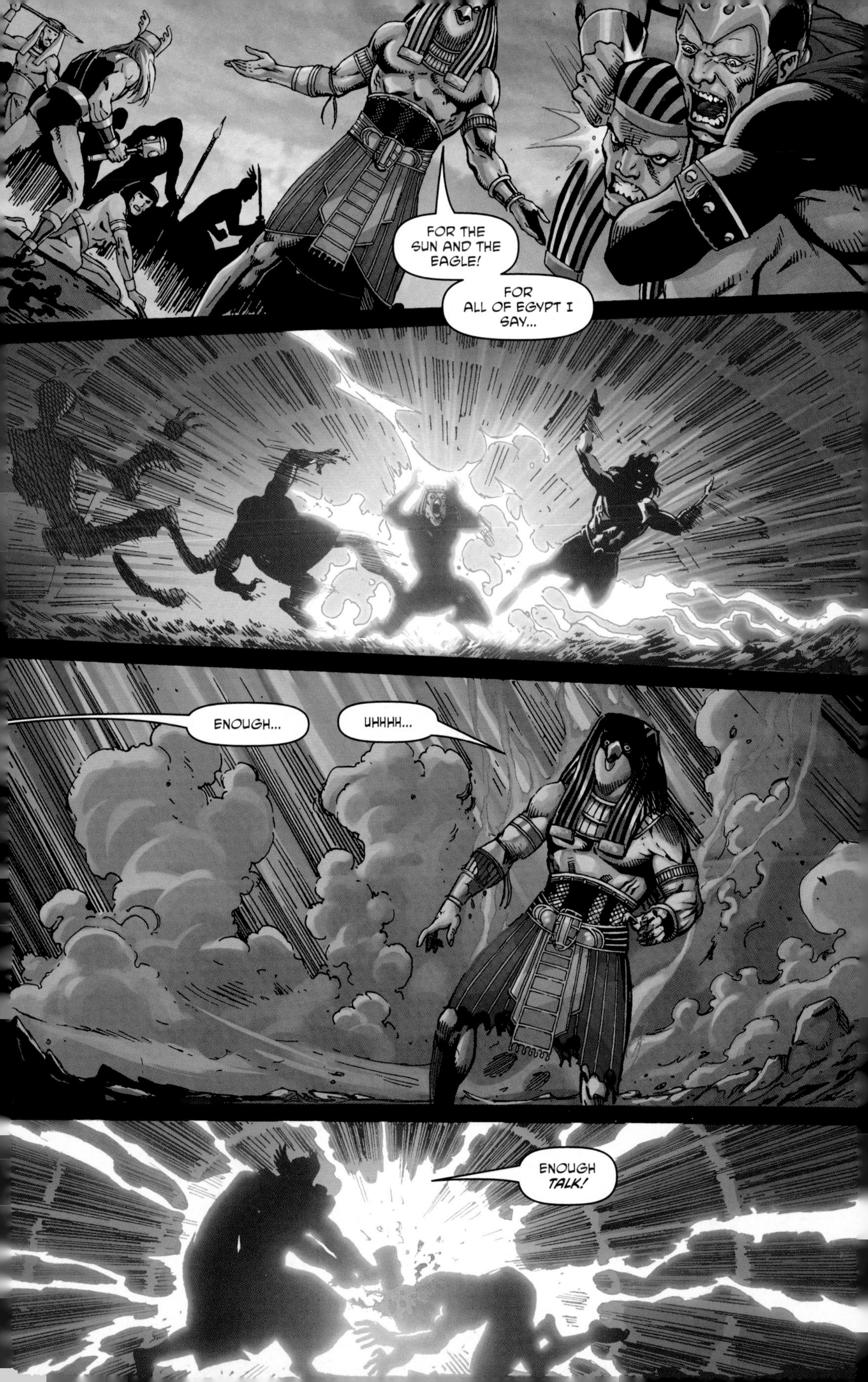
FOR THE SUN AND THE EAGLE!
FOR ALL OF EGYPT I SAY...
ENOUGH...
UHHHH...
ENOUGH *TALK!*

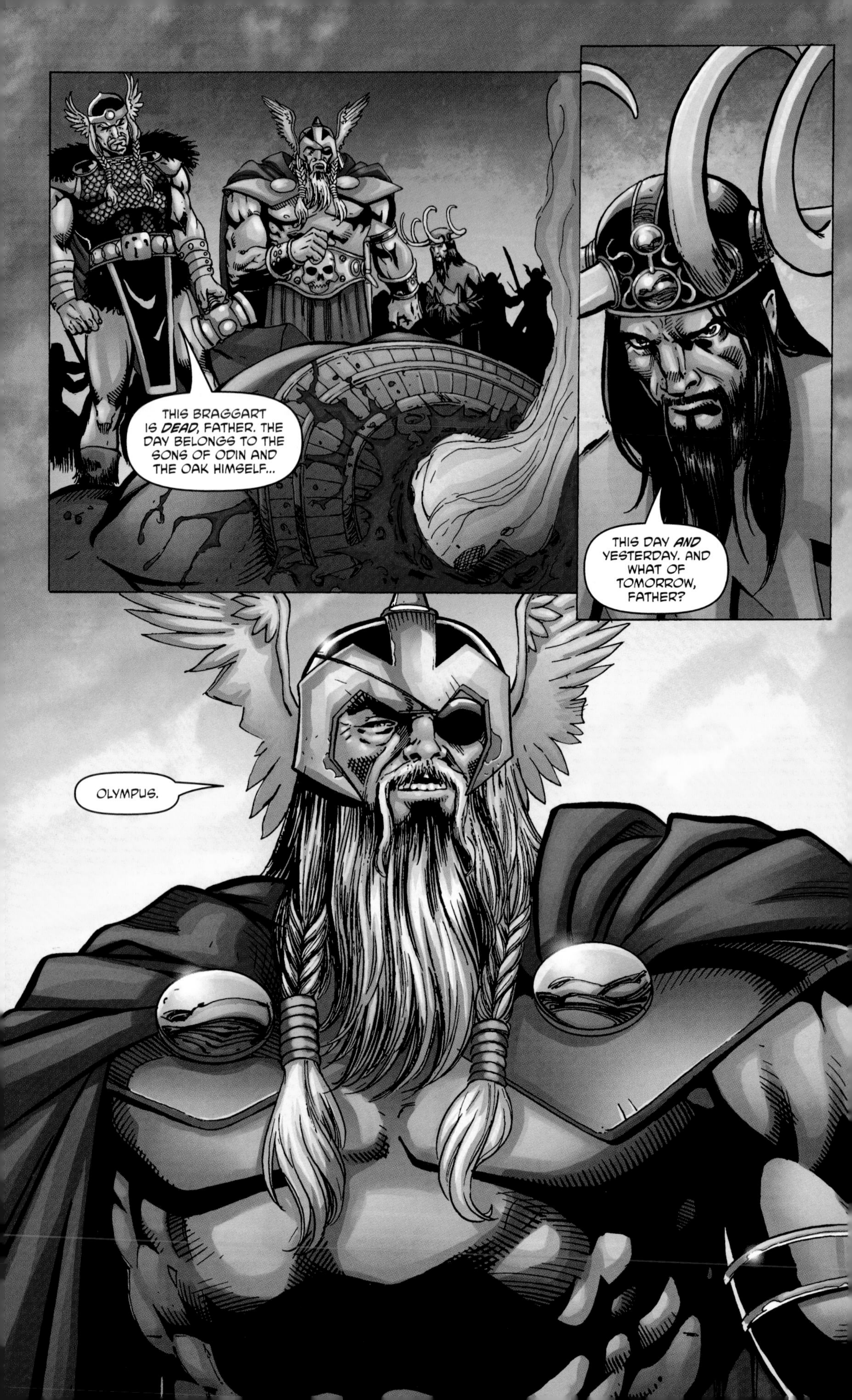

THIS BRAGGART IS *DEAD*, FATHER. THE DAY BELONGS TO THE SONS OF ODIN AND THE OAK HIMSELF...
THIS DAY *AND* YESTERDAY. AND WHAT OF TOMORROW, FATHER?
OLYMPUS.

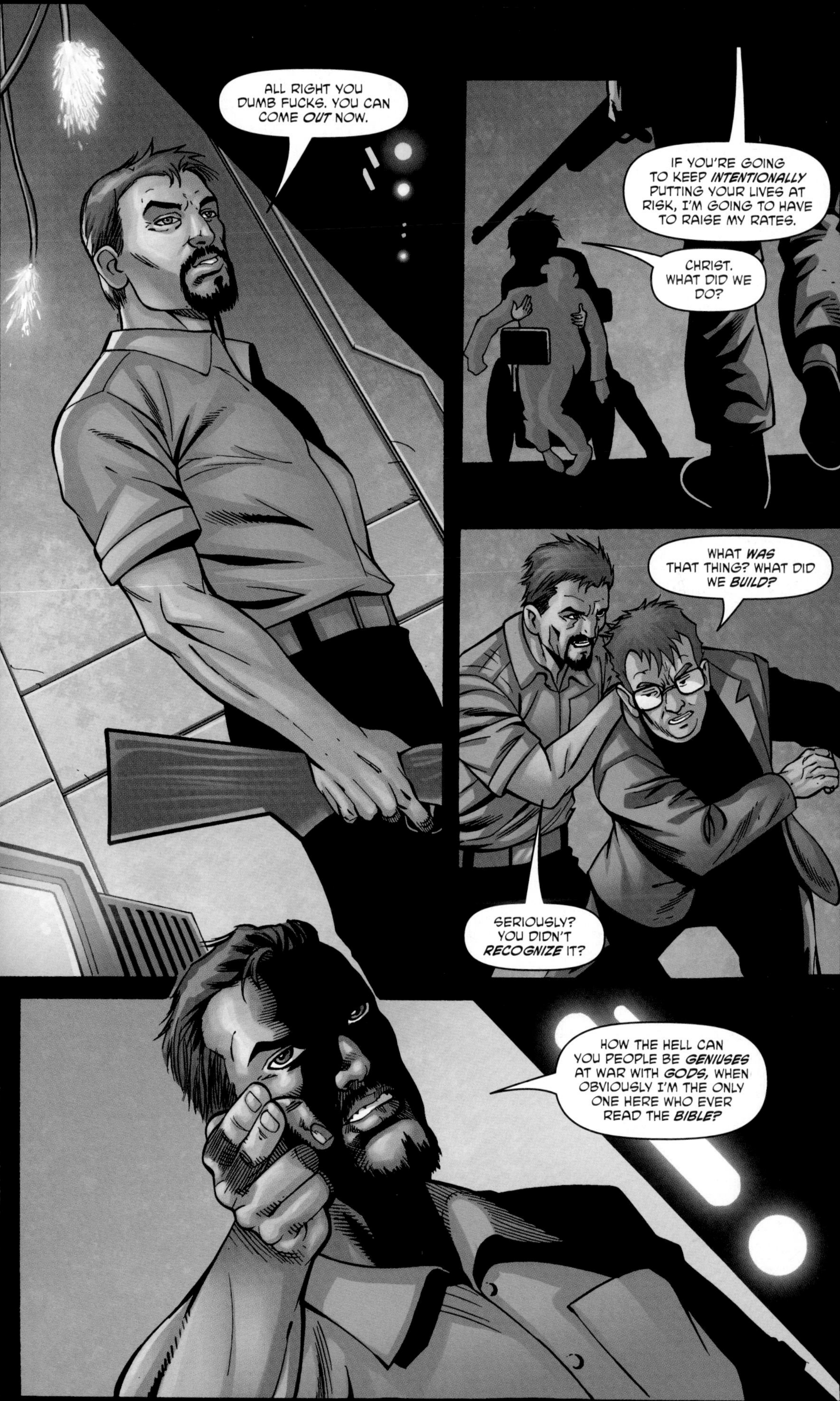

ALL RIGHT YOU DUMB FUCKS. YOU CAN COME *OUT* NOW.
IF YOU'RE GOING TO KEEP *INTENTIONALLY* PUTTING YOUR LIVES AT RISK, I'M GOING TO HAVE TO RAISE MY RATES.
CHRIST. WHAT DID WE DO?
WHAT *WAS* THAT THING? WHAT DID WE *BUILD?*
SERIOUSLY? YOU DIDN'T *RECOGNIZE* IT?
HOW THE HELL CAN YOU PEOPLE BE *GENIUSES* AT WAR WITH *GODS*, WHEN OBVIOUSLY I'M THE ONLY ONE HERE WHO EVER READ THE *BIBLE?*

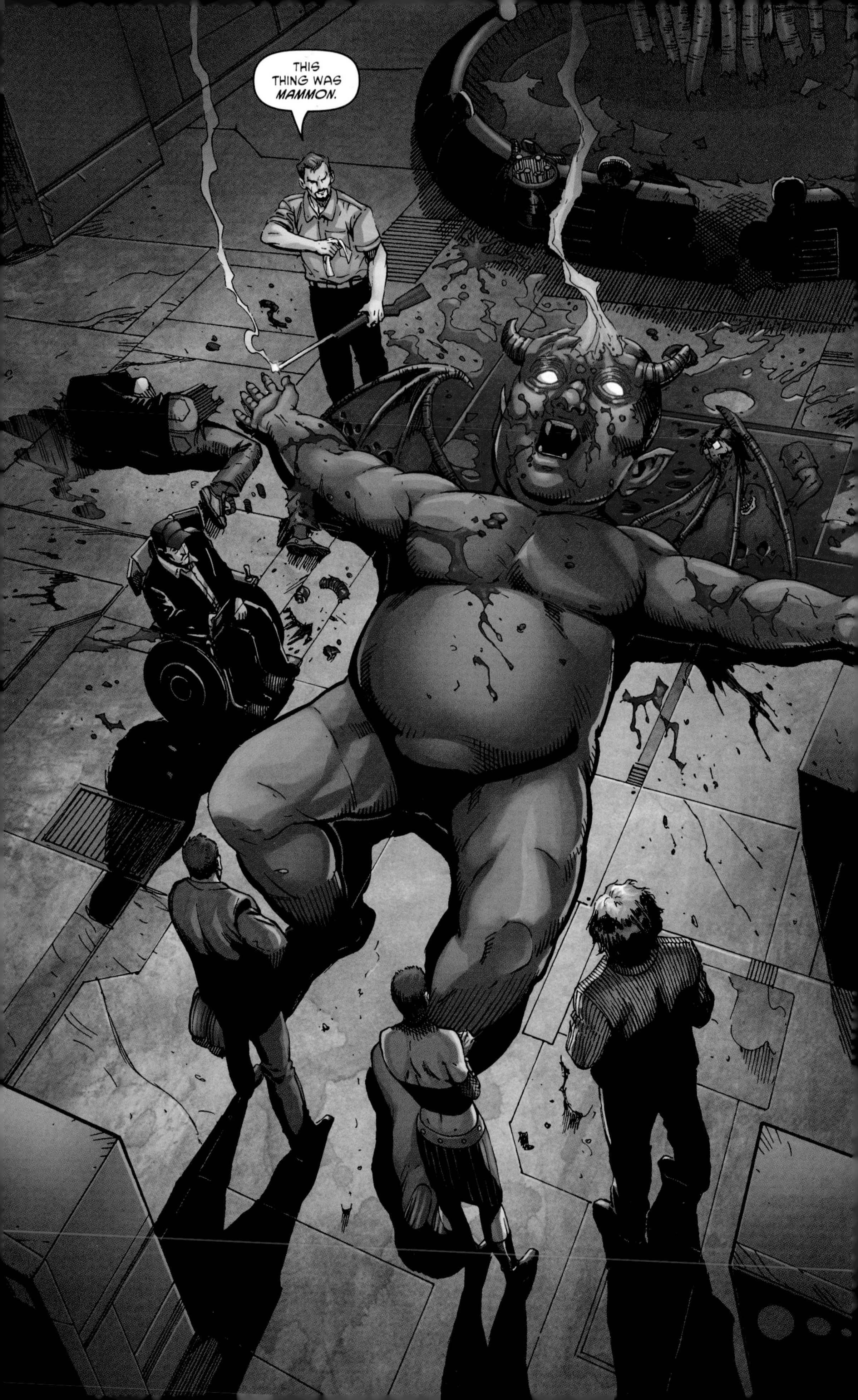
THIS THING WAS MAMMON.

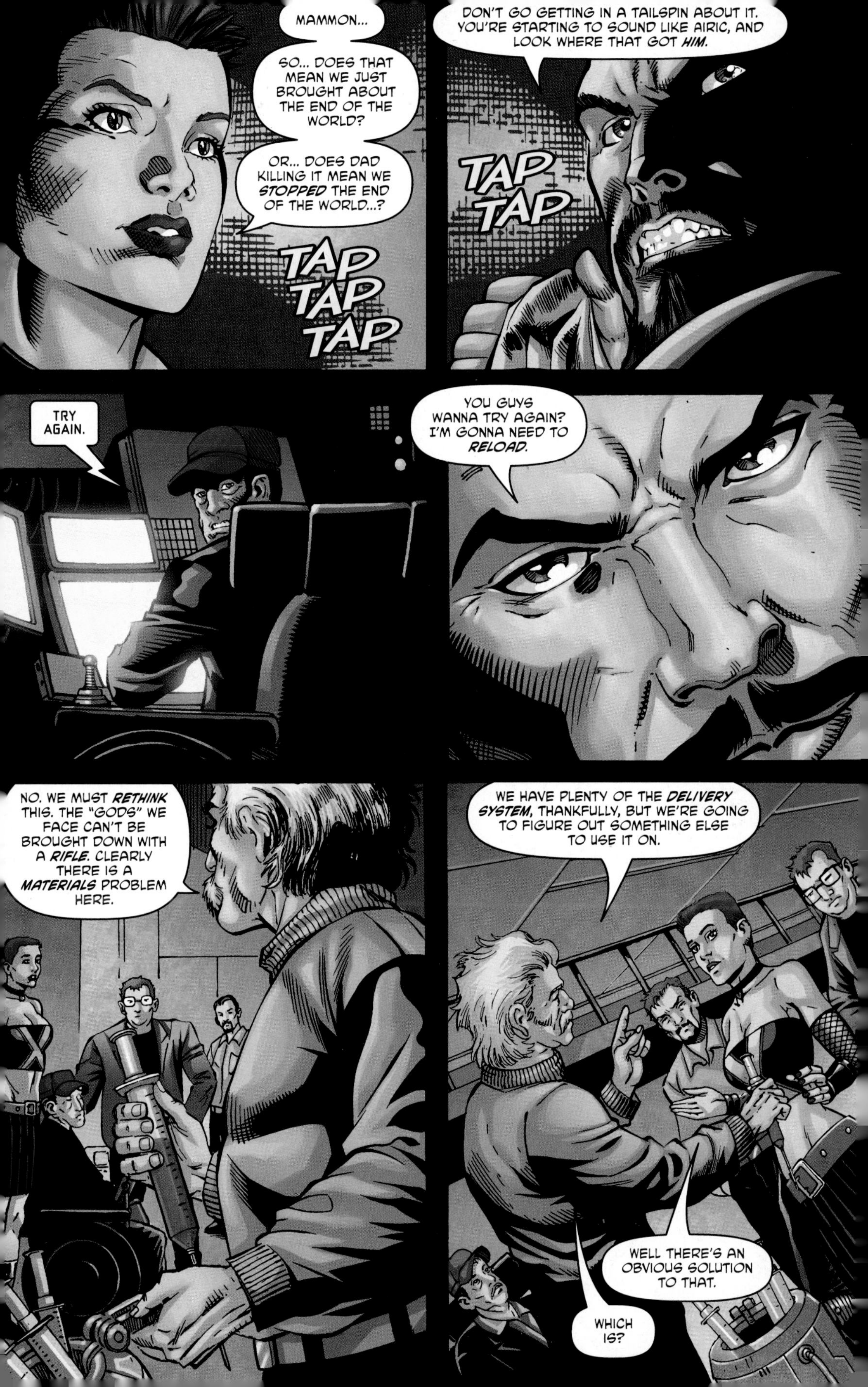
MAMMON...
SO... DOES THAT MEAN WE JUST BROUGHT ABOUT THE END OF THE WORLD?
OR... DOES DAD KILLING IT MEAN WE *STOPPED* THE END OF THE WORLD...?
TAP TAP TAP
DON'T GO GETTING IN A TAILSPIN ABOUT IT. YOU'RE STARTING TO SOUND LIKE AIRIC, AND LOOK WHERE THAT GOT *HIM*.
TAP TAP
TRY AGAIN.
YOU GUYS WANNA TRY AGAIN? I'M GONNA NEED TO *RELOAD*.
NO. WE MUST *RETHINK* THIS. THE "GODS" WE FACE CAN'T BE BROUGHT DOWN WITH A *RIFLE*. CLEARLY THERE IS A *MATERIALS* PROBLEM HERE.
WE HAVE PLENTY OF THE *DELIVERY SYSTEM*, THANKFULLY, BUT WE'RE GOING TO FIGURE OUT SOMETHING ELSE TO USE IT ON.
WELL THERE'S AN OBVIOUS SOLUTION TO THAT.
WHICH IS?

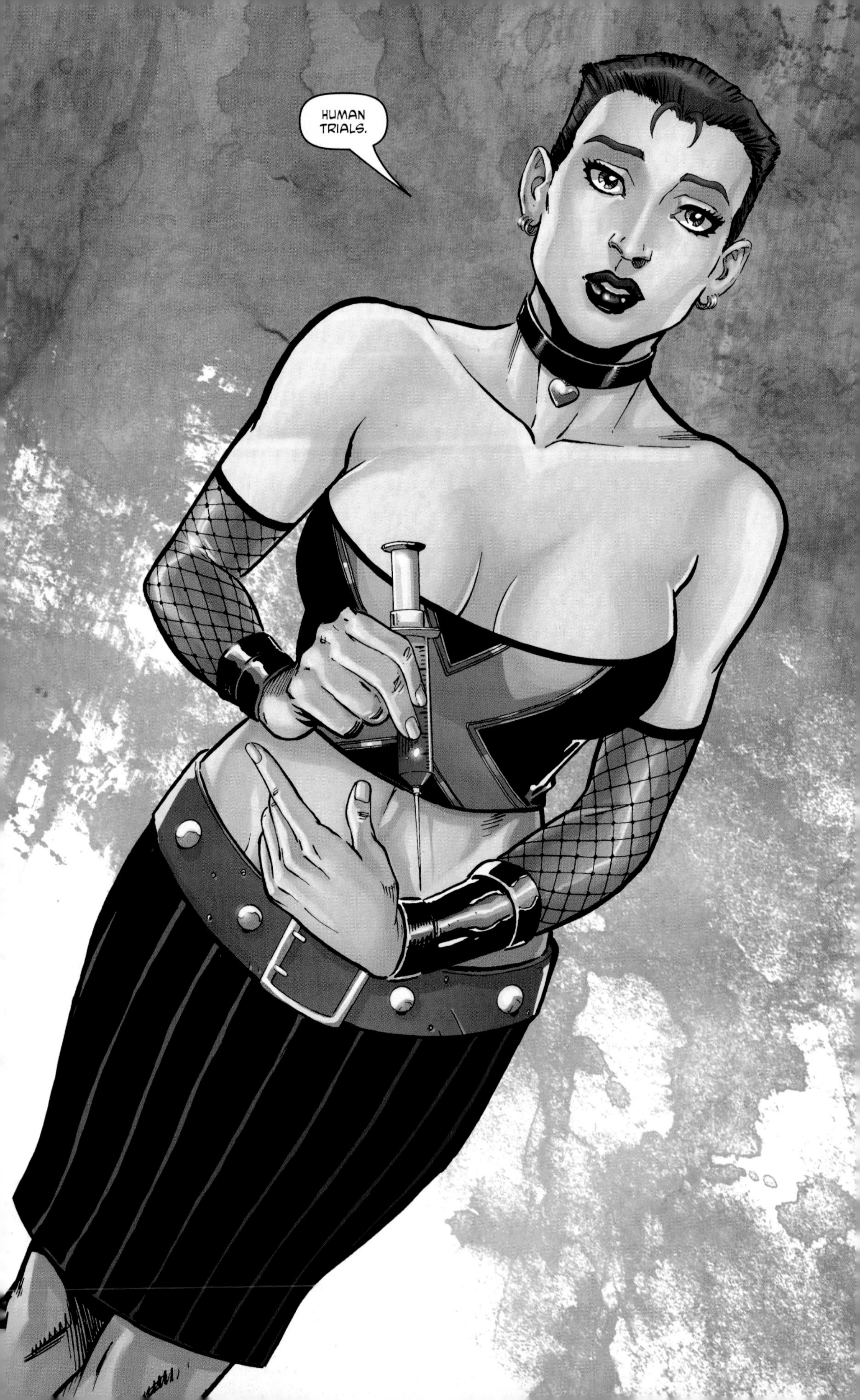
HUMAN TRIALS.

FIVE

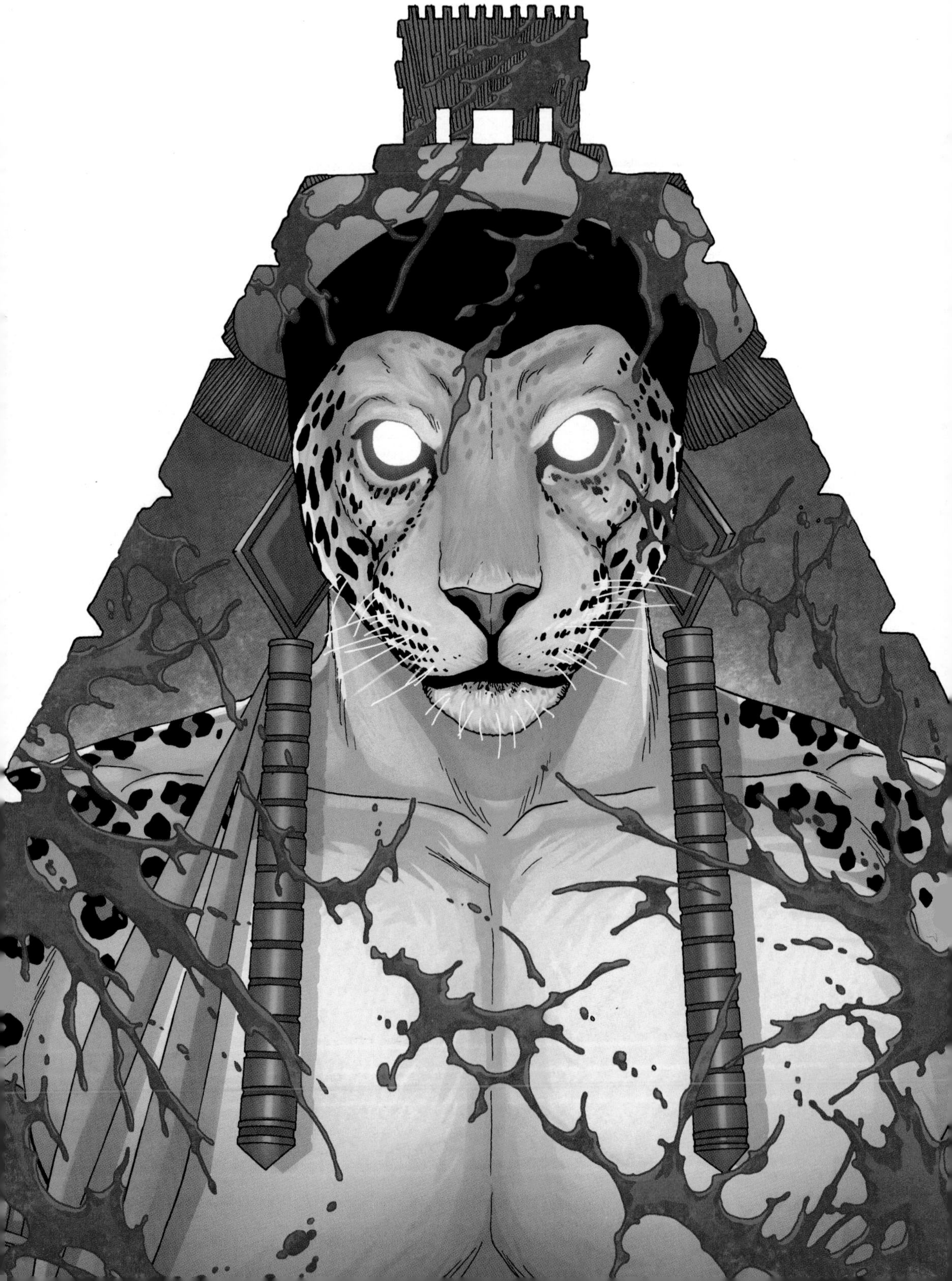

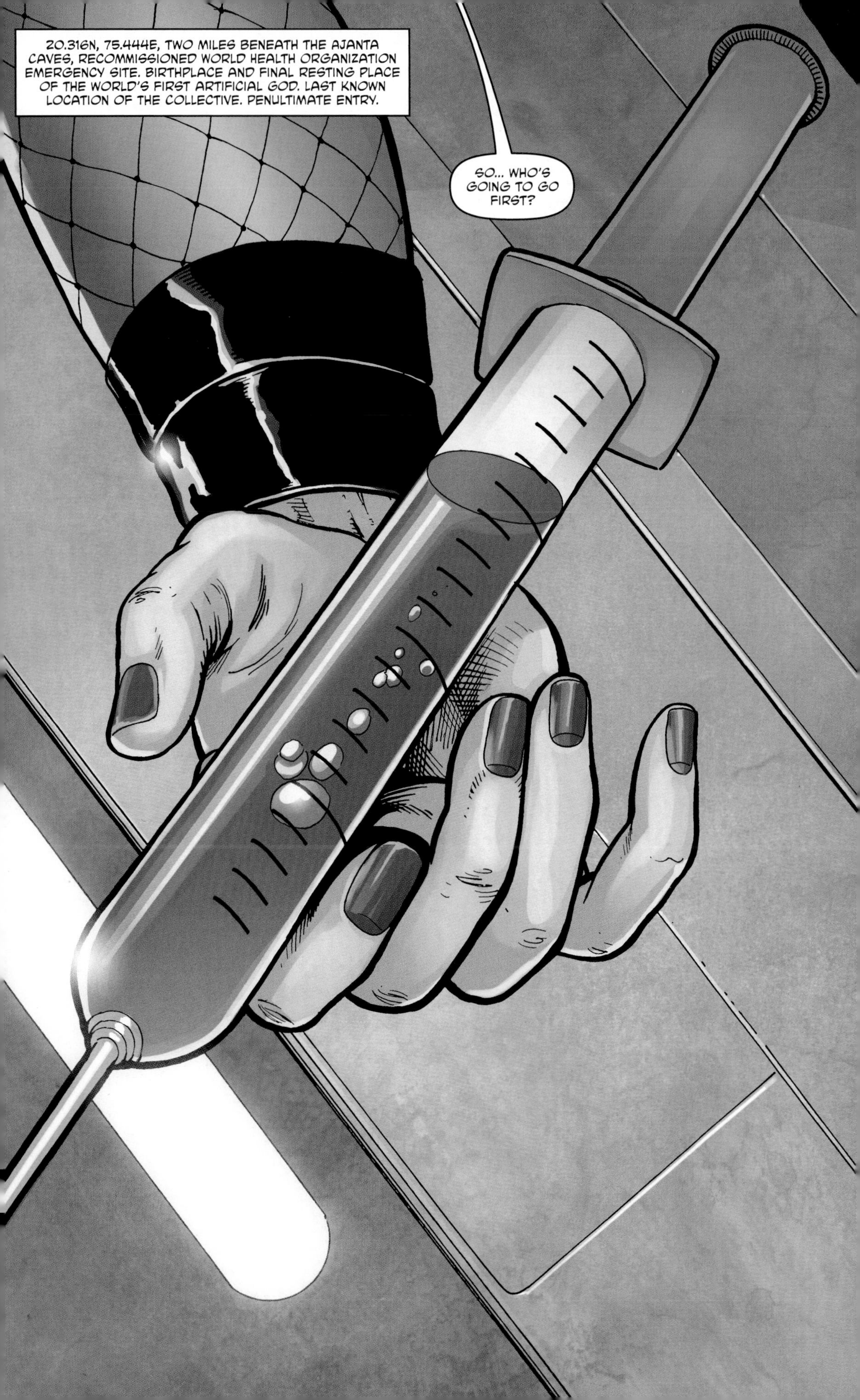
20.316N, 75.444E, TWO MILES BENEATH THE AJANTA CAVES, RECOMMISSIONED WORLD HEALTH ORGANIZATION EMERGENCY SITE. BIRTHPLACE AND FINAL RESTING PLACE OF THE WORLD'S FIRST ARTIFICIAL GOD. LAST KNOWN LOCATION OF THE COLLECTIVE. PENULTIMATE ENTRY.
SO... WHO'S GOING TO GO FIRST?

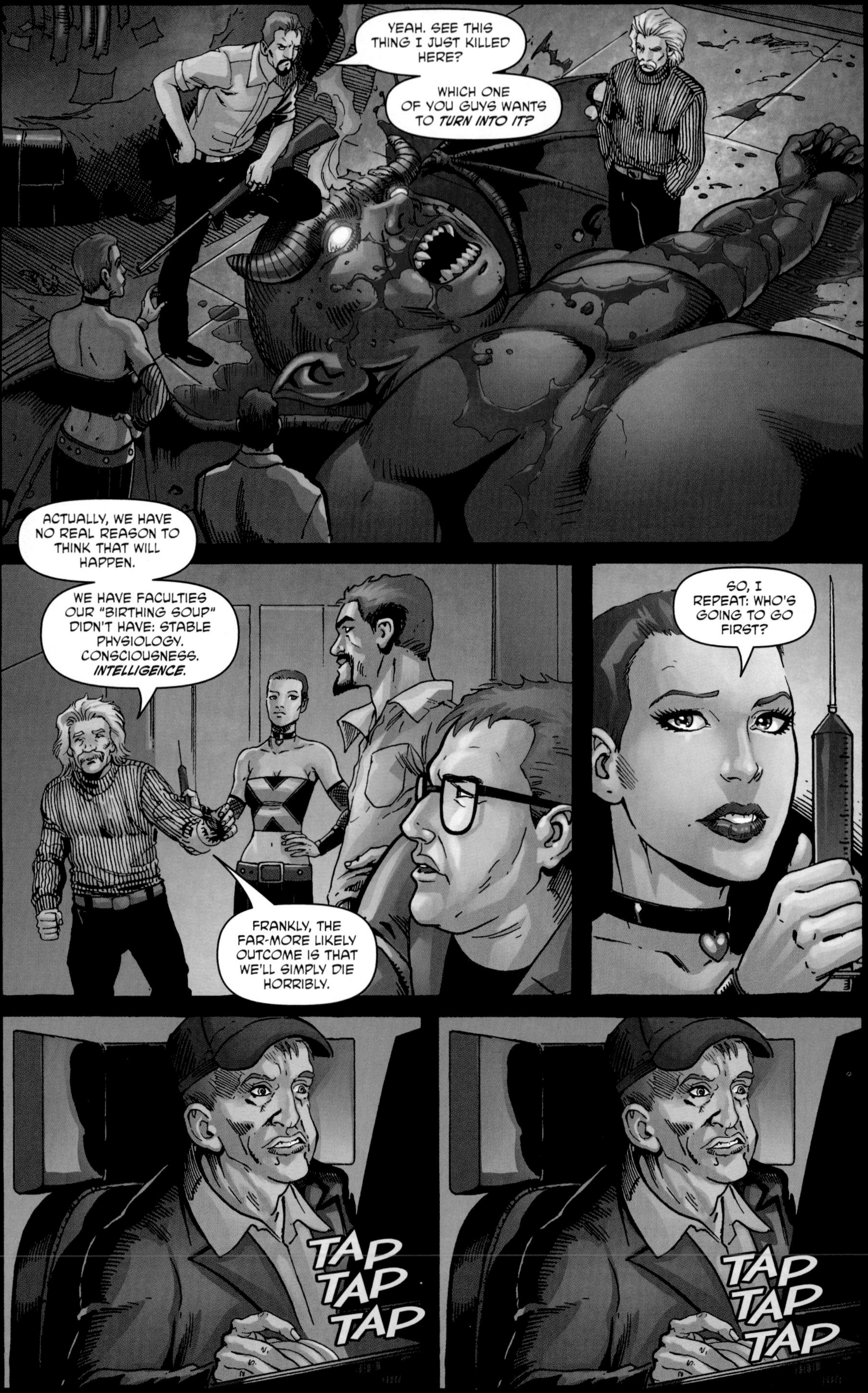
YEAH. SEE THIS THING I JUST KILLED HERE?
WHICH ONE OF YOU GUYS WANTS TO *TURN INTO IT?*
ACTUALLY, WE HAVE NO REAL REASON TO THINK THAT WILL HAPPEN.
WE HAVE FACULTIES OUR "BIRTHING SOUP" DIDN'T HAVE: STABLE PHYSIOLOGY. CONSCIOUSNESS. *INTELLIGENCE*.
FRANKLY, THE FAR-MORE LIKELY OUTCOME IS THAT WE'LL SIMPLY DIE HORRIBLY.
SO, I REPEAT: WHO'S GOING TO GO FIRST?
TAP TAP TAP
TAP TAP TAP

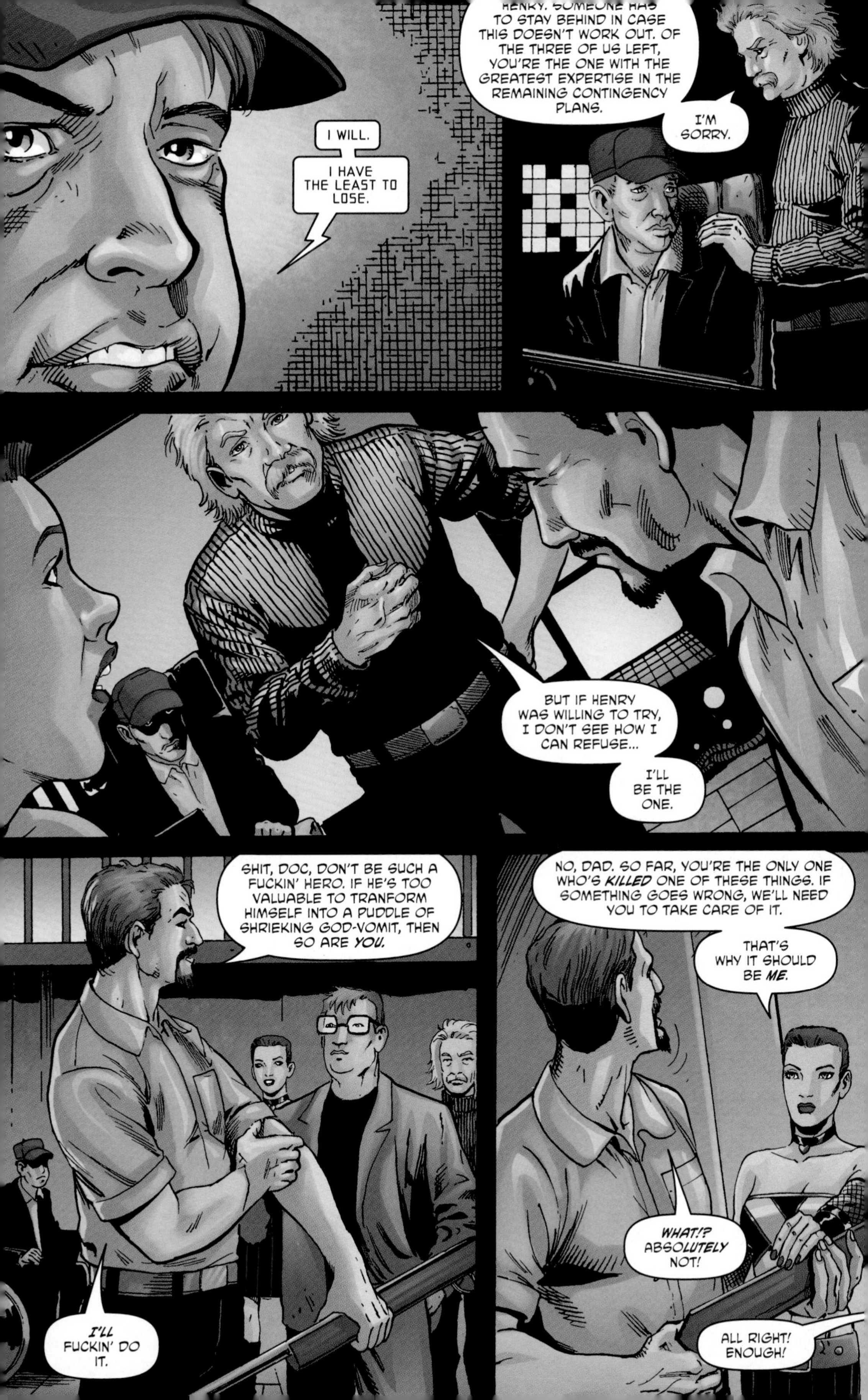
I WILL.
I HAVE THE LEAST TO LOSE.
HENRY. SOMEONE HAS TO STAY BEHIND IN CASE THIS DOESN'T WORK OUT. OF THE THREE OF US LEFT, YOU'RE THE ONE WITH THE GREATEST EXPERTISE IN THE REMAINING CONTINGENCY PLANS.
I'M SORRY.
BUT IF HENRY WAS WILLING TO TRY, I DON'T SEE HOW I CAN REFUSE...
I'LL BE THE ONE.
SHIT, DOC, DON'T BE SUCH A FUCKIN' HERO. IF HE'S TOO VALUABLE TO TRANFORM HIMSELF INTO A PUDDLE OF SHRIEKING GOD-VOMIT, THEN SO ARE *YOU.*
I'LL FUCKIN' DO IT.
NO, DAD. SO FAR, YOU'RE THE ONLY ONE WHO'S *KILLED* ONE OF THESE THINGS. IF SOMETHING GOES WRONG, WE'LL NEED YOU TO TAKE CARE OF IT.
THAT'S WHY IT SHOULD BE *ME.*
WHAT!? ABSO*LUTELY* NOT!
ALL RIGHT! ENOUGH!

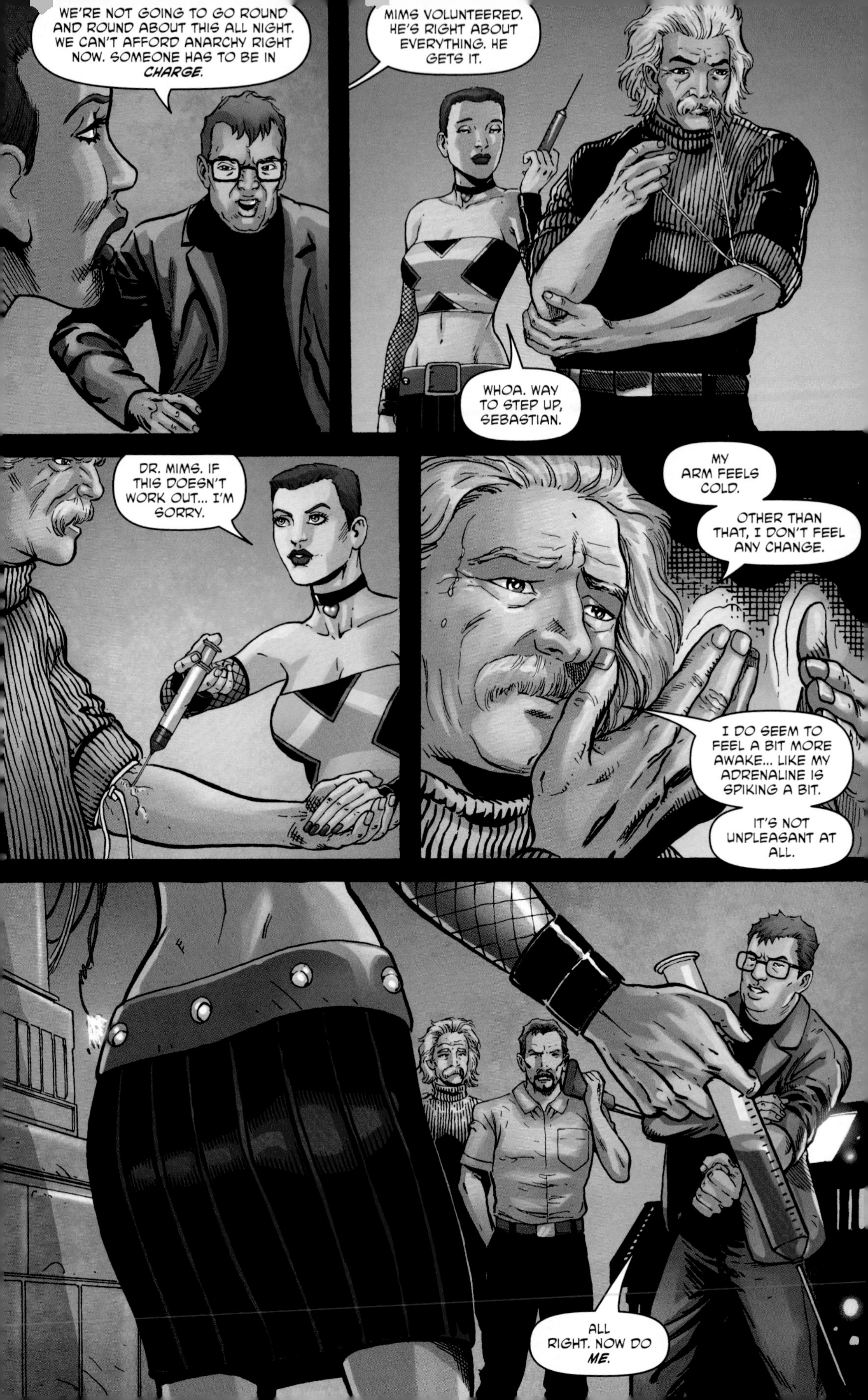
WE'RE NOT GOING TO GO ROUND AND ROUND ABOUT THIS ALL NIGHT. WE CAN'T AFFORD ANARCHY RIGHT NOW. SOMEONE HAS TO BE IN *CHARGE*.
MIMS VOLUNTEERED. HE'S RIGHT ABOUT EVERYTHING. HE GETS IT.
WHOA. WAY TO STEP UP, SEBASTIAN.
DR. MIMS. IF THIS DOESN'T WORK OUT... I'M SORRY.
MY ARM FEELS COLD.
OTHER THAN THAT, I DON'T FEEL ANY CHANGE.
I DO SEEM TO FEEL A BIT MORE AWAKE... LIKE MY ADRENALINE IS SPIKING A BIT.
IT'S NOT UNPLEASANT AT ALL.
ALL RIGHT. NOW DO *ME*.

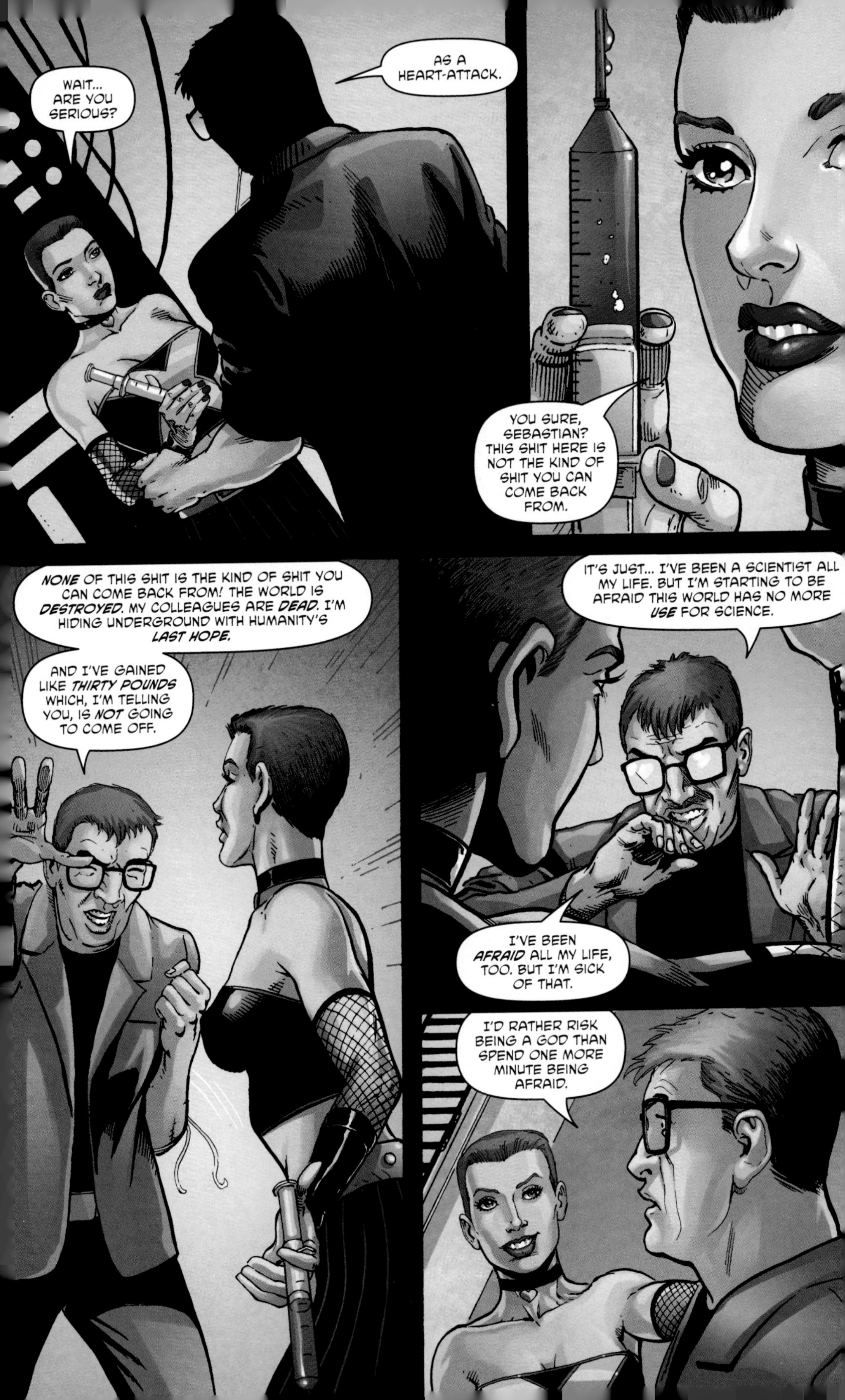
WAIT... ARE YOU SERIOUS?
AS A HEART-ATTACK.
YOU SURE, SEBASTIAN? THIS SHIT HERE IS NOT THE KIND OF SHIT YOU CAN COME BACK FROM.
NONE OF THIS SHIT IS THE KIND OF SHIT YOU CAN COME BACK FROM! THE WORLD IS DESTROYED. MY COLLEAGUES ARE DEAD. I'M HIDING UNDERGROUND WITH HUMANITY'S LAST HOPE.
AND I'VE GAINED LIKE THIRTY POUNDS WHICH, I'M TELLING YOU, IS NOT GOING TO COME OFF.
IT'S JUST... I'VE BEEN A SCIENTIST ALL MY LIFE. BUT I'M STARTING TO BE AFRAID THIS WORLD HAS NO MORE USE FOR SCIENCE.
I'VE BEEN AFRAID ALL MY LIFE, TOO. BUT I'M SICK OF THAT.
I'D RATHER RISK BEING A GOD THAN SPEND ONE MORE MINUTE BEING AFRAID.

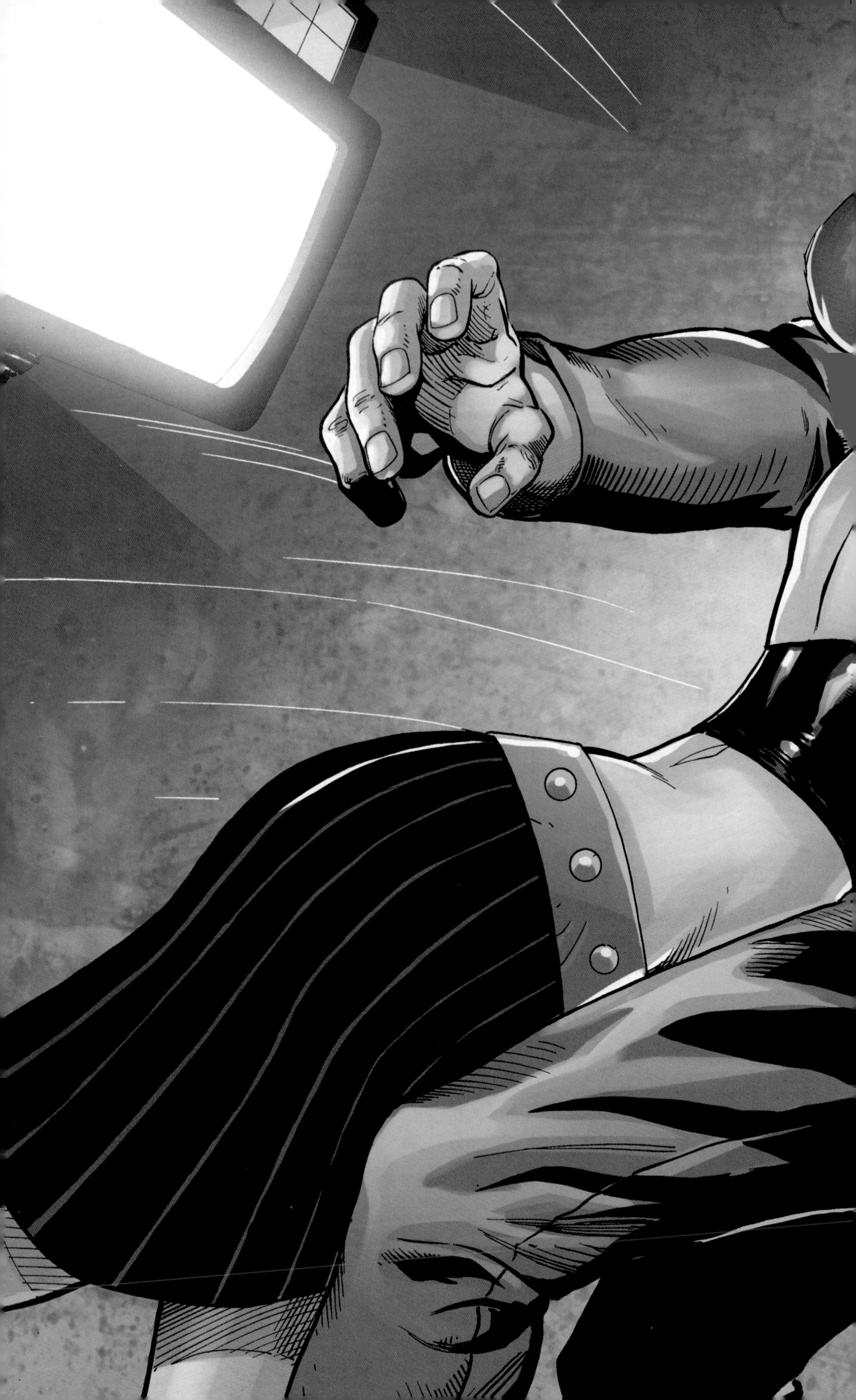

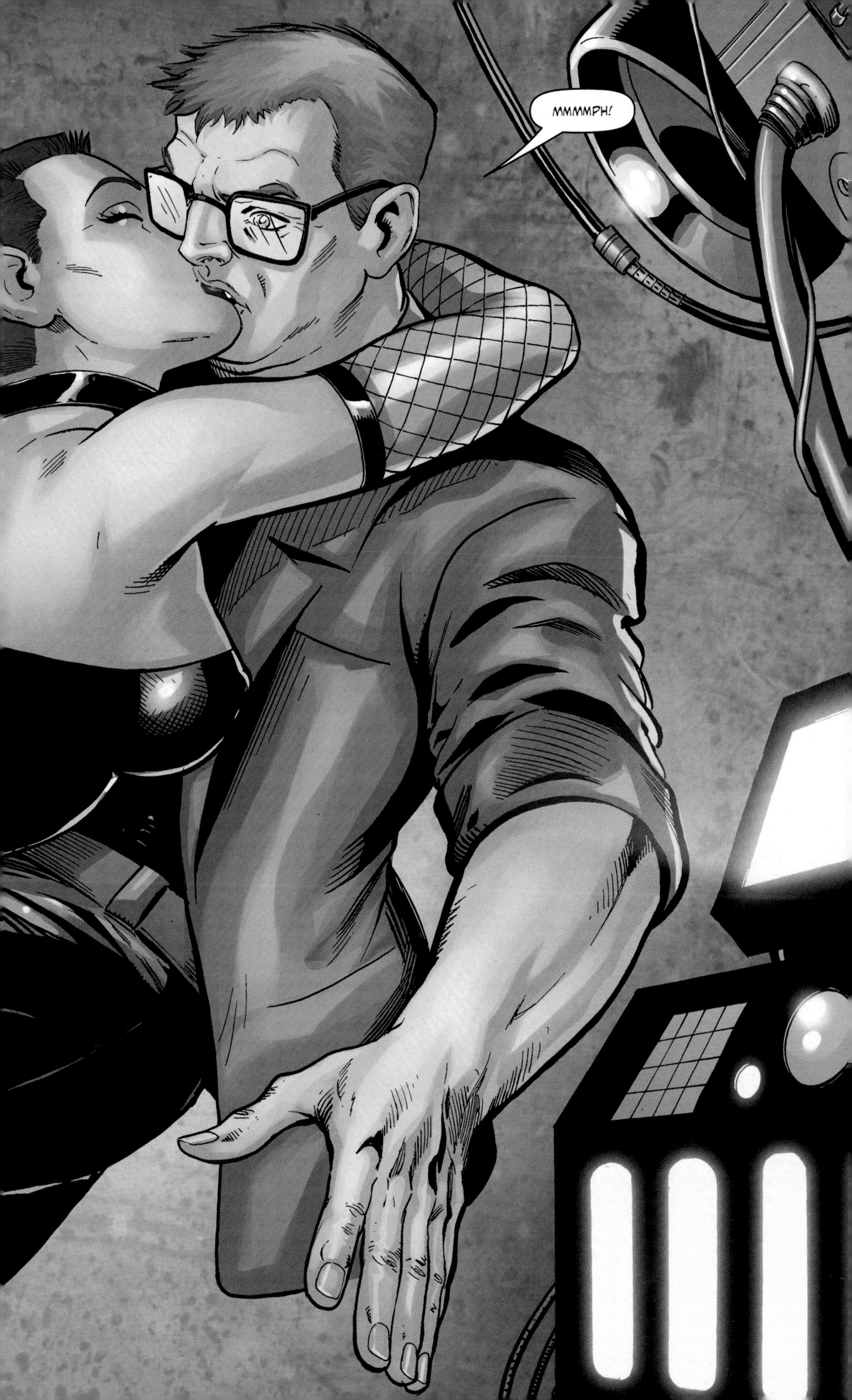
MMMMPH!

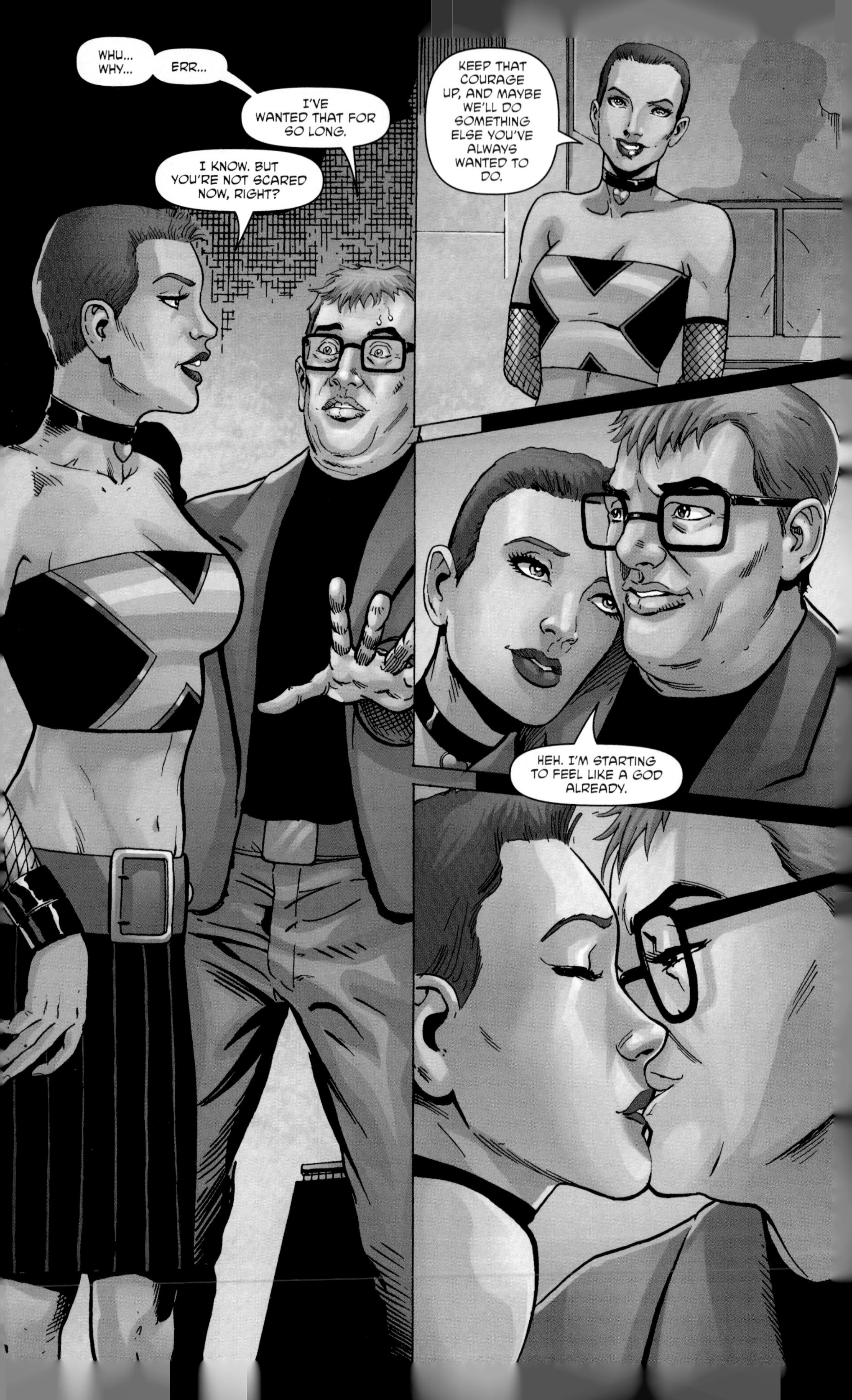
WHU... WHY...
ERR...
I'VE WANTED THAT FOR SO LONG.
I KNOW. BUT YOU'RE NOT SCARED NOW, RIGHT?
KEEP THAT COURAGE UP, AND MAYBE WE'LL DO SOMETHING ELSE YOU'VE ALWAYS WANTED TO DO.
HEH. I'M STARTING TO FEEL LIKE A GOD ALREADY.

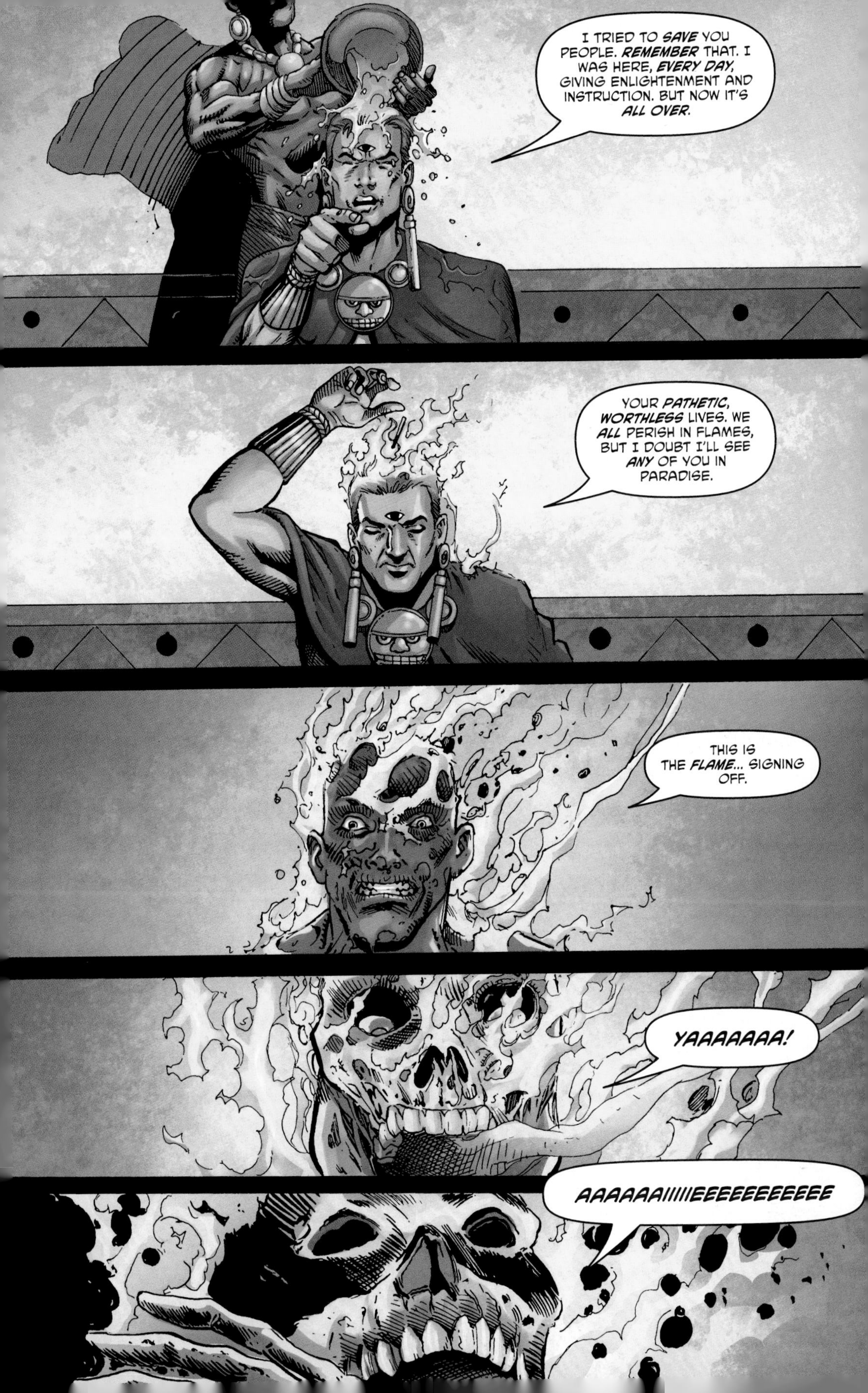
I TRIED TO SAVE YOU PEOPLE. REMEMBER THAT. I WAS HERE, EVERY DAY, GIVING ENLIGHTENMENT AND INSTRUCTION. BUT NOW IT'S ALL OVER.
YOUR PATHETIC, WORTHLESS LIVES. WE ALL PERISH IN FLAMES, BUT I DOUBT I'LL SEE ANY OF YOU IN PARADISE.
THIS IS THE FLAME... SIGNING OFF.
YAAAAAAA!
AAAAAAIIIIIIEEEEEEEEEEE

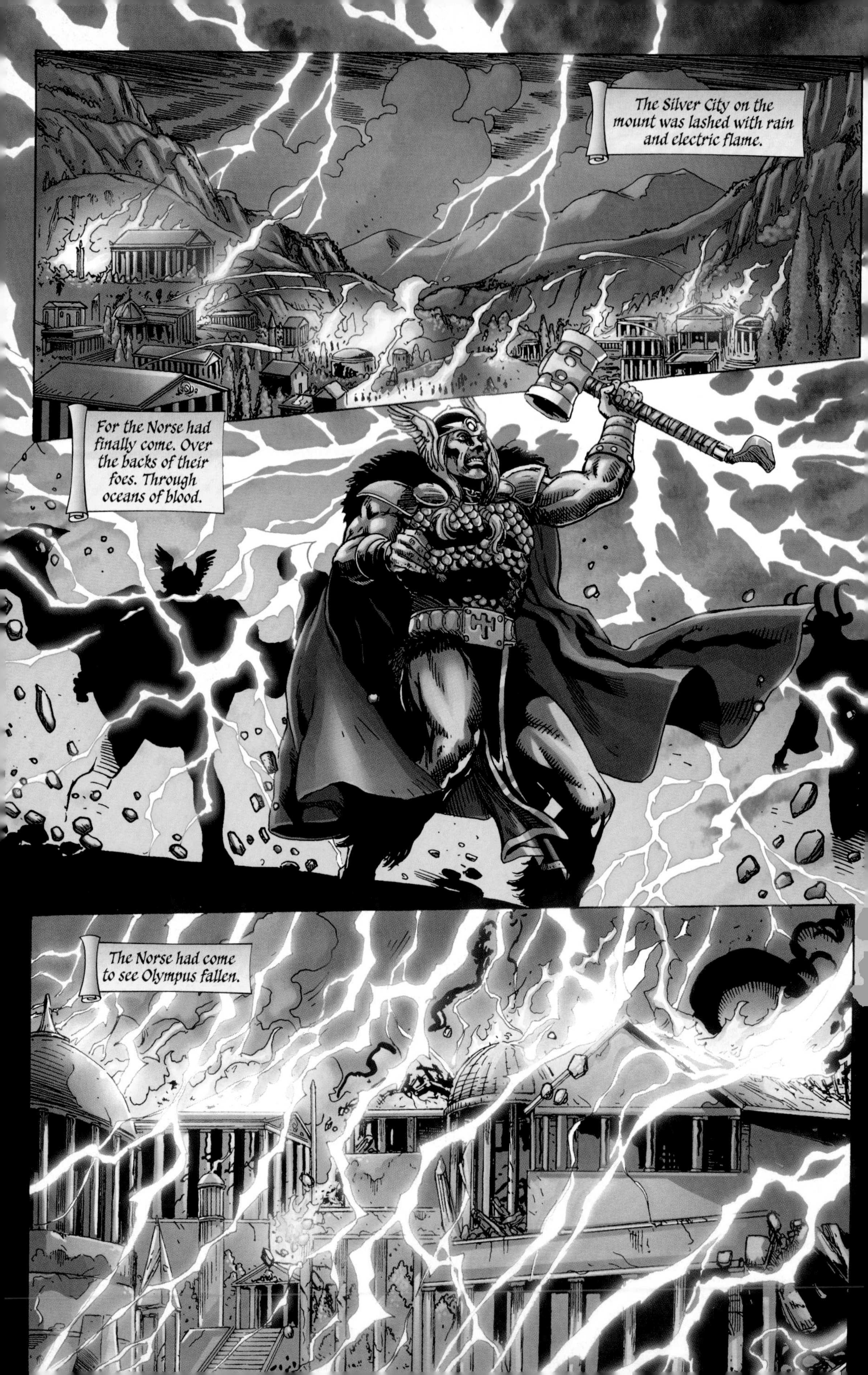
The Silver City on the mount was lashed with rain and electric flame.
For the Norse had finally come. Over the backs of their foes. Through oceans of blood.
The Norse had come to see Olympus fallen.

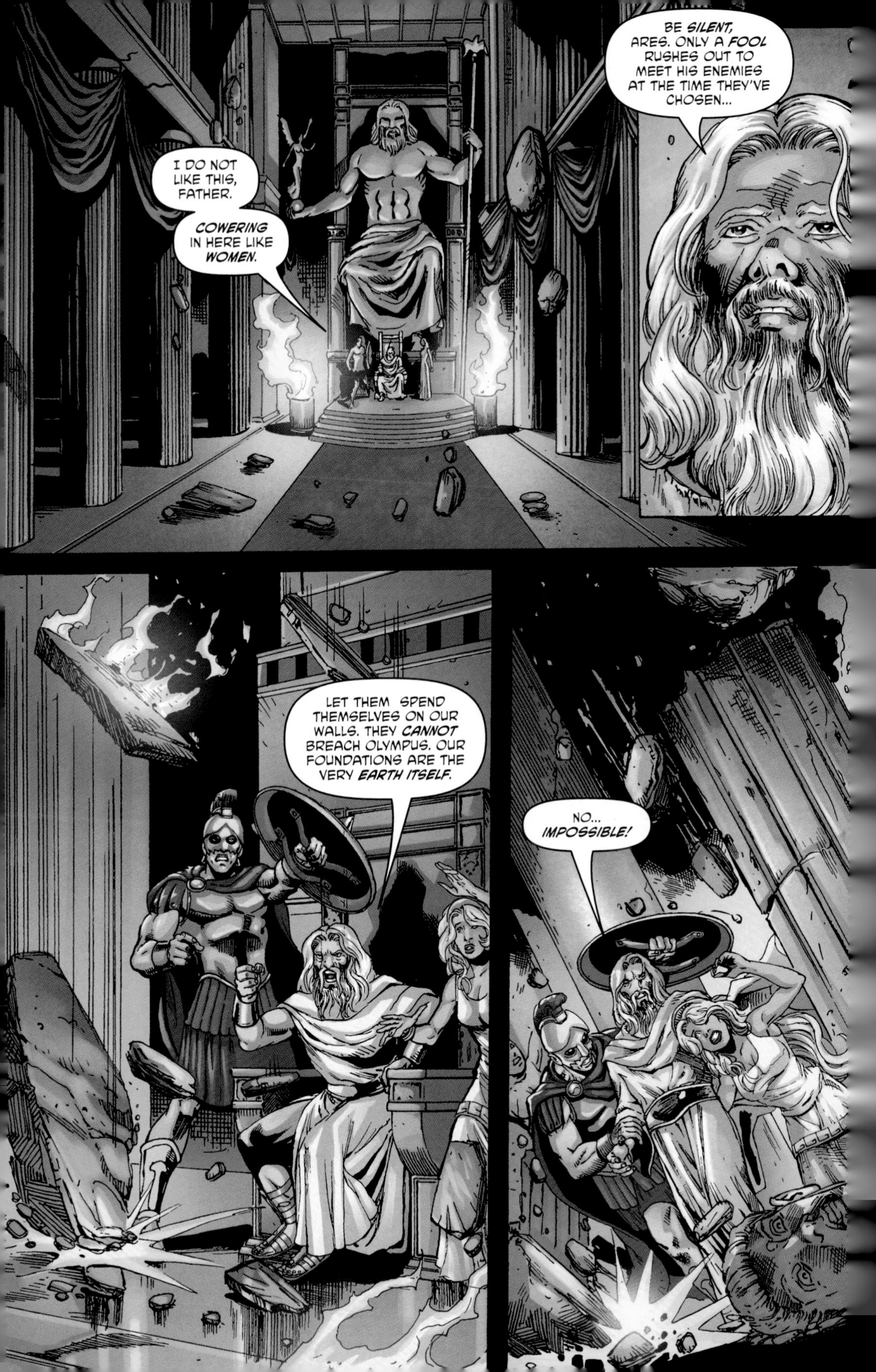
I DO NOT LIKE THIS, FATHER.
COWERING IN HERE LIKE WOMEN.
BE SILENT, ARES. ONLY A FOOL RUSHES OUT TO MEET HIS ENEMIES AT THE TIME THEY'VE CHOSEN...
LET THEM SPEND THEMSELVES ON OUR WALLS. THEY CANNOT BREACH OLYMPUS. OUR FOUNDATIONS ARE THE VERY EARTH ITSELF.
NO... IMPOSSIBLE!

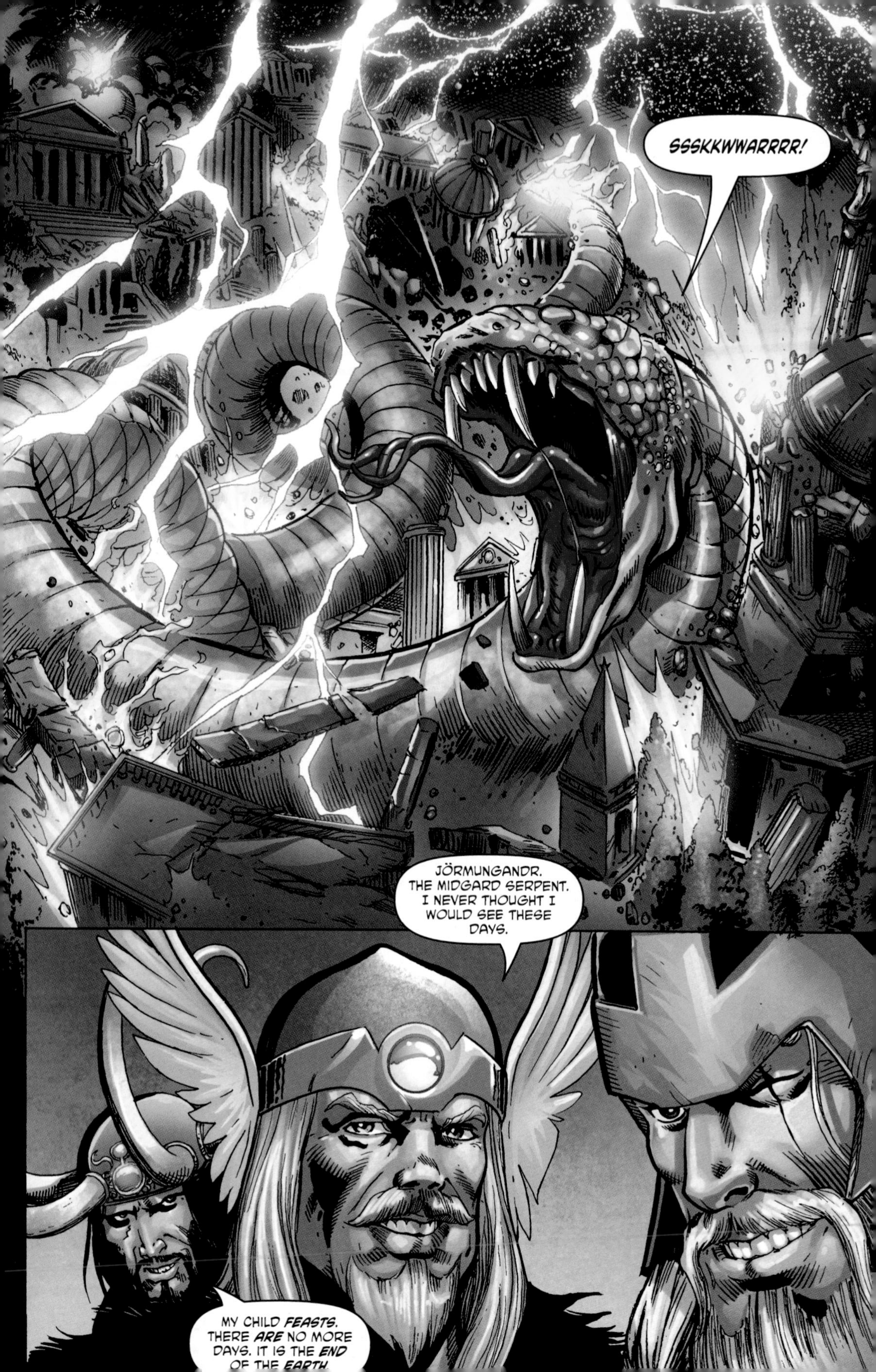
SSSKKWWARRRR!
JÖRMUNGANDR. THE MIDGARD SERPENT. I NEVER THOUGHT I WOULD SEE THESE DAYS.
MY CHILD *FEASTS*. THERE *ARE* NO MORE DAYS. IT IS THE *END* OF THE *EARTH*.

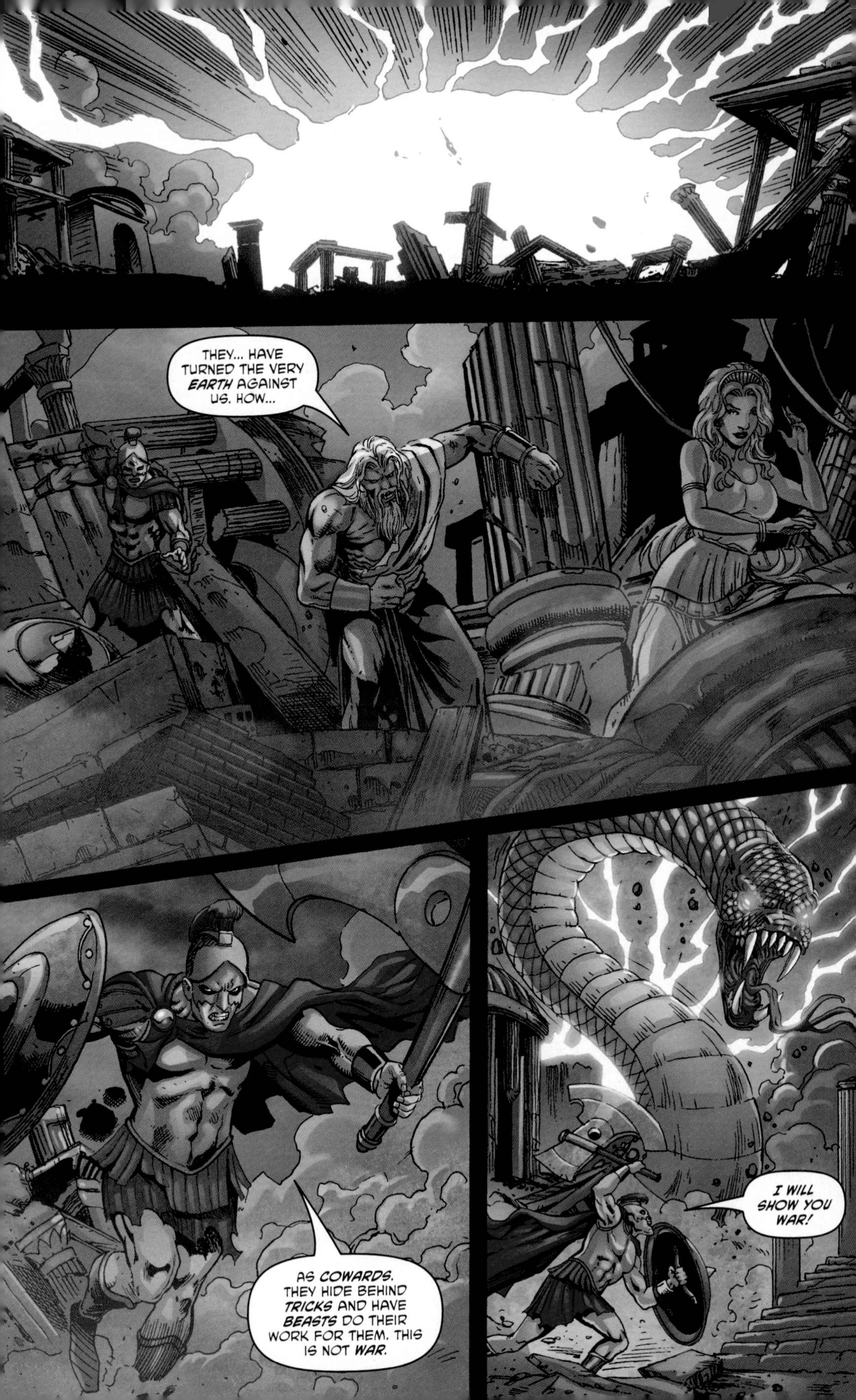
THEY... HAVE TURNED THE VERY EARTH AGAINST US. HOW...
AS COWARDS. THEY HIDE BEHIND TRICKS AND HAVE BEASTS DO THEIR WORK FOR THEM. THIS IS NOT WAR.
I WILL SHOW YOU WAR!

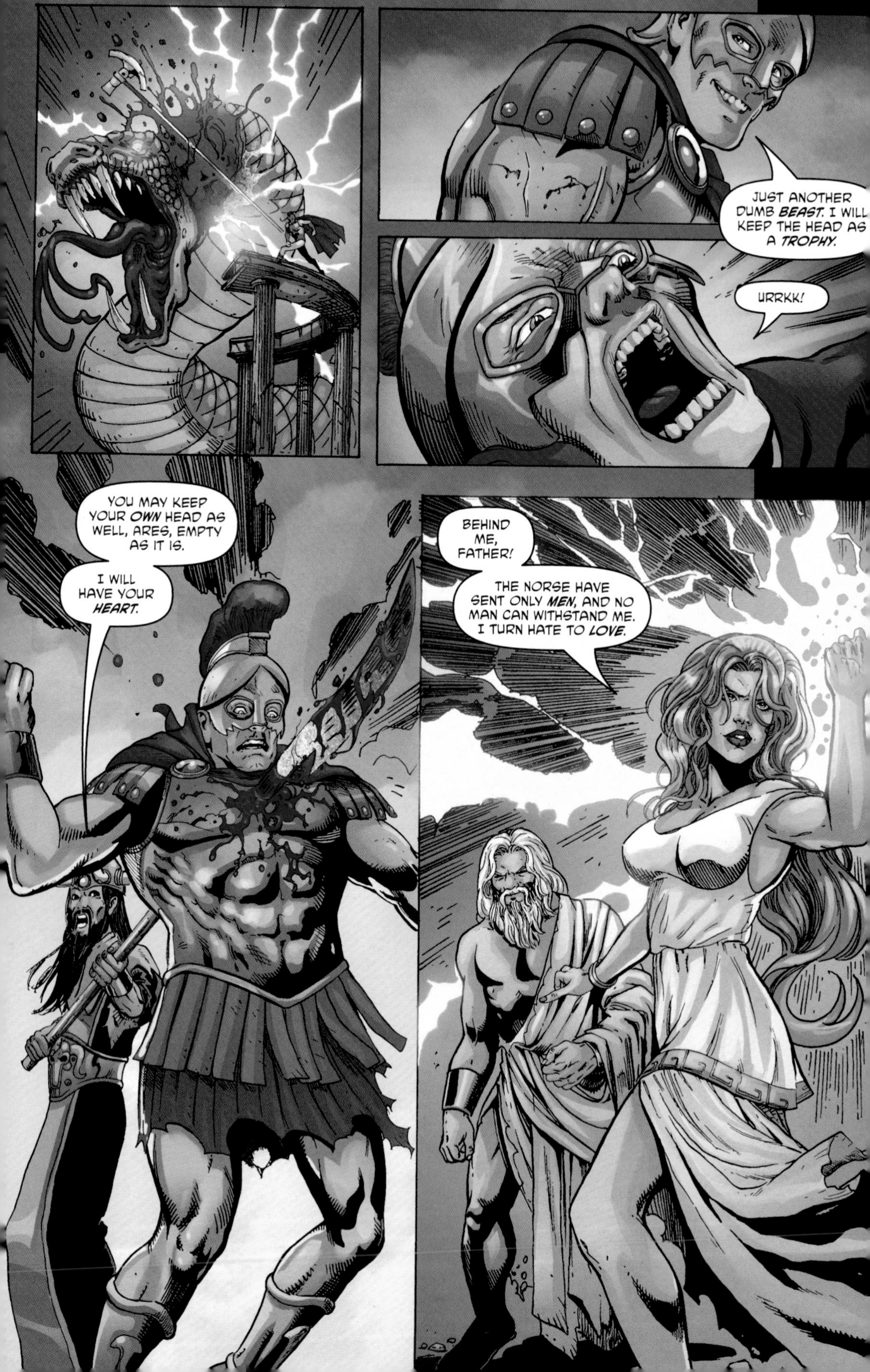
JUST ANOTHER DUMB BEAST. I WILL KEEP THE HEAD AS A TROPHY.
URRKK!
YOU MAY KEEP YOUR OWN HEAD AS WELL, ARES, EMPTY AS IT IS.
I WILL HAVE YOUR HEART.
BEHIND ME, FATHER!
THE NORSE HAVE SENT ONLY MEN, AND NO MAN CAN WITHSTAND ME. I TURN HATE TO LOVE.

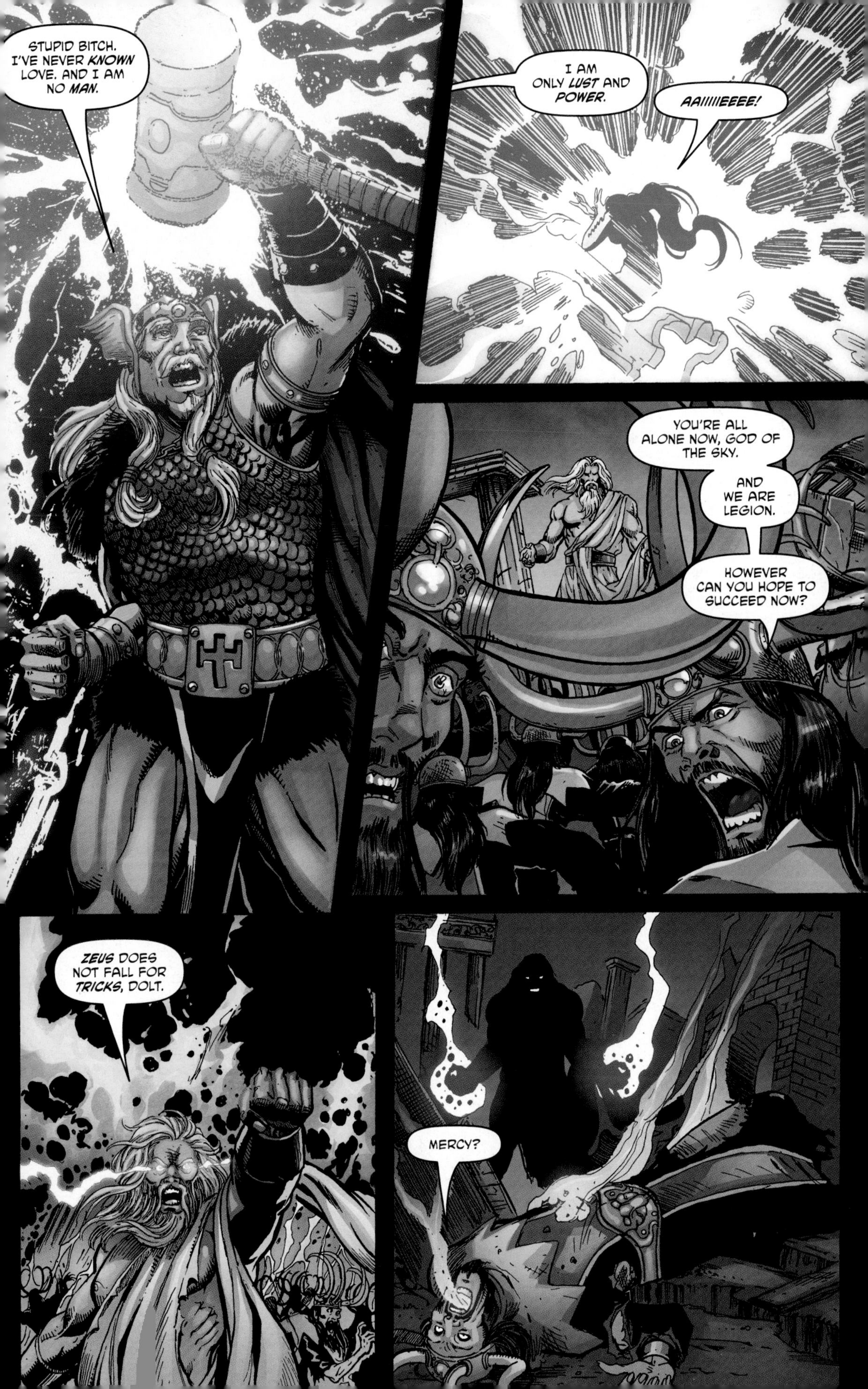
STUPID BITCH. I'VE NEVER KNOWN LOVE. AND I AM NO MAN.
I AM ONLY LUST AND POWER.
AAIIIIIEEEE!
YOU'RE ALL ALONE NOW, GOD OF THE SKY.
AND WE ARE LEGION.
HOWEVER CAN YOU HOPE TO SUCCEED NOW?
ZEUS DOES NOT FALL FOR TRICKS, DOLT.
MERCY?

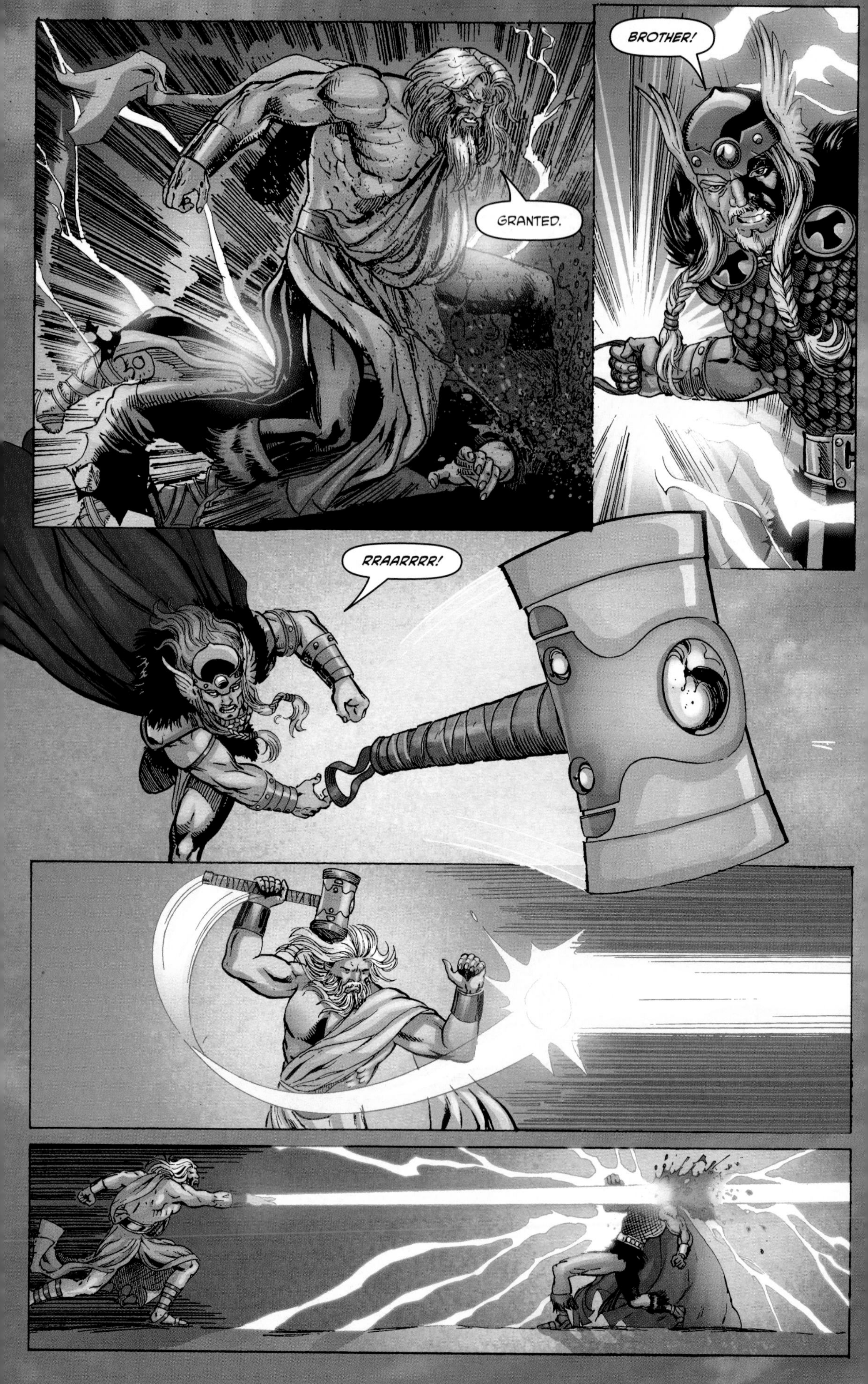
GRANTED.
BROTHER!
RRAARRRR!

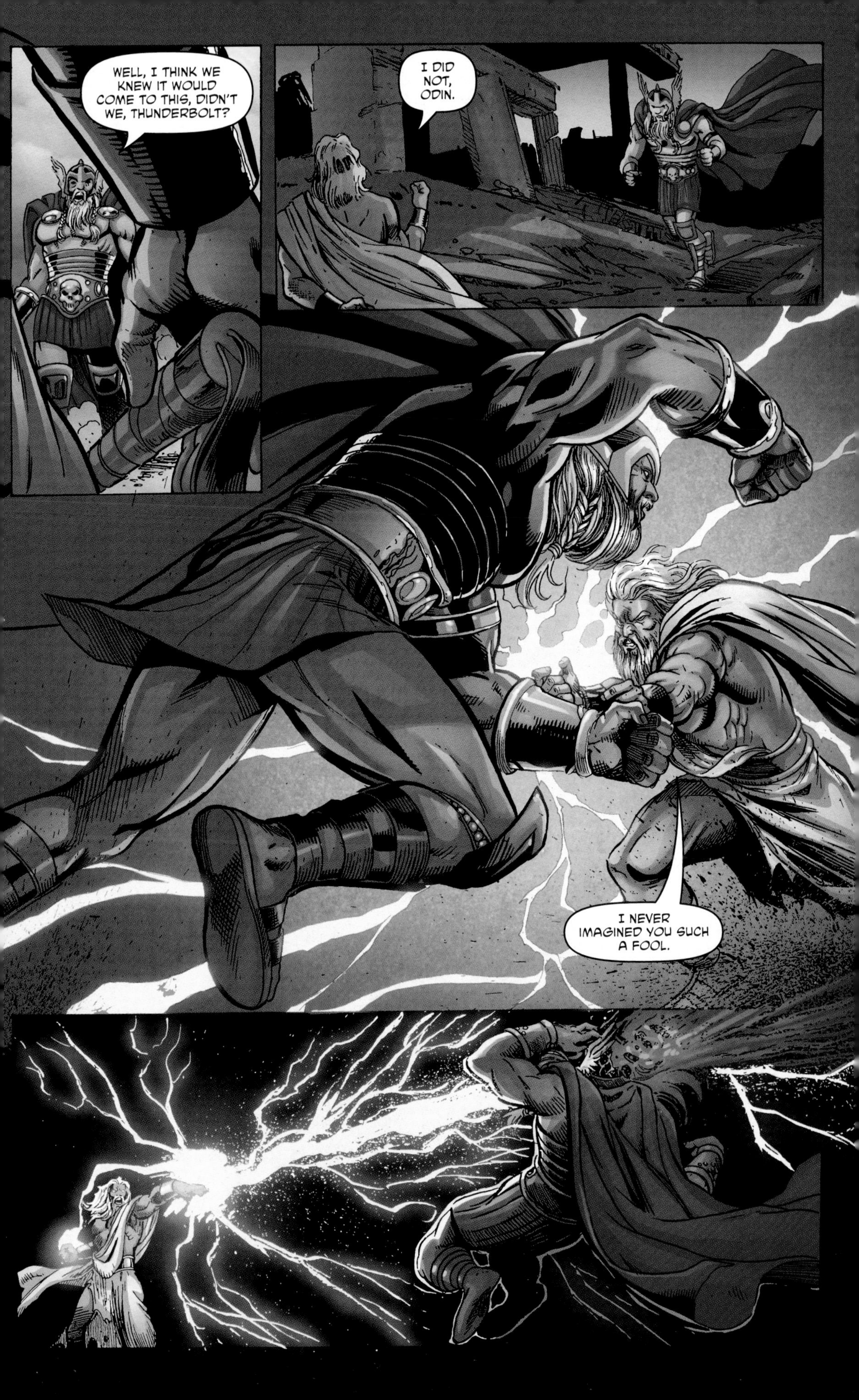
WELL, I THINK WE KNEW IT WOULD COME TO THIS, DIDN'T WE, THUNDERBOLT?
I DID NOT, ODIN.
I NEVER IMAGINED YOU SUCH A FOOL.

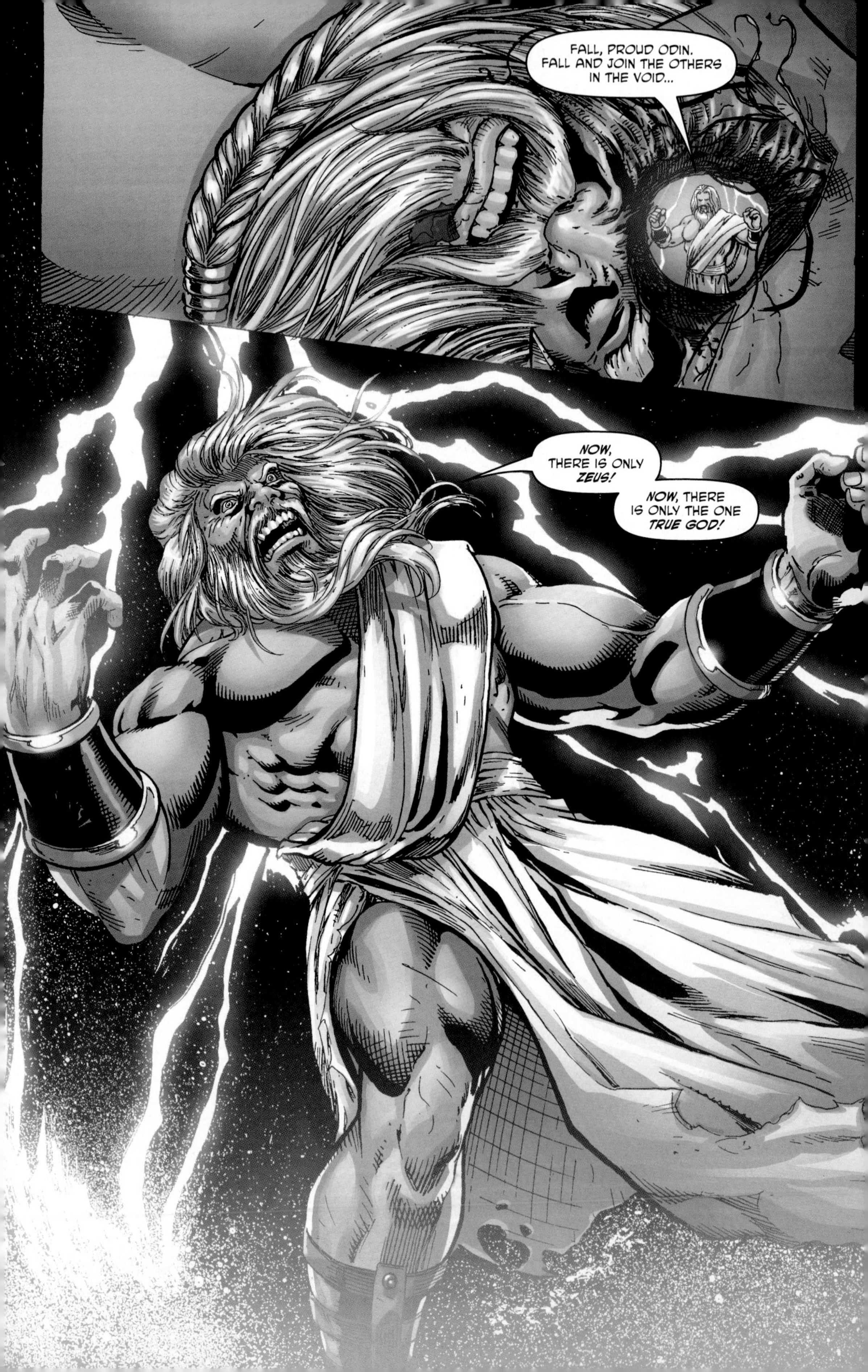
FALL, PROUD ODIN. FALL AND JOIN THE OTHERS IN THE VOID...
NOW, THERE IS ONLY ZEUS!
NOW, THERE IS ONLY THE ONE TRUE GOD!

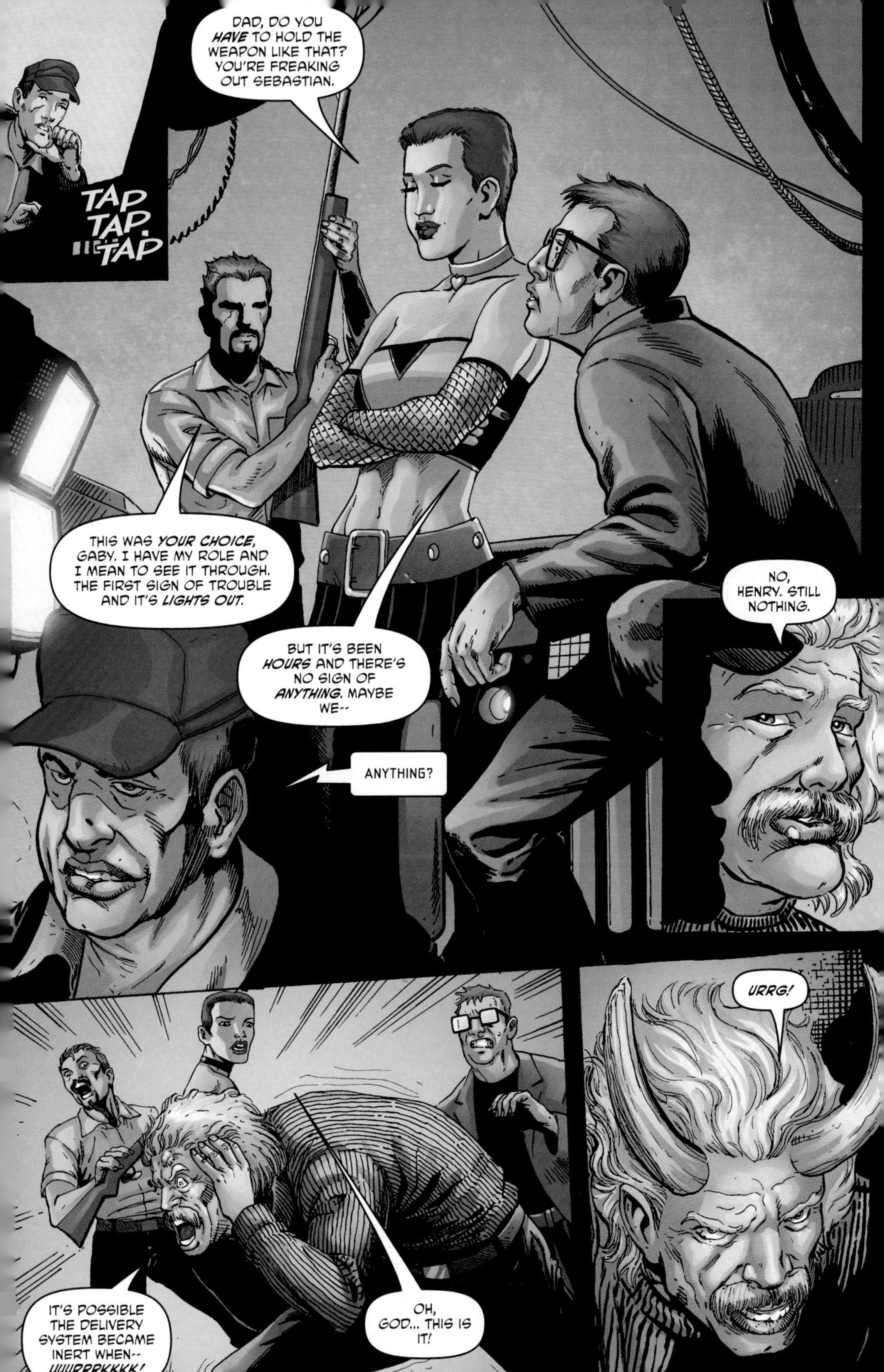
DAD, DO YOU *HAVE* TO HOLD THE WEAPON LIKE THAT? YOU'RE FREAKING OUT SEBASTIAN.
TAP TAP. TAP
THIS WAS *YOUR CHOICE*, GABY. I HAVE MY ROLE AND I MEAN TO SEE IT THROUGH. THE FIRST SIGN OF TROUBLE AND IT'S *LIGHTS OUT*.
BUT IT'S BEEN *HOURS* AND THERE'S NO SIGN OF *ANYTHING*. MAYBE WE--
ANYTHING?
NO, HENRY. STILL NOTHING.
IT'S POSSIBLE THE DELIVERY SYSTEM BECAME INERT WHEN-- *UUURRRKKKK!*
OH, GOD... THIS IS IT!
URRG!

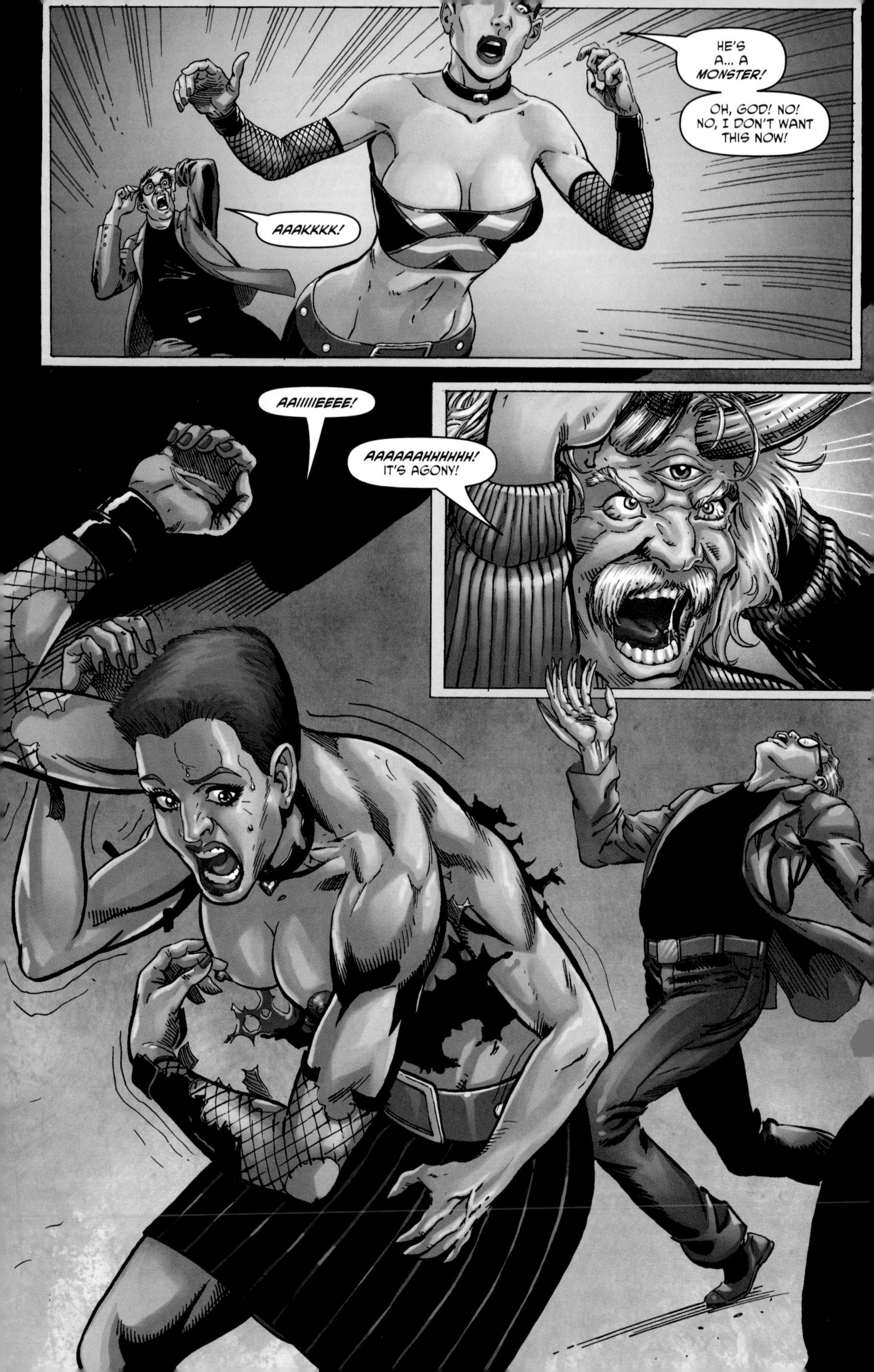
HE'S A... A *MONSTER!*
OH, GOD! NO! NO, I DON'T WANT THIS NOW!
AAAKKKK!
AAIIIIIEEEE!
AAAAAAHHHHHH! IT'S AGONY!

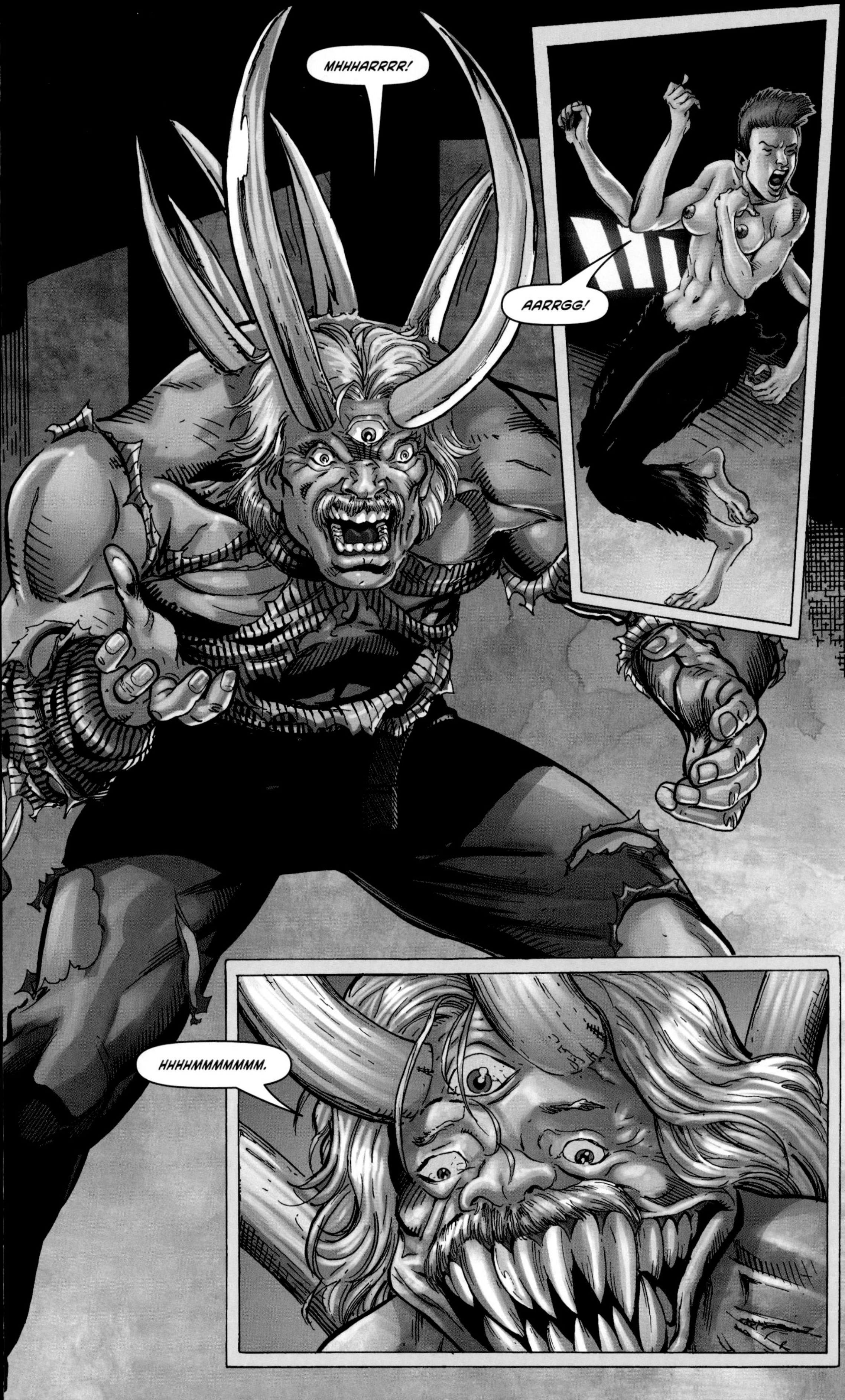
MHHHARRRR!
AARRGG!
HHHHMMMMMMM.

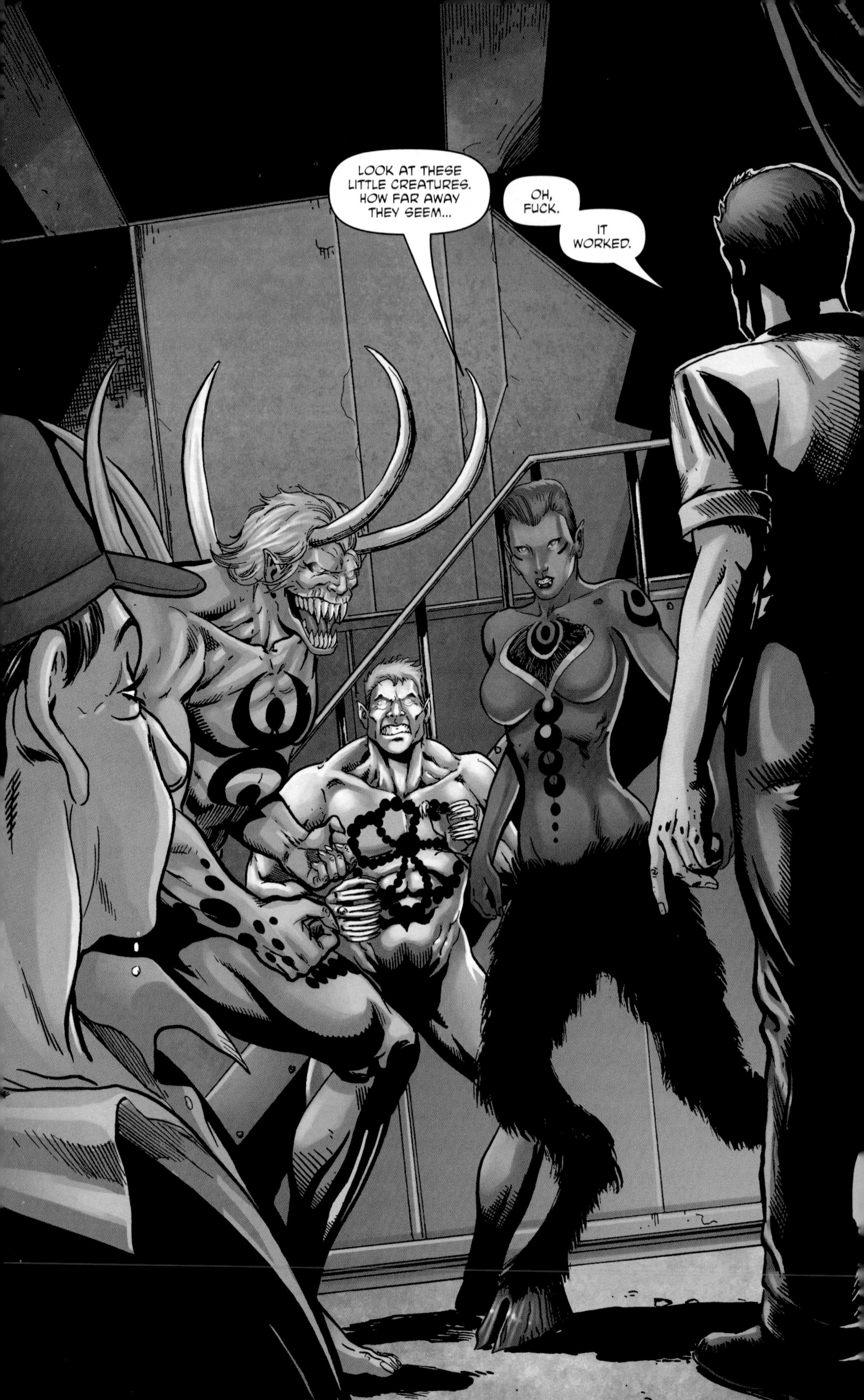
LOOK AT THESE LITTLE CREATURES. HOW FAR AWAY THEY SEEM...
OH, FUCK.
IT WORKED.

SIX

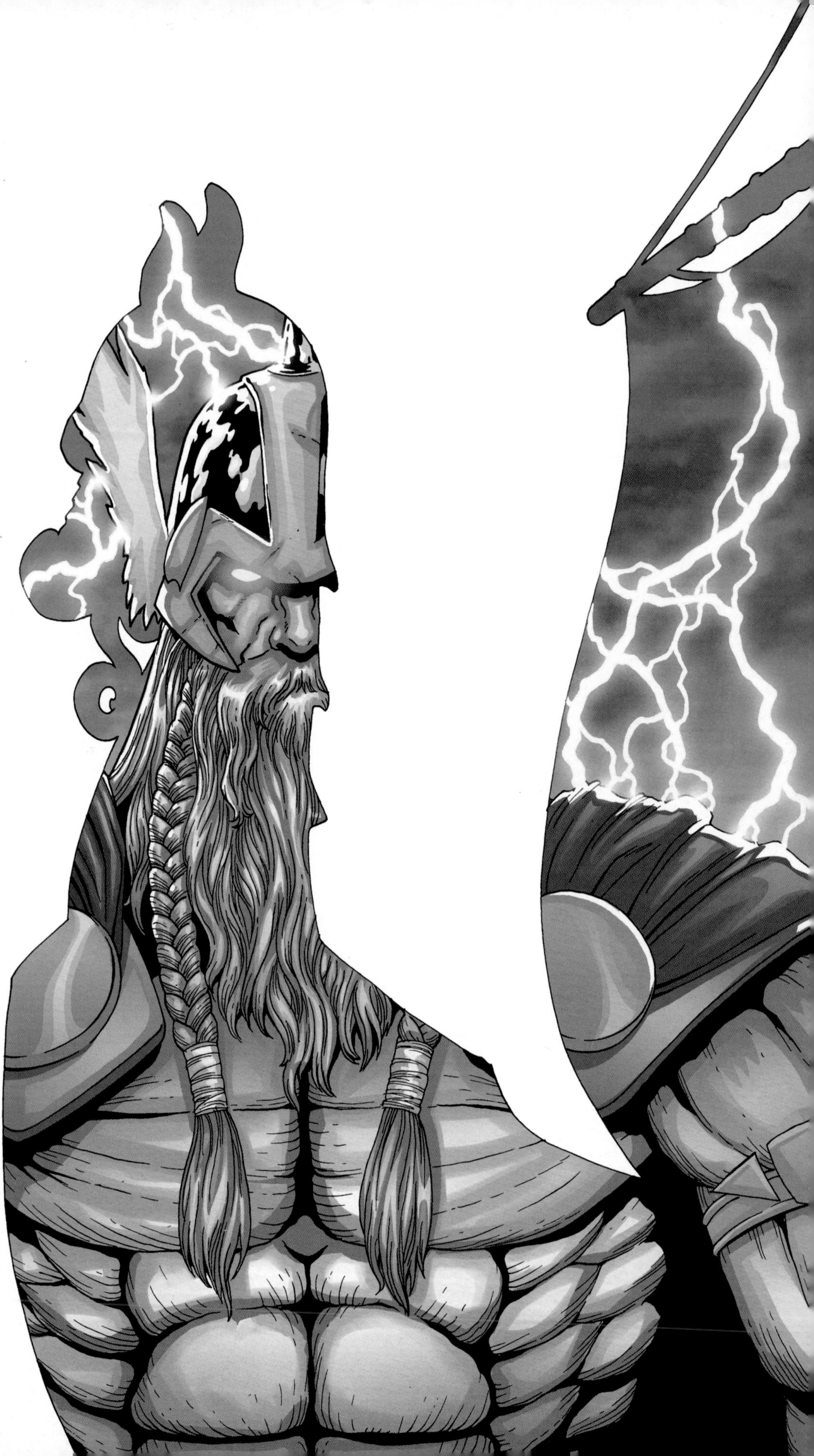

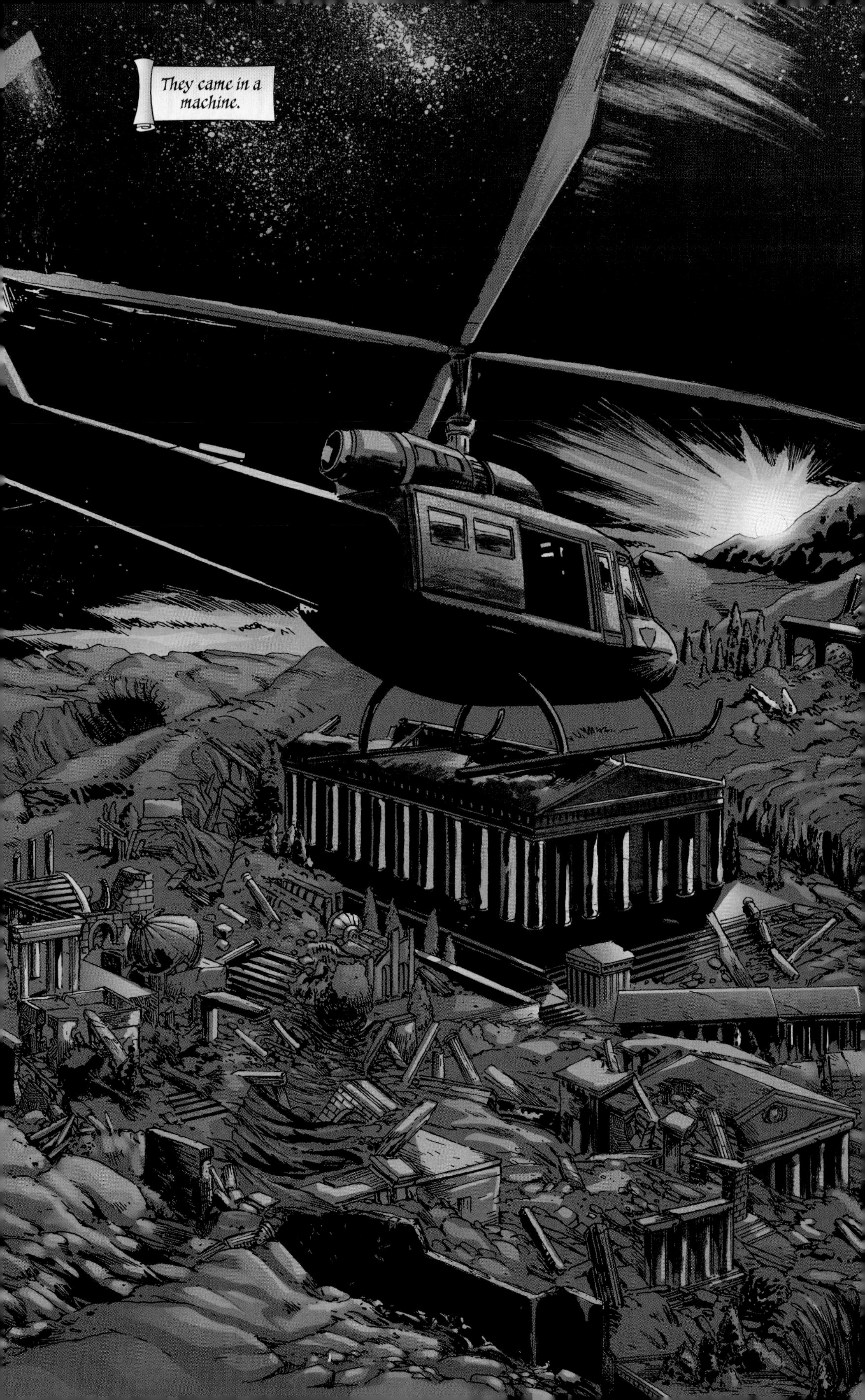
They came in a machine.

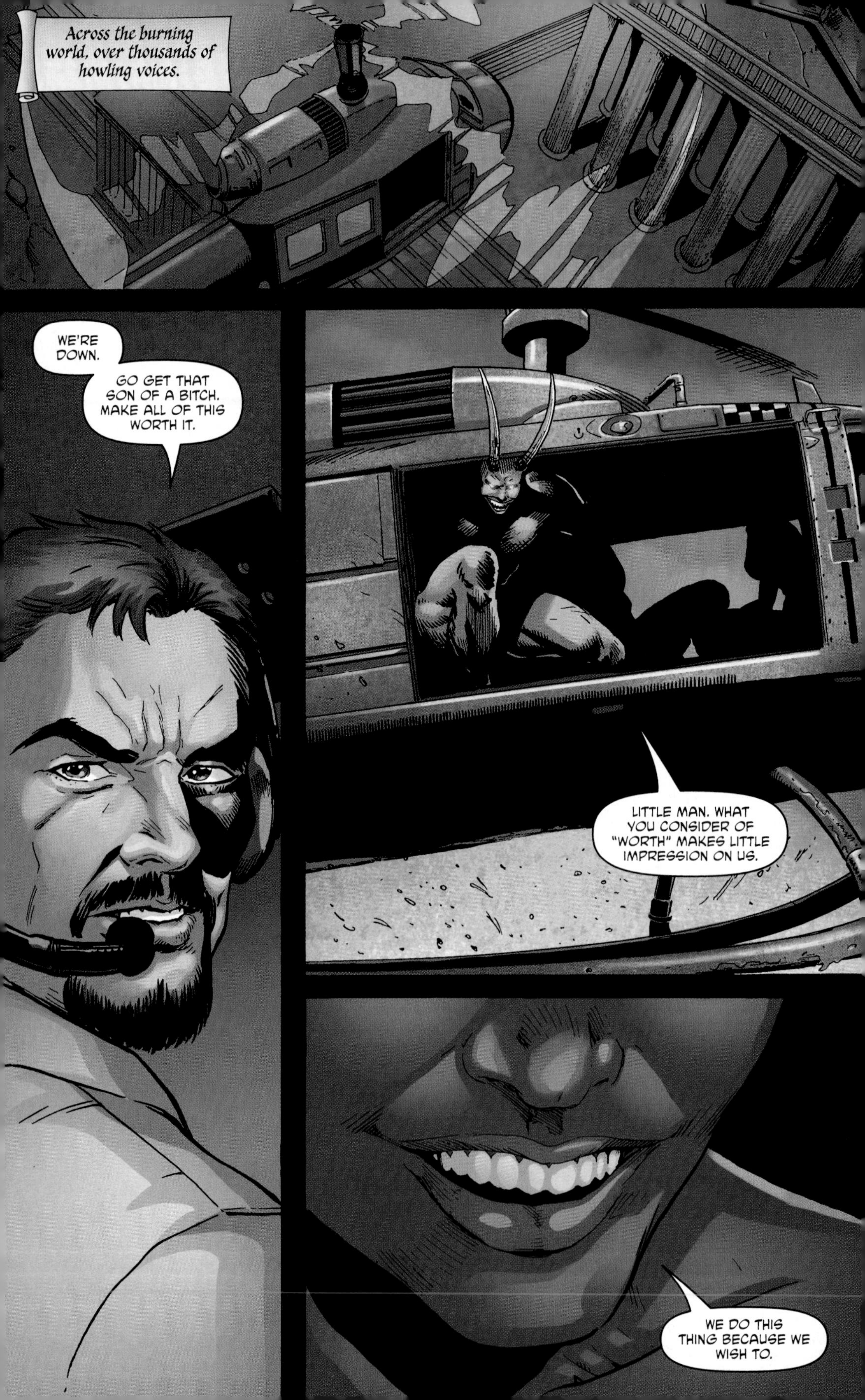
Across the burning world, over thousands of howling voices.
WE'RE DOWN.
GO GET THAT SON OF A BITCH. MAKE ALL OF THIS WORTH IT.
LITTLE MAN. WHAT YOU CONSIDER OF "WORTH" MAKES LITTLE IMPRESSION ON US.
WE DO THIS THING BECAUSE WE WISH TO.

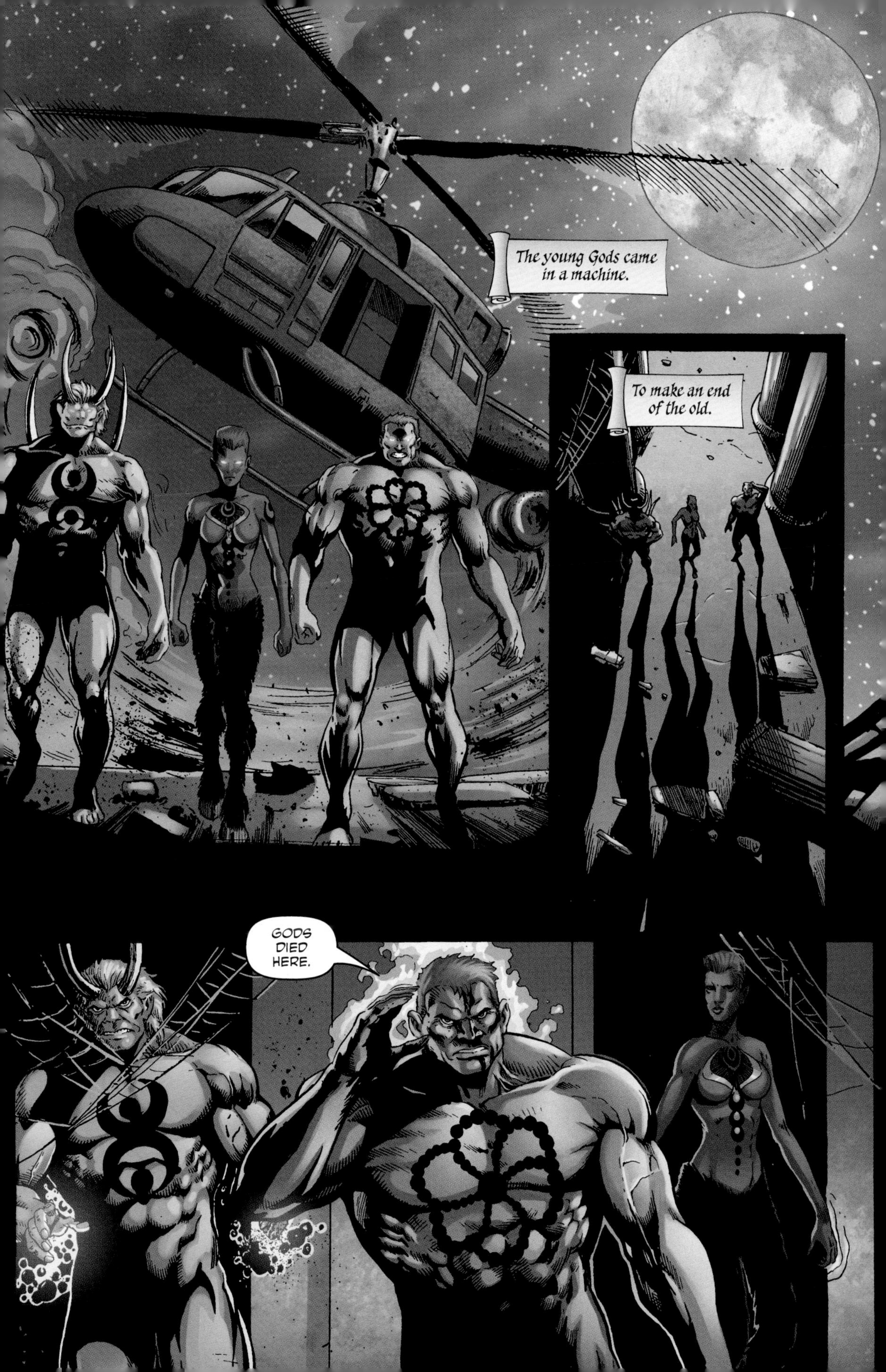
The young Gods came in a machine.
To make an end of the old.
GODS DIED HERE.

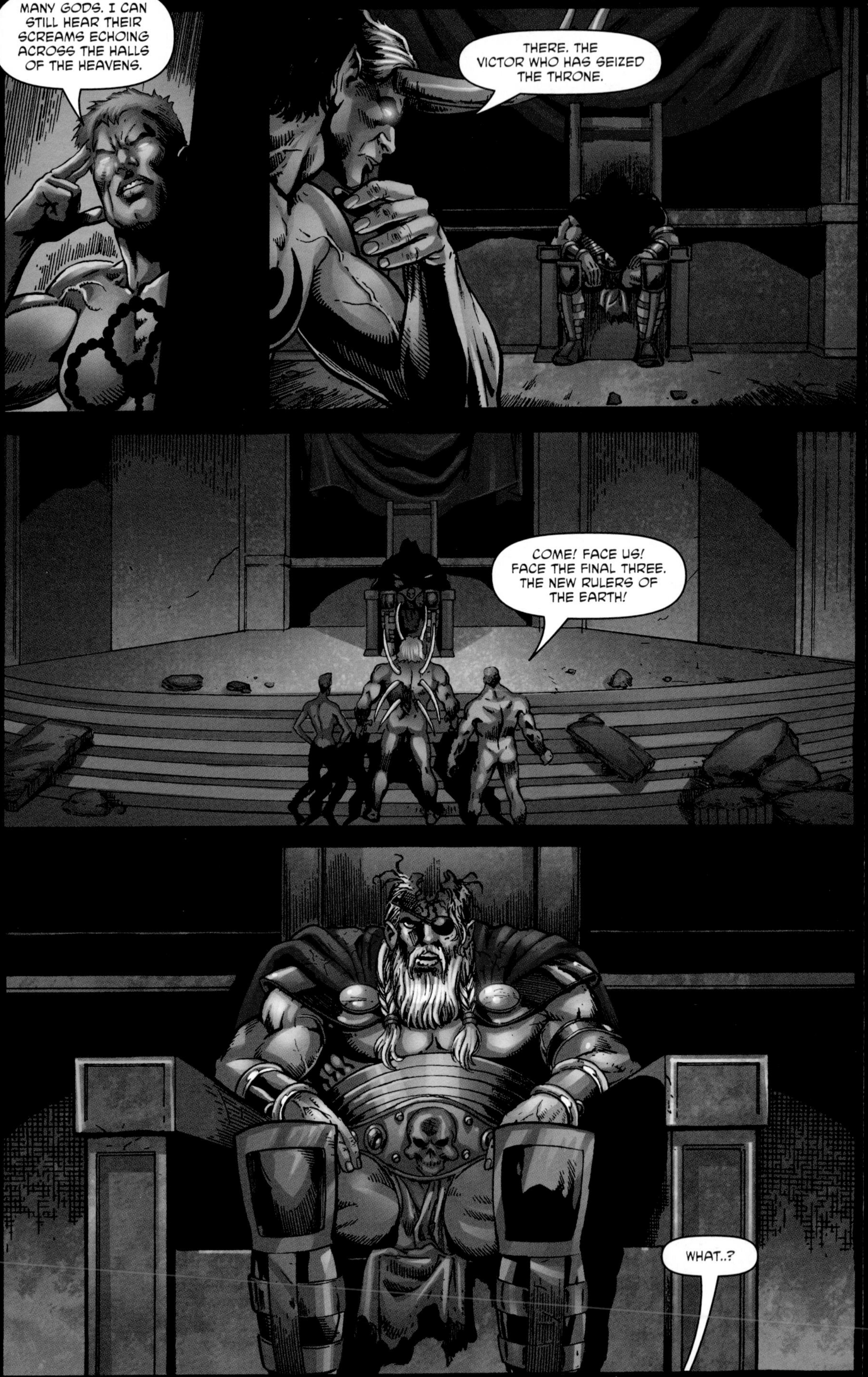
MANY GODS. I CAN STILL HEAR THEIR SCREAMS ECHOING ACROSS THE HALLS OF THE HEAVENS.
THERE. THE VICTOR WHO HAS SEIZED THE THRONE.
COME! FACE US! FACE THE FINAL THREE. THE NEW RULERS OF THE EARTH!
WHAT..?

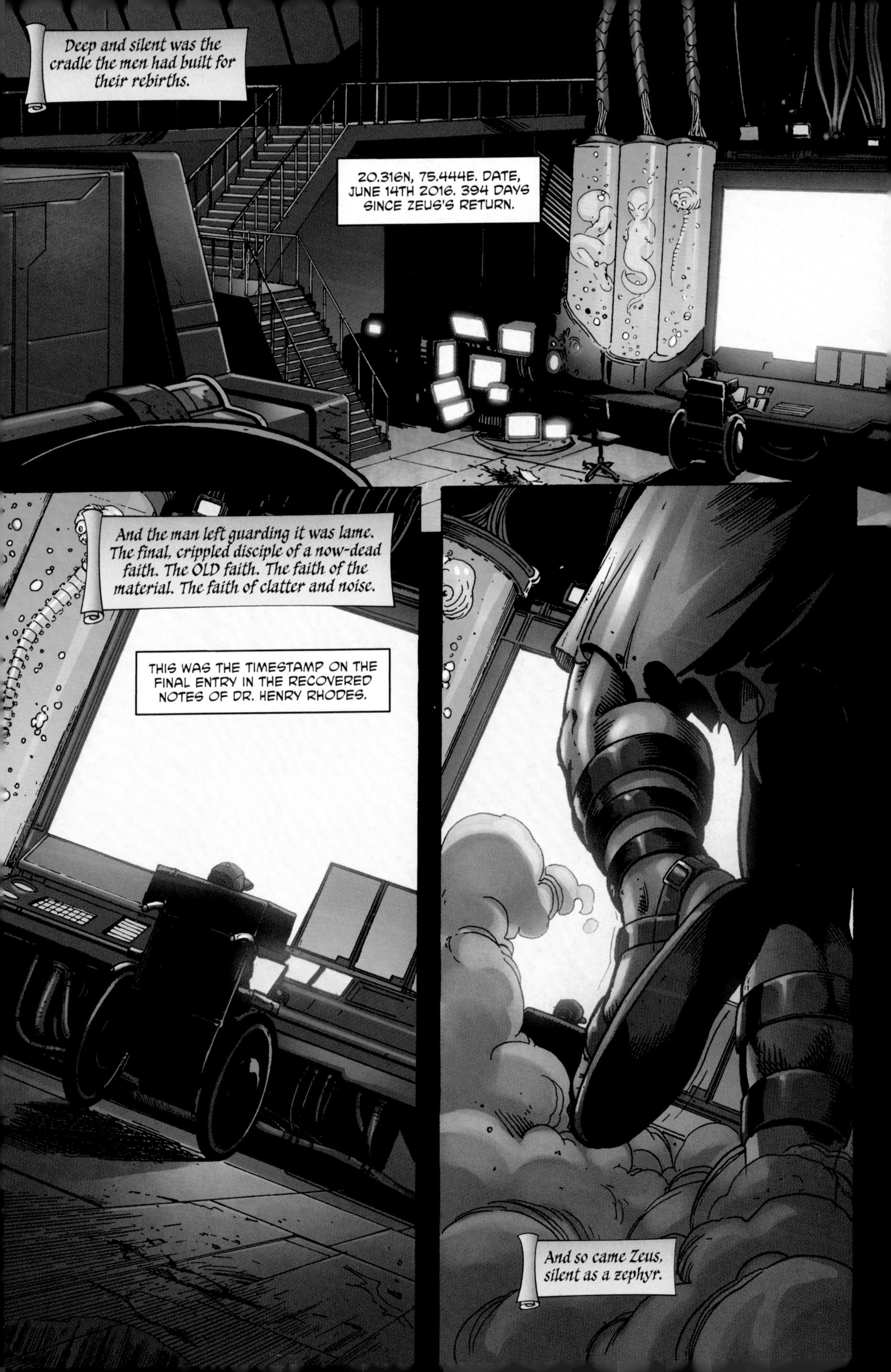
Deep and silent was the cradle the men had built for their rebirths.
20.316N, 75.444E. DATE, JUNE 14TH 2016. 394 DAYS SINCE ZEUS'S RETURN.
And the man left guarding it was lame. The final, crippled disciple of a now-dead faith. The OLD faith. The faith of the material. The faith of clatter and noise.
THIS WAS THE TIMESTAMP ON THE FINAL ENTRY IN THE RECOVERED NOTES OF DR. HENRY RHODES.
And so came Zeus, silent as a zephyr.

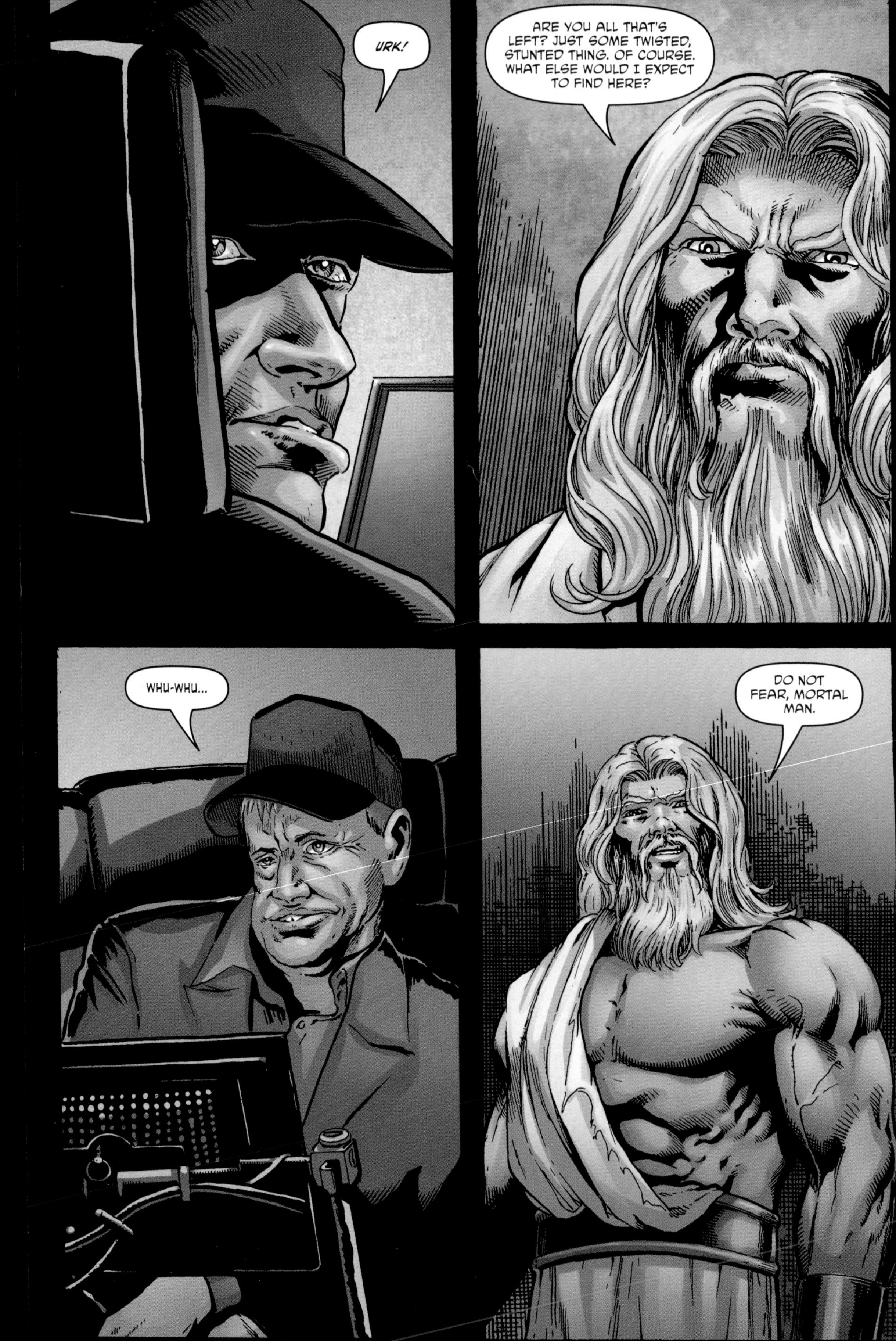
URK!
ARE YOU ALL THAT'S LEFT? JUST SOME TWISTED, STUNTED THING. OF COURSE. WHAT ELSE WOULD I EXPECT TO FIND HERE?
WHU-WHU...
DO NOT FEAR, MORTAL MAN.

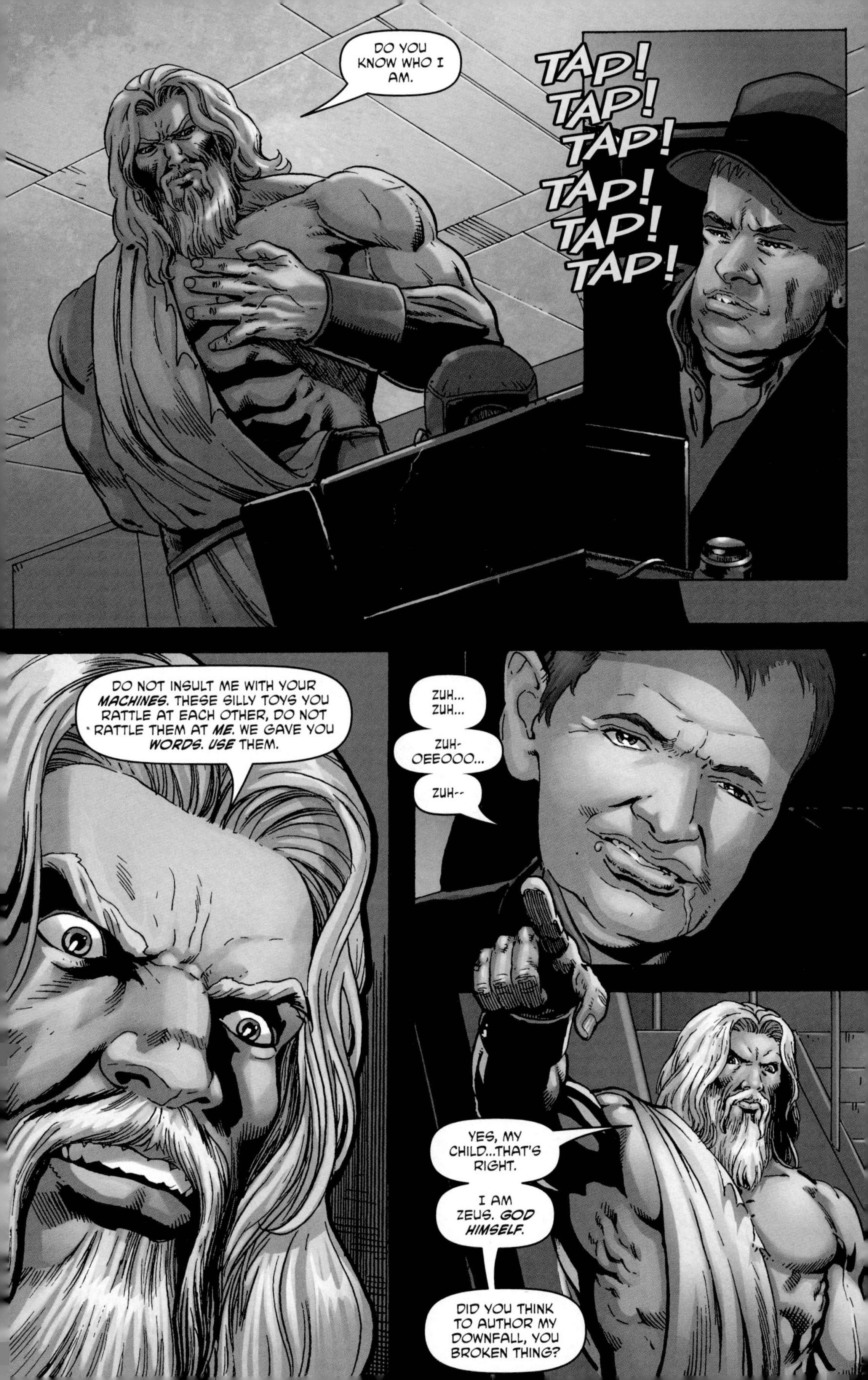
DO YOU KNOW WHO I AM.
TAP! TAP! TAP! TAP! TAP! TAP!
DO NOT INSULT ME WITH YOUR MACHINES. THESE SILLY TOYS YOU RATTLE AT EACH OTHER, DO NOT RATTLE THEM AT ME. WE GAVE YOU WORDS. USE THEM.
ZUH... ZUH...
ZUH-OEEOOO...
ZUH--
YES, MY CHILD...THAT'S RIGHT.
I AM ZEUS. GOD HIMSELF.
DID YOU THINK TO AUTHOR MY DOWNFALL, YOU BROKEN THING?

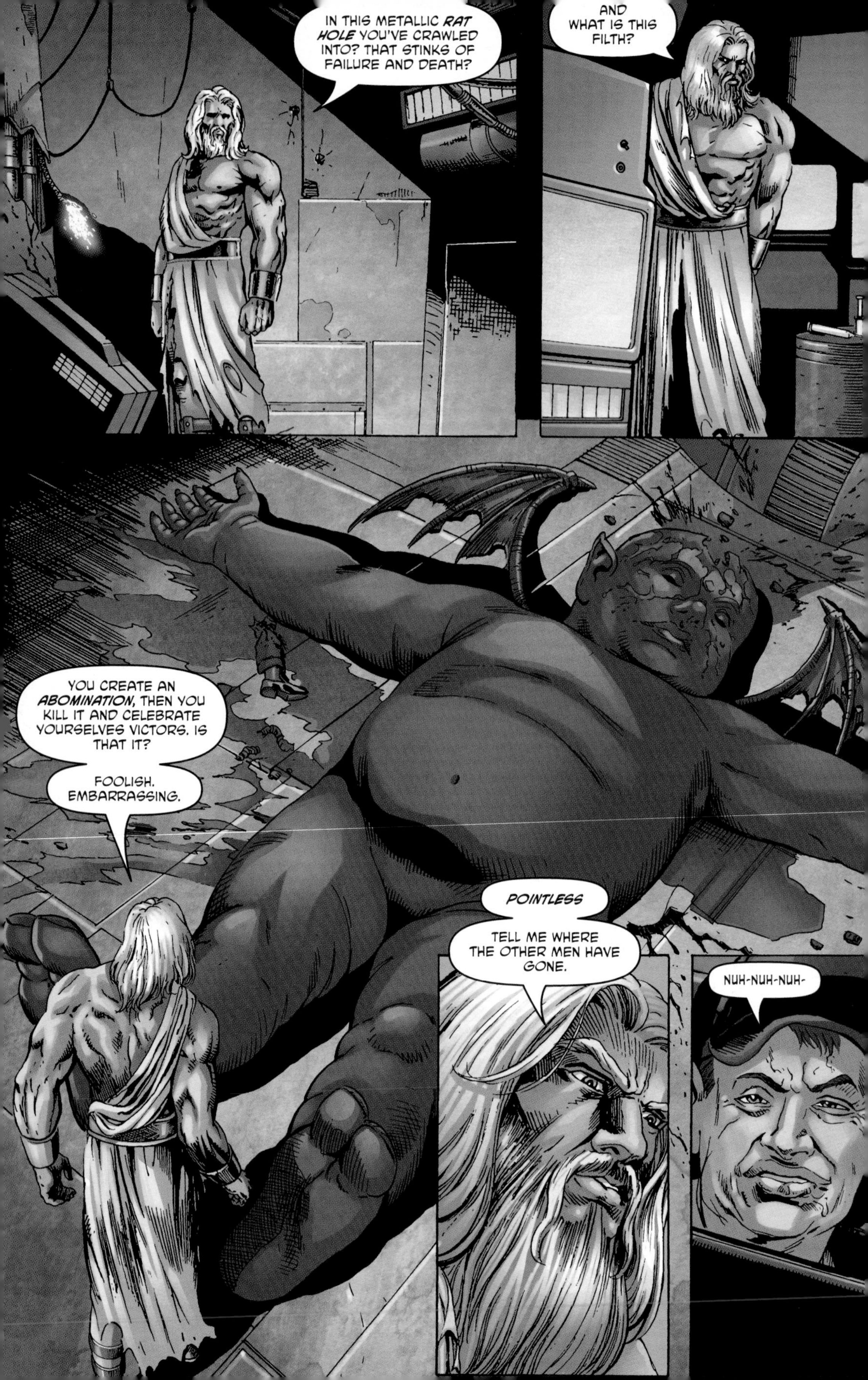
IN THIS METALLIC *RAT HOLE* YOU'VE CRAWLED INTO? THAT STINKS OF FAILURE AND DEATH?
AND WHAT IS THIS FILTH?
YOU CREATE AN *ABOMINATION*, THEN YOU KILL IT AND CELEBRATE YOURSELVES VICTORS. IS THAT IT?
FOOLISH. EMBARRASSING.
POINTLESS
TELL ME WHERE THE OTHER MEN HAVE GONE.
NUH-NUH-NUH-

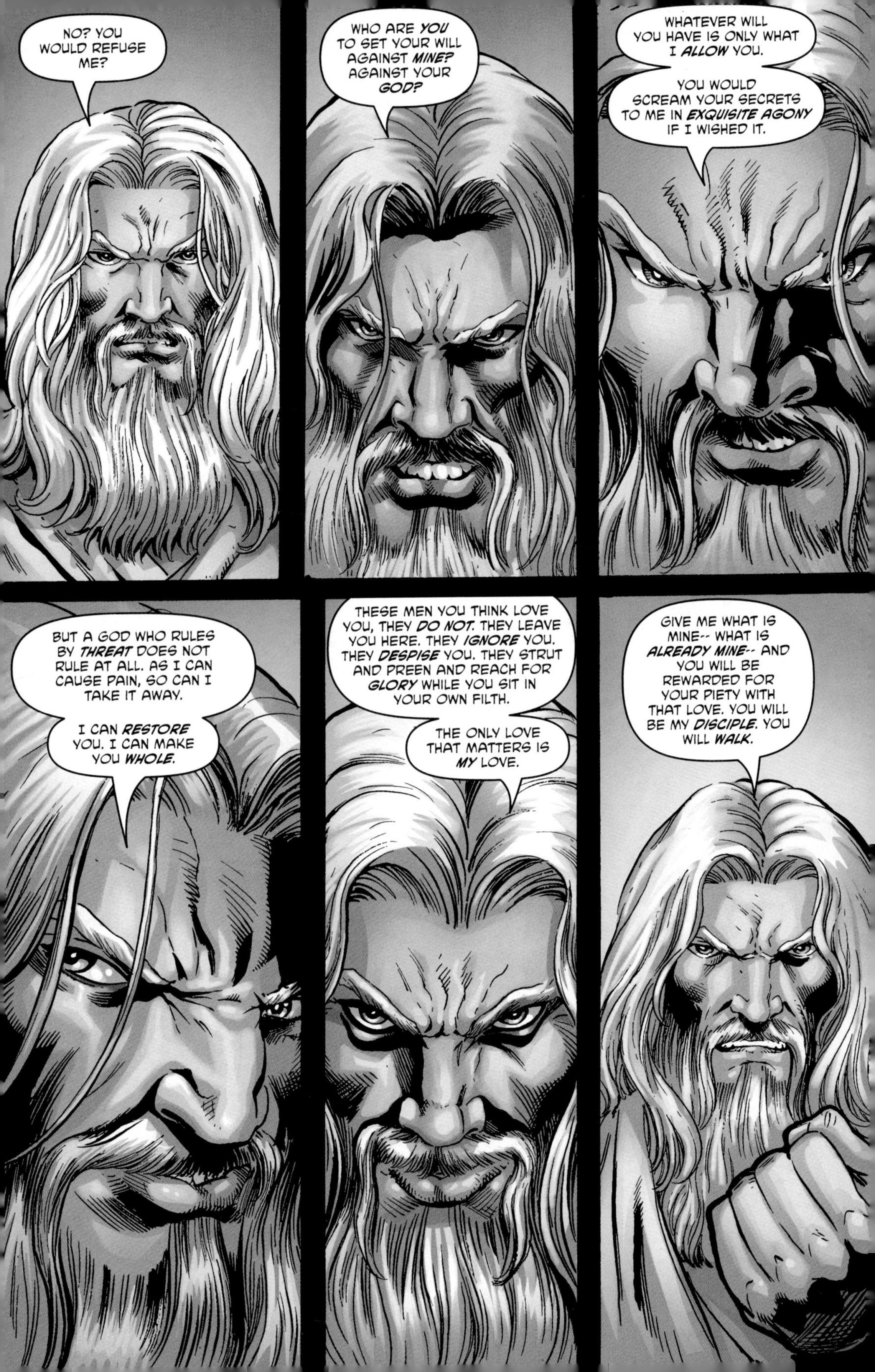
NO? YOU WOULD REFUSE ME?
WHO ARE YOU TO SET YOUR WILL AGAINST MINE? AGAINST YOUR GOD?
WHATEVER WILL YOU HAVE IS ONLY WHAT I ALLOW YOU.
YOU WOULD SCREAM YOUR SECRETS TO ME IN EXQUISITE AGONY IF I WISHED IT.
BUT A GOD WHO RULES BY THREAT DOES NOT RULE AT ALL. AS I CAN CAUSE PAIN, SO CAN I TAKE IT AWAY.
I CAN RESTORE YOU. I CAN MAKE YOU WHOLE.
THESE MEN YOU THINK LOVE YOU, THEY DO NOT. THEY LEAVE YOU HERE. THEY IGNORE YOU. THEY DESPISE YOU. THEY STRUT AND PREEN AND REACH FOR GLORY WHILE YOU SIT IN YOUR OWN FILTH.
THE ONLY LOVE THAT MATTERS IS MY LOVE.
GIVE ME WHAT IS MINE-- WHAT IS ALREADY MINE-- AND YOU WILL BE REWARDED FOR YOUR PIETY WITH THAT LOVE. YOU WILL BE MY DISCIPLE. YOU WILL WALK.

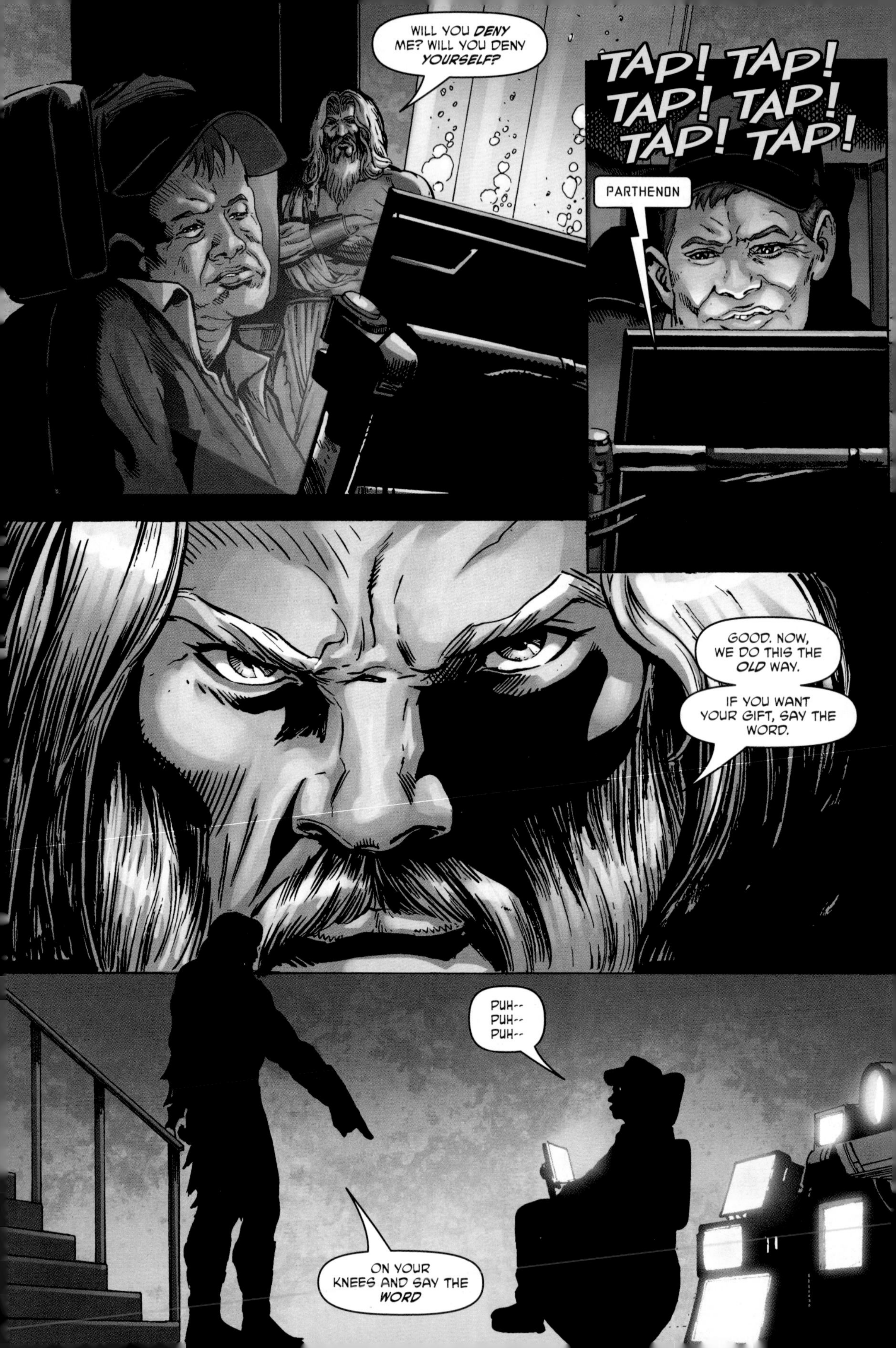
WILL YOU *DENY* ME? WILL YOU DENY *YOURSELF?*
TAP! TAP! TAP! TAP! TAP! TAP!
PARTHENON
GOOD. NOW, WE DO THIS THE *OLD* WAY.
IF YOU WANT YOUR GIFT, SAY THE WORD.
PUH-- PUH-- PUH--
ON YOUR KNEES AND SAY THE *WORD*

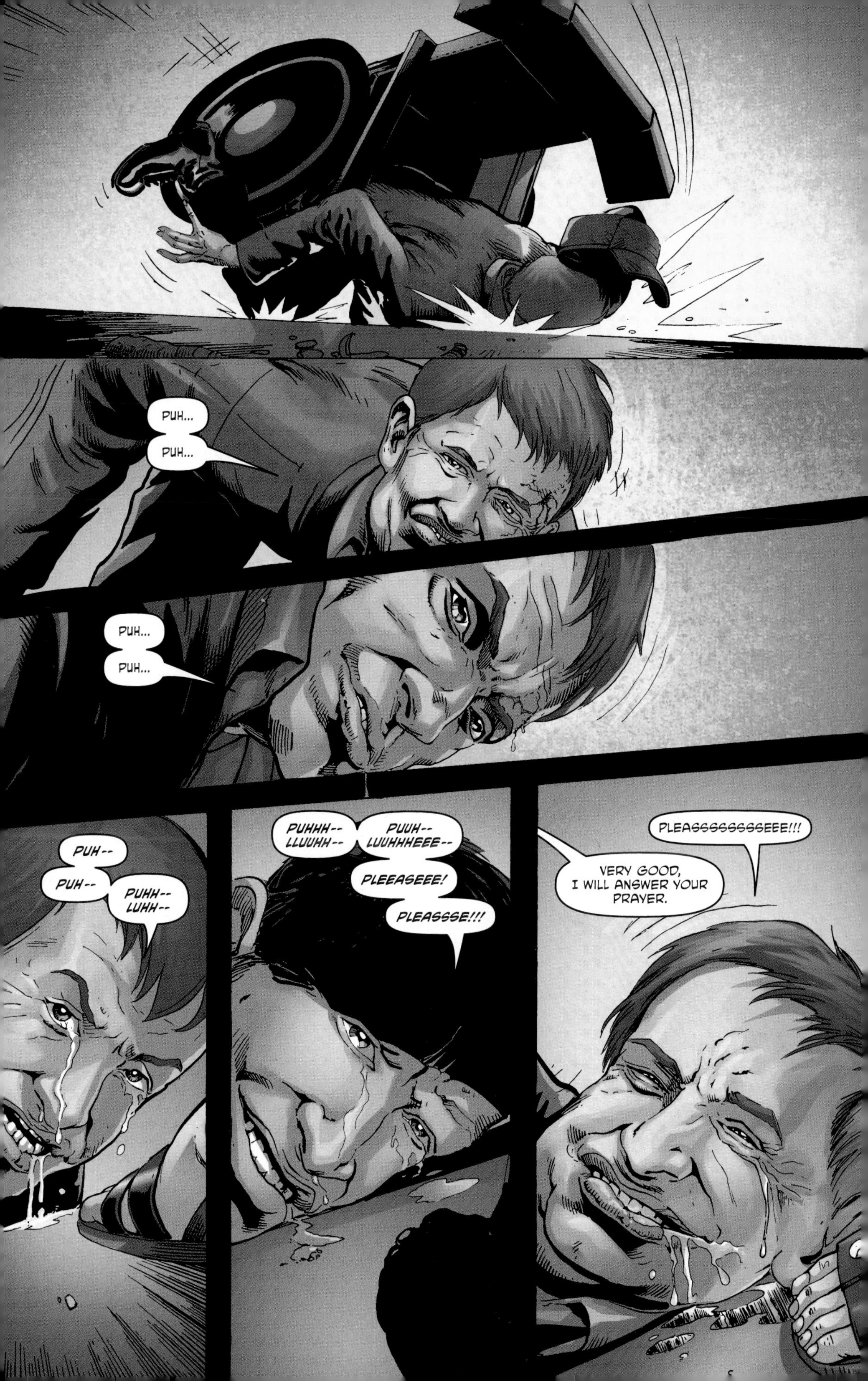
PUH...
PUH...
PUH...
PUH...
PUH--
PUH--
PUHH--
LUHH--
PUHHH--
LLUUHH--
PUUH--
LUUHHHEEE--
PLEEASEEE!
PLEASSSE!!!
VERY GOOD,
I WILL ANSWER YOUR PRAYER.
PLEASSSSSSSSEEE!!!

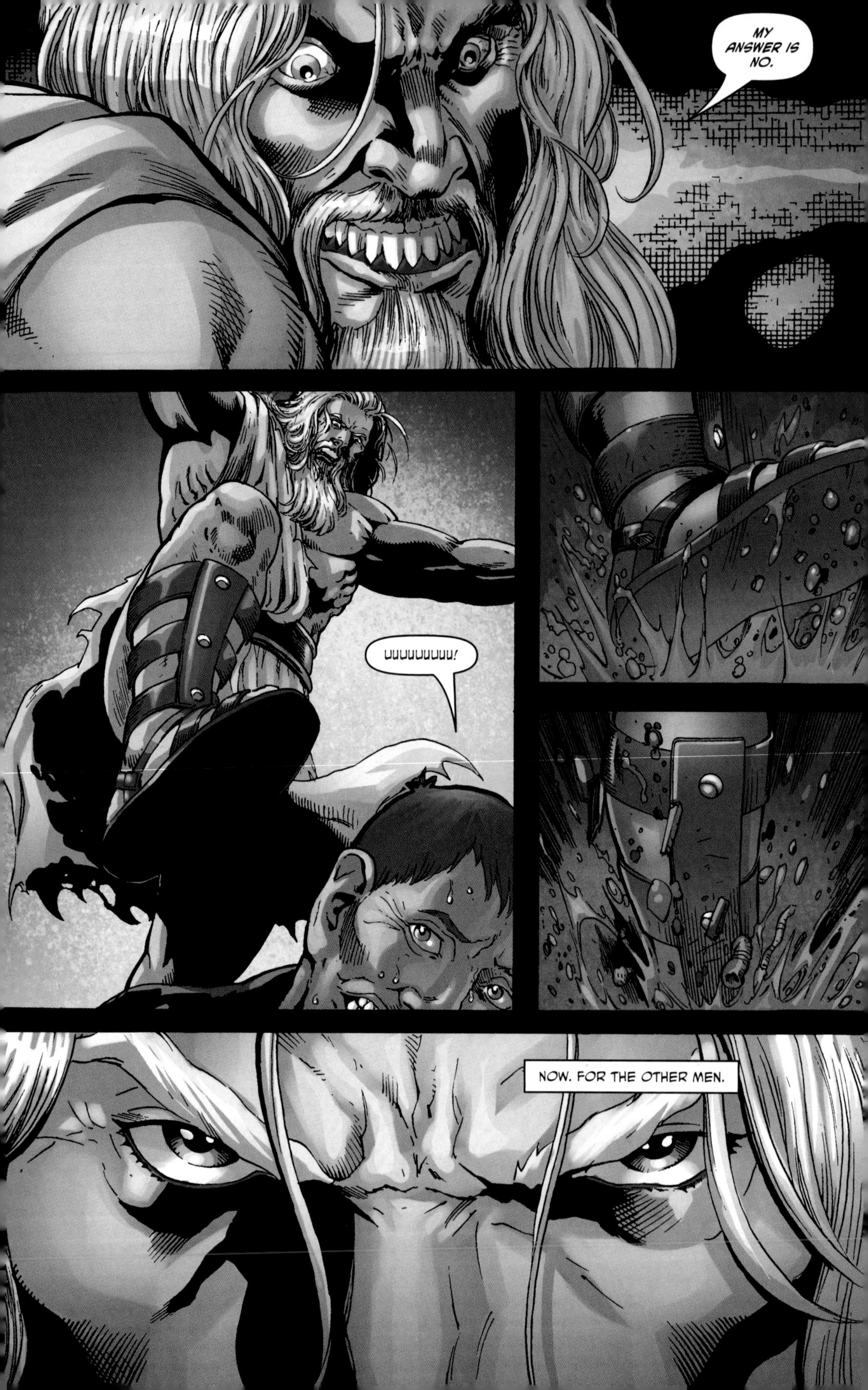
MY ANSWER IS NO.
UUUUUUUUU!
NOW. FOR THE OTHER MEN.

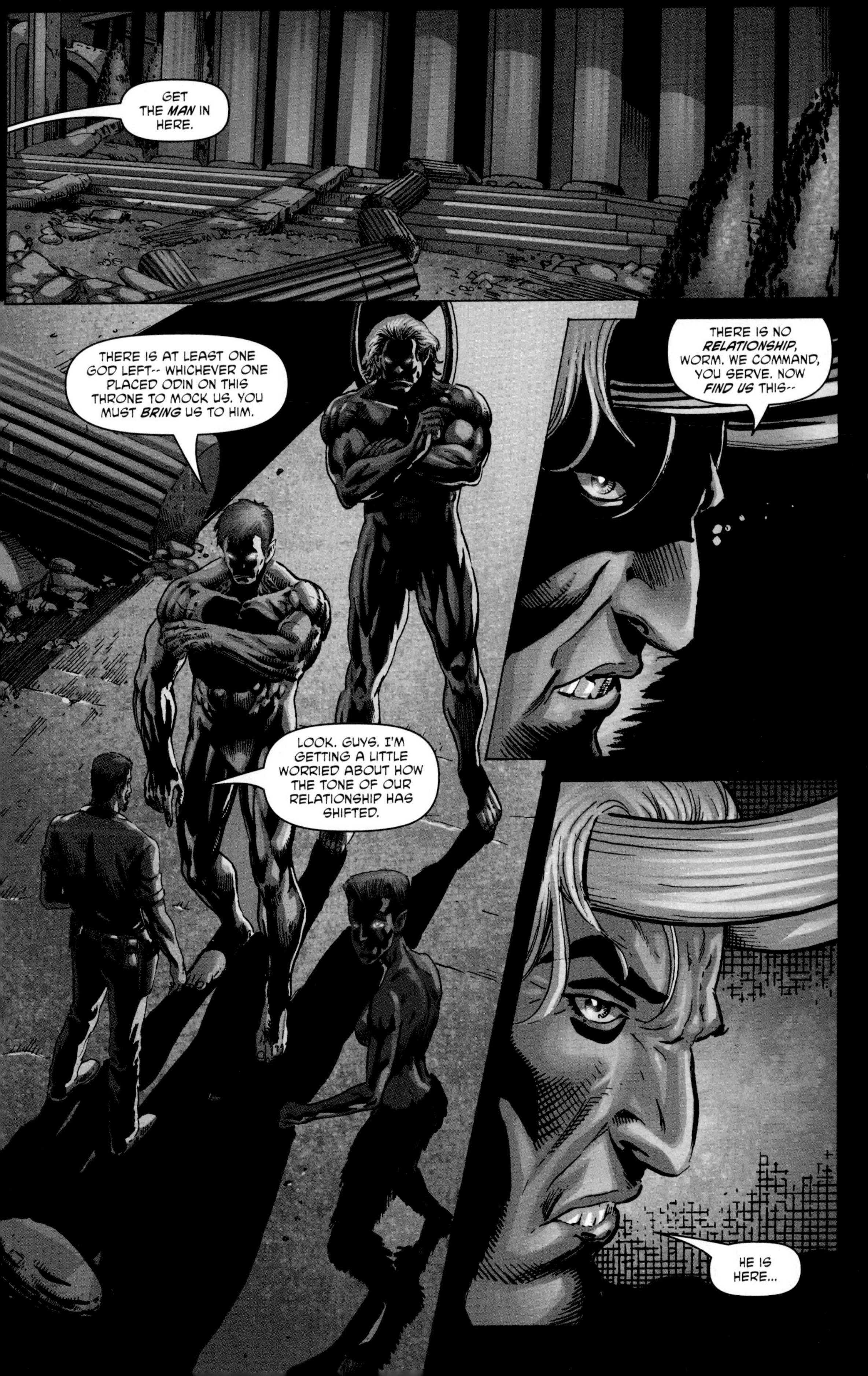
GET THE MAN IN HERE.
THERE IS AT LEAST ONE GOD LEFT-- WHICHEVER ONE PLACED ODIN ON THIS THRONE TO MOCK US. YOU MUST BRING US TO HIM.
LOOK. GUYS. I'M GETTING A LITTLE WORRIED ABOUT HOW THE TONE OF OUR RELATIONSHIP HAS SHIFTED.
THERE IS NO RELATIONSHIP, WORM. WE COMMAND, YOU SERVE. NOW FIND US THIS--
HE IS HERE...

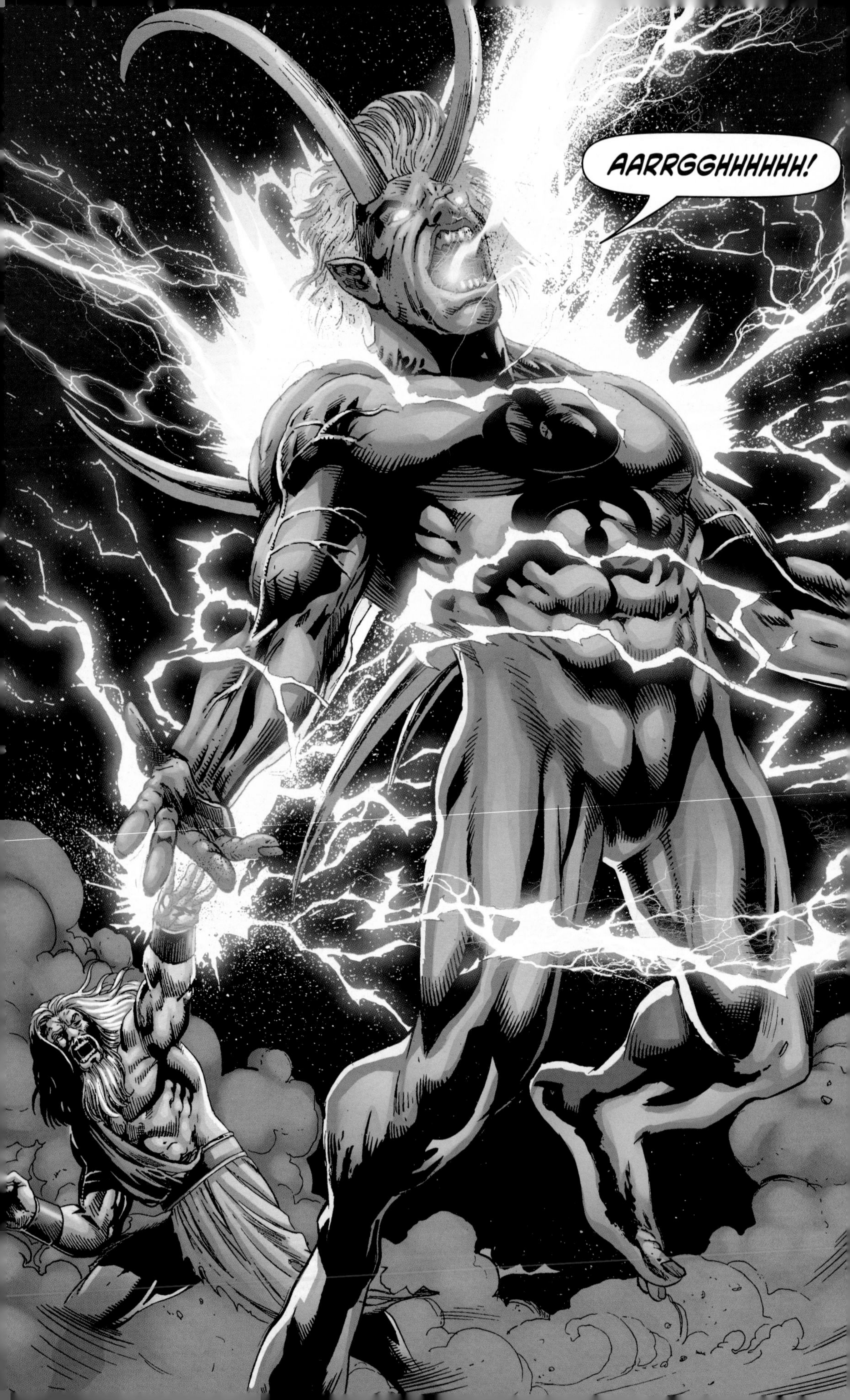
AARRGGHHHHHH!

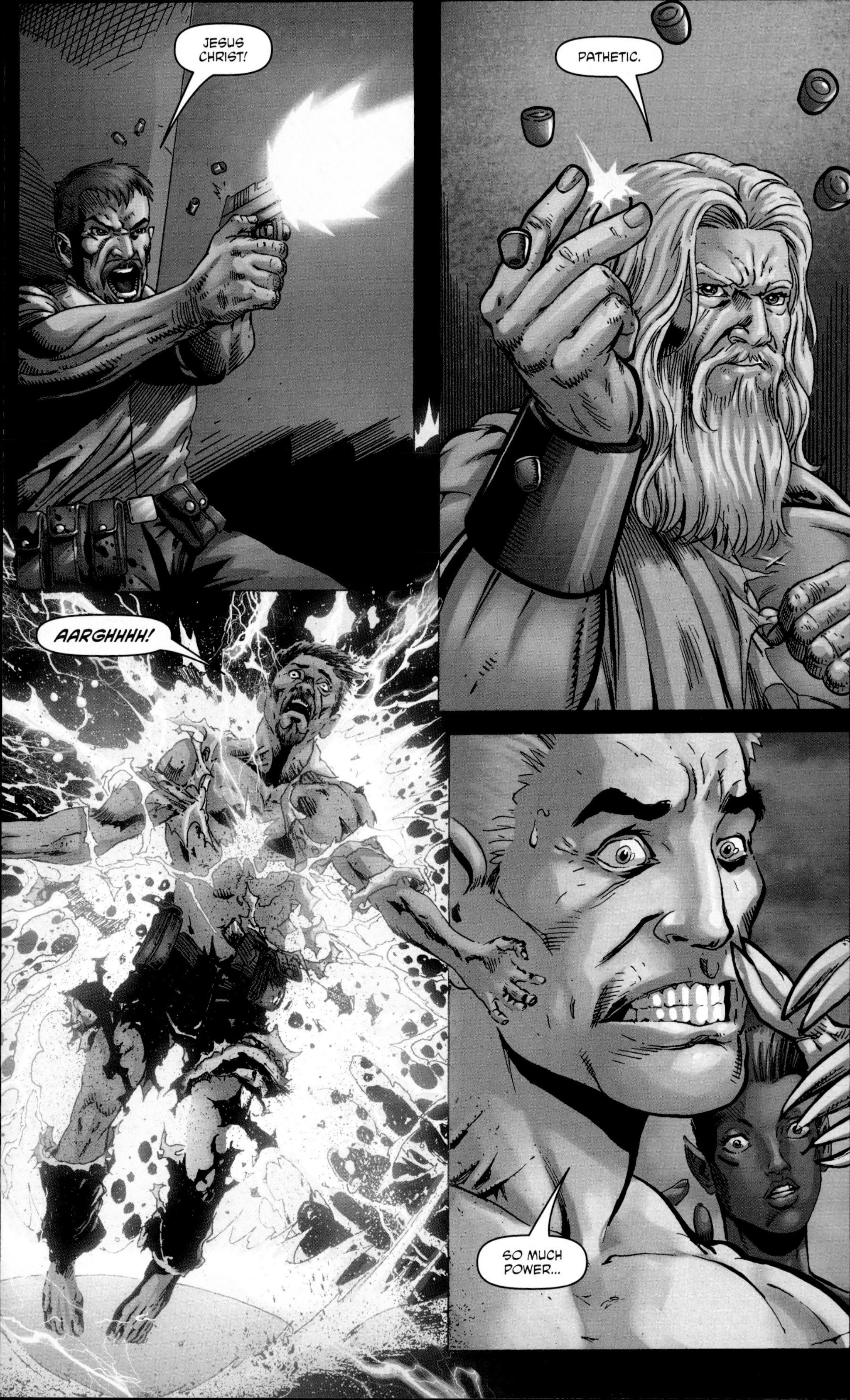
JESUS CHRIST!
PATHETIC.
AARGHHHH!
SO MUCH POWER...

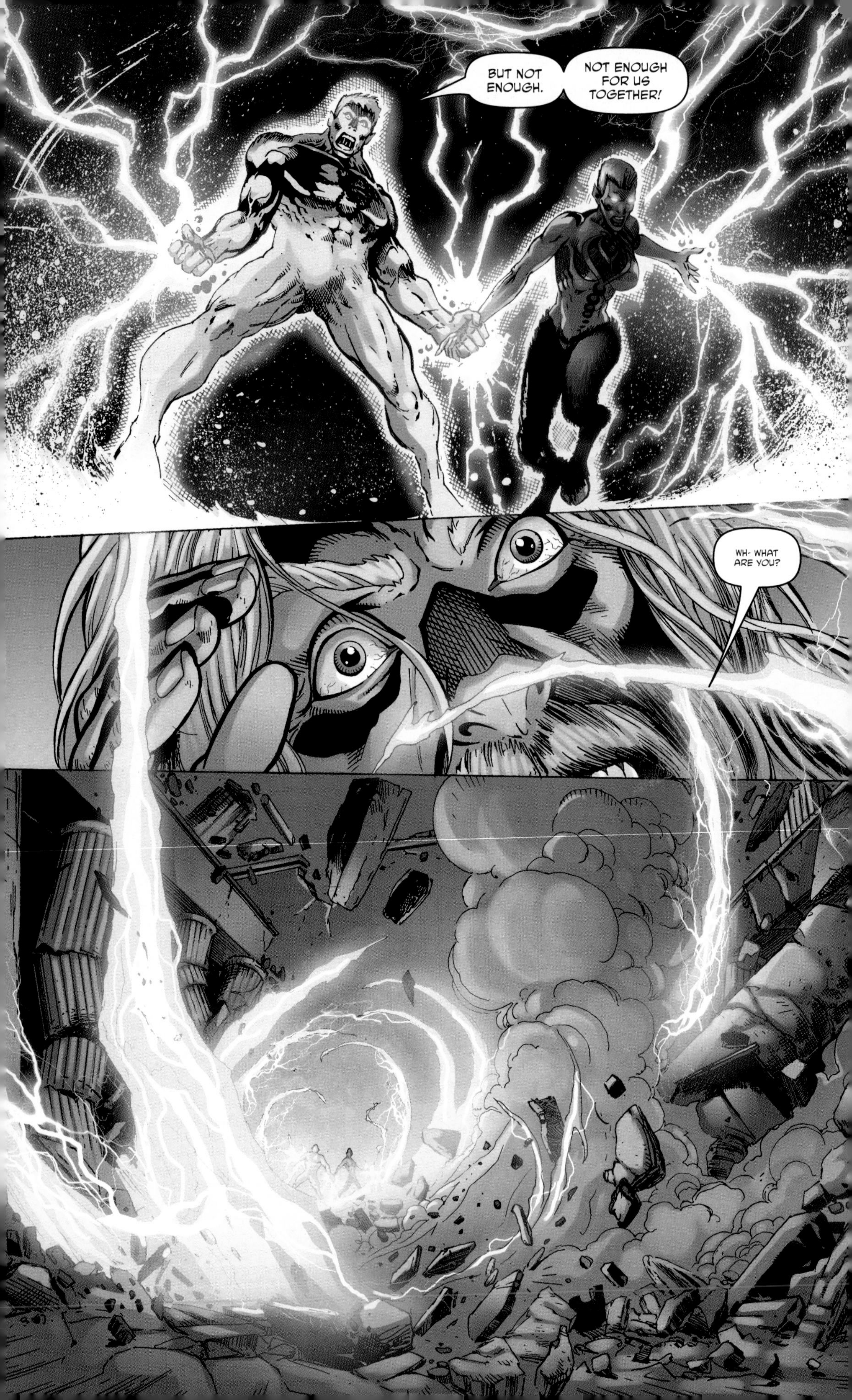
BUT NOT ENOUGH.
NOT ENOUGH FOR US TOGETHER!
WH- WHAT ARE YOU?

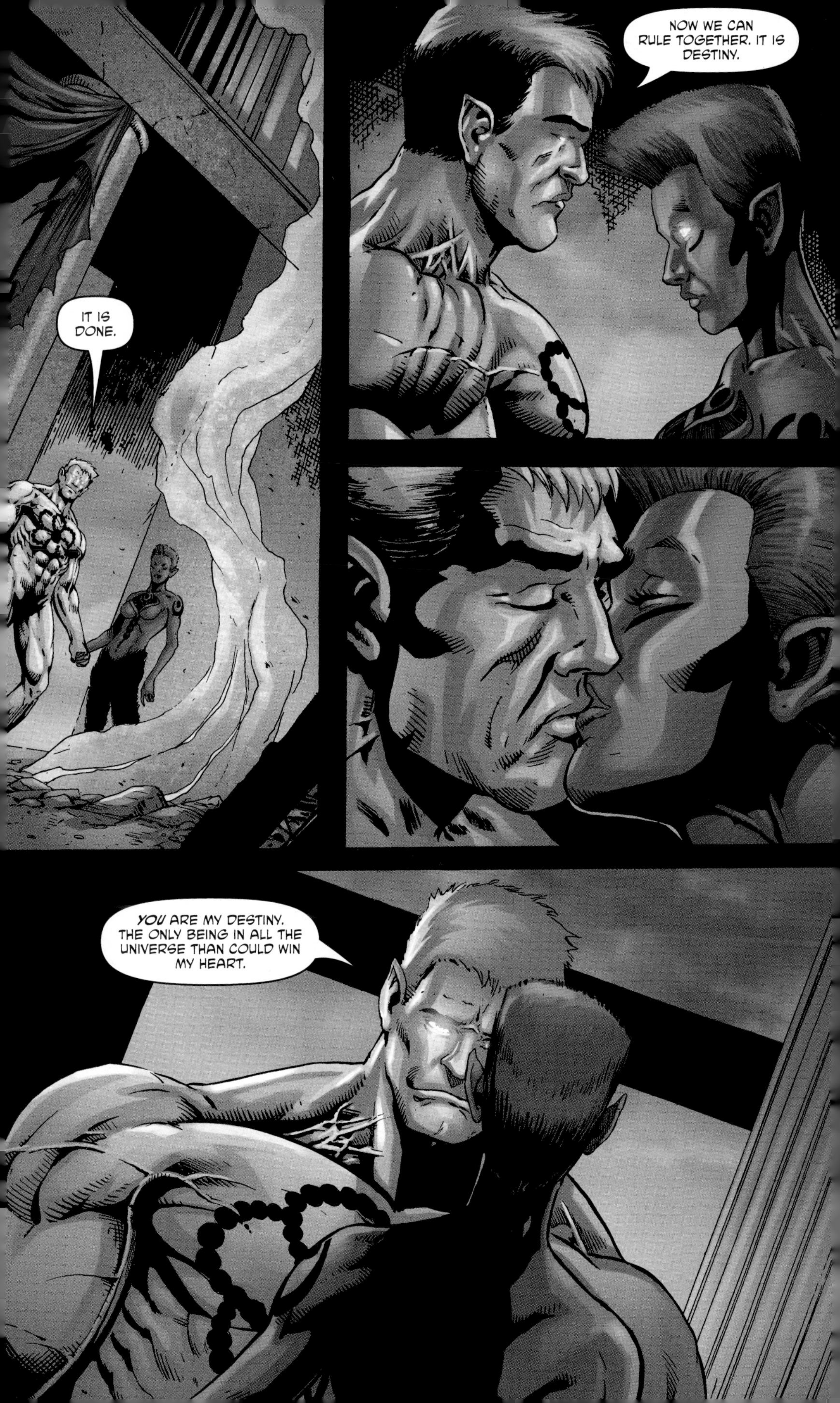
IT IS DONE.
NOW WE CAN RULE TOGETHER. IT IS DESTINY.
YOU ARE MY DESTINY. THE ONLY BEING IN ALL THE UNIVERSE THAN COULD WIN MY HEART.

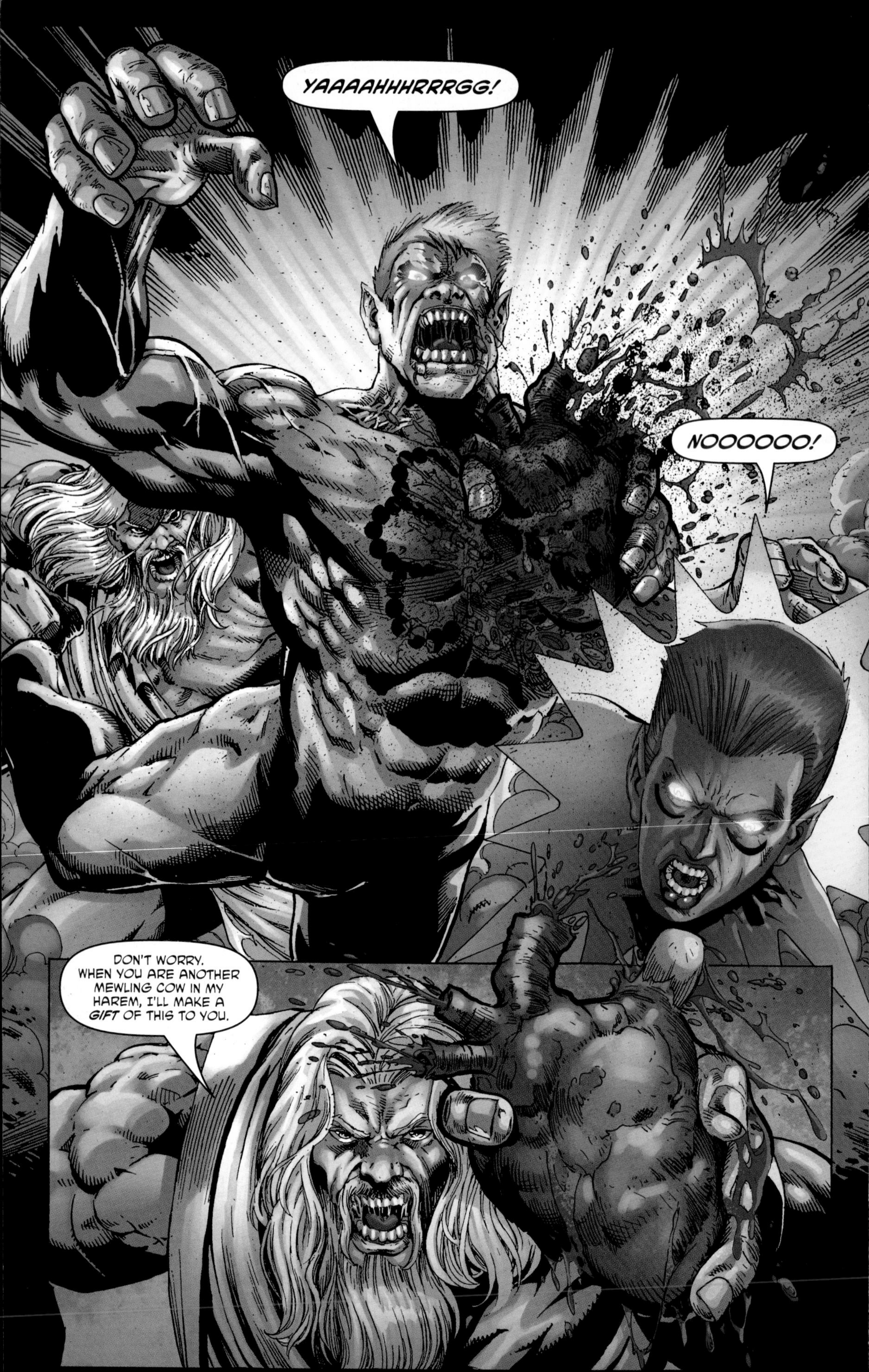
YAAAAHHHRRRGG!
NOOOOOO!
DON'T WORRY. WHEN YOU ARE ANOTHER MEWLING COW IN MY HAREM, I'LL MAKE A *GIFT* OF THIS TO YOU.

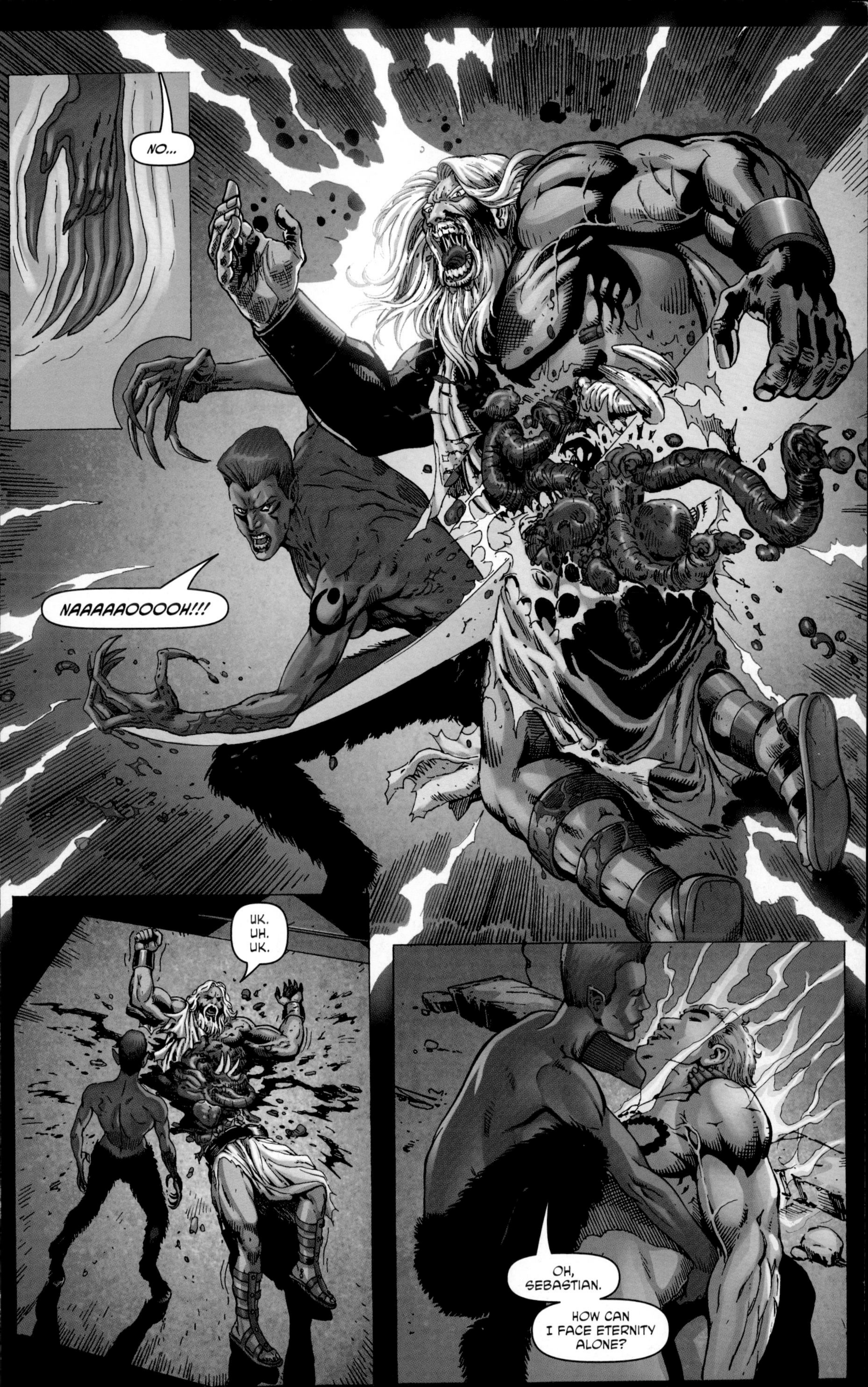
NO...
NAAAAAOOOOH!!!
UK. UH. UK.
OH, SEBASTIAN.
HOW CAN I FACE ETERNITY ALONE?

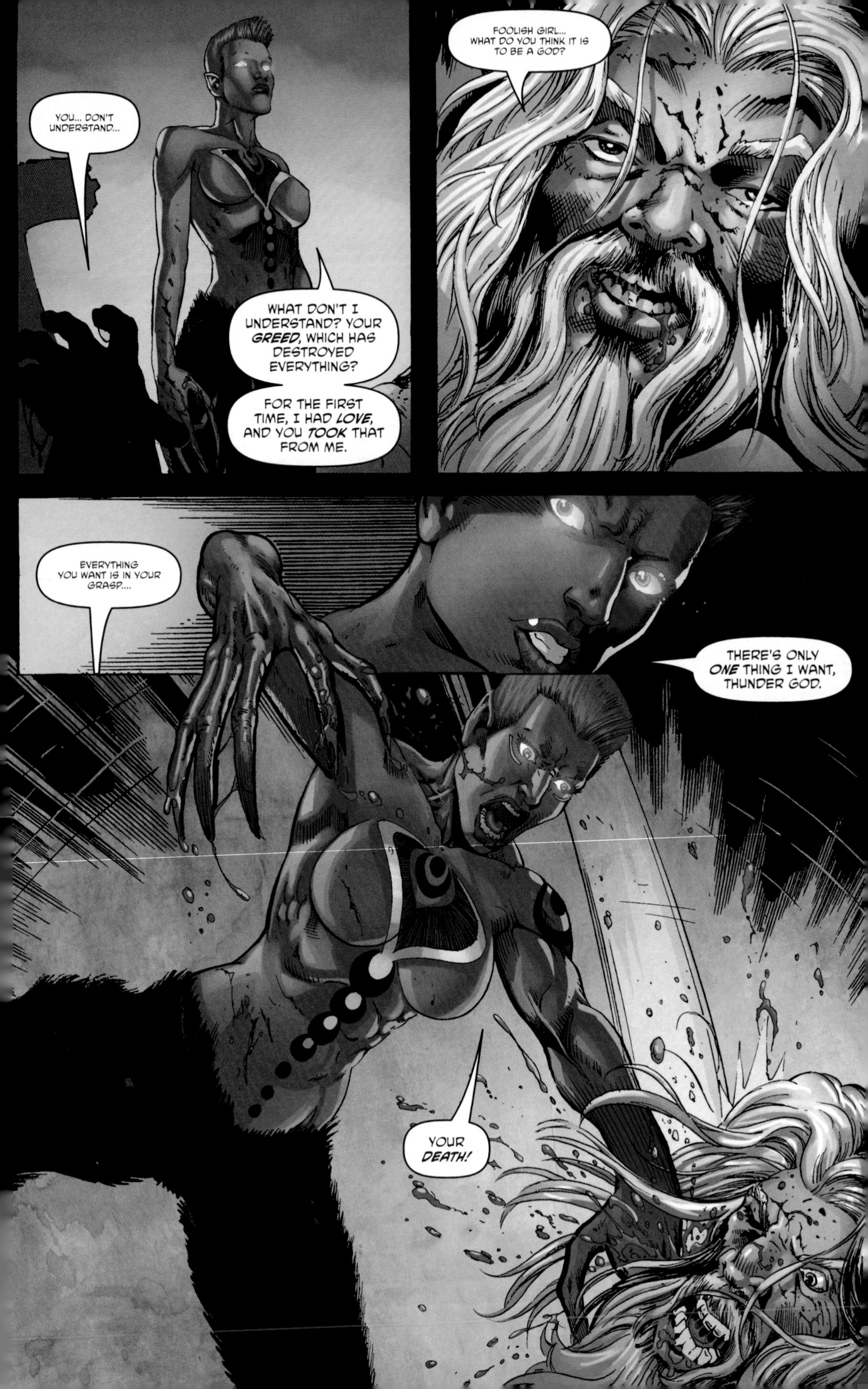
YOU... DON'T UNDERSTAND...
WHAT DON'T I UNDERSTAND? YOUR *GREED*, WHICH HAS DESTROYED EVERYTHING?
FOR THE FIRST TIME, I HAD *LOVE*, AND YOU *TOOK* THAT FROM ME.
FOOLISH GIRL... WHAT DO YOU THINK IT IS TO BE A GOD?
EVERYTHING YOU WANT IS IN YOUR GRASP....
THERE'S ONLY *ONE* THING I WANT, THUNDER GOD.
YOUR *DEATH!*

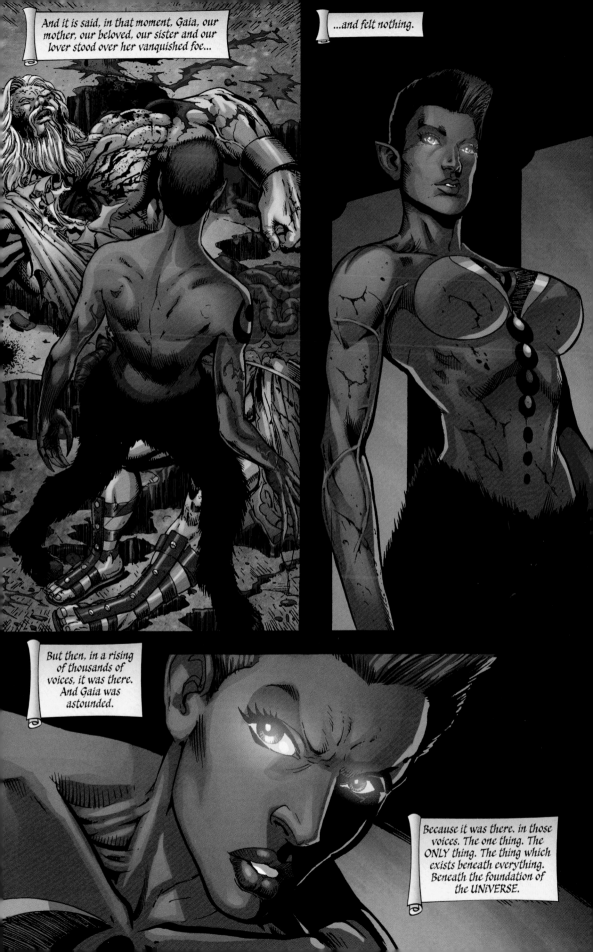

And it is said, in that moment, Gaia, our mother, our beloved, our sister and our lover stood over her vanquished foe...

...and felt nothing.

But then, in a rising of thousands of voices, it was there. And Gaia was astounded.

Because it was there, in those voices. The one thing. The ONLY thing. The thing which exists beneath everything. Beneath the foundation of the UNIVERSE.

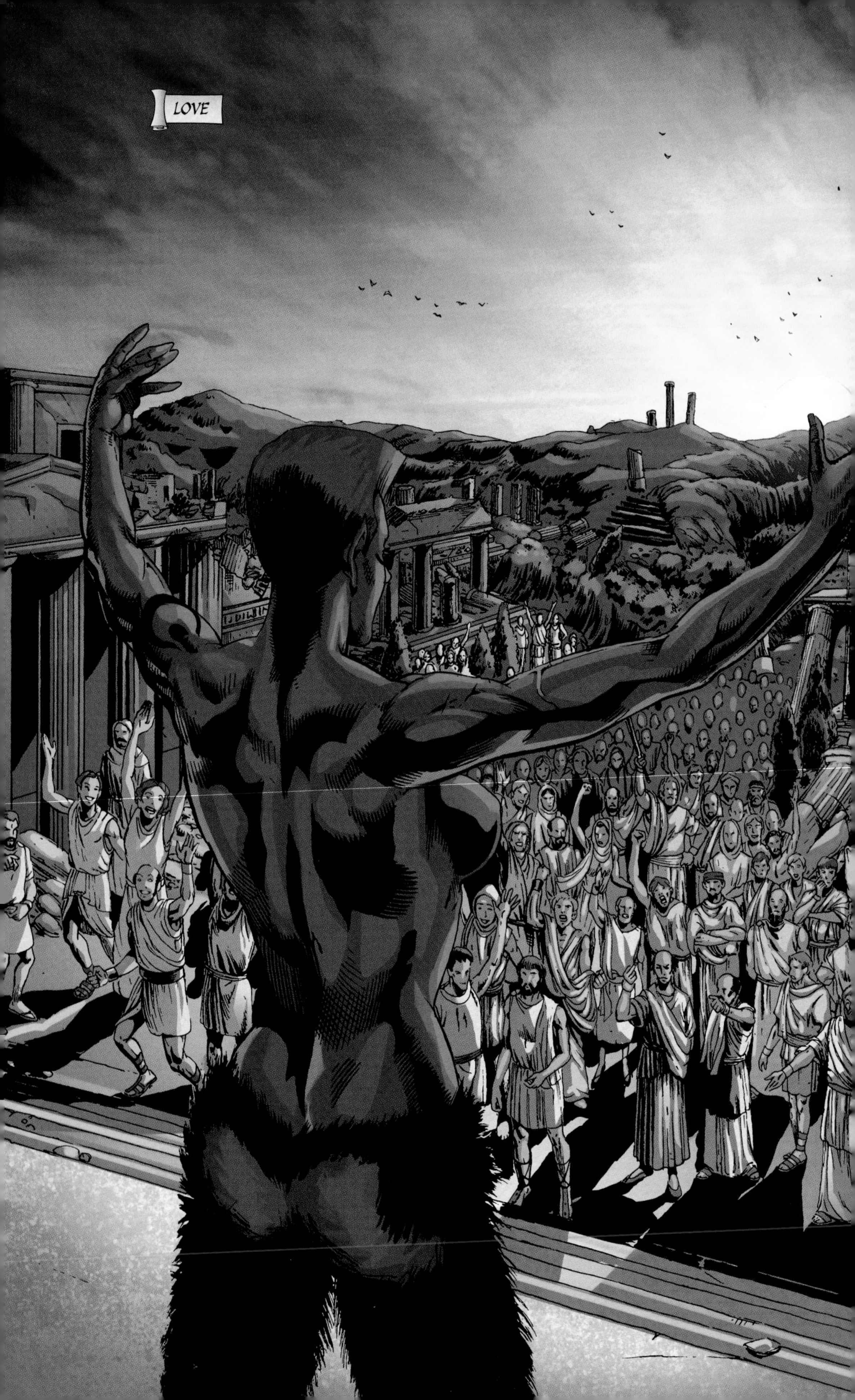
LOVE

INTERLUDE

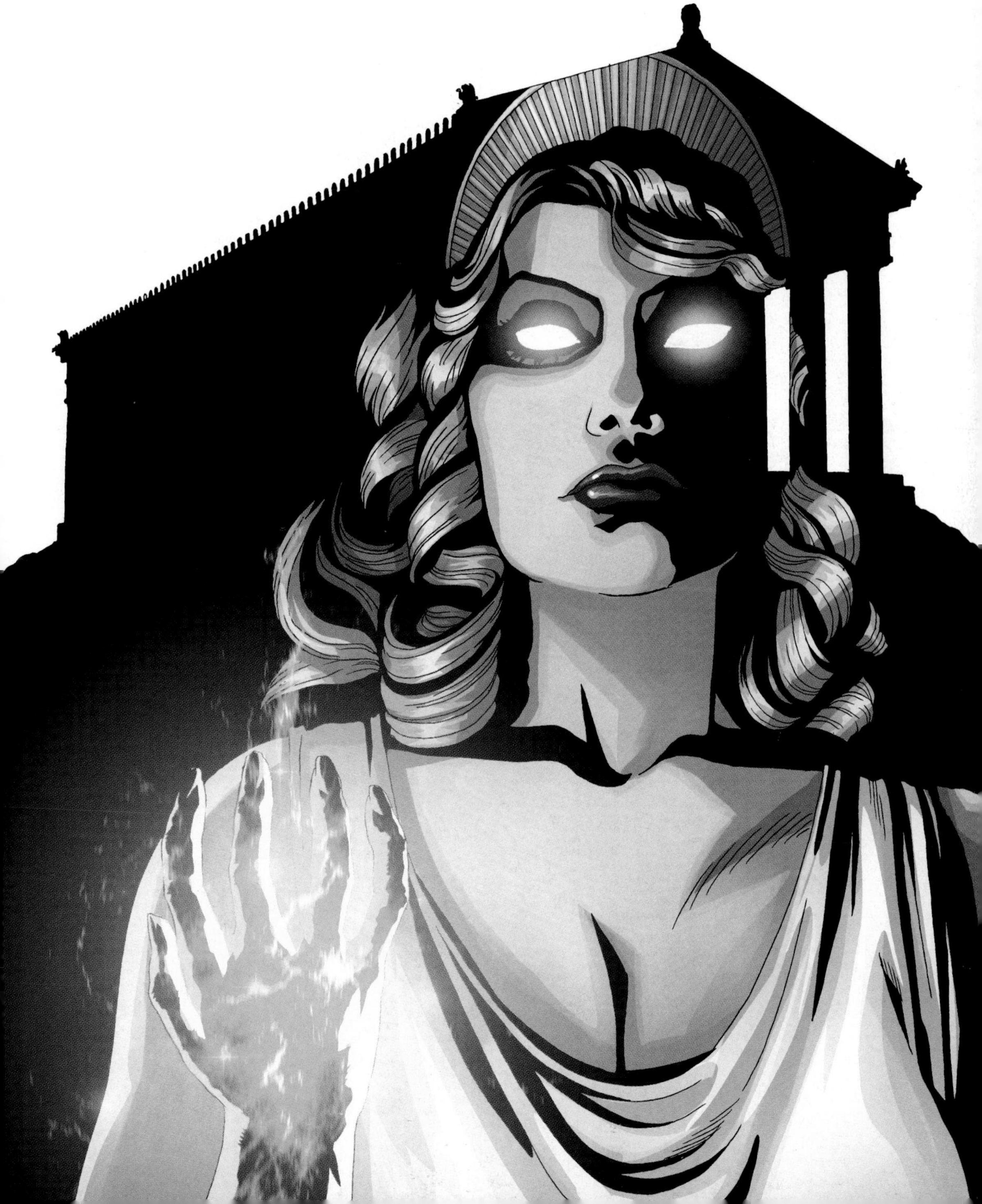

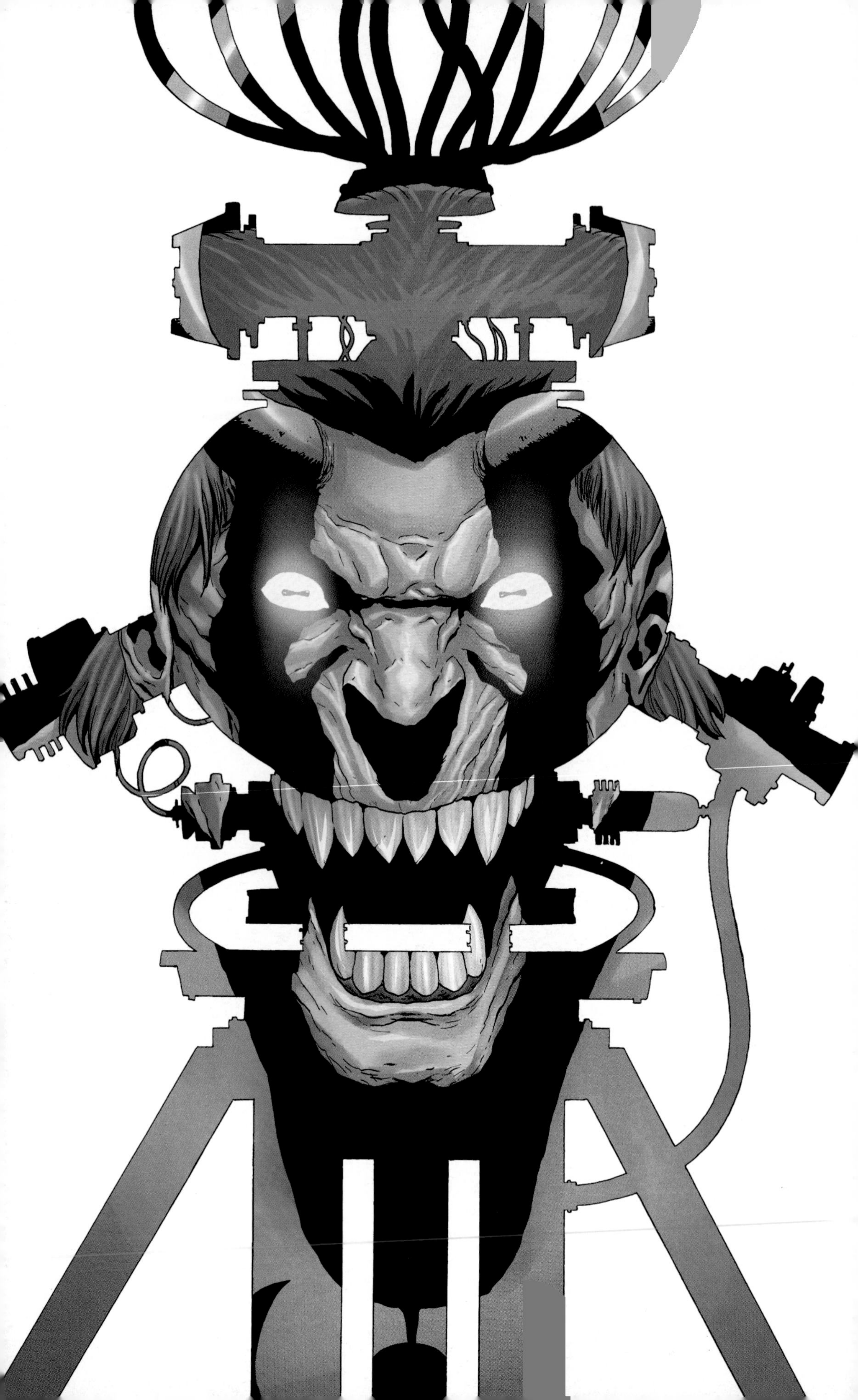

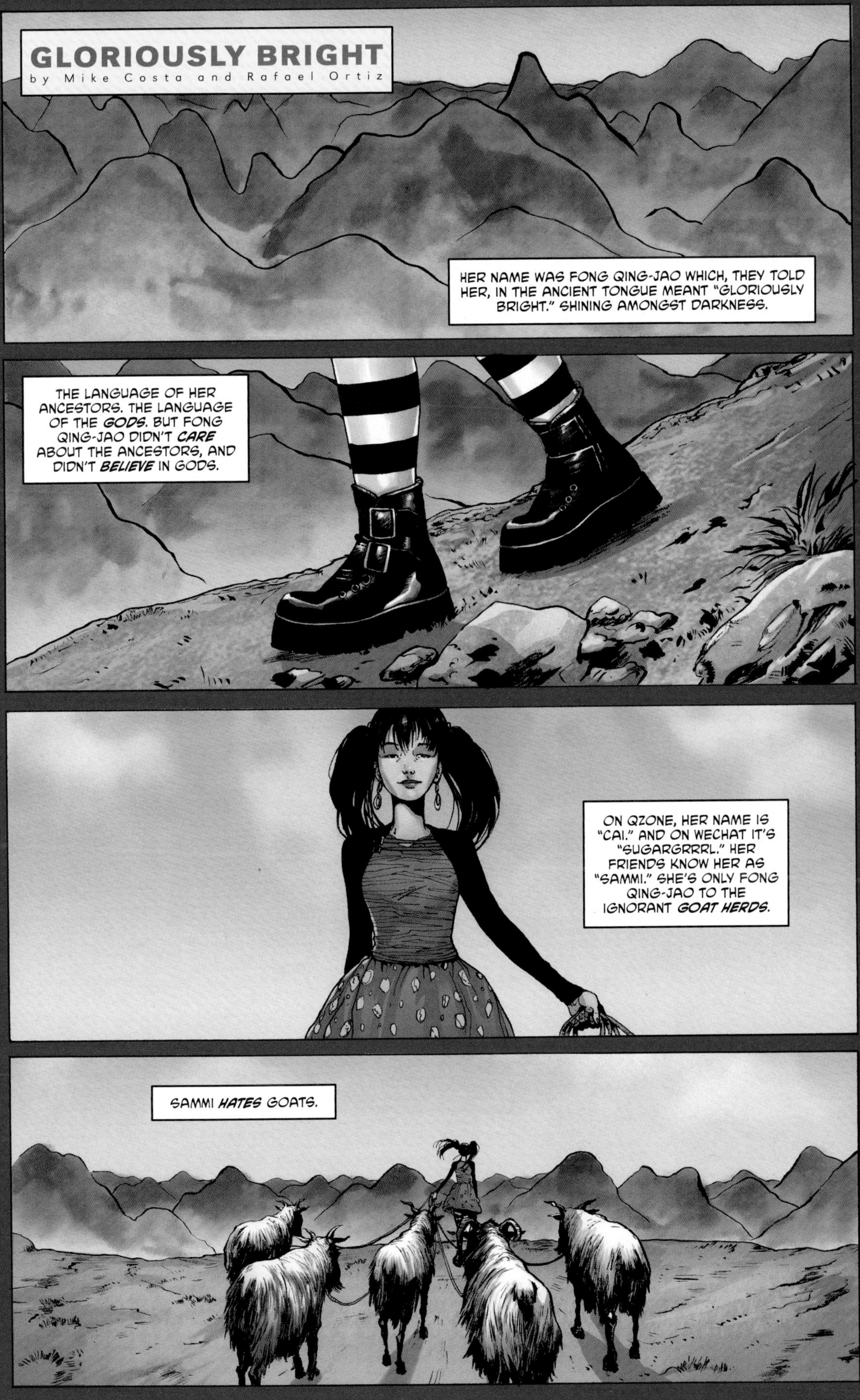
GLORIOUSLY BRIGHT
by Mike Costa and Rafael Ortiz
HER NAME WAS FONG QING-JAO WHICH, THEY TOLD HER, IN THE ANCIENT TONGUE MEANT "GLORIOUSLY BRIGHT." SHINING AMONGST DARKNESS.
THE LANGUAGE OF HER ANCESTORS. THE LANGUAGE OF THE *GODS*. BUT FONG QING-JAO DIDN'T *CARE* ABOUT THE ANCESTORS, AND DIDN'T *BELIEVE* IN GODS.
ON QZONE, HER NAME IS "CAI." AND ON WECHAT IT'S "SUGARGRRRL." HER FRIENDS KNOW HER AS "SAMMI." SHE'S ONLY FONG QING-JAO TO THE IGNORANT *GOAT HERDS*.
SAMMI *HATES* GOATS.

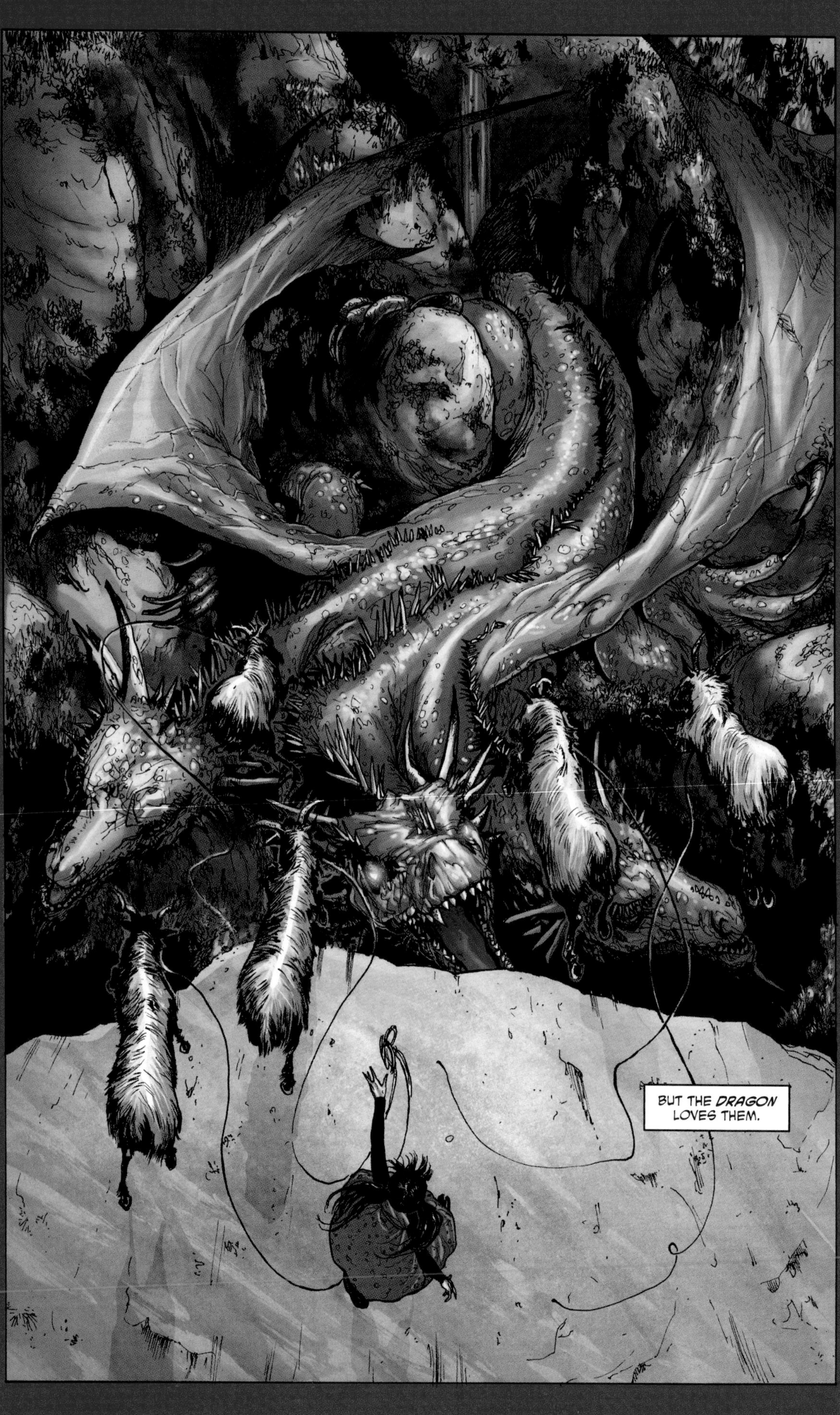
BUT THE DRAGON LOVES THEM.

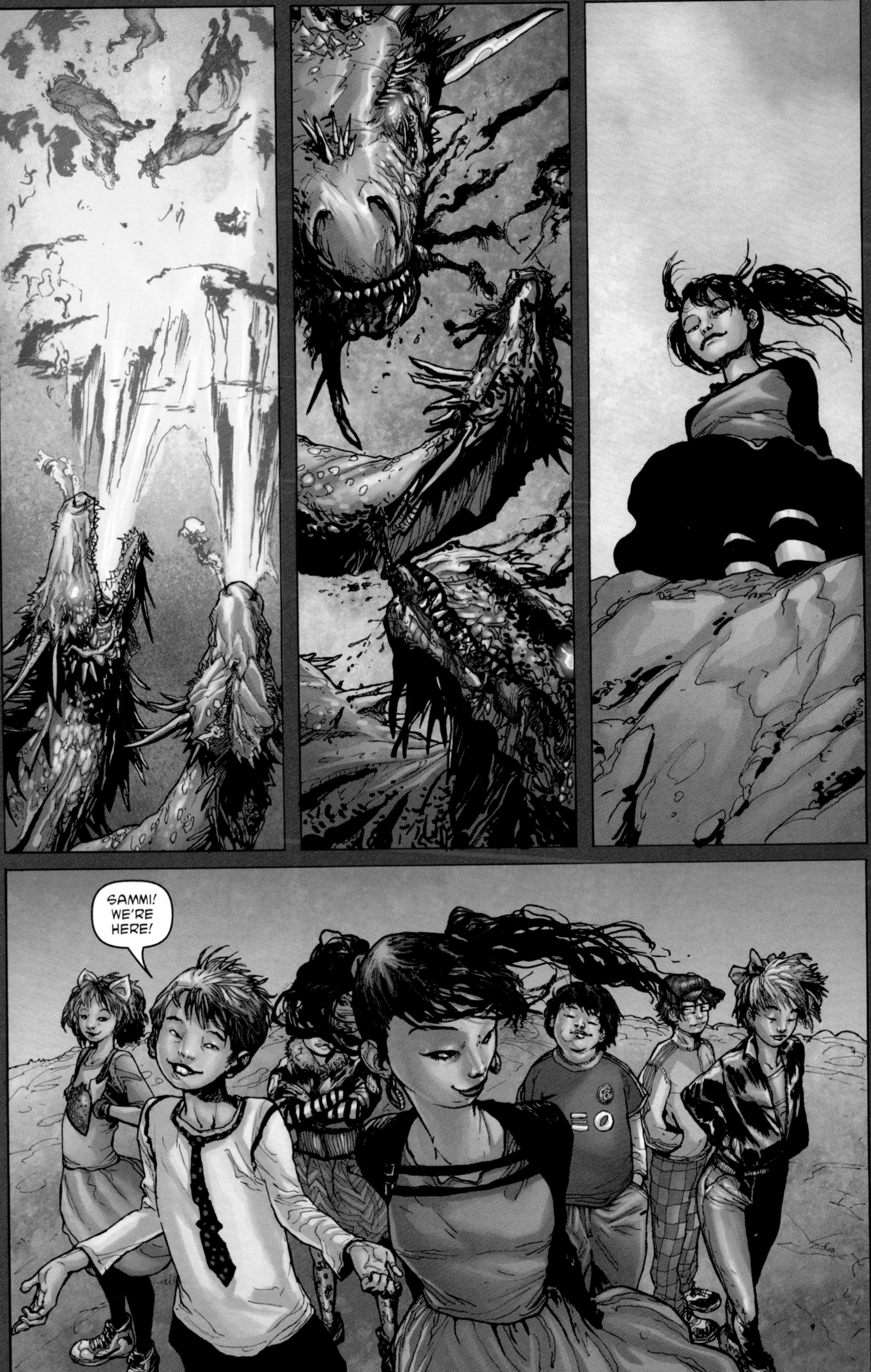
SAMMI! WE'RE HERE!

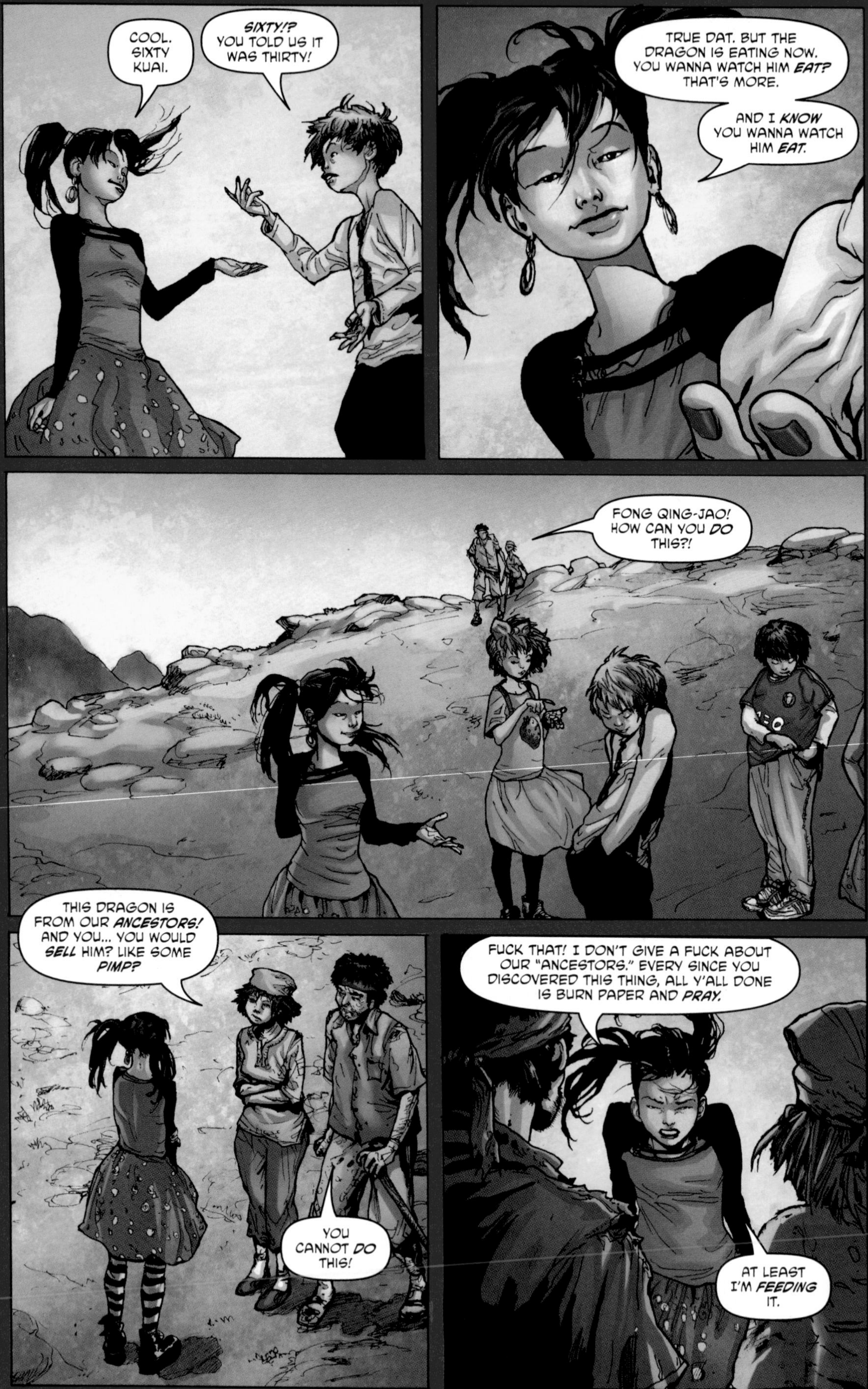

COOL. SIXTY KUAI.
SIXTY!? YOU TOLD US IT WAS THIRTY!
TRUE DAT. BUT THE DRAGON IS EATING NOW. YOU WANNA WATCH HIM EAT? THAT'S MORE.
AND I KNOW YOU WANNA WATCH HIM EAT.
FONG QING-JAO! HOW CAN YOU DO THIS?!
THIS DRAGON IS FROM OUR ANCESTORS! AND YOU... YOU WOULD SELL HIM? LIKE SOME PIMP?
YOU CANNOT DO THIS!
FUCK THAT! I DON'T GIVE A FUCK ABOUT OUR "ANCESTORS." EVERY SINCE YOU DISCOVERED THIS THING, ALL Y'ALL DONE IS BURN PAPER AND PRAY.
AT LEAST I'M FEEDING IT.

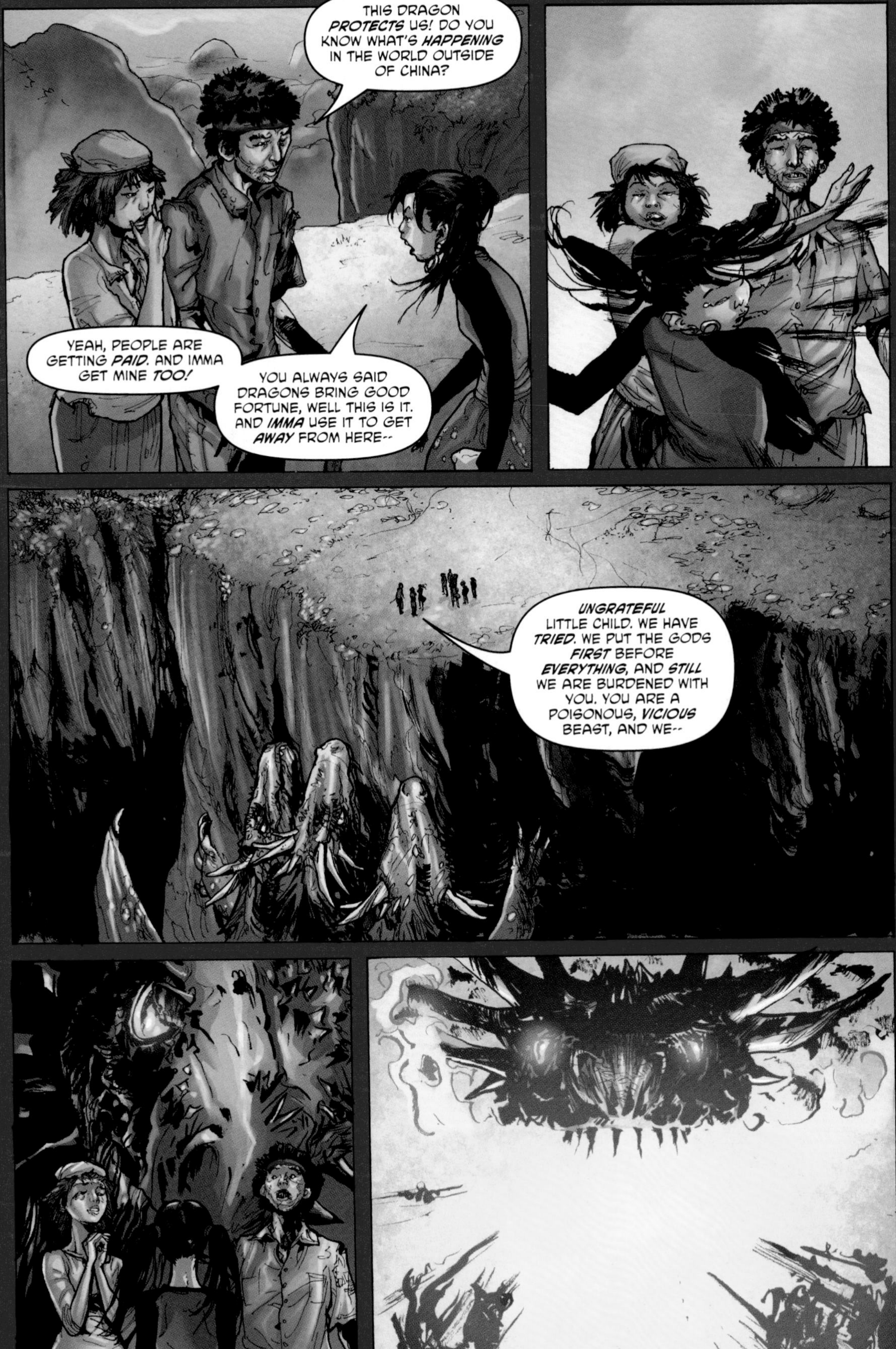
THIS DRAGON PROTECTS US! DO YOU KNOW WHAT'S HAPPENING IN THE WORLD OUTSIDE OF CHINA?
YEAH, PEOPLE ARE GETTING PAID. AND IMMA GET MINE TOO!
YOU ALWAYS SAID DRAGONS BRING GOOD FORTUNE, WELL THIS IS IT. AND IMMA USE IT TO GET AWAY FROM HERE--
UNGRATEFUL LITTLE CHILD. WE HAVE TRIED. WE PUT THE GODS FIRST BEFORE EVERYTHING, AND STILL WE ARE BURDENED WITH YOU. YOU ARE A POISONOUS, VICIOUS BEAST, AND WE--

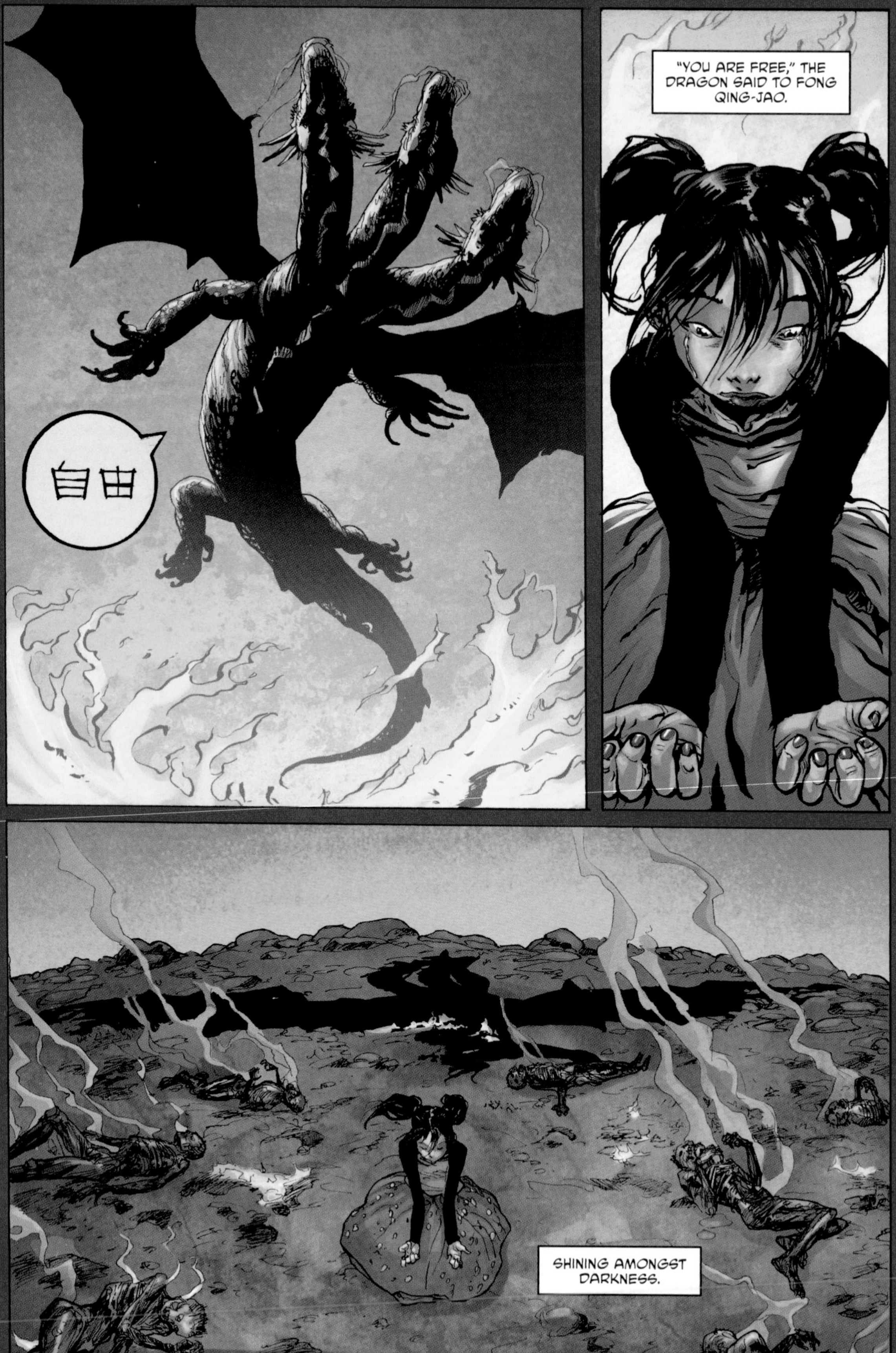
自由
"YOU ARE FREE," THE DRAGON SAID TO FONG QING-JAO.
SHINING AMONGST DARKNESS.

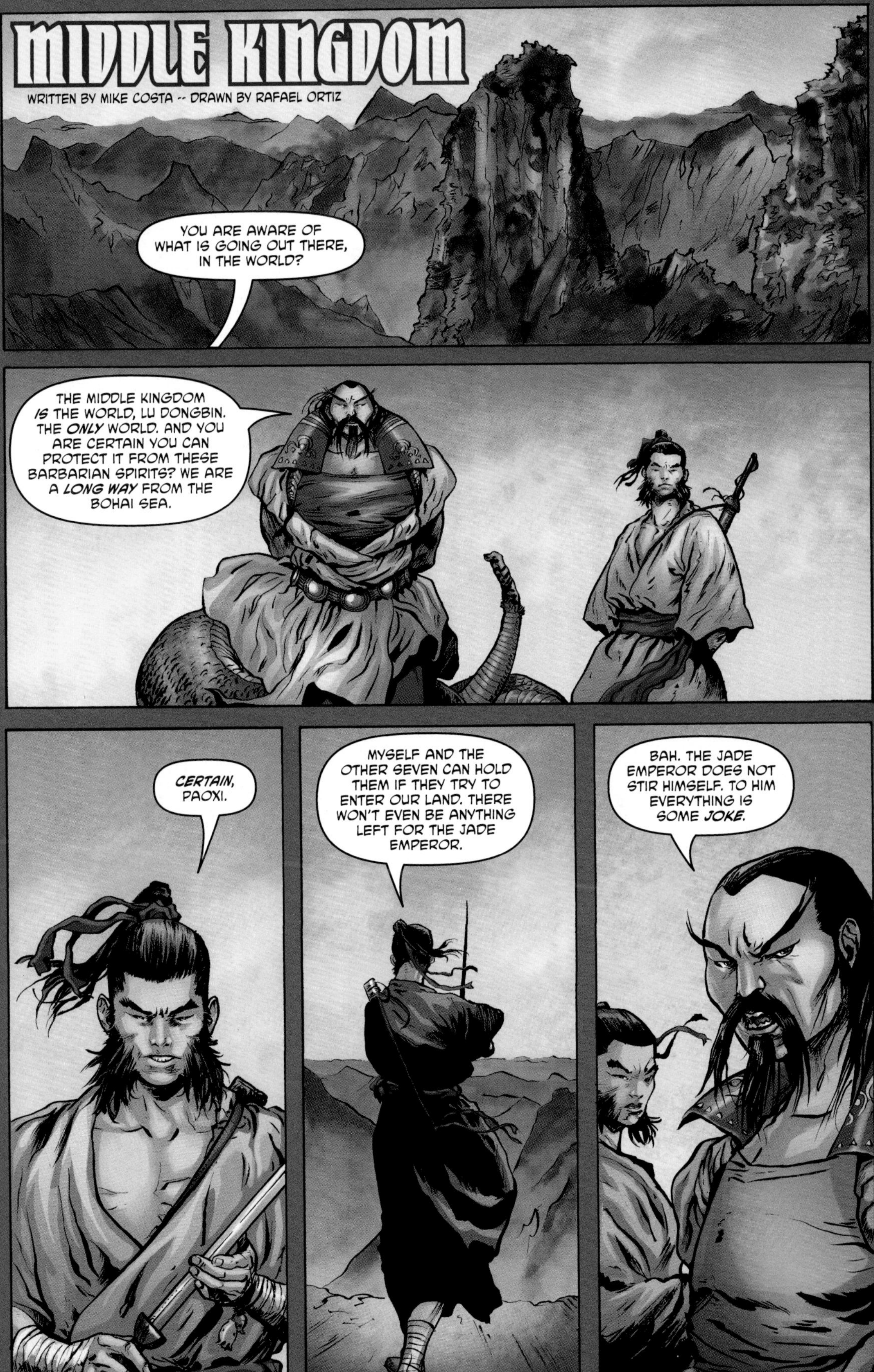

MIDDLE KINGDOM
WRITTEN BY MIKE COSTA -- DRAWN BY RAFAEL ORTIZ
YOU ARE AWARE OF WHAT IS GOING OUT THERE, IN THE WORLD?
THE MIDDLE KINGDOM IS THE WORLD, LU DONGBIN. THE ONLY WORLD. AND YOU ARE CERTAIN YOU CAN PROTECT IT FROM THESE BARBARIAN SPIRITS? WE ARE A LONG WAY FROM THE BOHAI SEA.
CERTAIN, PAOXI.
MYSELF AND THE OTHER SEVEN CAN HOLD THEM IF THEY TRY TO ENTER OUR LAND. THERE WON'T EVEN BE ANYTHING LEFT FOR THE JADE EMPEROR.
BAH. THE JADE EMPEROR DOES NOT STIR HIMSELF. TO HIM EVERYTHING IS SOME JOKE.

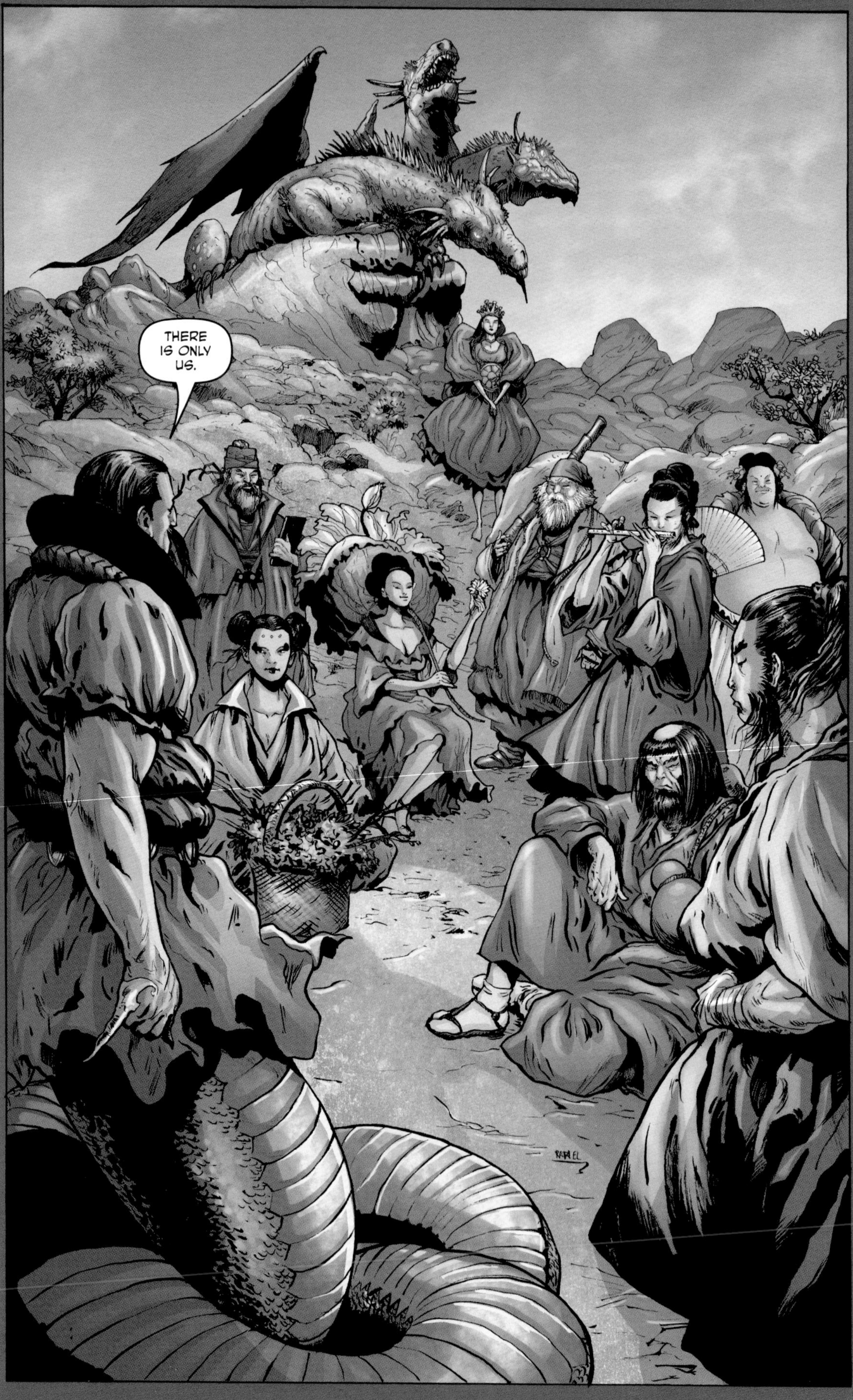
THERE IS ONLY US.

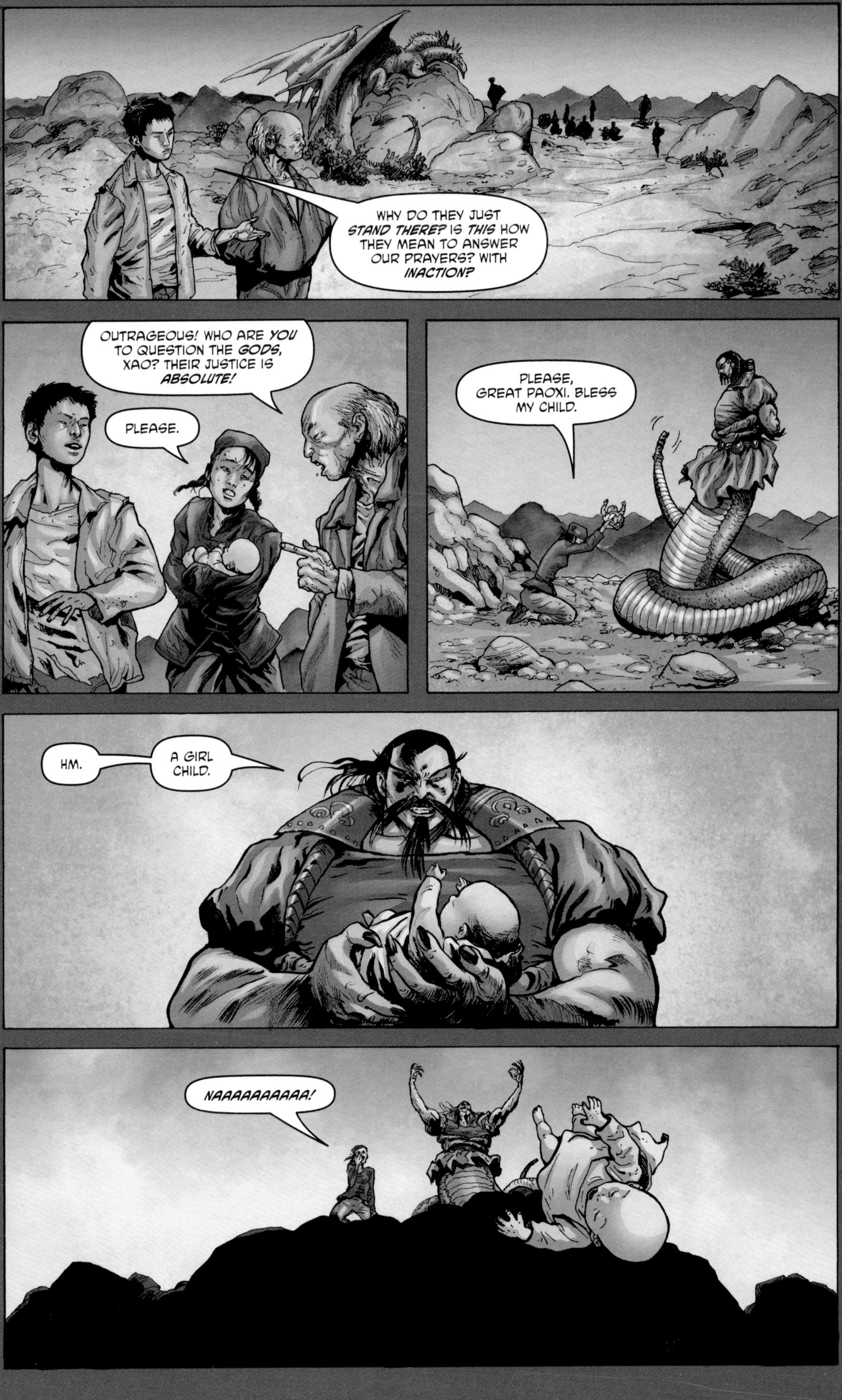
WHY DO THEY JUST STAND THERE? IS THIS HOW THEY MEAN TO ANSWER OUR PRAYERS? WITH INACTION?
OUTRAGEOUS! WHO ARE YOU TO QUESTION THE GODS, XAO? THEIR JUSTICE IS ABSOLUTE!
PLEASE.
PLEASE, GREAT PAOXI. BLESS MY CHILD.
HM.
A GIRL CHILD.
NAAAAAAAAAA!

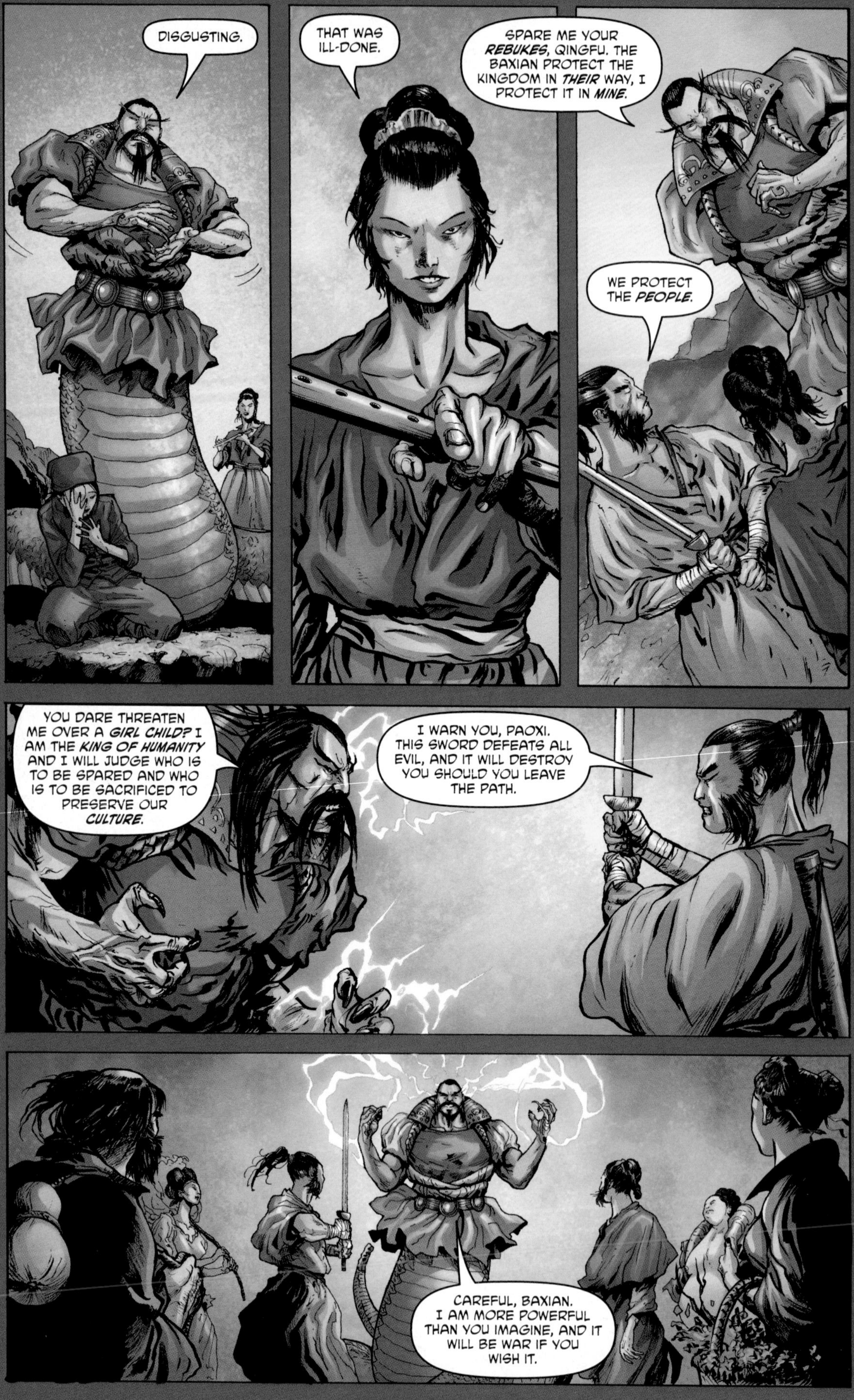
DISGUSTING.
THAT WAS ILL-DONE.
SPARE ME YOUR *REBUKES*, QINGFU. THE BAXIAN PROTECT THE KINGDOM IN *THEIR* WAY, I PROTECT IT IN *MINE*.
WE PROTECT THE *PEOPLE*.
YOU DARE THREATEN ME OVER A *GIRL CHILD?* I AM THE *KING OF HUMANITY* AND I WILL JUDGE WHO IS TO BE SPARED AND WHO IS TO BE SACRIFICED TO PRESERVE OUR *CULTURE*.
I WARN YOU, PAOXI. THIS SWORD DEFEATS ALL EVIL, AND IT WILL DESTROY YOU SHOULD YOU LEAVE THE PATH.
CAREFUL, BAXIAN. I AM MORE POWERFUL THAN YOU IMAGINE, AND IT WILL BE WAR IF YOU WISH IT.

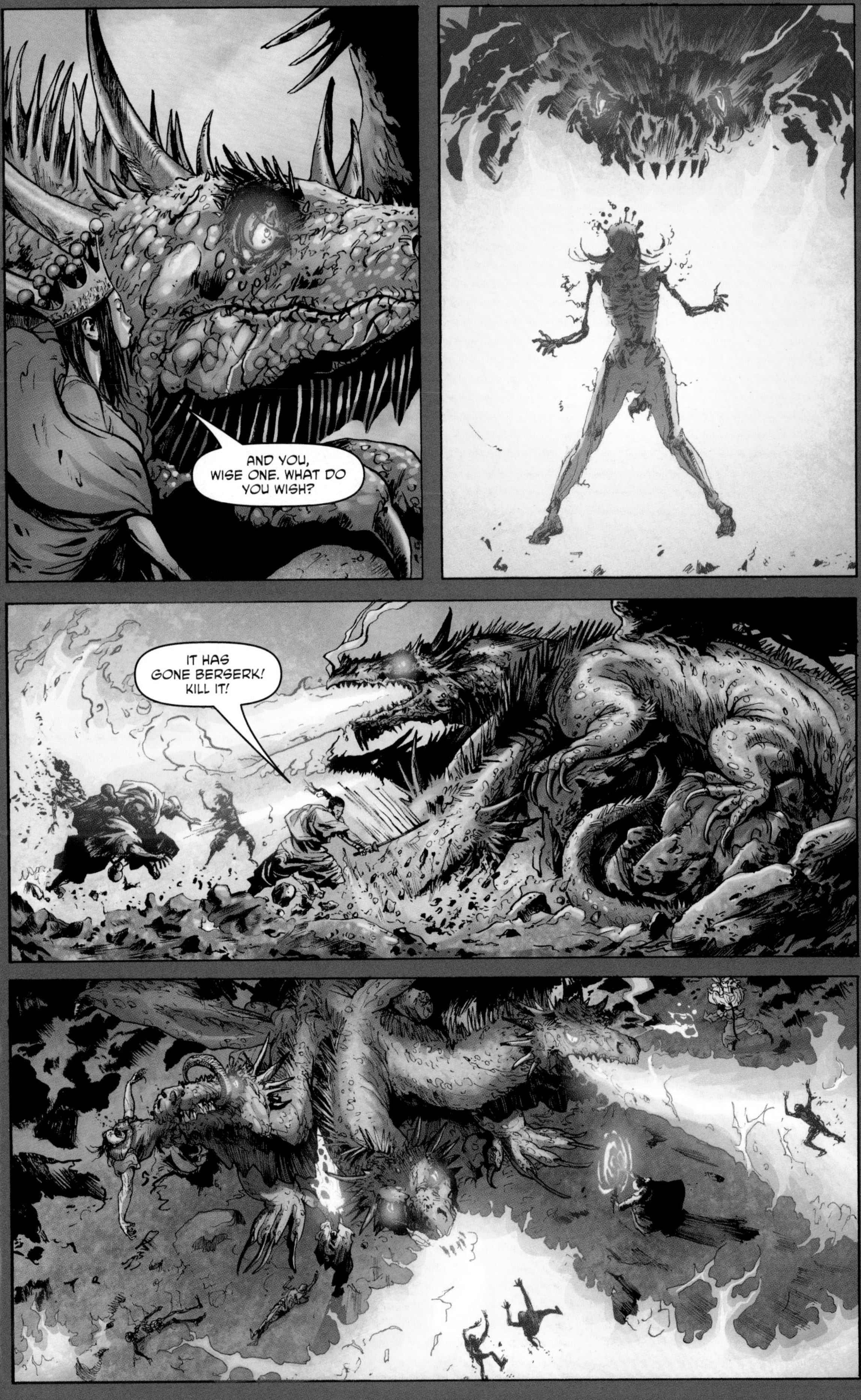
AND YOU, WISE ONE. WHAT DO YOU WISH?
IT HAS GONE BERSERK! KILL IT!

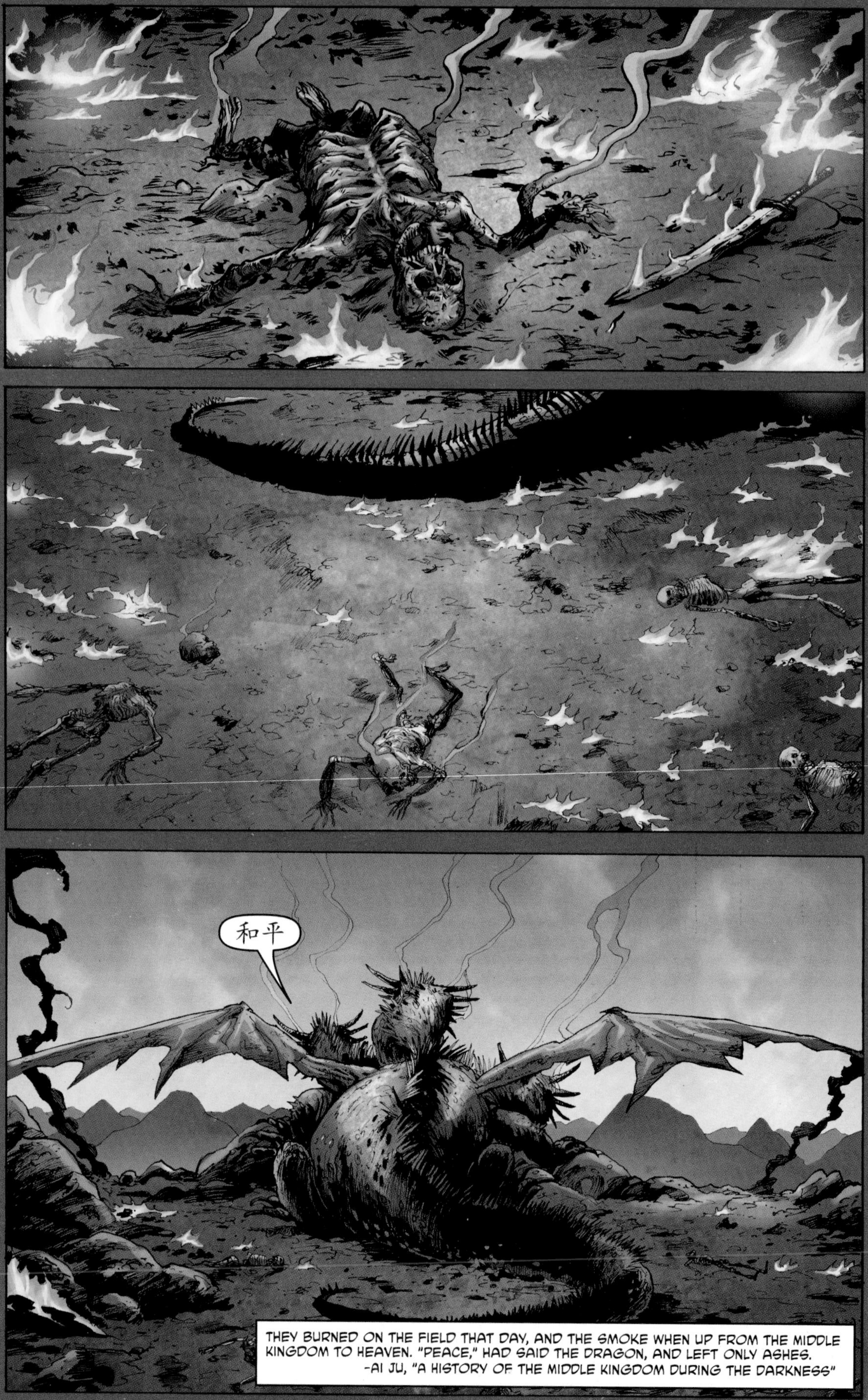
和平
THEY BURNED ON THE FIELD THAT DAY, AND THE SMOKE WHEN UP FROM THE MIDDLE KINGDOM TO HEAVEN. "PEACE," HAD SAID THE DRAGON, AND LEFT ONLY ASHES.
-AI JU, "A HISTORY OF THE MIDDLE KINGDOM DURING THE DARKNESS"